Stanislavski On Opera

Frontispiece: The ballroom in Stanislavski's residence at 6 Leontyevski Pereulok, which was used for both rehearsals and performances.

STANISLAVSKI ON OPERA

by Constantin Stanislavski

and Pavel Rumyantsev

Translated and Edited by
Elizabeth Reynolds Hapgood

Theatre Arts Books · New York

In Memory of

Elizabeth Reynolds Hapgood - February 27, 1974

Robert Mercer MacGregor - November 22, 1974

For a quarter of a century Elizabeth Hapgood as translator and Robert MacGregor as publisher worked together
to bring the thought of Constantin Stanislavski to the
world beyond his native Russia. Theirs was a close and
productive relationship all too rare in the world of pub-
lishing. This book is the last fruit of that collaboration.

The translator and publisher wish to thank Mme. O. Rossikhina and the pub-
lishing house of Iskusstvo in Moscow for the use of photographs from the
Stanislavski productions.

Contents

About the Co-author

PAVEL IVANOVICH RUMYANTSEV came to the Opera Studio of the Bolshoi Theatre in 1920, as a twenty-year-old youth who was still a student at the Moscow Cònservatory. His singing teacher was the then famous Director-in-Chief of the Bolshoi Theatre, A.I. Bartsal. The young bari-tone attracted Stanislavski's attention through his artistry, his mu-sicianship, his fine external qualities, and his enquiring attitude towards his art. New creative possibilities, of which he had no conception, opened up before Rumyantsev while working with Stanislavski, for, as he used to say, in the voice production department of the Conservatory the whole focus of the teaching was essentially on the placement of the voice, the correct producing of the notes given, without any regard whatsoever for the dramatic form of the work to be brought into being. Rumyantsev, however, did not immediately become a convinced fol-lower of Stanislavski's ideas. There were disputes between teacher and pupil, which in the end always led to reconciliation. It was, of course, not easy to follow Stanislavski, who admitted no compromise in art and who demanded from his pupils a most selfless and truly heroic devotion. In addition it must be remembered that the work of the Opera Studio was carried on under the difficult conditions of the early post-revolu-tionary years, conditions of economic ruin and severe deprivation. Among the papers of Rumyantsev there is a document dated December 9, 1920, to the effect that Stanislavski was interceding with superior authorities to obtain for one of the students, one Rumyantsev, a pair of galoshes because "he is obliged twice a day to walk a very long way to the Studio and as a result suffers from frequent colds."

Rumyantsev's range of interests was very wide; he was never willing to remain within the narrow precincts of his profession. He took long journeys and in 1930 he signed on as a member of the crew of the ice-breaker "Sedov," which was part of a polar expedition led by the famous scientist Otto Schmidt. This breadth of interest marked him off from most of his fellow singers, who were intent only on "problems of sound". It enabled him to become not only a many-faceted and subtle artist but a leading director, a member of the theatre administration and finally a writer on the theatre.

Rumyantsev himself participated either as an actor-singer or director, or sometimes both, in the majority of Stanislavski's opera productions which he describes. He started out performing character parts in student productions, but in the end he himself played the title role in *Eugene Onegin*.

From the theatre point of view he was perhaps the best of the many Onegins I have had the fortune to see on the opera stage. In certain parts in his repertory Rumyantsev was not able to achieve at once the wide vocal range required by the role, but he always· attracted the public by the subtlety of his inner design of the character, his finished phrasing, and the artistic perfection of his performance as a whole.

Rumyantsev's work as a director began when he took part in the staging of *Boris Godunov* and *The Queen of Spades*. Later he operated more and more independently, although still under Stanislavski's eye, when he put on *Carmen* and *Rigoletto*. Following this he worked in Leningrad, where he staged *Carmen* at the Kirov Opera and Ballet Theatre and taught at the Leningrad Conservatory. From 1945 to 1947 Rumyantsev acted as director in the Opera House of Sofia in Bulgaria.

Rumyantsev had the idea of compiling a book about the Opera Studio when the young group was in its initial stage. From that time forward Rumyantsev was never without his pad in hand, entering all of Stanislavski's remarks at rehearsals and in conversations with the students. He began to collect, too, all sorts of documents relating to the young opera theatre which could be of use to anyone doing historical research in the future. Gradually he accumulated a mass of material. But the facts and comments by Stanislavski brought together here are not based just on Rumyantsev's personal recollections. He also made extended use of notes made by his colleagues in the Studio.

Rumyantsev incorporated as well many documents left by Stanislavski, quoted his letters, diary entries, manuscripts, articles. Many of these documents are printed here for the first time.

Rumyantsev died suddenly in 1962.

Excerpted from an article by G. Kristi, leading Russian Stanislavski authority.

Translator's Foreword

THE FORTUNATE PEOPLE who were privileged to see any of the original productions of the Moscow Art Theatre, as directed by Stanislavski and Nemirovich-Danchenko, were profoundly aware of an all-encompassing harmony of form, a perfectly scaled integration of component parts, characters, moods, emotions. It was as though these plays were performed under the guidance of a master conductor with a genius for timing, balancing, containing, and releasing human feelings of every kind and colour.

One reason for this special gift of the two men who opened a whole new era in the history and character of the theatre is not hard to find. They were both deeply versed in music and eventually each in his own way realized his ambition to work in that field.

Stanislavski was trained by the great opera singer Fyodor Kommis-arjevsky and might have followed that métier with success had he not become a superlatively expressive actor.

Even so he always felt instinctively that music could greatly enhance the effectiveness of an actor since the work of a really good composer provides such a powerful base from which dramatic expression can derive not only stimulus but also a sense of direction.

So it was that towards the end of his active career he embraced with enthusiasm the opportunity offered him of establishing a studio, a training school for young singers of the Moscow Opera Theatre—the Bolshoi. Their vocal development continued under their own masters but to Stanislavski was left the absorbing task of molding them into a synthesis of singer-actor-musician. They had to be so imbued with the deepest possible significance of every note in an opera and feel themselves so entirely motivated by the music that they never needed to look at the conductor.

The first complete opera produced by Stanislavski was Chaikovski's *Eugene Onegin* based on Pushkin's novel in verse. It caused a great sensation, albeit the work on it was done under circumstances of great material hardship with no adequate stage facilities, scarcely any heating of the premises in which the singers worked, and even lack of proper food. This made the undoubted brilliance and impact of the completed productions all the more remarkable. It was a piece of rare good fortune that one of the members of that first group of singers kept a detailed account of how it was all done. In P.I. Rumyantsev's transcription of Stanislavski's words one is made to feel that the master himself is present as he propounds problems as they arise in production after production.

From this verbatim record many workers in the field of opera and drama will gain startlingly fresh insights, and may well feel themselves deeply indebted.

ELIZABETH REYNOLDS HAPGOOD

Note

THE OPERA STUDIO of the Bolshoi Theatre was founded towards the end of 1918, at the instance of E.K. Malinovskaya, the manager of the State Theatres in Moscow, and with the support of the Art Council of the Bolshoi Theatre. The goal assigned to the Studio was a renaissance of opera traditions and the raising of the theatre-cultural level of the actor-singers. The direction of the Studio was turned over to Stanislavski. To begin with, the work was carried on with singers from the Bolshoi. Then in October 1919 a group of young singers was taken into the Studio. The Studio put on three performances in concert form: *Werther* by Massenet (1921), *Eugene Onegin* by Chaikovski (1922), and *The Secret Marriage* by Cimarosa (1925). Later it was separated from the Bolshoi and after 1924 was called the Stanislavski Opera Studio. In 1926 the Studio was converted into the Opera Studio-Theatre and in 1928 into the Stanislavski Opera Theatre.

1

In the Opera Studio

IN JANUARY 1921 Stanislavski was offered an old private house, 6 Leontyevski Pereulok, which had escaped the conflagration when Moscow was burned in 1812. The facade is not distinguished in any special way, but from the courtyard behind it one discovers all the peculiarities of a nobleman's home dating back to the days of Griboyedov. There is a large two-storied addition which encloses an oaken staircase leading to the second floor. It is so old that the lower-floor entrance to the house is now below today's ground level. There are also little balconies which have been added, presumably in the first half of the 19th century.

This building was not only the last residence of the great theatre director but was also his working laboratory. About one quarter of the second floor is occupied by a large hall with columns (the former ballroom). It was here and in the room adjacent to it that the Opera Studio of the Bolshoi Theatre, which Stanislavski had agreed to direct, "settled". Lessons and rehearsals went on without interruption here from early morning to late evening. The piano was never silent except at night. In order to carry out his plan of incorporating his system of acting into opera, Stanislavski immersed himself completely in the world of music and singing.

All he had to do to go to rehearsals, which were carried out on strict schedule, was leave his study, cross a low-ceilinged vestibule with four columns, scarcely higher than Stanislavski himself, and enter the hall where rehearsals were in progress all day long. Every free moment he had Stanislavski would use to come over to see how the work was going on.

"Am I interrupting?" he usually said as he glanced cautiously into the large room. "Please go right on!"

But of course within five minutes he had taken over the rehearsal himself and was working away with the singers. This was extra instruction he gave the young players in addition to their regular training in his system of acting.

"First we must find a common language," Stanislavski would say, "then we shall try to combine the art of living a role with its musical form and the technique of singing. After that we shall try out the validity of our work in performances. But to reach the point of actual performance we must go through a lot of preparatory improvisations. These will be based on songs and individual scenes from operas."

This coherent program of work was necessary to the development of Stanislavski's method of training which was not yet generally accepted in our theatres—that came much later.

The proponents of "pure operatic singing", those devoted to the old routines, did not accept Stanislavski's ideas about opera and they did their best to prove that if a singer has a real voice he does not need any training in acting.

The makeup of this Opera Studio group also made Stanislavski realize that he would be obliged to begin his training with the simplest exercises and sketches. The group, aside from a very few singers from the Bolshoi (K. Antarova, V. Sadovnikov, A. Sadomov), was made up of youngsters from the Moscow Conservatory of Music.

In order to keep to the historical truth of the record it must be said that certain other well-known singers were in the Studio, but not for long. In connection with this fact Stanislavski said:

"You must remember that a strong group is formed not by outstanding singers, these will always be lured away from us by other opera managements with promises of big salaries. The core of our Studio will consist of good singers of what we may call average talent, but who love their work; cultivated singers and actors who are welded together into an ensemble, who cannot be thrown off balance by the temptation of becoming stars, or acquiring great personal fame.

"First we shall go through a course of preparation for opera which was not included in your conservatory training. Until you have finished that you will not be fit to set foot on our operatic stage, that is to say until you have chosen as the goal of your artistic life a kind of singing which is not only beautiful but also informed with that thought and inspiration. That kind of singing is without exception the true kind for all of you."

The theory of the Stanislavski acting "system", daily exercises to music, sketches acted out for the purpose of giving a basis to the most varied kinds of body positions, movements in space, the freeing of muscular tenseness and finally, the principal and most interesting work, the singing of arias and lyrical ballads (in the execution of which the students synthesized all the component parts of the "system")—all this preparatory work was done by the students before they began to put on any Studio productions.

Stanislavski in teaching others was at the same time learning himself. He listened with closest attention, for example, to the lessons on orthophonics and singing diction given by N.M. Safonov, who had the gift of brilliant exposition in analyzing words and the way to achieve expressiveness through them. He knew how to get a singer to feel very deeply the meaning of a lyrical ballad and how to use a variety of techniques, including diction and vocal training, to bring that meaning fully to life—in this he was supreme. Of course, one could always learn from such a great teacher as Safonov and we young singers listened to him avidly during our lessons and "sweated it out" with him at the piano, repeating dozens of times a phrase that did not come off right. Unfortunately he died in 1922.

Concomitantly with our practical work on the "system" Stanislavski gave us a course of lectures drawn from what was later to become *An Actor Prepares* and *Building a Character*. At that time Stanislavski was in the process of formulating those books.

Our studies lasted a long time, nearly five years (1921–1926), and continued side by side with the readying of productions. They were carried on by Stanislavski and his assistants. Later on, especially by the new young members, the Studio was called the "School on the Move."

In the early part of the existence of the Opera Studio Stanislavski was greatly assisted by his sister Zindaïda Sokolova and his brother Vladimir Alexeyev, who undertook all the preparatory training of the young singers.

Vladimir Alexeyev was a good musician. He had a refined sense of the rhythmic side of the acting of opera which occupies such an important place among all the other components of a performer in opera.

Stanislavski himself placed the greatest significance on rhythm: "No, you have not yet established the rhythm of this part of your role. You have not got it under control, you do not savour it. Ask the advice of my brother," he used to say.

Zinaïda Sokolova helped the students to create the inner score of a part; she had the gift of finding the subtlest shadings for that inner life. The whole pattern of "Tatiana's Letter" scene was worked out by her with N.G. Lezina; it was on the whole approved by Stanislavski and included in the production of *Eugene Onegin*.

The man who taught the Stanislavski "system" of acting was N.V. Demidov. He was well informed concerning the psychological foundations of Stanislavski's work and even helped him in the preparation of material for his books, a fact which the author registered with gratitude.

One half of each day was devoted to class activities and the other to the preparation of performances.

The first three scenes of *Eugene Onegin:* "The Arrival of the Guests at the Larins',", "Tatiana's Letter," and "The Meeting," were the basis for Stanislavski's practical work on the production.

Here he put two main objectives before the young actor-singers. The first was to achieve expressive, incisive diction, thanks to which they could convey clearly and colourfully the words they sang. "Fifty percent of our success depends on diction. Not a single word must fail to reach the audience." That was the "leitmotiv" of Stanislavski's work with singers.

The second objective was the complete freeing of their bodies from all involuntary tensions and pressures, for the purpose of achieving easy, simple handling of themselves onstage. It was to achieve this ability to free their bodies from excessive tenseness, especially in the arms, wrists and fingers, that daily exercises were devoted. They were all done to music in order to train the singers in making every movement consonant with musical rhythms.

In the process of projecting his voice a singer is obliged to tense certain muscles (of the diaphragm, the intercostal muscles, the larynx); that is to say these are *working* contractions which are necessary to the actual singing. It was the principal aim of a whole series of exercises prescribed by Stanislavski to make a distinction between the working contractions and superfluous tensions, thus leaving all the other muscles completely free. He was always on the watch for those unnecessary tensions in the body, the face, the arms, the legs of a singer while performing. When an artist is performing in accordance with his inner feelings he must not be impeded in his movements by muscular contractions. The singer's whole attention must be centered on his action.

"Actors onstage are often fearful that the public will be bored if there is not enough gesturing, and therefore they go through a whole lot of motions," Stanislavski used to say. "But the end result is random and trashy. On a large stage, especially, restraint is above all necessary and this can only be achieved if one has complete control over all of one's muscles."

"Thoughts are embodied in acts," Stanislavski taught us, "and a man's actions in turn affect his mind. His mind affects his body and again his body, or its condition, has its reflex action on his mind and produces this or that condition. You must learn how to rest your body, free your muscles and, at the same time, your psyche."

Exercises for the purpose of relaxing muscles from ordinary tensions in order to acquire plasticity of movement—easy walking, the ability to govern the use of one's arms and hands—were set down by Stanislavski as *musts* for a singer-actor of his school.

These exercises were conducted in a certain order: The students stood in a semicircle and, while music was played, went through various forms of gymnastics. Stanislavski told the musician in charge, one Zhukov:

"What we need is eight quarter notes for the raising of the arms, elbows, hands and fingers; also eight quarter notes for their relaxation and return to position. We want your help in harnessing the energy and then in releasing and relaxing it.

"First relax the muscles of the hands so that they are completely free and hang from the wrists as inertly as strings. Swing them backwards and forwards, separately and together," he said. "After that the fingers must be so relaxed that they dangle from their joints. Then raise your arm to your shoulder, free that from all tension, and then let your elbow dangle from its joint. Shake the lower part of your forearm from your elbow down lightly and freely."

To free the muscles of the legs it is necessary to stand on one leg, relax the foot of the raised leg, make it inert, watching mentally the lack of feeling in the toes. Then make rotary movements with the free foot. Stanislavski himself was so accustomed to these exercises that while he was seated, for instance at a rehearsal, he would twist his free foot and test its flexibility. These exercises enabled him to have a light, mobile way of walking, for which he was famous up to the time he was very old. He was fond of repeating that "a flexible foot and toes are the basis of lightness of walking."

While holding one's leg off the ground, relax the tension of the whole shank and gently rotate the knee joint. Then raise the leg, bend the knee, relax the whole, and slowly let the leg down.

In relaxing muscular tensions in the neck, one throws one's head forward and then by movement of the body causes it to roll from side to side. Then, seated on a chair and having relaxed the neck muscles, one throws one's head backwards and lets it roll around at will. While executing this exercise one imagines oneself in a state of sleep.

To relax the muscles of the shoulders and chest, the torso should be slightly inclined forward, with arms hanging inertly, and the waist muscles quite free.

After these exercises one could gradually relax all the muscles of the body and drop to the ground like a sheaf of wheat.

"These exercises," said Stanislavski, "develop a sense of tranquility, of self-control and power, as well as the clear understanding of one's muscular structure."

There were, of course, some singers who deep down in their vocal being considered that the exercises of the relaxing of muscular tensions were quite superfluous, that they bore no relation to singing. "For singing mannequins such exercises are indeed superfluous," said Stanislavski, "but for living human beings, if they wish to remain such on the stage, they are imperative."

One must note that it was impossible to imagine all of Stanislavski's exercises as fun, as fascinating things to do for the participants. At times there was stubborn, monotonous repetition, grinding work done for the sake of art. Yet even to this dull monotony Stanislavski maintained an attitude of enthusiasm and enjoyment as great as when he was carrying on a rehearsal. And he exacted the same kind of joy in work from everyone else.

Daily training in how to walk with graceful fluidity was obligatory before the beginning of any rehearsal; the exercises were necessary as a means of softening and warming up the body, the physical apparatus of an actor. "The singer-actor needs them fully as much as he does his daily vocalization exercises," Stanislavski would say.

The exercises in smooth walking were begun to very slow music. In the course of two measures in very slow time (adagio) only one step was made so that the weight of the body imperceptibly and smoothly passed from one leg to the other without the slightest hitch. The sole of the student's foot and the movement of the toes played a great part in this beginning exercise.

"Your feet must be very soft springs in order to carry the weight of your body smoothly. Remember the example of a horse, of the highly trained Orlov breed of trotter—you can put a glass of water on his back and it will never spill. Try to achieve that kind of smooth, gliding, airborne way of walking, so that you too would not spill a glass of water carried on your head," remarked Stanislavski.

Gradually the tempo of our walking was increased; a step was taken to a half measure, then a quarter, finally an eighth—yet even at the greatest speed the smoothness of movement had to be maintained, even when we reached the point of almost running. "Without a well-developed capacity to walk an actor might just as well have no arms either," said Stanislavski.

Similar exercises for arms and hands were conducted in much the same way as is done in ballet training, except that the movements made had to be based on some inner purpose. Stanislavski did not recognize any beauty in gesture or pose for its own sake; he always insisted on some action behind it, some reason for a given pose or gesture based on imagination.

"Make out of every gesture some act, and in general forget about mere gestures when you are practicing. Action is all that counts, a gesture all by itself is nothing but nonsense."

A great deal of significance was attributed to dancing and all the actor-singers were obliged to be able to dance: mazurkas, waltzes, polonaises, schottisches—we had to be able to dance them all. All the dances in Eugene Onegin were performed by the whole cast: singers, chorus, soloists.

Fencing was used as a necessary part of physical training to prepare an actor for the execution of all sorts of actions on the stage. Stanislavski valued fencing especially because dueling with rapiers obliges an actor to be able to combine the working tensions of his legs and whole body with an extremely flexible lightness in the use of his arms, especially his hands, and this can be accomplished only by sharp attention to the condition of his entire physical apparatus.

But the main point about fencing was, for Stanislavski, the fact that each duel was the best possible training for concentration of willpower and attention, for the development of an inner interrelationship with a partner, for the always necessary study of one's opponent.

In all our exercises Stanislavski insisted on inner justification for whatever we were doing at a given moment. This applied as well to vocalizing as to diction, to the logic of speech as to physical exercises —fluid movements, dancing, fencing. He always determined that we prepare "given circumstances", some imaginative idea that we were to carry out during our work.

He never allowed a single, even most elementary, technical exercise to be done "in general", just for the purpose of going through a form.

"I do not understand just what you are doing now," he would say, while watching our hand exercises. "If you are trying to make beautiful movements in space by using your softly curvaceous arms while your imaginations are fast asleep and you do not even know it, then what you are indulging in is empty form. Try to fill it up with something out of your imagination. Give each exercise some purpose of its own, and combine everything you do with feelings with regard to the action.

"I do not at all understand for what reason you are doing this exercise, why one arm is above your head and the other is wound around your body—if there is nothing else to it, it's just 'ballet'." Ballet in quotation marks was what he called "beautiful" poses which lacked all inner meaning, and he often said the word "ballet" in a rather venomous tone.

In this way the Stanislavski "system" of acting was gradually introduced into all the preliminary training of the singers. It began to be a great help to us much sooner than we expected, because we mistakenly thought that all the exercises for the relaxation of muscles and physical freedom of movement, taken just by themselves, were something quite different from lessons in the "system".

"All of your exercises, even those which may seem the most mechanical, must be related to the 'system'; that is to say they must have some creative relationship to what you are doing," said Stanislavski during one of our lessons in learning how to walk smoothly.

There is a deep cleavage here from the method of training artists in places where the Stanislavski "system" is given as a special course not related to any of the other disciplines.

Everyone knows, after the publication of *My Life in Art, An Actor Prepares,* and *Building a Character,* how much hard work was put into the development of Stanislavski's acting technique, and what high standards and demands he required of himself in his lifelong search. It was these strict standards that Stanislavski placed at the base of the daily work he did with his students in his Opera Studio. Hence his motto: *Art demands sacrifices.*

I recall once the expression of dismay and anger on his face as his students said to him: "We are not going to rehearse tomorrow, it's a holiday."

"What kind of artists are you if you work only on week days and then rest on holidays? What are you taking a rest from? Creativeness? A true artist works every single day, every hour of his existence, all his life, because he cannot live without creativeness."

Self-indulgence, let-down, compromise with work—all these were repugnant to Stanislavski. He felt it his duty to instill in all his students the same attitude towards their work, the same artistic taste and love of work that he exacted from himself.

He asked each student in detail why he had come to the Studio, what he expected to learn there, what relationship he saw between singing and acting, what it was he had been dissatisfied with in his earlier training. Any stereotype answer such as "I would just like to work here" did not satisfy him at all; even the youngest, shyest girl was forced to tell him what her attitude was towards art because he looked upon every applicant as a potential artist.

He searched keenly into the soul of every untutored, inexperienced student to see if he could discover even a grain of artistry which could be nursed along, because it was essential if the voice and the suppleness of the body were to develop. This attitude on Stanislavski's part produced a genuinely creative atmosphere in the Studio. It was part of the training of every student actor-singer.

The first lessons he gave to the singers involved very simple physical actions: set a chair in a given place, hide a letter, sit for three minutes facing the public—in other words the kind of exercises commonly used in training actors in the "system".

"What is this 'system'?" Stanislavski would ask the singers during their first lesson-rehearsal. "There are those, you know, who think it can be used to create talent. But this is not so! The 'system' is a sort of guidebook to help the soul become more creative. It is addressed to the soul so that it will accept what the author feels at a given moment in the works he has created. When the author and the actor coalesce in a part, a creative miracle has been performed. The 'system' helps the actor to express what the author wished to say.

"It also helps the actor to develop his physical apparatus so that he can reproduce in artistic form what his soul has created. Then there is another highly significant point to be added: The 'system' is a form of science which an actor usually disregards because he pins his hope on inspiration from 'on high', thinking that it will be provided when needed.

"Very good," he added ironically, "anyone who has never acted on the stage is welcome to try this out."

There was an awkward silence for a bit while Stanislavski carefully looked over all the students sitting around him as if he were studying them. Finally a young woman singer rose from her chair:

"What should I do?"

"You can take your chair up onto the stage and place it facing us."

Of course the young woman realized that just to move her chair was not enough and that she had to carry out some objective. She began by looking around, then set the chair in a certain place, walked two or three steps away from it, looked around again, then apparently ran out of ideas and looked fixedly at Stanislavski who smiled and asked:

"Well, have you finished your scene? Can we close the curtain?"

"I don't know what to do next."

"What you did do, I don't understand anyway," said Stanislavski.

"I bought a new chair."

"That I did not grasp. In fact I rather thought you wanted to get rid of the one you had. In any case, go ahead and do something, anything you like."

The young student sat down on her chair, thought for a few minutes, took a mirror out of her handbag, began to put on some lipstick and smooth her hair. Then she did a little work on her eyebrows and eyelashes. Everything she did was perfectly natural and right. She was doing with assurance things she was accustomed to doing every day.

"All right. Now what was your purpose in what you were doing?" asked Stanislavski after she had finished her makeup and was looking rather guiltily at him.

"I am trying to carry out my objective correctly."

"Very well, it's a good thing to have an objective, you cannot come out onto the stage to do something 'in general'. On the stage we must have life but not only that, it must be the life of your imagination which you make real for us. An actor himself must create that life, produce it through his fantasy. To be an actor you must in the first instance possess a developed, rich sense of fantasy. Your creativeness will begin only when you have in mind the words 'if it were so'. Without that 'Magic If', without fantasy, there can be no creativeness, no matter how well you execute simple physical actions on the stage.

"Take these same simple physical actions and set them in various 'given circumstances'. Take what you just did with the makeup on your face and play it twenty different ways and let each little sketch be put into different 'given circumstances'. Use your imagination to think up many little plays; the action will be the same throughout but its purpose in each case will be different. Never repeat an exercise without a fresh objective.

"In all your beginning exercises you must be developing your imagination. Without that faculty an actor can do nothing on the stage.

"As a means of extending your imaginative powers you will have to invent all sorts of 'given circumstances'. Using the magic formula 'if things were so and so', surround yourself with imaginary objects and always answer for yourself the questions: 'Where, when, for what reason or purpose is this?' When you create an imaginative life for a part, when you know all the facts concerned with it and you enjoy this—then it becomes a reality."

To this the young woman answered:

"But before I can do all that I must first of all know how to present things truly, to act."

"No. First of all you must create the circumstances suggested by the 'Magic If'. For instance: suppose you are a bride and are about to go to church to be married. If that were so how would you look at your face in the mirror, how would you make up your eyes, arrange your hair and so forth? Or if you were a sixteen-year-old girl starting off to a ball, how would you do all these same things?

"Creativeness is of great interest, so is an actor's imagination. It is at the very heart of our work. You did everything correctly but there was no art in it. So that is the first thing you must learn."

Then turning to another student Stanislavski said to him: "You chose the objective of coming home tired from your work and said to yourself 'I'll have some tea!' That is all truthful and lifelike, but lacks interest. It cannot set the actor on fire. The truth he portrays must be artistic."

To which the young man replied:

"But it is hard to act without words. Now if I had any lines to say I would show more feeling."

"No," said Stanislavski, "words are not an end in themselves. We shall first learn to move about, to act. Any routine actor can recite his role, that's not difficult to learn. He can have as many cliché intonations as he will have automatic muscular reactions. But what we have to learn is how to move, how to sing or dance or mime, whether we use actual words or not.

"There are actors who are mortally afraid of making mistakes. And this is always apparent on their faces because they go through their roles extraordinarily cautiously. A timid actor needs only to make a tiny slip and he is already lost. He must develop the self-control to be unafraid of making a slip into falseness, then he can instantly return to the path of truth."

"Take as the subject for your imagination the most insignificant thing, for instance a button on your coat sleeve. You will be able, by giving it your sharp attention and concentration, to oblige it to stir your imagination and keep it intense for as long as you choose.

"An actor on the stage does not believe in the object itself but in his relationship to it. Therefore no matter what prop you are handling I shall believe in its reality on the stage if you establish the right attitude towards it and are sincere."

Stanislavski's talk was broken off at this point and the students went onto the stage, that is to say into the centre of the hall, to execute a series of improvisations. In all these the objectives with which Stanislavski had begun his lesson were carried out.

After her discussion with Stanislavski the young actress who had improvised on the stage with her chair realized that it was not enough just to believe in your physical actions—you had to "wrap" them in imaginative "given circumstances." She began again, and the onlookers then slowly realized that she had undertaken a journey by ship. By the frightened look in her eyes it would not be difficult to surmise that the ship was beginning to roll. She tried to stand up and walk along the deck, but suddenly she felt there was something false about all this and that the onlookers were ironically whispering to each other, so she abandoned the sketch. Stanislavski who was watching her with an interested smile exclaimed with disappointment:

"Oh, why did you stop? It was interesting to me and the rest of us to watch you get back on the right track, but you were too weak-willed. You lost your head out of fear of being overly criticized, a feeling that is still inside you. You wanted to do everything well but you did only the first part right. Then that super-critic inside you brought out your false self-admiration. The kind of self-criticism you need is the kind that ferrets out what is untrue in order to let you create what is true. It searches out what is bad but for the purpose of correcting it, not merely in order to tear you down. First and foremost you must see and feel what is true and make that your point of departure. The capacity to see what is good, what is beautiful, is a necessary part of an actor. That is the yardstick you must apply to yourself.

"Self-criticism is necessary too but it should be properly directed. Remember for the future that there will always be some things that are poor in your acting and you must reconcile yourself to this. Art is not a fixed ideal. Art is constantly on the move. Pushing yourself off from the letter 'A' you reach the letter 'B' then 'C' and so it goes on forever. *The ideal of perfection is infinite.* As soon as an actor says to himself: 'I am "ideal"', he is done for, he has left the path of art. Nevertheless in criticizing yourself and others, while you may see what is false and bad you must also know how to see what is good."

The best sketches which Stanislavski proposed were the ones done to the accompaniment of music, so that the students could listen to the rhythm and the character of the music and give their improvisations a definite content and exact form as suggested by the music. The musician who improvised the music for the sketches knew, of course, the content of the plot and how to develop the course of action; he was also able to introduce meaning into what was being done, together with the most varied nuances, by his use of both rhythm and musical form. The actor then had to be delicately sensitive to these musical hints and he also had the job of introducing his own improvisations, moving in faithful conjunction with what he was hearing. Such exercises require very keen response on the part of an actor to the music being played—music which he does not know in advance, and to which he must wholly subject himself, thus developing sharp attention as well as musical sensitiveness. Such musical exercises also must be played by a skilled improvisor with a wide range of fantasy. An ordinary musician would only ruin the delicate texture of this kind of work.

"From the instant the music begins you are completely in its power. Your nerves, blood, heartbeat must all be in accord with the rhythm proposed by this music. Yet to seize this rhythm, live with it, let it permeate your whole being, is no easy matter. One must proceed by degrees. The simplest thing is to beat the measures, the stresses. That is the easiest to accomplish, yet this affects only, as you might say, the extremities, the periphery of your body.

"It is not this rhythm which will determine the essentials of the composition played or your life as part of it. I am speaking here of the inner rhythm which makes you act differently, breathe differently. It is the thing that carries away your emotions, arouses them, giving them both keenness and power.

"This music gives the tone of your feelings. These feelings, if truthfully evoked, acquire power, resonance, so to say. So listen most carefully to the music. You have to hear in it the reason for what you are doing and *how* you are to do it, so that your every imperceptibly unobtrusive movement will be in harmony with the music. This should not be obvious; all that the eye sees is harmony in keeping with the sounds made by the orchestra and your own voice. It is the achieving of this particular kind of harmony, embodied in you on the stage, that is the whole basic idea of opera."

The principal objective which Stanislavski set for his young singers was a union of their musical, vocal technique and of living their parts in the flesh. This latter required a subtle sense of musical rhythm in order to produce fluent physical movement of the actor's entire physical makeup.

Stanislavski also demanded of his singers the greatest possible vocal expressiveness, and to develop this he used many romantic ballads.

The successful execution of these ballads presupposes a wide variety of vocal shadings to convey the composer's ideas; therefore Stanislavski considered this work as a necessary preparatory step in the direction of preparing a role. It was not by chance that the first public appearance of the Opera Studio was in a concert consisting of "romances" by Rimski-Korsakov.

The rehearsals preceding this concert formed a great part of the teaching Stanislavski himself gave. I recall a few of them.

I see a young woman singer leaning lightly on the lid of a concert grand piano, standing in front of Stanislavski. She is singing a romance by Rimski-Korsakov called "Serene, serene is the sky blue sea". She had learned this ballad earlier when she was still in the Conservatory. Every shading indicated on the music was absolutely preserved, and the ballad was sung in accordance with all the customs and rules of the music-hall singers of those times—that is to say, her eyes were fixed above the heads of the audience as she seemed to see something imaginary but familiar far off in the distance. The muscles of her face were tensely fixed in a contrived smile (the usual "mask" for all singers in those days) which was intended to convey an impression of lightness, a complete lack of any effort in singing the high, lilting notes of the song.

The singer stands in the curve of the instrument, leaning her right hand lightly on the polished black surface while her other small hand hangs freely at her side. She stands quietly, putting the weight of her body on one foot. We were all quite aware, from our work with Stanislavski's sister Zinaïda Sergeyevna Sokolova and with him, that pressing one's two hands together over one's heart, as if to express powerful emotions, was *out*, and that one should not stand on the stage firmly on both feet as if at attention (note classic statues in this regard), that there must not be the slightest tenseness in one's neck (God forbid that one should raise one's shoulders while singing). Besides, we were told, if one's elbows or wrists are tense he is practically nailed down and that's the end of his creative powers. This young singer's brow is serene, and that is important too because it means she has not turned to stone.

The very young singer stands so relaxed, so naturally in front of Stanislavski as she finishes her song. Slowly she changes and looks at him with a little embarrassment as he, still smiling, watches her as steadily as he did while she was singing; he seems to be expecting something more. Then, crossing his knees and coughing slightly, he rubs the back of his right hand with one of the fingers of his left in a gesture we knew was preparatory to expressing himself.

"Well, well, that was very nice. I see before me a pretty young woman, whose carriage is easy, indeed slightly flirtatious. Her voice is resonant, well polished, but what she was singing about or why she came over to the piano . . . quite escapes me. Did she wish to show us her looks? Here I must speak quite austerely and even resentfully, because I am going to speak the whole truth. The reason for this is that if you do not, at the very outset of your pursuit of art, devote yourself to that art with your whole being you will just roll downhill along the road to platitudinous, routine ham singing, and you are not likely ever to return to that art's fundamental truth.

"I have digressed a bit but this is an essential factor in the life of an actress, unless all she wants to be is a commercial performer."

This term "commercial performer" was one Stanislavski used frequently when he wished to express his highest degree of disdain for an actress who did not comprehend her great obligation to her art.

"Explain to me what you wished to convey by this ballad, what thought impelled you to choose this particular song, to sing it, what there was in it that attracted you?"

The young singer did not reply with much clarity; she liked the music very much although there were too few words and the song was too short; she did not have time to express the feelings which are inherent in it.

"First search out the logic of the thoughts, that paves the way for the emotions. First of all you must have a clear comprehension. Read the verses, and say what the principal factor in them was that moved Maikov and Rimski-Korsakov, and tell us what you understand in them."

The young singer read the lines:

> Serene would be the azure sea
> If undisturbed by the rising storm
> That rages and dashes billowing waves
> Upon the beach.
> Serene within my breast would be
> My heart if suddenly
> Your image did not rise and rush
> Upon it with more force and speed
> Than any storm.

Then added:
"I wish to convey that I love him:"

"Whom?" asks Stanislavski. "Do you see him? Know him? Or are you talking in general terms?"

"No, I haven't thought about this yet."

"Then that implies a kind of 'generalized' love, a sort of rubber-stamp love, nothing but a sweet smile! This means your imagination has not yet been put to work, you have not so much as glimpsed anything behind the words or beyond the music.

"Now let us proceed point by point. What thought has the author implanted in your mind? The blue sea would be serene if there were no storm which would dash waves onto the shore. Thus all would be serene in my soul if your image did not rage through it like a storm. Now look at this idea from every angle, develop it, embroider it. Ask yourself why you compare your soul to a sea. When does this happen in one's life? Do you wish that this sea, that is to say your soul, should always be tranquil or, on the contrary, do you long for a storm? To this end search through the poem and decide which words are more important and which are less so."

"I think the important words are 'at peace my soul would be within', and 'your image'."

"Then ask yourself if you would rather not have his image pass before you, meaning that you would rather not remember him."

"No, of course that cannot be so since I love him. He is always in my thoughts."

"Then it is a good thing that your breast throbs stormily, not serenely, or do you regret your lost peace?"

"That I still do not know."

"Listen to the music. It will reveal what lies behind the text, your innermost thoughts."

So they listen to the song; the pianist plays but she does not sing; the line of the vocal score is reproduced.

"The music which accompanies his image rages like a storm, but with great joy and illumination," says the singer.

"That means then," says Stanislavski, "you take joy from this disturbing element and, further, you are not satisfied by your state of tranquility. Yet when you sang, you sounded as though you regretted this intrusion on your peace of mind. Now it seems that you will be obliged to convey your joy in having that peace overwhelmed by a strong wind like the sea, by his image which is swifter than a passing storm. Note how well the poet and the composer have coalesced here to produce one single emotion.

"Maikov has some 'r's' in nearly every phrase and Rimski-Korsakov rises to a culminating point on the word 'swifter'. Continue to listen to the music: that is the centre of your feelings even after you have ceased to sing. It is the same old theme of love assailed by storms. Love overwhelms one like a sudden thunderstorm.

"Now we have cleared up a few points. Repeat the song and try to be very clear in acting in accordance with each word. Make a pattern with the words: the sea is serene until the storm blows up; that is how my soul would be, at rest, if it were not for your image, for my memory of you. But do not attempt to draw on your emotions."

The young woman sings the ballad again and is inwardly quite concentrated, as though she were listening to something going on inside herself. Stanislavski watches her eyes very closely.

"There," he says, "that is the first step. You still must pay attention to the words. They still lack flavour. 'If no storm. . .' is too slurred. You must keep practicing, repeating it dozens of times, and the same with the next line about the dashing waves. These are intricate combinations of sounds, so you must go over and over them until they are crystal clear, so that all the sounds come out of their own accord, effortlessly. Remember too that all labial sounds must be distilled with special care, by constant repetition.

"Now listen carefully: you have just given me a rather clear statement about how serene the sea would be if there were no storms and how at peace your soul would be if he did not appear. But this is still not art. It was produced with well polished craftsmanship. It makes a faint impression: musical form and a musically-trained voice can create a facsimile of art, they can affect the hearer and, for a moment or two, they may stir his imagination. Most singers are satisfied to do no more than that because they consider that is all that is called for. They have reproduced the form of a composition in which the rhythmic sequence and combination of sounds will, of course, give a glimpse, a suggestion to the hearers of the composer's intent. I can catch the drift of his meaning and vaguely sense what he wishes to say.

"But to reveal completely to me, the hearer, what else is underlying here, the things I cannot perhaps seize in this most brief romance—that is what an artist must do for me.

"To achieve this your singing must be transformed by a musical statement into a confession made by your heart. You must take the place for me of both the poet and the composer, you must infuse into me your own creative emotions, your state of being. All the elements of your inner life must be set to work. Then you will bring to life the author's idea, his theme. Where is the key to this? It lies in what we call the 'Magic If' and one's 'Object of Attention'.

"Let us now follow the logic of the idea, putting ourselves into the circumstances of the moment—with fantasy for a sail and thought for a rudder. You will enter into a life shaped for you by your own imagination. After this, feelings will begin to flow of their own accord. Your thought will be profound, your fantasy rich, your feelings broad. A shallow idea, a poor imagination will not give rise to any feelings. In this last case your result will be ordinary, it will not be a piece of art.

"Now answer these questions put to yourself: Who is he? And who are you? Why are you gazing at the sea? Where does this happen? When? The clearer all these circumstances are the richer will be your imagination concerning them and, consequently, your way of rendering this song will be altered, will take on a fresh aspect.

"Next, answer your question as to who 'he' is, this image, flashing storm-like through your soul. You need not tell me about this. He may remain your secret, the secret of the artist, but it is all important that all this should be abundantly clear to you yourself, then if you wish you may express all the details.

"If you are a Greek woman, Aspasia for instance, the sea is a familiar, an intimate, element of your life. But if you are from the North and are looking at the sea for the first time, your attitude towards it in this song would be entirely different. If you are a modern woman and have just come to a seaside resort, there would be a third variant. The point is to arouse your imagination, to feed your fantasy. This is all a part of the 'Magic If'.

"The second part is the 'Object of your Attention' towards which your inner vision is trained. What do you see when you sing about the sea and about him?"

"First I envision the kind of sea I saw last summer. . . ."

"You have every right to do so. All that is necessary is that the image be clearly limited and definitely defined. Sing it again."

The singer begins but is interrupted by Stanislavski.

"No. You did not concentrate yourself. Every second must be of the greatest value to you. There is no time to gather yourself. Concentration must be instantaneous. From the very first note of the musical introduction you are all attention; this enables you to be carried away to the sea."

After listening once more to the song, which now seemed somehow extended in length and breadth, and to have acquired a special expression, Stanislavski lets the young singer go with the words:

"Now go to work, dig down deeper into the song, enhance the highlights and the shadows the way painters do. You still have a lot of problems: the person on whom your attention is fixed, the words, the many images showered down on you by your fantasy deriving from your own life experience and your reading. But forget all that once you begin to sing. Stick close to the focal point of your concentrated attention on which your mind vision is riveted and leave all the rest to be worked out by your subconscious. Throw all the bits of food into your pot and when the time comes it will of itself be ready—that is, if you will be logical in your thoughts and actions."

Then turning to the rest of us he says:

"I am very glad to listen to these ballads that are little known, rarely sung. Our singer, Galya, is right to choose one of them. It is easier then to find one's own path and avoid the influence of having heard performances by other singers. Singers usually imitate the mannerisms of great performers and for that all they need is to have a good aural memory. I know about this from my own experience.

"Out of eight lines of verse you have to construct a whole dramatic story. As yet, you are unable to cope with this, but charm, youth, a fresh voice, a forthright manner will go far to create the illusion that you have almost done so. All these are qualities with which you are already endowed. What is left for you to do is the hard task of polishing to a high brilliance your own artistic gifts and learning how to adapt them to your work.

"For your first exercises it is important to choose a good text. This is of great help to a young singer. From this point of view Rimski-Korsakov will provide you with taste and fine discrimination. Chaikovski, on the other hand, often chooses weaker verse. Take for example his 'He loved me so. . . .' The music, to be sure, makes up for the triviality of the poem, yet if you listen carefully you will sense all its thinness, so it requires more effort on the part of a singer to make something out of the verse and endow it with some worthwhile meaning."

Stanislavski's sister, Zinaïda, gave the preparatory training to the young singers, breaking ground as it were, getting songs ready to present to Stanislavski.

We always thought that we had accomplished a great deal in these preparatory sessions and secretly each one of us expected to make a big impression on Stanislavski by the artistry of our performance. We dreamed of his saying: "Bravo! Well done! I have nothing to suggest. You have done all the work needed!" and of his leading the young singer with smiling eyes back to his or her chair. Yet dreams of this sort were nearly always dashed to the ground with the last chord of the music. Oh the tears that flowed in our impatient expectation of quick success and artistic recognition, and how much patience and perseverance were drilled into us on our way through Stanislavski's school.

The working atmosphere in the Opera Studio was strict, exacting, yet it elated and enthused all who worked with him despite all the deprivations we had to suffer in those difficult post-revolutionary years. These deprivations did frighten away a few singers who chose to abandon the ascetic atmosphere of Stanislavski's school in favour of quick public success.

"Well, what is the work laid out for today?" is Stanislavski's first question.

"We have to give some help to Vladimir Verbitski," says his sister Zinaïda.

"Very good. Come to the piano, Verbitski." A young, tall student with twinkling black eyes moves over to the instrument. At first glance he does not seem to be in the least nervous and very simply sings whatever Stanislavski asks for. Is he really not nervous at all? Of course he is. But we all are aware of the secret of how to hide or rather to overcome such excitement. Stanislavski himself taught us that.

"There are two kinds of nervousness: one is creative and the other panicky. Treasure the creative excitement and learn to overcome the panicky one. You can overcome it by means of concentration. The stronger your nervous excitement the more firmly you must attach your attention on some object and not allow yourself to be torn loose from it. If you can rivet your attention on something, anything, at the needed moment it will mean that you have learned how to manage your excitement. Even a button on your jacket can save you from unnecessary and harmful nervousness. It can put you into a state of 'public solitude'."

At this juncture Stanislavski tells us about his meeting with an aviator by the name of Utochkin. After Utochkin's first flight over the Moscow hippodrome Stanislavski went over to him through the crowd of spectators surrounding him. Stanislavski, as a director of plays and an actor, was interested in what his sensations had been during the flight. Was he frightened? How had he dealt with his nervousness? Utochkin replied that he had not been concerned with fear or nervousness because he had had "no time to be afraid"; he had been too busy keeping track of all the instruments and levers, of which there were a great many.

"So I realized," said Stanislavski, "that the enormous concentration he put on all those panels of instruments had saved him from any nervousness. That is what we actors have to do too when we take off on our own creative flights."

In general this comparison of the creativeness of an actor with the flight of a plane, and all our exercises in tuning up our physical and inner apparatus—his "system" of acting, so like the preparation for a flight by an aviator—figured often in his work with us. He drew examples from what might seem the most unlikely phases of life, the most unexpected and faraway aspects of nature, as if to underscore the communality of the laws of nature in all the aspects of creative activity.

We now know why Vladimir Verbitski is so collected, we know why he naturally and attentively keeps his eyes fixed on a poplar tree out in the yard as if it were an object of particular interest to him. "You're doing very well," is what we think. But Stanislavski, as soon as he hears the first notes of the piano, stops the singer.

"You have a very potent means for holding your attention here in this music, and yet your eyes are fixed on a poplar tree in the yard. Do not miss a single note, project yourself into the depths of every sound created by Rimski-Korsakov, unriddle them and you will find there is no better means of concentration than this of quieting yourself and allowing yourself to be carried over into the life created by you and the composer. You are making use of exercises set for you in the very beginning of your work here. But when you are on the stage do not ever look upon yourself as a student. Now you are an artist and the complete master of this hall and all of us in it, who find ourselves under the spell of your creativeness."

Now the singer transfers his whole attention to the music. Before he begins to sing, there are two bars written for the right hand alone, playing repeated thirds in six-eight time. It is as though the piano were imbuing him with the rhythm of his own heart; then after listening to these thirds the singer at once begins his song: "Of what do I secretly dream in the silence of the nights."

The rippling notes and the passive six-eight rhythm produce a mood of contemplation, while requiring of the singer a lightly lyrical agitation of his feelings. At least that is how it seemed to all of us present. The text of the ballad, written by Maikov, would seem to be quite clear:

> Within the silences of night, my secret dreams,
> Within each hour of the day, my thoughts—
> Shall e'er remain obscured from all,
> Even from thee my heart's own verse.
> My airy friend, the joy of all my days,
> Even to thee I dare not trust
> The visions of my inmost soul—
> Lest thou betray whose voice it is I nightly hear,
> Whose face it is I see at every turn,
> Whose eyes do ever light my way,
> Whose name it is forever on my lips. . . .

The finale of the song does not end on the usual high tone but ends quietly on a meditative note as the last word is sung.

"Well, what have you to say for yourself?" asks Stanislavski.

"It is difficult, of course, for me to say anything, yet it seems to me that I do understand the meaning of the song althought I cannot say to what extent I was able to convey it."

"What meaning?"

"The idea that love must be a secret from everyone and that one may not confide it even to verse," the young man begins to explain.

"That would indeed seem to be the case, yet it is as dry as a report read in court. First of all, who are you? I somehow felt that you are some kind of respectable papa who is afraid that someone will find out a secret passion of his. You do not grasp and as yet do not understand the most important fact: You are a poet whose verse is the joy of his days!

"The music, the melody, is full of throbs and agitation, despite its relatively smooth flow and serenity, but you do not hear this as you should. Thus you do not disclose the depths of the soul of this song. Inside, it is full of ardor. Just think, all life, day and night, every instant is filled with it, you speak her name over and over. But all we hear is some kind of positive, academic singing.

"Now you go over there and hide yourself behind one of those columns [the rehearsal was taking place in the large hall with the columns where *Eugene Onegin* would be staged a year later], let us have just a glimpse of you. Then sing this ballad as if you feel you have to keep your love a secret from us all—yet this secret is such a delight to you that you cannot restrain yourself from talking about it all the time. Go along now, don't stop and think about it but let it rip, come what will!"

Vladimir goes over to the columns and half hiding himself from our sight he begins to sing. Stanislavski keeps prompting him in a whisper:

"These triplets are not mere notes, they are the beating of your heart. See how it throbs!"

The first part of the ballad ends with the words: "This shall be a secret from all men", after which the piano repeats the familiar lilting melody with a broad sweep.

Here Stanislavski stops the singer:

"No! It is very important that this be a secret from everyone. Sing as if all the others are unworthy of knowing your wonderful secret.

"And you," he says turning to the pianist, "must play as if you yourself were involved in this secret. After all you are here now in the place of Rimski-Korsakov."

Now to all of those present the song sounded different, it was now filled out with inner emotions, it sounded as though it were an intimate talk between two souls. It was only in a few phrases that the voice of an overwrought soul rang out into space.

Stanislavski then asks the happily excited young singer how he feels.

"As if I were singing an entirely new song."

"Why? Because you were able to grasp the right inner rhythm of the verses and the music. The whole point lies in that inner rhythm. It is the close companion of your feelings and, when rightly understood, it will evoke in its train all the right emotions.

"You were also aided by the simple device of secreting yourself behind the columns, hidden away from us. As you continue to work on this song, think of yourself as a poet and although you say you cannot confide your secret even to your own verse, you nevertheless are actually creating a poem. Thus you are doubly inspired: by love and by your expression of it in a poem, and as a result you have the love of a poet. That is the core of the ballad.

"In all ballads, no matter how brief they may be, there is the seed of a larger piece of work. In each there is a plot, conflict, solution, and a through-line of action and given circumstances all leading to a super-objective. It is the aim of each actor-singer to gain the right understanding of the surrounding circumstances and to know how to choose the right colours in which to reproduce them."

The work that Stanislavski was doing at this time was most intensive. He was the principal director of plays and productions in the Moscow Art Theatre, and he acted in some of the plays himself. He kept Mondays and Thursdays free for work in the Opera Studio. If, at any other time, he had a free day or evening he immediately sent word that he was coming over to work in the Studio.

Then anyone who was at the Studio or could be quickly sent for was included in the session with him. Stanislavski obviously enjoyed working in the atmosphere of music. At the same time he was learning how to write about his work for his future book *My Life in Art*.

"How lucky you singers are," he used to say as he settled himself in his armchair in the big studio workroom. "The composer provides you with one most important element—the rhythm of your inner emotions. That is what we actors have to create for ourselves out of a vacuum. All you have to do is to listen to the rhythm of the music and make it your own. The written word is the theme of the author but the melody is the emotional experience of that theme.

"You must come to love the words and learn to bind them to the music. An opera actor is only creative when he produces sound in visual form. Make it a rule for yourselves: not to sing a single word to no purpose. *Without the organic union of words and music there is no such thing as the art of opera.*

"Now let us listen to 'The Upas Tree', if you please."

The pianist begins to play this gloomy short aria by striking heavy bass octaves that sound like overwhelming blows. That is also the way that Vassili Vinogradov's beautiful bass voice begins to sing.

Having listened to the song, Stanislavski's comment is:

"You only hint at the theme, you do no more than lift a corner of the curtain, you do not uncover the whole majesty and terror of the picture. In a word you have not yet truly heard or seen into Pushkin's lines."

Here Stanislavski rises suddenly from his chair, and stretching his long arms before him like the paws of some kind of sphinx, fixes his heavy-lidded, half-closed eyes on some far-distant point. His face seems hewn from granite and inspires awe.

When the pianist, who is watching him closely, plays the introductory chords he begins to sing. The words now sound awesome. The

text of the song is entirely different. All the vowel sounds are deep and the first phrase suddenly takes on a new and ominous sense. The second phrase at once makes us feel that we see some elemental, lava-like earth.

After that when he pronounces the words about the single upas tree as a "fearsome sentinel of doom", a great cosmic world opens before us. "The upas tree is terrible," Stanislavski emphasizes, "and it stands alone in all the universe."

> Out in a desert parched, bereft of life,
> Rearing itself from sun-caked soil
> The upas tree stands erect, alone,
> A fearsome sentinel of doom.
>
> Nature with arid thirst
> On day of wrath gave birth
> To this tree acurst
> Gave it dead leaves and
> Filled its roots with venom.
>
> The poison filters through its bark
> Under the noonday blaze
> At eve it hardens to a thick,
> Transparent resin.
>
> No bird flies near, no tiger comes,
> Only black storms envelop it.
> All shun this tree of death
> And flee from it in horror.
>
> Should an errant cloud mayhap
> Sprinkle its dormant leaves,
> They too drip poison into the
> Surrounding sand.
>
> Yet a man with ruthless mien
> Sent another man, his slave,
> To this grim tree of death.
> By morning he brought back the poison.
>
> He brought the deadly resin and a branch
> Of wilted leaves, his face bathed in sweat
> Which coursed over him in icy streams.
>
> Under the vault of his lord's great tent
> The poor slave brought his load, grew faint, fell dead
> At the feet of his unconquerable lord.

Into this venom the sovereign
Now dipped his arrows
To carry doom to all who lived nearby
And far beyond his borders.

We were ready to believe that we were listening to a new language. What was this: Pushkin's writing? Or could it be that Stanislavski could so re-create words? Both things were probably true. Yet it was only now that we clearly conceived all the poison, evil, disaster, terror, doom of which this tree of death was the dread symbol. Yet the amazing part of it was that despite the terrifying picture which had loomed before us, we were ourselves not terrified; there was so much power of art and such a sense of indestructibility about Stanislavski, who seemed to have become the sentinel of doom, that we did not fear this elemental evil. Perhaps we were feeling pride in the powerful artist who for an instant disclosed to us the profundity and pictorial power of this creation of Pushkin and Rimski-Korsakov.

"I might make a mistake farther on so that is why I stop," says Stanislavski, and, passing his hand over his face as if wiping it, returns to his place in his armchair. "I show you this not so that you will copy me or follow the logic of my thought: Each one can and should do it differently and in his own way."

Vinogradov now takes his place again. How frightening to stand where Stanislavski has just been and sing what he has just sung!

Yet this is not really so. Everyone knows Stanislavski's rule about work: Whatever you do on the stage, whether you act, sing, express your emotions, embody your character—you must first do your work correctly and only later on do you render it more beautiful or lustrous. If one of us is absorbed in reaching some simple and clear object in a believable way, he has nothing to fear; there will be no critical or ironical looks beamed in his direction. That is why Vinogradov boldly moves to the piano and instantly follows, as it were, the hot trail just blazed by Stanislavski, who now becomes a careful prompter. He is as filled with feeling as the singer himself, suggestions constantly trembling on his lips:

"When we come to the line, 'Should an errant cloud mayhap sprinkle its dormant leaves. . .' why is there such a soft, caressing melody, and warm *piano?* The rain cloud is a thing of joy, it brings refreshment to the world. . . . But now you must instantly change about, as you sing, to say the rain is poisonous. You see, the upas tree converts even good into evil. Repeat the words about the cloud. You have finished the exposition of the theme, you have conjured up for us a realm of death. Now human beings and their relationships come into action. You are presenting a large and very dramatic piece of poetry, it

is a whole play in itself. Imagine yourself to be a Pharaoh who has sent his slave to fetch the poison. This poison is obtained at the price of the slave's life. A despotic power drives people to their death. The more terrifying that power is the more we shall loathe it. And there is the gist of the thought contained in the poem: We must hate evil.

" 'Yet a man with ruthless mien sent another man, his slave, to this grim tree of death.' Convey that command which is contained in a commanding look.

"At the words 'The poor slave brought his load, grew faint, fell dead', Rimski-Korsakov wrote a descending fall of notes full of suffering that very distinctly portrays the fatigue, illness, dying of the slave. Sing each word to the last letter," says Stanislavski. " 'Brought his load, grew faint, fell dead'—there you have three large acts. Always remember that the first sign of a good singer is the fact that he sings each word, and consequently each phrase, to the very end.

" 'The poor slave brought his load, grew faint, fell dead at the feet. . .'—now pour into the broad melody all the pain of giving up one's life and do so with large strokes, but gently and with consideration for the dying man. And then rap out each syllable of the rest of the phrase: '. . .of his unconquerable lord.' Let these dry, rapped-out syllables serve as a description of that sovereign."

The singer repeats the individual phrases several times and the rehearsal goes forward at a rapid pace.

"Now come to the third unit of action: 'Into this venom the sovereign now dipped his arrows to carry doom to all who lived nearby and far beyond his borders.' Note how Rimski-Korsakov contrives to pass the theme of the poisonous upas tree to that of the sovereign: the composer uses the same melody for both. You now have the sovereign in your mind's eye. Your words are few but there must be a great deal of thought behind them. Nekrasov put this well in his expression: 'Words are condensed, but thoughts expand.' That aphorism should serve as a device for the work of all singers.

"As for the end of the ballad, there is little for me to say to you. Usually the finale goes along correctly of its own momentum if you have thought your way through to it correctly. There is one thing to remember—the expressiveness of the words. They must paint pictures for my imagination of the life created by the author. But how shall I, the listener, be able to visualize these pictures if you, the conveyor of them, do not see them? You must infect me with the desire to see your pictures, images, and I shall follow your example and also create images in my own imagination. Act through the words and the music on my imagination and not just on my eardrum. To achieve expressive words and produce them in the style of a Shalyapin you need to possess first-class diction.

"Now sing it all through from the beginning and feel your way to the goal that you aim at throughout the whole ballad. Gather together the component parts and slip them like the chunks of a shashlyk on the spit of the main idea. Slaves perish—sovereigns retain their power. The death of the slave who fetched the poison enables the despot to spread death to neighbouring countries. Hence hatred towards a poison-spreading, death-dealing despotism runs through the entire song."

After a successful rehearsal we often sat around and talked. Stanislavski used to tell us about singers he had known; most often he spoke of Shalyapin, with whom he was on friendly terms. Stanislavski liked to take out his key chain and rattle it. (Why he had so many keys in his pocket no one could guess because his doors in his study were always unlocked!) At such times he liked to joke and when our young singers began to dance he smiled at their free and easy ways. This lent an atmosphere of great simplicity and hominess to the school.

The purpose of finding the "core" of a short ballad, of revealing the bright, packed imagery, thoughts and feelings exalted above those of daily life, was to develop in a singer the sharp eye of an artist and the subtle sensitiveness of a poet-musician.

Each song of this kind worked out by the students was a kind of whetstone on which they sharpened their feelings, minds, tastes, and techniques for their futures as actor-singers.

Stanislavski laid a special, really serious stress on any ballad chosen to be worked on, even the shortest, and he was unconditionally committed to the careful study of the thought and character of the author's composition. "Why did you choose this particular song?" "What is it that you wish to convey by it?" Such were his questions and they had to be answered with more sense than just the stereotyped: "Because I liked it." For Stanislavski every ballad was an artistically achieved statement.

Take, for instance, the very short ballad of Rimski-Korsakov called "In the hills of Georgia." Characteristic of it are languid, tenderly sad Eastern intonations and a majestically melancholy form. The singer's difficult task is to convey the power of Pushkin's "radiant sadness". It cost Stanislavski a great deal of hard thinking to infuse this work with meaning so that the ninety seconds it took to sing it became significant both to the singer himself and to the people who heard him perform.

We see the student who has just sung the song standing in front of Stanislavski. There is nothing in the ballad to "show off" the singer; there are no ringing high notes that he might drag out, there is no long *fermata* at the end in which to put all kinds of "feeling".

As the ballad was just sung, no one seems to have been affected by it. Everyone feels this including the performer himself, Kudinov, who is now looking, with an uncertain smile, at Stanislavski. But the latter is very good-natured: the effort and the ineffectualness of the young singer are too obvious.

"Yes, yes, what you need here is the power and grasp of a Shalyapin," says Stanislavski at last. "But we just don't possess them. Therefore all we can do is to learn how to follow his example. The result may not be too brilliant in power and expressiveness, but it will be true to the nature of the composition.

"Now ask yourself: what is the essential element without which the heart of this ballad may not be expressed? What action, yes *action* not mood, of your soul, is at the base of your emotions and interpretation of this song? What must be now the substance of your life? Study the Pushkin text most searchingly. It is a ballad, a subtle, transparent watercolour drawing. To convey its content one needs not simple contemplation, a vacant eye and faded sound, but a very strong sense of energetic, inner activity, a vivid imagination, all masked under the restrained tenderness which permeates the whole ballad. Pushkin has no faded words, thoughts or images. And Rimski-Korsakov was well aware of this. He puts the Pushkin words into the foreground. That is why his accompaniment is made of such light, transparent music. That is also why the melody and the logical significance of the text are so closely bound together. This ballad is a model of the care taken by the composer for the precious words of the poet. At no point in this song does the composer sacrifice the text to any external vocal effects. This much is a general introduction to the character of your performance. How will you now concretely attack the problem of singing the ballad?"

"I shall study the verses and first of all penetrate their meaning," comes the bold reply of the young singer.

"Very well, continue," says Stanislavski.

"There are two parts, two themes: there is nature and there is I myself with my feelings."

"Generally speaking, that is true, but you must always seek out first the human being. His thoughts are the foreground and through him, his reactions, nature will participate.

"Next you must know: What man? After all you are in this case Pushkin himself." This statement by Stanislavski quite takes the singer aback. "You see, you are talking about your *own* depressed spirits, your *own* sadness, your *own* love. Thus the depression, sadness, and love of Pushkin are now yours." When he sees the bewildered face of the young singer and hears the suppressed giggling among the other students at the idea of Kudinov being transformed into Pushkin, Stanislavski goes on to explain :

"Of course, you will remain yourself, Kudinov, and when I give you the role of Pushkin it means that your thoughts and feelings should be affected as if you stood yourself in the place of Pushkin. Do you know under what circumstances he wrote these lines?"

"I do. Pushkin was travelling through the Caucasus to Arzrum in 1829 and wrote them on the way. They are evidently addressed to Natalia Goncharova [Pushkin's wife]."

"Good. If you will fill in the rest of the circumstances of the ballad with the figments of your imagination that will be good. But above all stick closely to the text."

The singer begins cautiously to read the verses: "Over the hills of Georgia lies a dense fog and night. . . ."

Stanislavski stops Kudinov at once.

"Do you visualize this picture? You may no longer just read the words aloud. Now all the words of this poem are cherished by you. We are all here now on a street in Moscow but you are to transport us to faraway Georgia, crossing nearly the whole of Russia, climbing the great range of the Caucasus mountains, carried along by horses. And you are alone, which is something one's particularly aware of at night. And note too it is not just the time of night but there is a dense fog lying over the land. There is something motionless about this, something numbing except. . . ."

"Nearby the tumult of the Aragva river," says Kudinov.

"Which means you are on the banks of the Aragva, which alone in the impenetrable night pursues its tumultuous course. See how laconically a great picture has been shaped. How you must treasure every single word so that it may reveal a picture. Then what does the poet feel in this setting?"

"I am sad and yet my heart is light," reads on Kudinov.

"Wait. Do not babble your words," says Stanislavski as he stops the singer. "This whole dark picture is summed up in the poet's confession that he is sad. Nor could it be otherwise. This is perfectly natural and just as it should be. But suddenly, quite unexpectedly, this dark picture is illumined by a shaft of light. The poet is sad but his heart is light; his sadness contains not only some light, it is filled with it. And notice too that three times he repeats the words: thou, thee, only with thee. What an affirmation of life! On what a bright note of joy he ends.

"If we read on carefully, we shall see that Pushkin in his state of reflection (what man as he travels does not think of the woman he loves?) draws a conclusion of great significance showing the power of the poet's ardent heart as it overcomes the depressions and agitations of life. This song is about much more than longing for the beloved. It is about the great heart of the poet that you will sing. . . ."

We listened, enchanted and inspired by Stanislavski's thoughts, and realized that there was no such thing as inexpressive, dull ballads but only a shallow approach in our thinking about them. Therefore if we were to do justice to Pushkin, Rimski-Korsakov, Chaikovski, we had to develop our imaginations and indeed become poets ourselves.

"You singers have the capacity to convey the deep thoughts of a poet and all the significance of any ballad," said Stanislavski as if he were reading our minds. "Words, reinforced by music, have a magic power. All you need is to pay attention to the words and they will resound with extraordinary power—this is something an actor can never achieve in drama. But you must consciously enunciate your words and the melody and not let them just slip uncontrolled from your tongue.

"Let us listen to what Rimski-Korsakov does to words, to every syllable, how he designs the intonation of the music. Now please sing the first two lines."

After a melancholy chord that seems to hang lifelessly in the air, the singer begins the familiar introduction to the ballad. The thought contained is now clear but when he tries to clothe it with his singing Stanislavski is obliged to stop him again and point out the long and difficult path towards true expressiveness.

Stanislavski's own wealth of miming, his expressiveness and gestures so enriched the thought and the images contained in the ballads, he made all so clear that one wanted to begin to sing again at once before the impression cooled, before this magnificent moment fled, so that one could seize upon and take firm hold of the pattern sketched by him.

Yet to grasp all this in one sweep is not possible in art. It is only to one of limited mind that it would appear possible to create something so splendid in a flash.

"That happens only once perhaps in a whole lifetime," said Stanislavski. "At least it happened to me only once, when I was playing Ibsen's character, Dr. Stockman. I had an instantaneous insight into all the slightest details of his life—I did not have to search any farther."

But when our singer, so inspired by Stanislavski, has sung no more than two lines of the ballad, he is gently stopped.

"In the first place you are not altogether concentrated, you do not have in mind what it is to listen at night to nature, in unfamiliar surroundings at that. Secondly, and as a result of this, your words are not entirely motivated. No images arise out of them as yet. That means that your sub-text is insufficient. If that is true a prime factor is lacking: the rendering of the author's intent through your own emotions." In saying this Stanislavski smiles understandingly because he sees how distraught and upset the singer is. Then he asks: "Why is this so? Because you wish to embrace everything in one grasp. Therefore you must learn to make an analysis, so that you may know with what to

begin. Begin with a firmly and clearly fixed object on which to concentrate. *All your art will stem from that, so let this be an established
rule for you.*

"Now exactly where is your centre of attention, of what does it
consist?"

"My past, a night in the mountains in the Caucasus," says the singer.

"Very good. But the point, of course, is to make these memories
concrete. You must have a clear remembrance in your mind of similar
circumstances. Arouse your fantasy and your 'emotion' memory."

"I never was in the Caucasus but I have been in the Crimea, and
travelled once by night from Sevastopol to Yalta. That is all I have in
the way of memories."

"Then recall that and also bring back anything else germane to this
ballad, books you have read, poetry, pictures you have seen and tales
you have heard. Sometimes a painting seen with special interest may
yield more food for your feelings than a whole lecture. So bring back to
your imagination as much material of this sort as you can. We need it in
building our 'given circumstances'. Some things are provided by the
author: night, mountains, a river and, far away in the North, a beloved
one. But in your imagination you must make them all very vivid, as if it
happened to you only yesterday. When you will have produced these
circumstances in your own imagination and come to believe in them,
then we too shall believe in your feelings. We cannot know what you
see in your imagination but we shall be drawn by your inner visions and
we, the spectators, will paint in our imaginations our own pictures,
under the impact of your creative inspiration."

"But I have so little time for the beginning," says the singer. "There
is only one chord, and then it is necessary to paint at once a complicated
picture."

"Then remember how things happen in real life. Do you actually
need so much time to create a vivid picture in your imagination of this
or that event? You are told that just now an airplane crashed, some
people you knew were killed, and instantly you imagine a whole picture although you have never witnessed the crashing of an airplane.
Why is this so? Because it is all very close to your feelings, you are much
involved, inwardly activated. In such a case do you need much time to
concentrate? Your own nature does this instantly for you. An actor must
learn this process and how to be guided by it. How long did it take you
to envisage that tragic picture? One second, perhaps two, and then you
immediately were concentrated on studying the details and being
affected by them. What is the key to this? Your intent attention!

"So it is in the present instance: your attention fixed on an object
forces you to go deeper and deeper into the imagined picture. The

difference here is that you must *guide your attention. That is why an actor finds it important, indeed imperative, to stick to this rule: An actor must be able in a single instant to fix his attention on the object presented, so that he may react to it with true feelings, and also he must be able as quickly to turn off his attention and cut out his emotions, returning to his own life.*

"This implies virtuosity in the handling of your attention. If an actor says, 'I entered into my role so completely, was so powerfully affected by it that I began to weep and could not stop', then he must be warned that he has taken a wrong turn. That way lies hysteria. That is not art. We must understand the emotions, and have a technique to control them. Write that down and add it to your rules. Why not write everything down? Do you rely on your memory? The point is not whether your memory is splendid or not too good. The thing is that the creative capacity of an actor and a singer is a *science*. You have to study, develop it, as you do other forms of science. Unfortunately, few realize this. But let us go back to our Caucasian ballad."

Listening to Stanislavski, the singer is standing by the piano, profoundly immersed in his thoughts. His face is utterly serious. When the first tentative, sad chord is played at the start of the ballad, his eyes travel slowly to some distant place seen only by him, far beyond the walls of our hall, and then, as if obeying some inner urge he begins very simply and gravely to sing.

"Over the hills of Georgia lies a dense, dark night." Then we hear the harmonic sounds accompanying the words, "Nearby the tumult of the Aragva river." The melody here is like a beautiful cascade of sounds, rising lightly afterwards to the words: "Before me. . ." until over the hearts of his listeners a warm wave seems to rise and fall. We cannot take our eyes from the unhandsome, round face of the singer, now so informed with meaning. We wait to hear what he will sing next, how it will be, as if we have quite forgotten that we know the contents of the ballad.

When he sings: "I am sad and yet my heart is light," suddenly we all feel released from the tense anticipation in which we had been held. Stanislavski, who has been leaning forward in concentrated expectancy, his face most earnest in expression, now suddenly throws himself back in his chair and says:

"You began correctly and made us all listen to you. But then you lost the thread of thought and began to 'colour' your words. You 'are sad' and immediately you put on a sentimentally silly little smile, 'yet my heart is light' with an artificial lighting up of your face. This is arrant overacting from an inner vacuum. That is because you abandoned your focus of attention. But you should follow the text, the thought. After all, when a man is sad his heart is heavy, but you say sadness is shot through with brightness. Therefore here the words 'light', 'brightness', 'thoughts of thee' take on a special significance."

The singer begins once more at the beginning and although all the words come out distinctly, one feels a studied effort on his part and Stanislavski is again dissatisfied. He tries to find a new approach to the singer's psychology.

"Now you are mechanically emphasizing the important words. It is not your thought which is in action. You seem to be pushing the words forward. For whom are you singing this?"

"I am talking to myself. I am alone."

"You mean you are reflecting? When a man reflects, when he communes with himself, there is nonetheless a kind of dialogue; it is as though his mind is conversing with his heart. Consequently, the monologue will contain hesitancy, doubts, firmness, weakness, and stubbornness—all the elements of an ordinary argument. Your reflections need to be more profound. Address them to her. Where is *she*?"

"Very far away, in the North, in Moscow."

"Note that the poet does not say his thoughts are full of her: He uses the word *thee*, thus addressing himself directly to her. You see how inattentively we are still reading and weighing the text. Now if you will turn your thoughts directly to her across a great extent of space this will oblige you to pack more action into your words and thinking, as if impelled by distance, to make them carry over to her. The volume of your voice is not of any avail in this. So what then is the focal point of your attention?"

"She is—I must sing to her."

There could be no question about it. He sang in quite a different way. We felt this not only through the sound of his voice but also the expression in his eyes that were set on some far, faraway point. This "distant look" in a singer draws everyone to him, it arouses a desire to speculate about him, it arouses a desire to speculate about what he is seeing, what moves him so.

Stanislavski listened to the whole of the ballad, never taking his eyes off the singer. It was obvious that he too was rather moved, but he was sparing in his praise although we believed that he was satisfied with the responsiveness of the singer.

"Now you are on the right trail. It remains for you to put a high polish on the song, by detailed enunciation of every word, every vowel, while at the same time conveying the thought they contain and the beauty of the music.

"Sing the beginning again so that you will realize the direction of the work still to be done."

He sings the first two lines of the ballad and then Stanislavski stops him.

"All that we shall say about this song, the separate lines, words, images, vocal shadings—all that will be stored up in your subconscious. Therefore the more you reflect on the contents of the piece, turning your attention to the very finest shadings of sound, the richer will be your storehouse.

"In this compare your work with that of a painter who first makes a drawing and then lays on the colours. Good painters are known by the richness of their palettes, by the succession and combination of the most delicate halftones."

"But I follow all the shadings indicated by the author: all the *piano, crescendo, ritardando* marks. I do not know what other shadings I should look for."

"I am speaking of shadings of words and sounds, nuances which cannot be set down in the score, yet they are the very ones that impart a soul to the composition and it is through them that the artist becomes manifest."

As he goes on to speak of the differentiation to be made in vowels in order to increase their pictorial, phonic power we realize that all this is not immediately acquired and the singer himself shakes his head doubtfully, evidently hesitating to believe in his own ability to achieve it.

"Now, don't think too much about it," says Stanislavski. "Start right off, or else you will fall into the habit of excessive introspection and will be afraid to sing. All right, you will make mistakes, but what of that! You will exercise your willpower and not be balked. Actors often say: 'I see, I understand. I'll do that next time.' But no—go ahead and do it *now.*"

These words stir the singer into action and he begins to sing. From time to time he stops when a word does not come right and sings it over and over.

Whereupon Stanislavski, who is keeping close track of him, cautiously prompts him. As the creative and artistic impulse takes hold of the singer, Stanislavski sees to it that he does not lose his way.

Next we have a ballad quite different from the preceding. It contains no description. It consists of words exchanged between two men; it is practically a small aria from an opera. And we are puzzled by how to take hold of it.

"Let me hear it, please," says Stanislavski, setting his pince-nez on the bridge of his nose.

A serious young baritone goes over to the piano, gives a sign to the accompanist, and with grim and immobile face he begins to sing "The Messenger," a song composed by Rimski-Korsakov to words from a poem by Heine:

"Up and to horse! Through thicket and plain, haste to the castle of Duncan."

The precipitous, galloping music runs through almost the whole length of the song. It is only the last four lines that have a despairing accompaniment as the action nears the tragic dénouement.

The content of the ballad concerns a young knight who rouses his servant and sends him at night to King Duncan to find out which of his daughters Duncan is marrying off. If it is the black-browed one all is well, but if it is the one "with bright brown braid" then let the servant bring him a cord for a noose.

The whole ballad is very agitated, impetuous in character. Nervous sixteenth notes to each quarter note of the accompaniment give the impression of a wild gallop and at the same time a wildly-beating heart waiting for its doom.

The *recitativo* line for the baritone is also set in the spasmodic, galloping tenseness of the accompaniment. Towards the end of the song the hoofbeats die away in long chords, like the heavy swinging of the pendulum of fate. The Knight speaks in gloomy, thoughtful tones: "Go then to the marketplace and buy me a cord, ride back at a walk and be silent. I shall understand!"

The whole song lasts barely one minute but what a tempest we sense in the soul of that man!

The baritone sings the ballad. We can see that he is afraid to "overact" and incur the wrath of Stanislavski so he avoids doing anything extreme or extraneous. His face remains impassively gloomy from beginning to end as he studiously produces each note, each word.

"For whom did you sing?" asks Stanislavski with a sly expression.

"For you" is the reply.

"Am I your servant? As a matter of fact you could have made me feel I was your companion. But this I did not feel."

"No, that is not what I meant. I simply recounted the story to you."

"In other words, you were not addressing anyone in particular. You did nothing but stir the air and sang to the microbes in it."

"I know that I did not have a focal point of attention. It makes you feel awkward, to stand at the piano when you have to act as if you are on the stage."

"But this *is* your stage now. Once you went over to the piano and undertook to re-create a piece of the life of a human soul—that puts you on the stage. Acting beside a piano is a most subtle and difficult thing to do. The reason is that all depends on fantasy, on yours as an artist, and ours as spectators. Now sing me the song again. I shall be listening."

The singer begins over again. Stanislavski listens with absorption, his eyes on the floor. At the end he sits motionless for a few seconds, then stands up briskly and says:

"You prompt me, I do not know all of the words yet." Suddenly with the first chord of the music he is transformed. His face is pale and he leans over the table in front of his chair gazing at the floor as if in the shadows he saw something which made him exclaim in a desperate voice: "Up and to horse! Throught thicket and plain, haste to the castle of Duncan!"

Then as he leans over still farther he goes on in a hissing but musical whisper: "Go to his stables, and wait! If anyone comes, enquire. . . ." Suddenly, as if he can no longer hold back his secret, he straightens himself and in a desperate tone, almost a cry, he sings: ". . . which of his daughters Duncan is giving in marriage."

We had the sensation that it was night, that we were in dimly lighted stables, straw on the ground, a lantern on the wall, horses moving restlessly in their stalls, and, in the corner, the Knight's servant just aroused from his sleep. The Knight himself is a half-clad youth; his eyes are wild, burning with fear and despair as he speaks to his servant.

"If it is the black-browed one. . ." Stanislavski goes on in a choked voice, "then fly back. But if it is the other, with the bright brown braid. . . ." Here his whole great figure is staggered as if under the impact of a painful blow to his heart: ". . .if it is the other with the bright brown braid. . ." He finishes the phrase with a broad and sweeping tone of despair, then sinks into himself with the words: "No need to hurry then, my friend."

The word "friend" is spoken as if it means the end of everything.

After this come two long-drawn-out chords. He seems quite bereft of emotion, bent over, absorbed in himself, and sings almost with indifference: "Then go thou to the market," and adds, with a kind of inner brutality: "buy me a cord" (the word sounds terrifying as he sings it), "come back at a walk and be silent!" As he says "be silent" he looks for the last time at his servant and it sounds as if that is the most important of his orders. At the end he sings very simply, collectedly: "I shall understand!"

We sit there motionless, frightened, really alarmed by what we have seen. The fear stems in part from the tragic content of the song, the dreadful fate impending, and so vividly projected. But in the main we are stunned by the power of the instant outburst of drama which Stanislavski has shown without the slightest preparation or evidence of effort.

Settling back in his armchair, Stanislavski remarks quietly:

"I have given you this demonstration not for the purpose of having you copy me but in order to teach you how to follow the logic of what I did. Each person will pursue that line in the light of his own understanding, taste, and talent.

"Now let us analyze what is to be done in this ballad. Of course it is more of a piece from an opera than a short song, and it calls for a dramatic, 'Shakespearian' interpretation. You need great inner technique in order to seize at once the intense inner rhythm of the scene and its focal points: your servant, the image of the wedding, your own death. But you do not get your rhythm *after* the music has begun—there is not time for that. You must set your rhythm ahead, *before the music starts,* as though you were yourself determining it for the accompaniment. Therefore the ballad should already be taking shape in your feelings before the first note is played on the piano.

"Here it is necessary, and I use this word very sparingly, to have the *temperament* of an actor. It is that temperament which permits you to arrive at the needed rhythm and continue with it unabated to the end. This high point of impact is arrived at not through force, which would blur it, but through powerful expressiveness. Included in this too is the use of pauses which are fully as significant. Actually the power to make his pauses pregnant with meaning reveals the true actor. Only a powerful temperament can fill out a large pause. Shalyapin was famous for that. In fact the Shalyapin pause as well as his diction have become classic.

"Do not seek out temperament inside yourself but rather look for the most moving parts of a piece, find the right rhythm, exercise active willpower, and all this will combine to bring out your temperament, if you have any.

"But do not force or do violence to your feelings if your soul does not catch fire. The most dangerous thing you can do now is to cripple your faculties by overloading them beyond your strength—that leads to hysteria and muscular cramps resulting from over-tenseness. Make this a rule: *The more dramatically powerful a scene is, the greater the call on your inner forces, the freer your body must be.* While you are singing watch your hands with especial care: no clenched fists, no twisting of fingers. If you ball your fists you are done for because you will have shut in your temperament, driven it deep inside."

One rehearsal day the following short conversation took place.

"Why are you not showing me something?" Stanislavski asked a quiet young man as he came across the vestibule from his study to our rehearsal room. The vestibule contained a window, decorated with four small white columns, which looked out into the courtyard. A round iron stove stood in one corner. This space was where we sat and smoked, as irresponsible youths, while waiting our chance to stand beside the piano and offer proof as to whether or not we were worthy of Stanislavski's time and effort spent in trying to make actors and artists out of us.

"I have been given a ballad to sing and I don't know what to do with it. I don't like it, but all the good songs have already been distributed. Your sister told me that this is a good ballad but I can make neither head nor tail of it."

Stanislavski looked at the bewildered and disturbed expression on the young man's face and said:

"Well, you sing it anyhow, if you know it."

"Oh, I have worked over and repeated it so often I am bored by it." And then he walked with considerable embarrassment to the piano.

The ballad did indeed appear to be rather baffling both in form and content. Rimski-Korsakov had made a short musical monologue out of verses by Maikov. He composed it in a stylized form of antiquity, with highflown speech placed in a very beautiful *recitativo*, accompanied by opalescent harmonies.

When the song was over no one seemed to have understood what it was about and we waited to hear what Stanislavski would say. He was silent for a bit and then turning to us all he made this comment:

"I like this ballad, there is a lot of flavour in it, but it requires the right approach. This will prove most instructive for you," he added, turning to the singer.

"This is a preparatory study of a young man in Ancient Greece. It is almost in the style of a poem by Sappho. All singers should enlarge their horizons and broaden their culture. Now read me the verse. . . ."

> In the grotto I awaited thee—
> The promised hour came and went
> Daylight soon spent
> Drowsed into twilight;
> The aspens dozed, the halcyon birds fell silent.
> Yet all in vain!
> The moon glided forth and flooded
> The firmament with silver . . . vanished. . . .
> The night melted away and Kephale's beloved,
> Eos, leaned over the gates of rosy, new-born day,
> Shaking down from her tresses golden grains,
> Pearls and opals, into the dark blue plains
> And forests. . . . Still thou camest not. . .

"Is the thought in this verse clear?" asked Stanislavski.

"I comprehend that it is a question of useless waiting all through the night. But the song is very brief."

"That is the point at which music performs miracles and you should learn how to make the most of this magic power. In music sometimes four measures can create the impression of very extended expectation. But you have not used the pauses and the rests. Anyhow, one cannot sing by metronome. A metronome and true creativeness cannot possibly coexist."

The singer repeated: "In the grotto I awaited thee. . . the promised hour."

The phrase has a strong accent on the words "awaited thee" and on the "pro-o-mised hour," when the melody rises in an ascending scale and ends on a D-flat. This is an advantageous note for a baritone, and very effective though sometimes treacherous.

Stanislavski said to the singer:

"What you have to convey is a long, passionate time of expectancy and this one phrase should make you fall in love with the song. Sing it quite freely; it is *recitativo* in character. 'In the grotto I awaited thee'—put a strong accent on 'awaited thee' and follow it with a rest. Then very slowly go on to 'the promised hour'. With each syllable your voice slowly rises to the last word, 'hour'; then hold it as long as you can and let it fade away to nothing.

"Is there a rest there?" Stanislavski asked.

"Yes, indeed there is," interrupted the accompanist.

"Then use it for all it is worth, and in an artistic way. Let this note at first have a joyous sound, then as it diminishes it will grow sadder and sadder until it finally dies away. Meanwhile, with this one phrase you will paint a large picture. A melodious word can be magical. You as yet do not appreciate the full power of such a word nor are you able to exploit its richness."

The singer then attempted to follow the plan so vividly laid out by Stanislavski but the treacherous D-flat was his undoing. One heard only a tentative note which made one think of a man on a tightrope in the circus. But there was no sense of elevation about it, no colour as yet.

"No, that's not right," said Stanislavski. "You're not firmly seated in your saddle. You are simply intent on this one note and are focused on it, whereas your attention should rather be fixed on a black-eyed Grecian maiden.

"Carry each phrase to its conclusion. Extract everything you possibly can from it. Do not throw all the component parts into one heap but study each one separately. How many units do you have that belong together in ideas?"

"I think there are five: the first, *I was waiting;* the second, *the day ended,* everything went to sleep; the third, *the moon rose and set;* the fourth, *dawn broke;* and the last, *thou didst not come.*"

"Just see how simple that all is. And as a result you have a very large program of waiting. But let each unit, the moon, the dawn, be carried to its conclusion quite separately from the rest. Do not let any one of them merge into any of the others.

"Then there is the inherent desire but that is for the future. That would be too difficult for you at present. Now what you have to do is to establish the character of the song, its style. This is no suburban ballad. It is all half divine, half mythological. That is why the words are so stately. However, in order to avoid all fake pathos, study the song from the point of view of your own feelings. That will be the first step. Later you can add character.

"And do not forget your diction. It is very special here. Above all proceed with logic and plant yourself firmly on that."

At the same time that the students were working on ballads they were given their first rehearsals onstage of opera scenes. Two scenes were chosen which were in more or less finished form. One was part of the prologue of *The Maid of Pskov* and the other the prologue from *The Tale of Tsar Saltan*, both by Rimski-Korsakov.

In both cases, the former being dramatic and the latter comic in content, there were characters and situations which required real acting. As this was to be the first production of the Opera Studio, awaited by all musical and opera-going Moscow, the performance would be not only important but decisive. Many theatre people had heard of Stanislavski's experiments with opera and were looking forward with interest to their public presentation. Some were prejudiced against them and some were filled with hope and lively expectation. The wings in Moscow's theatres were full of rumors about Stanislavski's method of work with singers, since partial descriptions of it leaked out and gave ammunition to those who were against and those who were for change.

Despite the controversy Stanislavski was anxious to try out the results of his work in public.

All in the Studio understood the dangers and responsibility inherent in this first production—the singers were new, unknown, so that their names were linked only with that of Stanislavski. In those years he enjoyed immense respect and popularity yet there were always stubborn opponents.

"Now see to it that you don't disgrace me," said Stanislavski in a half joking way to his students.

It must be said at once that Stanislavski's way of teaching acting and of directing was so powerful that the audience listened to *The Maid of Pskov* prologue with bated breath, and they laughed loudly at the comic *Tsar Saltan*. Of course the young singers were not real masters of their art but they were sustained by the method and inspiration of Stanislavski.

In the beginning he presented these opera scenes without costumes and makeup. In this way he wished to underline the fact that the young singers were in a close, direct relationship with the public. Although this natural and free way of performing was not new in drama theatres, it was an unheard-of innovation for opera singers, who usually sang at a great distance from the audience with a large forestage and the orchestra pit between them.

These first public productions of the Studio took place in the summer of 1921 on the Moscow Art Theatre stage. They were given along with the first showings of the Vakhtangov Studio (*The Miracle of St. Anthony* and *The Wedding*). In addition to this public test of the singers' achievement there was another point of significance. The fact that the Opera Studio was offered the use of the Moscow Art Theatre stage greatly enhanced the importance of these performances both in the eyes of the public and in those of the singers themselves.

During that summer season we underwent a short course in discipline which tempered our great joy with many bitter tears. Stanislavski with generous hand had showered on us his discoveries in the world of his art, but he was equally generous in handing out punishments for the least infringement of ethics or discipline. At the very first rehearsal we heard the terrifying, reverberant voice of Stanislavski issuing his warnings throughout the silent theatre.

Stanislavski's tirelessness and persistence during rehearsals had become well known, but it was now for the first time that we faced the tremendous demands he made on performers. We saw what it cost in work and energy to produce something on the stage that would be simple, life-like, fluent and convincing. We also realized that the work of an actor must be constant and unflagging.

Stanislavski usually watched rehearsals from the sixth row in the orchestra. When a rehearsal appeared to be drawing to a close he would move into the first row. But when the young actors stumbled into a blind alley in their search for the right path, when the eyes of the women began to fill with tears and their voices quavered, then he would take a chair and sit right on the stage and with his indomitable will he would get them to the point where they could leave the rehearsal in a happy mood, not only because they had learned something new but also because they had achieved a firm grasp of it.

This first performance of the Opera Studio was called *A Rimski-Korsakov Evening*. It began with a "Gloria" sung by the whole company in honour of Rimski-Korsakov. They stood on the steps leading from the proscenium to a platform which had its own curtains. To one side was a bust of Rimski-Korsakov on a pedestal surrounded by flowers.

On the forestage itself there were two rows of heavy, old-fashioned armchairs and a piano. The "Gloria" was accompanied by flourishes of trumpets from the wings and was sung by the young artists facing the bust. They then sat down and the main program began.

It was rather unusual in form. All the participants were on the stage in their previously rehearsed positions. Some remained seated, others stood as they sang their ballads with only the slightest hint of staging. It was a test to show if they could behave impeccably in public while remaining within the compass of the thoughts and feelings of the song. Stanislavski's main injunction was: "sing these ballads in public but do not sing them at the public."

When the concert ended there was a blackout during which the performers themselves removed the furniture (this in itself had had to be rehearsed many times because it was done in complete darkness). When the lights went up a second curtain opened and they gave the excerpt from *The Maid of Pskov* prologue, scenes from *Christmas Eve* and *The Tale of Tsar Saltan.*

The next production was *A Pushkin Evening,* composed of the first three scenes from *Eugene Onegin,* and the prologue to *The Tale of Tsar Saltan,* with text by Pushkin. The three scenes from *Onegin* had been prepared in the previous winter season, although the first one actually played by the Studio was the one called "Tatiana's Letter". From this kernel grew the eventual production of the whole opera. It was in this scene that Stanislavski's concept was most fully executed, and the inner world of Tatiana was conveyed in such a way that the whole attention of the spectators never left the face of the actress-singer.

For Chaikovski the essence of the Letter Scene is the revelation of Tatiana's soul, conveying all the shadings of her thoughts and feelings; it is this scene which defines the character of the whole opera. When Stanislavski grasped the meaning of this scene and was able to convey its essential quality, he held the key to the entire production. Although the three scenes from *Eugene Onegin* in this performance were played before bits of scenery borrowed from plays in the Moscow Art Theatre repertory, the director's plan was fixed from then on.

The performance concluded with a dramatized version of a "Homage to Pushkin" written especially for the occasion. To the music of a ceremonial procession the singers set a bust of the poet on a pedestal and sang their praise to him.

In balancing the account of this first season of the Studio it is necessary to say that it was not yet an epoch-making event in the theatre life of Moscow. Still there were a number of experts who realized that in these "sketches", in Stanislavski's special approach to opera, in his efforts to blend the music with the words and both with the rhythmic movements of the actor-singers, they could experience new reactions to well-known operas. The various pieces shown in this first season of so-called "sketches", particularly *The Maid of Pskov* prologue, *The Tale of Tsar Saltan* and the Letter Scene from *Eugene Onegin*, were outstanding.

The entire action of the short prologue to *The Maid of Pskov* consists of Vera's story revealing the painful secret of her infidelity to her husband, and his unexpected, precipitate return. Then comes the dénouement which gives the whole event an unforeseen twist. If this scene is presented in the usual operatic way it is extremely difficult, indeed all but impossible. The wife's five-minute-long tale recited from the forestage is very like the Letter Scene in *Eugene Onegin*, and in this instance Stanislavski, as previously, resorted to extremely stark solutions. The young wife's whole tale is told while she is reclining on a bench by the stove.

The unexpected return of her husband fills the stage with furious action, the culminating point of which is Vera's attempt to throw herself out the window. During this entire scene there was not one superfluous movement by the actress which would draw the attention of the spectators away from her face. This called for the most delicate kind of inner technique.

The unfolding of Vera's temperament while she remained in the same place throughout the whole tale was masterly in its enthralling effect on the audience.

This brief scene conveys the dark days of the reign of Ivan the Terrible when human passions were rampant, and the opera reproduced quite faithfully the atmosphere of times long past.

The tone of the Letter Scene was quite different, yet Stanislavski sensed what its essence was from the very beginning. Just as in operas on historic themes he had to fight against histrionic posturings in fancy, period costumes, in the *Onegin* he ran head-on into all sorts of operatic clichés developed in the traditional productions. It was Stanislavski who uncovered the noble simplicity, the purity of soul, which were the very essence of Tatiana's life and love.

The comic line in the opera *Tsar Saltan* was clearly marked. The actors were completely truthful in projecting their feelings but there were lightly underscored gestures and a sharply expressive staging which brought the characters alive but at the same time gave the sense of their being in a fairy tale. The slothful, self-important, overdressed Cook and Weaver, the evil Babarikha, the solemnly stupid Tsar, and the bright-eyed, Cinderella-like Militrisa, in a hemp coverall and bast shoes, running around with either pails or armfuls of firewood, provided contrast and stirred the audience to the realization that "a fairy tale is a lie, yet there is a hint of truth in it. . . ."

The appearance of Stanislavski's students in two drama-concerts was, according to him, in the nature of an opening gun and made it possible for him to test their strength for full productions later on.

One of these test productions was Massenet's *Werther*, which was gradually put into shape by Zinaïda Sokolova. Stanislavski added the finishing touches and preliminary performances without scenery were given on the stage of the Moscow Art Theatre. Later on it was included in the repertory of the Opera Studio and was taken on tour in Leningrad, where it alternated with performances of *Eugene Onegin*.

The underlying idea of the *Werther* production was to point up the contrast between, on one side, the lower-middle-class, patriarchal way of family life in Germany, with its limited home interests, Sunday churchgoing and daily visits in the evening to beer halls, and the romantic, wildly protesting Werther on the other. This clash ran like a red thread through the whole production and brought Massenet's Werther closer to Goethe's Werther; in fact they almost were fused.

The alternating shifts between the semi-comical, naive, dull-witted smugness of petit bourgeois life in a German provincial town and the poetic moods and dramatic tension of the scenes with Werther and Charlotte were pointed up not only by the staging and the external decorative accessories but especially by the deepened contrasts and the psychological life of the two leading characters. The clear exposition of the logic of the conduct of the principals lent them an unexpectedly new and vivid basis which took them out of the rut of ordinary operatic routine. Stanislavski had a great deal of work to do with the singer who had the role of Werther. He had to have a lyric tenor, one free of all the saccharine clichés of his profession. His Werther must be full of virile inner power. As a result his music, which at times had seemed too soft and shallow, began to make a quite different impression.

In this production there was a whole series of brilliantly expressive and poetically entrancing mise-en-scènes, which, as so often in Stanislavski's work, acquired a profound, symbolic significance. This production has long since been forgotten, yet in it Stanislavski produced the most delicate shadings in the inner and outer conduct of his actors—something which is so lacking in many operatic productions of works with profound psychological content.

In summing up the theatrical season of 1922–23 the newspaper *Izvestia* wrote: "But what deserves especial mention is the appearance of the Studio of the Bolshoi Theatre which has been for three years chiefly under the guidance of Stanislavski. They gave *Onegin* and *Werther* and stirred up on all sides the most contradictory interpretations and opinions. This is very much to the good. Both productions are striking in the deep truthfulness of the stage action which closely follows psychological emotions. Before such an achievement in the field of opera we can only bow down. One can safely guarantee that nowhere on the whole earth is there or has there ever been such an approach to opera. We can be happy over the good fortune of the young people who were lucky enough to go through this training. There was no one among the young artists who struck us as being phenomenally gifted by nature with a special voice, but the depth of their dramatic achievement at times had an impact that was breathtaking."

In this early period of the Studio's existence we must also include the production of Cimarosa's *The Secret Marriage*. It was prepared for presentation to Stanislavski on his return in the fall of 1924 from his tour abroad.

The choice of this opera was not accidental. It enabled the Studio to embody Stanislavski's principles of operatic art in the style of 18th-century opera. It also gave the singers an opportunity to practice Italian singing and *recitativo*. In this opera there are many repetitions of certain musical phrases. If they are to have true liveliness they must be informed with logic and not mere formality, the singers must possess a high order of technique, the ability to provide a real basis for the words and music, and do all this within the difficult framework of classical composition. The libretto in itself provided a well-made, intriguing comedy plot. If, as Stanislavski always asserted, "One cannot be a really good singer without excellent diction," here in this opera the singer was compelled to have crystalline diction combined with highly polished charm. At the base of Stanislavski's work here was the objective of achieving a true comic style. *The Secret Marriage* was the fountainhead of a series of Italian comic operas which reached its culmination in Stanislavski's production in 1933 of *The Barber of Seville.*

The singers in *The Secret Marriage* were called upon to portray a dissolute old man galvanized into a suitor, a puffing, overage spinster seething with passion, and a miserly, ambitious, stupid-but-sly father of two prospective brides. These roles, despite the sincerity with which they were played, became in effect caricatures with subtle touches of farce. Stanislavski enjoyed dipping into these parts, although they scarcely seemed appropriate for him with his subtle psychological grasp of dramatic and poetic situations. He was however strongly drawn to plays bordering on the grotesque and in this field his fantasy was limitless.

Of course, in demonstrating, he himself played *all* the roles in *The Secret Marriage*, but above all he adored playing tottering old men with vacant eyes. He played the aged Count with stiff legs barely propelling him, and a face bereft of intelligence with a baby mouth and smacking lips. Half blind, more than half deaf, he apparently retained only the capacity to chew on something tasty or suck it. Tall as he was, others supported him. The whole picture was such a complete satire of the Count's dissolute past that his desire to marry Donna Geronima (of course for the sake of her dowry) brought a roar of laughter from the audience and roused their expectation of further humorous events.

The play was written in accordance with the canon imposing unity of action, place, and time. The architectural feature of the columns dividing the stage from the audience in the Opera Studio's hall was adapted into a theatre set by the scene designer and painter Kravchenko. The columns were converted into square structures, part of the vestibule of a massive stone pile, the walls of which were ornamented by frescoes in the rococo style. Two staircases between the columns led up to the private rooms of the owners of the house, and a single door gave entry to the room of the younger daughter. A fireplace and portraits on the walls helped to reproduce an 18th-century atmosphere.

In this opera there are only six characters in all. Consequently each role had to be taken by an actor-singer capable of handling it with the lightness and gaiety of a comedy part. Without that *The Secret Marriage*, which is a brilliant musical comedy, is robbed of all meaning. That is also why, in all probability, the opera is not often given. It requires a genuine ensemble of acting and singing. The delicate lacework of Cimarosa's opera is full of exquisite musical and vocal detail and requires of those who perform it a highly developed sense of form. A singer's conduct on the stage—his thoughts, feelings, movements, along with his singing—are held in a corset of form which does not allow of deviations or liberties, regardless of the airy gaiety and even buffoonery of the unfolding plot.

This gay comedy with all its lively melodramatic peripatetics was played at top speed, at a good comedy tempo. It was not a production of great significance, but it demonstrated with accuracy the basis of Stanislavski's opera reforms. It was a refined miniature, the merits of which were not immediately obvious and were noted only by spectators of attentive and keen perception.

2

Eugene Onegin

ON THE 15TH OF JUNE, 1922, in the house where Stanislavski lived after the Revolution, the first performance under his direction of Chaikovski's opera *Eugene Onegin* was given.

This production was extraordinary from the point of view of the ideas then in vogue about how to present an opera. The setting consisted principally of a kind of portal made up of the four columns which divided the ballroom of the old mansion into two unequal parts. The smaller part including the columns served as the stage and the larger was for the audience. A heavy gray curtain divided the one from the other. The portal with the four columns, with small but carefully planned decorative effects, was converted into the façade of the Larin home, into Tatiana's bedroom, into the Larins' dining room, and even into the opening near a forest where the duel takes place. The players were all young students of the Opera Studio and they acted in their ordinary clothing. There were no dress suits, wigs, no makeup, no footlights and the audience sitting only a couple of paces removed from them seemed to be participants in the action on the stage. In the wings, Stanislavski stood pressed into the indentation of a window and held the ropes governing the curtain. From watching his now smiling, now suffering facial expressions it was obvious that he was part of the performance and was involved in what was transpiring on stage.

The music for the performance was provided by a piano out in the part of the hall where the audience sat. The whole production went along with the smoothness of a well-prepared concert. The singers, who were well in command of their roles, threw no furtive or anxious glances at the conductor.

The small vestibule outside the ballroom which also led to Stanislavski's apartment was filled in the intermission by the audience and the students of the Opera Studio not engaged in the performance.

This performance contained in miniature all the essential elements of a complex theatrical production: wings, lights, sound effects, accurately planned intermissions, shifts of scenery. All this was handled by students who were learning the technical mechanism of a theatrical production.

Despite the apparently home-made, modest quality of the staging, it nevertheless contained that all-important factor for which the theatre existed—truthfulness of human emotions.

After this performance both the press and the spectators agreed that the depth of thought, the thrilling excitement of feelings, the enchantment of Pushkin's verse and Chaikovski's music were here conveyed more fully and with greater finish than in any former productions of this opera.

This application to the art of opera of the experience and knowledge of such a great student and reformer of theatre art as Stanislavski was most brilliantly successful. It was evident that if he continued and developed his work in this field he would create an opera theatre, the foundation for which was laid in this production.

The first performance of *Eugene Onegin* goes back many, many years now, but as a classic story read in one's youth, that production remains, in all its detail, forever in our memories as the essence of genuine artistry. It has the right to be termed a classic.

Scene One: The Arrival of the Guests

As the last soft *pizzicato* chord from the strings was ending and the curtain was drawn to the quiet rhythm of the first duet the audience saw the façade of the Larins' simple country home. On either side there were small terraced steps leading down into the auditorium, open windows and in front of them a few lilac bushes. Sitting on the top of one terrace was Madame Larina, the lady of the house, and at her feet on one of the steps sat the old Nurse. The scene was reminiscent of a painting by Maximov: the house, the two elderly women, the silhouettes of two girls near the window on the right—one at a harpsichord, the other standing beside her. All this against a background of impeccable Empire style, the classic lines of the columned portal of a country estate belonging to a noble family—all so evocative of the past, of laconic, exquisite simplicity.

There was no hint in the scenery of the rolling landscape of Central Russia, no park or pond, no river on the horizon, in fact none of the picturesque accessories with which scene designers so often overburden this scene in order to impress the audience. How minuscule singers have seemed for centuries against such massive backgrounds!

In his setting Stanislavski pursued a course directly in opposition to established custom. The onlooker's first impression was clearly that of the almost tangible, cozy, calm life in the Larins' home. It was left to him to imagine the old park which Madame Larina and the Nurse are looking into with admiring eyes, the sun setting over the tranquil fields, the sound of peasants singing as they come home from work. The soul of the onlooker was as easily caught up in the world of Pushkin's characters as if he were reading the story.

Yet to achieve this simple effect on the stage—to walk about, sit down, converse, sing, *live* it all in the foreground of the stage—all this required immense technical training in acting, fluency of body movement, and sound musicianship on the part of the singers. At such close range the audience saw not only each movement of an actor's body, each turn of his hands, but also the slightest change in the expression of his eyes. He had to bear himself in public with irreproachable control. Ordinary operatic performers were unable to meet such tests. An excessive ebullience, usually considered evidence of commanding the stage, would be here a fatal exhibition of tactlessness.

The staging planned by Stanislavski proved such that the singers could not have carried it through without his help, without special physical and spiritual training. That is why the work of the director in such a production is above all that of a teacher in the highest sense of that word. In every production Stanislavski began with tuning up the singers' "creative mechanism", beginning with improvisations and ending up with the polishing of the individual role. Starting from the clear hypothesis that the actor is the master of the stage, he categorically insisted on its application to opera. To obtain and maintain this mastery he urged his singers to continue their training beyond his "preliminary" work with them, every day, every hour, throughout their lives.

Fortunately we are able to follow the style of Stanislavski's work and can grasp what, to the superficial or indifferent observer, might be incomprehensible—the salient features of his creative line of thought. This is a most precious legacy which has not yet been fully examined and is still not understood by many specialists in the theatre.

Let us then proceed along the principal line of Stanislavski's practical work in opera, the direction taken by him in his artistic concept of how to synthesize in an organic way the music and the drama of Chaikovski's composition. Let us follow the logic, indeed the *necessity,* of the performance as developed by the singers in accordance with the musical and dramatic requirements of the composer, and see how the staging was evolved naturally by the performers themselves in keeping with the logic of their own requirements in living their parts. The director Stanislavski is out of sight in such a performance, leaving the actors quite to their own. Still they hold in their hands the thread of Ariadne—Stanislavski's system of acting—which keeps them on the right path, protecting them from the dangers of muscular rigidity on the one hand, and on the other of "playing up" to the public, flirting with it, mincing about, and all the cliché habits so common to opera singers whose only goal in the past was to show themselves off to advantage and try to outdo all their fellow singers on the stage.

"An actor must earn the right to appear downstage," Stanislavski used to say, "and the way he does this is through learning how to metamorphose himself into the character he is playing. If he can do this, let him step forward. Then he should be in the foreground all of the time because I as the spectator enjoy his creative ability. Yet it is obviously tactless to come down to the front of the stage without knowing what you are going to produce when you get there."

So here we are in front of the Larin home and the people who live there. Now Stanislavski gradually introduces them to us, the audience; how carefully and accurately he has planned it.

The opera opens with a duet sung by Tatiana and Olga ("Have you heard?"). One might imagine that the public should see them at once.

"No," says Stanislavski. "The leading characters, especially Tatiana, cannot be presented in such an insignificant way. Her entrance must make a powerful impression."

So this calculating director first lightly catches the interest of the spectator. We see Madame Larina and the old Nurse, who, as they sit on the terrace, join the audience listening to Tatiana and Olga singing inside the house in the living room. We realize that there is no reason for the girls to come out and show themselves to us. They are practicing their duet.

"This section serves to introduce us, the onlookers, into the unclouded, simple life of this family. Who should do this? Of course those who set the tone of that life, the older people, the mother and the Nurse. . . . Do you see what our objective should be?" asks Stanislavski.

Can there be any relationship between the lyrical music in which the voices of Tatiana and Olga are delicately interlaced with the triolets of the harps, and the cooking of jam which the simpleminded directors of the 1880's included as characterizing the life in the Larin home? The impression of a meditative, calm, thoughtful stillness is so clearly palpable in the music that one cannot possibly bring to mind great pots of boiling jam, even if the stage directions in the libretto do indicate that jam is being made.

In any case Stanislavski was always quite sceptical about such stage directions in plays or opera libretti. He considered that they were put in by people with little knowledge of the stage. This was usually done during the first production and then printed that way. We have no notion who wrote in the libretto that jam was being made, but we can state quite boldly that there is no indication of this in Chaikovski's music.

The light of the setting sun falls athwart the white columns of the façade of the house. Madame Larina and the Nurse are resting after the household labours of the day as they listen to the singing of their beloved girls floating out to them from the living room.

It is not at all easy to sit in front of an audience and do nothing except listen. It requires great artistic skill. In fact Tatiana and Olga had to sing their duet over and over many times before Madame Larina and the Nurse could achieve that calm on the stage which conveyed at once the relaxation of two elderly women, their satisfaction with the life surrounding them, their tender love for the two girls, their philosophy gained through a lifetime of experience that habit is as good as happiness.

Yet, besides, they had to show that they were two distinct types of people: the lady of the house with her strict upbringing in a noble family of the beginning of the 19th century, with all her manners and sentimentality, and the Nurse, a peasant woman, a serf, a warm-hearted, kindly person very like Pushkin's own old nurse, Arina Rodionovna.

It was to these almost imperceptible shadings in attitude that Stanislavski's first lessons were consecrated. He bent every effort to get from those two actresses the kind of conduct on the stage that would instantly convey the right tone for the whole performance.

Madame Larina is sitting in an old armchair with an antimacassar doily, and the Nurse is at her feet, in the very foreground, only a yard inside the curtain.

"No, you must sit so that I can feel that your whole body is resting and that you are completely at ease. Get rid of all unnecessary muscular tension throughout your body," insisted Stanislavski.

The actresses try out various poses adapting themselves to the setting and to each other.

"But remember," he says to Madame Larina, "that no matter how you relax your body, you still retain your lifelong habit of keeping a straight back and holding your head high; the bend of your elbow and the softness of your wrists and hands will show in your way of sitting. Even if the Nurse loosens up her bent spine completely and lets her work-roughened hands, her stiff old fingers, hang down you will still remain trim. It is the way in which you lift your lorgnon from your lap, carry it to your eyes, how you use it to point out this or that, that will indicate to me how you were brought up and how you brought up your daughters. Now look at me through your lorgnon as if I were an utter stranger, point out something in the park to the Nurse, reflect for a bit, toy with your lorgnon thoughtlessly. You can make the lorgnon a sort of extension of your arm, it is such an habitual accessory, rather like a cigarette in the hand of a confirmed smoker.

"Now listen to your daughters singing. Do you love them? Are you proud of them? But above all don't look smug or conceited. Your aristocratic upbringing requires a certain restraint in the expression of your feelings. How will you exchange glances with the Nurse when a certain passage pleases you particularly? After all, you yourself know music and when you were young you used to sing. . . .

"Do you feel," he then said, turning to the Nurse, "what it means to you, for instance, to turn your whole body around to look in the direction of the window? It is an undertaking for you, you feel a stab of pain in your back, your hips are so stiff the turn is difficult to make. Now you turn, then get up and go into the house. Oh no! You cannot possibly do it that quickly. When an old person has been sitting for a while in one position his back and legs seem to stiffen, they must be gradually brought back into motion, they must be warmed up to act, the back must be carefully straightened and only then is it possible to walk. And on each step up you must plant both of your feet, the way children do.

"Until you feel quite at ease inside yourself and there is no tension in your body or in your attitude to Madame Larina, whom you have known for some thirty years, you cannot begin to sing. Begin with the simplest things; think of how you would sit there, listening, looking at her if you had been her old nurse. There is no need as yet of any emotions and feelings. What you have to do is put your fantasy to work. It will begin to act the moment you begin to ask yourself, 'Where, when, why, etc.', and in this way you will create a whole past for yourself. Yet this is a large and complex undertaking. You will have to work at it constantly and for as long as you sing the role of the Nurse. Right now, however, put the question to yourself of how you have spent this day. Then, in accordance with what you have done in the course of this imaginary day you will find the *only* way for you to sit there and act. But remember that you really must *visualize* that imaginary day and not just reel off words about it.

"Very well. Now you are resting: Try to remember what it feels like to come home and rest after an overburdened day. Let me see you get up and come from inside your home to your places here and sit down as you would in real life. When the curtain opens you will be sitting there in front of us onlookers and you will make us feel how you came here and why you are sitting in such attitudes."

After the actress has played this exercise a dozen times, it becomes very convincing. Then Stanislavski says:

"You must always come onstage having begun to act your roles in the wings, before you reach the audience."

It was by means of the most varied exercises of this sort that

Stanislavski taught his actors how to get into their parts before they
went onstage, and not just automatically follow the pattern of the
staging set by the director for fear of any accidental slips that might
upset the self-possession of the other actors and interfere with their
complete absorption in the music.

"The music of the duet will provide you with the necessary tranquil
rhythm; your every movement, even the slightest, will be in rhythm
with the music, provided you are saturated with it, breathe it in with
every breath you draw. At that point you will feel the complete aesthetic satisfaction of being able to create your role and we shall feel the
same in watching you do it."

Now we no longer have before us two actresses with nervously
restless eyes, full of embarrassment, we have two new women with
whom we are not yet acquainted. Madame Larina is wearing a pale
violet dress with a light summer shawl on her shoulders and the Nurse
has on a shaggy shawl over a simple dress and a dark, peasant-type
kerchief tied around her head. They are both absorbed in contemplating the quiet evening, the old park, and in listening to the sound of
singing coming from within the house. Now and then they glance at
each other and smile. Probably they are thinking of bygone days and
from the expressions on their faces and their gentle smiles you can tell
that their memories are bright and tranquil, as are the evening and the
singing of Tatiana and Olga. Now the first half of the duet is finished and
Madame Larina begins to recall her memories: They are singing . . . and
I used to sing. . . The Nurse replies, remembering the time when Madame Larina's husband was still her fiancé. . . . Then the daughters
continue with the second part of the duet. A quartet ensues but usually,
in most productions, no one ever knows who is singing what or to
whom.

This quartet is an artful blending of two duets: there is the dreamy,
slow "Did you hear?" and the *recitativo* exchange of memories of their
past between Madame Larina a⁻d the Nurse.

It takes great vocal skill to keep the comparatively rapid exchange
between them, interrupting each other as they do, from slipping into a
sort of chatter, and to preserve the liveliness of the dialogue along with
the tranquility of the atmosphere with which the music and the whole
scene is imbued.

Here Stanislavski used a hitherto unknown means of handling an
operatic ensemble. Usually the musicians' main concern is only to keep
the voices in balance and follow the composer's melodic line. Yet if the
music is the sole concern, it would be entirely too difficult to think
about diction and stressing the clear meanings of the words in such a
complex interweaving of voices. Usually what happens is that the
content of what each person in the ensemble is singing is sacrificed to

the purely musical form. The goal Stanislavski set was that while keeping strictly to the musical text the thoughts that motivated the performers during the quartet and duet should be conveyed to the audience with equal clarity. As the notes in the music, so the words must come across both *forte* and *piano*. The words in any musical phrase which were essential to the clarification of the thought in it had to be produced with exaggerated precision so that the consonants would cut through the sound pattern, and the words that were of minor importance, even if they fell into stronger phrases of the music, should be sung with muted, subdued diction in order that they not interfere with the dominant theme. This is what Stanislavski called "word control." Every singer had to know exactly the melodic line for which he was responsible in any ensemble, just when and where he was to carry the "word-thought" and where he was to tone down his own diction in order to let his partner's words come through more clearly.

First we heard Tatiana and Olga sing the first part of their duet. We understood what they were singing. Then the quartet began. Here we had to understand what the older women were singing, therefore the diction of Madame Larina and the Nurse had to be sharper, more emphatic, while that of the two daughters was subdued so that their words, which in this instance were not of prime importance, did not outweigh and obscure the meaning of those sung by their mother and nurse. Tatiana and Olga rather "thought" their words, yet the musical pattern of their parts was precisely maintained. By means of this method Stanislavski was able to achieve complete clarity of expression for every single member of an ensemble and each role was preserved in its entirety. What usually happens in these ensemble scenes in opera is that the singers "stop acting", follow the conductor's baton beat for beat, and then when they have finished their bits they "begin to act" again. Any such way of singing was absolutely unthinkable to Stanislavski's system of acting. In accordance with that, even during ensemble singing the inner life of a character could never be interrupted even for a moment. This way of singing is achieved through intense inner concentration on the point to be conveyed, through a skillful and accurate rendering of the text. Naturally the technical grasp of the music itself had to be paramount so that the participants of the whole ensemble were able *to listen to* and *be listened to* by each other and not be glued to the conductor's baton or listen only to themselves.

One main condition that the singers had to abide by was that the conductor must be seen only through "side vision", that only an occasional check by a sidelong glance at him was permitted. While onstage they were never to be tyrannized by his baton. They had to feel his presence, sense his own inner rhythm just as he had always to sense and understand the rhythm of the actor-singer whom he was accom-

panying. That general inner rhythm governing the stage at any given moment is something which has to be worked out jointly between the singers and the orchestra. Naturally the conductor has the leading role in achieving this but just as the director has to be absorbed into the performance onstage, so the conductor must never be a despot. He should be the sensitive, responsive friend of the singer-actor.

With the quiet ending of the first quartet came the next number—the arrival of the peasants. This is a crowd scene with dances and the occasion for a brief diversion.

Some of the leading people in opera, musicians, scene designers, stage directors, are guided by such considerations as: "The public enjoys theatrical spectacles. Let them have a broad, colourful picture, give them a holiday atmosphere, dances. Crowd scenes build up a mood." Therefore many opera theatres which have at their disposal large choruses, a corps de ballet, and numerous supernumeraries feel it incumbent on them to convert an opera into a colourful "divertissement"; and the greater the applause after such a number, the more satisfied they are with their own achievements. Thus they imperceptibly, by catering to the public, set our operas back a century to the times when Dargomyzhski was only just beginning his struggle to introduce realism on the operatic stage in protest against the costume-concerts which went under the name of operas. All this has been written about by Serov, Stasov, and Chaikovski. Then Stanislavski, devoted to a struggle against the old opera conventions and the visiting-star system, created a new theatre which asserted the principle of ensemble acting and refined artistic taste. He demonstrated the way in which the theatre can exercise a cultural training force when it really makes an effort to reveal "sincerity of emotions, verisimilitude of feelings", as Pushkin described them, or to serve the purpose of "showing the life of a human soul" on the stage, as Stanislavski put it.

In opera there are two contradictory approaches to crowd scenes: The first relates to the occasions when the mob is a natural and dramatic part of the substance of the opera and is therefore essential. The other is when the crowd is used as a "divertissement" and does not forward the action of the plot but rather hinders it. In productions adopting this latter, customary approach, in the second scene in *Onegin* when the peasants enter right after the idyllic opening scene with the "kind landowner", Madame Larina, they go into a boisterous country dance. At the finale of this dance they freeze into poses with their arms and legs stretched out in all directions as if practically begging the audience to applaud them. The condescending public is usually quite ready to oblige with handclapping and the self-satisfied ballet dancers go off into the wings, having shown complete indifference to Tatiana although both these scenes were written for *her*.

"How are we going to put on *Onegin* in this hall?" Stanislavski is asked—the question concerns the original space in which the opera was rehearsed. "There isn't room enough for the peasants to make an entrance and dance."

"And why do they have to dance in the early scene in *Onegin?*" was his reply.

"But that is the customary thing: the peasants bring to Madame Larina the first sheaf of grain cut."

"Are we supposed to be putting on an agricultural opera? All that is simply dragged in by the nose. Does Pushkin make any slightest mention of such a rite? He could not possible have produced such a cheap, pinchbeck scene. This is nothing but an incrustation due to time, a sop to saccharine sentimentality. I am not at all certain that even Chaikovski cared for having a folk dance in the first act, but he was under some compulsion to gratify the taste of the theatre in his day. Such a scene with the peasants destroys all the exposition of the plot necessary to the beginning of the opera and therefore it is anti-artistic." Our celebrated conductor did not object to Stanislavski's reasoning and agreed to cut the chorus and Madame Larina's thanks for the songs.

Stanislavski never imposed his opinion arbitrarily. He never said: "We will make a cut here and we will not play this scene." He expounded the necessity for such a decision and convinced his actors by his irrefutable logic.

"In this first part we have created the atmosphere of the tranquillity of country life in which Tatiana lived. Now we have to present her to the audience. This moment of introducing the main character is extremely important.

"According to the librettist we have, immediately after the duet of Madame Larina and the Nurse, the arrival of the peasants with songs and dances, while somewhere in the middle of the crowd scene Tatiana is supposed to emerge. This approach quite blurs her entrance. Especially so since the meditative Tatiana, right after the wild dancing, begins to sing her first, significant phrase: 'When I hear those songs how I love to let my thoughts carry me away . . . far away'. Therefore let us have the peasants not come onstage but pass by behind the house. As they return home from their work in the fields let them sing that song, 'How my poor feet do ache'. This will prepare the mood needed by Tatiana for her first phrase.

"Incidentally, we have too little space to allow a whole group of people to pass in front of the house. Our set is built around the principals and not for the chorus. That is one reason for our boldly making this cut," Stanislavski explained. "We shall just throw out the chorus of dancers and singers. By doing this we shall strengthen the main line of the play. Any dances at this juncture would be merely a distraction and

would prevent our revealing the main thread of the plot—the line of Tatiana."

Later on it turned out that it never occurred to anyone in the audience that anything had been left out of the performance, or that anything had suffered from the omission. On the contrary, the scene gained in finish from the streamlining.

To go back now to the stage. The duet of Madame Larina and the Nurse is over. The movement of the music dies away on a long-drawn-out note played by the double basses. The two old women sink deep into their memories of the past.

From somewhere far off a single voice is heard. One must listen carefully to discover where it comes from. The voice gradually grows in volume as it comes closer. The soft harmonies of the chorus merge with the melody carried by the tenor and by the time we hear the second couplet, "How my hands ache," we sense clearly the approach of a chorus coming to the house. This effect took a great many rehearsals to produce. It was necessary to find just the right place for the chorus, otherwise the singing would appear to come from the first wing.

At the singing of the second couplet by the chorus Olga lightly runs out on the terrace and then stands still, listening to the song. After that she quickly kisses her mother on the cheek and dashes off in the direction of the peasants. Her impetuous appearance at once characterizes Olga for the audience.

While we are making the acquaintance of Olga the chorus has come quite close to the house and would seem to be on the point of coming onstage. With the words, "How could I forget my dear one," the orchestra comes in to support the harmony of the chorus. This is a strong moment as the music from the orchestra swells forth, and on this wave of sound Tatiana appears in the doorway.

She stops on the threshold as if inhaling deeply the music of the folk song. She simply stands there and listens; yet in the combination of the music from the orchestra, the resonance of the chorus, with the quiet appearance of a slim young girl brought out onto the stage by a peasant song, we sense such a wealth of emotional content that despite its utter simplicity the scene becomes deeply significant.

The chorus drifts away, the sound of the singing dies down and is lost in the distance. Tatiana is still listening intently as she slowly comes forward to the balustrade at the edge of the terrace, as if she were being drawn by the dissolving melody. Now she is standing directly in front of us. She is simply dressed in a modest white gown, unadorned with ribbons or flowers. She holds a little book in her hands. Her quiet, thoughtful presence has already impressed itself on our memory. And although we have known her only for a brief moment, it seems as

though we have been looking at her for a long time and really know her. In this careful, skillful, and impressive way he introduced his principal heroine. Now she is quite prepared to take up her cue: "When I hear those songs, I love to let my thoughts carry me away . . . far away." And we are witnesses to this dream of hers.

"What do you bring with you when you come out onto the stage?" That was Stanislavski's principal question to every actor. And until you were able to give him an answer about the life in your role, your past in it up to the moment of your appearance, he would not permit you to step onto the stage.

"Listen to the overture," Stanislavski says to the singer who plays Tatiana. "Right here your role begins. Your music is there, and all the questions you put to life. Can you feel what it means to stand on the brink of emotions, of impulses you have never before known, when all around you things begin to seem different as though you were looking at them for the first time, and with different eyes? Can you feel this presentiment of the abundance of life, which is like the opening of a rosebud? In a moment it will burst forth into bloom. With this in mind, ponder your first words 'how I love' and above all 'away . . . far away'. This should contain for you a special, a magical meaning. This is your secret. You may not reveal it to us, but you must have it in you. That is what you must bring when you step out onto the stage.

"You cannot squeeze into a role through a chink in the door. In fact this would do violence to your own nature. You must come to *feel the role in yourself and yourself in the role*. At the moment when the role of Tatiana was given to you she did not exist as yet. There was only you. You will not get anywhere until you find out who and what you are, until you are familiar with all the circumstances which are bound up with this image of Tatiana. That person is an actor who can put herself into any mood. At first follow the course of simple physical actions. I do not care which way you move, stand up, or sit down; all I care about is what your imagination does."

In 1922 when K. E. Antarova was rehearsing the part of the Nurse she wrote down the following words of Stanislavski to the actress playing the leading role:

"You *are* Tatiana. You are standing in the wings and preparing to sing the first phrase of your duet, 'Have you heard?' If you did not come out of your dressing room as Tatiana, if you did not greet those you met along the way in your character, if, as you were putting on your makeup, you did not have your vigilant attention fixed on the dark winter evenings when the Nurse used to tell you fairy tales, if your heart does not beat in rhythm with Tatiana's . . . the stage, when you enter it, will not be the home where you have lived for so long, you will not be able to produce the colorations in your voice which are so completely enchanting, or reflect in them the newly-awakened forces of love in a pure, young creature."

Stanislavski worked long and arduously with the singer to draw her into that special state in which the audience first sees Tatiana. This is not just a meditative mood, not just troubled concentration, and there is nothing in it of sentimental flirtatiousness. What he was trying to achieve was a state of utterly modest simplicity and complete lack of any exaggeration.

"This is the state of an artist on the stage when he has nothing to 'act up' about. Because he is so absorbed with his own inner objectives, thoughts, concerns—all the action is inside him.

"See to it that you do not convey the impression by your conduct that you are simply out-of-sorts, slightly indisposed, as your old nurse with her simple mind might think," was Stanislavski's warning to the singer-actress. "It will be even worse if we are led to believe that you are worried about some household matter. You must strike us with the poetic quality of your state. Your imagination, as an actor, should lift you up out of everyday existence and carry you off into the life created by the fantasy of Pushkin, Chaikovski, and you. Listening to your own inner promptings, to what is transpiring inside of you, you will find something akin to the creative state of the poet who listens to the mysterious voice of his muse. . . ."

Now the actress has come onto the stage and nothing must interfere with her inner life; all we must do is to keep close watch on her, her face. She stands by the balustrade of the terrace, facing the auditorium; she seems to be following in her mind's eye the group of peasants passing by the house. In her hands she holds a small book, a French novel.

"As an actress you are immediately faced with a most difficult problem—you are standing in front of the public but you *must not sing at that public.* An actor from our theatre may not simply sing at an audience. That is a complete denial of our theatre. Our approach in art is directed at an *object.* Every actor, like every human being, has some object towards which his thoughts, his attention, is drawn when he embarks on any creative work.

"What is your object to be? You may sing to your mother, but that will lower the level of your thoughts. You may sing to yourself, your mind may commune with your heart. You wish to clarify the state you are in. Remember how it is in ordinary life when you talk to yourself on some serious subject or other. Until you have worked out your own technique hold fast to some object as you stand in the forefront of the stage (this may take a year or two to learn) because you are forbidden to stand facing the public and to address it directly. The doorframe to the right and the left of you must be the limit of what you see."

This problem of looking at the audience, of singing at it, was a subject of unremitting discussion during the twenty years that Stanislavski worked on operas. He considered this habit one of the worst and most hampering in the work of opera singers.

Tatiana has scarcely finished singing her first phrase when impetuous Olga again darts in from the wings. She sees her daydreaming sister and instantly (she does everything in an unexpected way) she hides behind a lilac bush and then steals out, almost crawls out, and to the accompaniment of a harsh chord jumps onto the terrace and frightens Tatiana. "Oh Tanya, Tanya, you are always dreaming. . ." From then on through the whole aria ("I am not given to languishing sadness") there is a playful, almost childish scene in which Stanislavski has Olga frolic around, full of pranks, in a mise-en-scène showing her to be indeed a playful child.

"Try to cheer and distract Tatiana with your aria. Translate your words into action. Invent any number of little pranks to divert her. But do it all very gently, without pressing—none of the actor's hysterical carrying on or forced animation! Think of some gay thing to do and do it in earnest."

At that Olga went over and stood on the very edge of the steps, balancing her body so that she would not fall off.

"That's just the thing for Olga," exclaimed Stanislavski happily. "Remember that it is only when a person does a silly thing seriously that it is really funny. This is something you see very often in the circus. A child too takes his pranks very seriously. He will try to spit three times in exactly the same spot. A quasi-child—that is what Olga is. Yet they nearly always act Olga as if she were saying: Look at me, I am just a silly girl.

"Just as you finish your first phrase, the orchestra echoes it with a spirited little chirping sound, pim-pam, and does this after each one of your phrases. And the sixteenth notes before you come back to your first phrase—they are clearly like a game of tag. Now snatch Tatiana's precious little book away from her, tease her. But then at the end of your aria turn modest, return the book, and then sit down on the arm of your mother's chair and caress her. But do it all in rhythm and especially avoid any coquetry or seeming to say to us: See what a good girl am I!

"Actors are always wanting to emphasize, to press down on the loud pedal, as if otherwise you could not reach the audience. That is not so! It is a very general mistake made by actors. The main thing is to be sincere, naive, and 'radiate' your feelings. Your arms and legs cannot express anything by themselves. Physical actions can do no more than set you on the right road. But how you will travel along that road into your part—that is of the greatest interest to us."

In this way Stanislavski slowly, gradually, stubbornly removed the hard shell of coquetry, sentimental pretense, "cuteness," and that saccharine quality which is so often resorted to on the stage to characterize high-spirited youth and quasi-childlike sincerity. This was what Stanislavski deprecatingly called the "rubber stamp of a high-power coquette". And it was a long time before he would let the actress playing Olga continue with her role, not in fact until he was positive that she was on the right track.

At this point the focus of interest shifts to Tatiana. The Nurse has risen from her chair, where she has been sitting for so long that her back is stiff. She straightens herself and moves towards Tatiana: "Tanyusha, Oh, Tanyusha, what is the matter with you? Are you ill?" But Tatiana goes back to reading her book and merely says, over her shoulder: "No, Nanny, I am well."

This is just an everyday exchange, but in an opera when you add singing voices every phrase can be made into an aria. Here Stanislavski carefully shapes each sung phrase so that it comes out simply, exquisitely, and in a gently musical way.

"Why should you turn such a caressing phrase of concerned interest ('Are you ill?') into a whole aria, and worse than that make the syllables all long and drawn out?"

"But the composer has set this in a high *tessitura* and that's what stretches it out."

"Still if you put the accent on 'Are you ill?' the implication is that you are *not* ill, therefore you are well. How would you say this in ordinary life? Go over this phrase again."

It was only when the singer could speak the phrase naturally while keeping to the logic of the intention that Stanislavski allowed her to sing it.

Stanislavski never passed over the slightest, even seemingly insignificant phrase. He would never rest until the whole was carefully molded, and so clearly sung that every bit of the thought contained in it was perfectly clear.

"You opera people," he used to say, "sing in syllables, and at best sing words, but you must learn to sing thoughts. The more clearly the thought behind the words is revealed in your singing, the better your voice will sound, because it will evoke your emotions, and backed by real feeling your voice becomes ten times as effective. Words, rendered more beautiful by music, arranged in graceful melody, acquire a most vivid significance and power in your singing. If you merely produce them mechanically, the words are deformed in direct ratio to speaking them illiterately on the stage.

"What made Shalyapin great? His ability to remove accents where none are needed; he preserved the complete melody, the feeling behind the words, with loving enjoyment. That's what made his words so delicious when he sang them. So pronounce the phrase about Tatiana's health simply—after all it is an everyday question—for there is no impending catastrophe as yet, and Tatiana is not threatened with an untimely end. But you put so much voice into this phrase when you sing it that we are frightened to death about her."

The transient scene between Tatiana and the Nurse is interrupted in the opera score by the appearance of the peasants and Madame Larina's "Thanks, good friends, for the songs", and that, of course, draws our attention away from Tatiana. But since Stanislavski did not have the chorus come onstage it was possible to come directly to Olga's line: "Mama, look at Tanya", which after the Nurse's worried question reinforces our attention on Tatiana.

"Here you can act out a whole scene. The worried mother fears her daughter is really ill. You must rise at once from your chair: where's my lorgnon, let me look at Tanya more closely, see what it is she is reading. You are short-sighted. Go over to her, look her in the face. When your daughter says: 'I am reading something very interesting!' here is a fresh cause for concern! What is she reading? Should she be reading such a book? Then after having carefully examined it you can give a little sigh and prepare to lecture her. While you," Stanislavski now turned to Tatiana, "show us here in the words 'Oh, how they suffer' (and take the 'Oh' on a high note) all your compassion, your painful concern, your trembling foreboding of love. Every high note is high because it is charged with content, deriving from the emotions underlying the words, otherwise it is just a plain little sound.

"You use this note, as it were, to interpret to your bewildered mother what love really is. Later on we shall see Madame Larina in the role of educator of her children. She is very like the head of an institute for well-born young ladies with her self-important, rather comical manners."

Stanislavski himself then took the lorgnon, crossed his arms, pressed his lips into a cupid's bow and began to sing his lecture on conduct: "That's enough, Tanya. . ." He toyed with the lorgnon and then expounded Madame Larina's train of thought.

"Time was when I like you read such books, was *excited* by them". Here the lorgnon acted it all out. At the word "I" it pointed lightly towards Madame Larina's heart; at the word "you" it pointed lightly towards Tatiana; and at "excited" it made some circling patterns in the air. All was expressed by the manner of his carriage and way of speaking; it was all as delicately refined as the accompanying music. The scene ends with the words: "...I found that in real life there are no heroes, and I am at peace." Here the lorgnon executed a flourish in the air, which left no doubt as to the fact that such novels were a lot of fictitious nonsense. The scene lasted in all a minute but it was enough to establish a vivid image of Madame Larina.

As soon as her mother assumes the role of governess Olga settles herself in her armchair and swings her feet, and that brings Madame Larina down to earth. "There is no use in acting so demurely. See, you forgot to put away your apron...." Chaikovski underlines very well the difference in character and temperament between Madame Larina and Olga. The *recitativo* reflects the mother's measured speech and alternates with the daughter's impetuous flow of words.

There is a light accent from the kettledrums after Olga's words: "Well, when Lenski comes, we'll see". The sound seems to be far away and strikes a note of warning.

The group of women for a moment listens to something far off. Then comes a light and delicate turn as the next scene looms: the excitement of the arrival of guests. The definite end of one scene and the clear shift to the next was something Stanislavski cared about a great deal. He kept reminding us:

"Listen to the music and be accurate in keeping all your actions on the stage in measure with it. Just as distinctly as the orchestra finishes one phrase and begins another do you divide the fractions of the staging. You finish one phrase, there is a slight pause, as in the orchestra, then you start the following one. Don't let the one blur into the next. Don't let them overlap one another."

Now comes a scene of confusion as the guests arrive. The approach of their carriage is indicated by the movement of the eyes of the actors onstage, which are concentrated on the right side of the auditorium, that Lenski has come and with him Onegin. There is a lot of running nearer, tension mounts, then the words: "Indeed it is he! But he is not alone.... Who can it be with him?" The Nurse reenters and explains that Lenski has come and with him, Onegin. There is a lot of running back and forth and excitement. Tatiana moves only when she says: "Quick. I must get away."

Such scenes in ordinary operatic productions show people supposedly in a hurry, but actually standing quite still to watch the conductor's baton and not miss their cues. This kind of scene is really very difficult to act because it requires from all the singers an impeccably accurate knowledge of the music and of all of one another's cues. Each one should be able to sing for all the rest, for only then can he feel free to move around on the stage and find his way in an external pattern that corresponds to the music.

Stanislavski assigns to each singer one or more objectives in terms of physical action which are logical and necessary to the development of the scene. These actions are to be executed within the framework of a musical phrase, in the same rhythm as that phrase, and this requires many rehearsals to perfect. Thus in addition to the musical score we have side by side with it the score of physical actions in a definite rhythmic pattern. In the course of rehearsals these rhythmic movements must fuse with the vocal expression. To this end it is necessary to study most carefully the musical rhythm of each phrase. This is done by means of special rehearsals devoted to rhythm. "The rhythm must go right through you" was a frequent saying of Stanislavski's. The rhythm rehearsals proceeded on the old principle of "What is difficult becomes habitual, what is habitual becomes easy, what is easy is beautiful."

When a rhythm is learned so that it fuses with the movements of an actor, it will not seem obvious or calculated, and he is then free to produce that harmonious synthesis of voice, drama, and music which was Stanislavski's chief goal in staging an opera. In fact he wrote about his bringing together of the three basic elements of opera in his book *My Life in Art.*

Careful study of the musical patterns in the score and careful training in the rhythmic aspect of his movements affords one more inestimable advantage to the actor—he is free and independent of the conductor's baton. The music is so thoroughly studied and all actions on the stage are so closely knit into it that the actor-singer becomes his own conductor. The separate entries in his role become quite simple because of the solid relationship between the words that are sung and his own physical actions. All a singer has to follow is the general rhythmic structure as set up by the conductor.

Stanislavski was convinced that the preparatory work on a singer's rhythmic movements on the stage should be carried on side by side with his work on diction and his daily voice training.

In the excitement over the arriving guests Tatiana at first starts to run inside the house but then quickly turns and dashes offstage into the garden. Madame Larina must take off her apron, throw it onto a table inside the house (the Nurse running by snatches it up), then she, Olga, and the Nurse move the big armchair away from the centre of the terrace and push it into a corner. Olga straightens her mother's cap and curls, but does not let Tatiana out of her sight, so that she can run after her, overtake her, and drag her back onto the terrace. All this is rehearsed so painstakingly that no one looks around at the conductor for cues. It is all done at a quick rhythm of sixteenth notes that purl along buoyantly in the orchestra, flowing down like a cascade, then instantly cease, cut off by one large chord. With this chord Madame Larina and her daughters are transfixed in mannered poses with their hands carefully folded in the way dictated by good breeding. You would never guess that the girls had just been running about.

If there is to be excitement, then let it be real. Stanislavski was not one to be afraid of bold contrasts between the placid, proper conduct of the women, especially Madame Larina and the Nurse, and their foolish, confused scampering just before the arrival of a well-known gentleman from St. Petersburg. Now Lenski and Onegin are about to enter: the main hero of the piece will appear.

In the score of the opera, after the chord which ends the music for the scene of confusion, there is a pause. The pause, not a very long one, precedes a broad musical phrase in which we are to sense the quiet self-confidence of the elegant Onegin.

"Is it possible to make a real pause here such as they do when there is a famous guest artist?" Stanislavski asks the conductor.

"Of course, if it is necessary for the action onstage. In fact the composer has put in a full stop."

"Very well then, let us give the whole of it to Lenski. Later the music obviously belongs only to Onegin. We must single out the entrance of the main hero. So let us have a big pause after which Lenski makes his entrance."

Lenski is happy and proud. He comes in quickly, crosses the whole stage and runs lightly up the steps of the terrace where he kisses Madame Larina's hand. ("Don't forget to bow to the young ladies," puts in Stanislavski.) Then he stops, looks in the direction of the wings from which Onegin is on the point of emerging. It is only after this that the Onegin music begins and he makes his entrance.

In this way Stanislavski marked out significantly the main male characters: the impetuous Lenski and the composed, indifferent Onegin, and each one came in on the rhythm of his mood.

Many and varied were the exercises given: how to walk and turn, how to approach the ladies. The men were all invited to dances in Moscow in order to put some polish on them and to help turn them into civilian and military gentlemen of the time of Alexander I. Stanislavski himself demonstrated all these refinements of manners and at the same time went through these exercises with his students to the accompaniment of music. He demanded more from Onegin of the social graces than from anyone else. He laid down the law: No matter how fine a baritone you may be, if your body is not trained to respond to the demands of Onegin's times you will not be able to sing the part. It is not difficult even with an inadequately placed voice to be taught to sing the role of Onegin, but to come to visit the Larins and play the disillusioned

Bryonic hero, to be a subtle poseur, and at the same time a socially accomplished person who would never commit an impolite act—all that is not so easy.

"In addition you must try to acquire a certain lightness and elegance, a poetic quality, a capacity to please, to exude charm."

We, the prospective Onegins, were taught how to walk in a ballroom; we were presented to the ladies; we tried to recall what it means to come into a strange house, to see many new things, some of them slightly ridiculous, but to remain imperturbable and perfunctorily polite. It is a very difficult role, completely a character part, but the colouring of Onegin's characteristics must be painted with the elegance and delicacy of a watercolour. It was only then that I fully realized what the Conservatory of Music had not taught me and how many things I still lacked when I sang Onegin there and was praised for my performance.

"Acquire first of all complete freedom as an actor and as a result of this you will possess a calm relationship to all that surrounds you." That was the first objective Stanislavski set for Onegin. "When you have that, go on to look for your pattern, your enjoyment of your own imperturbability—that will add the social polish. Then add a few drops of disillusion and affected indifference. Seek out the rhythm of a disillusioned man; that is the key to the way he carries himself."

This instruction may not be intelligible to everyone, but it explains the constant demands Stanislavski made with regard to the technique of an actor's carriage on the stage. It was something we were always working on. As we walked about we had to feel our toes and especially the springiness of the big toe as our weight shifted from one step to the next. This gave us a certain plasticity, a fluency, a *legato* of movement as musicians call it.

"The central theme of Onegin is his *search for fulfillment*. He was destined to recognize it, but not to be united with it." That was Stanislavski's definition of the main point of the role of Onegin.

"That through-line of action makes him a poetic character from the beginning of the first act; he has in him the poetry of the search for love.

"Of what does his social manner consist?" Stanislavski asked. "If it is noticed that you look down on provincial society, that would be bad. If you have come down to the provinces on a visit and appear to be delighted and full of life, that would also be bad. You must always act with dignity and elegance. Choose among the instruments in the orchestra those that help you, allow you to feel your own elegance. Take your first entrance. What an exquisitely undulating line is provided by the violins: the orchestra plays your music in three-quarter time, almost like a waltz and you come in against that rhythm but still in time. The two-quarter rhythm—your step—should, in merging with the three-quarter beat of the orchestra, give a sense of controlled calm. Do not try to find any special gestures for this part. Your arms will hang relaxed but never parallel. The best, the most correct way to play the role is without gesticulating. Gestures are not refined. They are muscular. In general, bear in mind not to act with big gestures. Most often you should use medium gestures and above all small ones added to the play on your face and the expression of your eyes.

"Now, forget about the technique of acting," Stanislavski would say at the rehearsals before an actor made his entrance in the part of Onegin. "Technique is only of value on the stage when you forget all about it. You have only one objective in your first scene—to look at Olga and Tatiana and please them. Everything else will emerge from your subconscious if you carry out your simple objective which is bound up with your arrival in a strange house and the making of new acquaintances. In this matter you must proceed with your own feelings deriving from your personal experiences in life."

Much of this advice flashes through your consciousness as you are moving about in your dressing room, walking down the stairs, crossing the dark stage to take up your position in the first wing on the left, from which you will emerge onto the brightly lighted, sunny terrace of the Larins' home.

As you feel the spring in your step, your snugly-buttoned coat that fits you like a corset, your head slightly thrown back against your stiff high collar, and the starched frills of your shirt pressing against your cheeks, you already sense that you are another person, somewhat different from the one that came to the theatre two hours earlier. Still, you are aware of an inner self that is checking on you.

"But that cannot be in accordance with our system of acting," you say to yourself. "You must enter the role of Onegin so that you forget yourself, but I keep remembering and watching myself. I must ask about this."

"Of course, you cannot forget even for a moment that you are onstage," said Stanislavski. "The actors who say that they immerse themselves so completely in their roles that they do not remember anything, they are so overwhelmed by emotions, are just making hysterical remarks. That is a morbid condition and actors should be completely sane. Tommaso Salvini's dictum to the effect that an actor laughs and cries but never loses control of himself because an invisible monitor is always present in him, is a law for our creative work. This 'equilibrium' which enables an actor to laugh and to weep and at the same time watch himself do these things is the essence of art.

"Also bear in mind," said Stanislavski, "that an actor always has the urge to 'perform' as much as possible, to increase as it were his salary. But you must remember that ninety percent of your 'performing' comes from tenseness. That is where the relaxation of muscles is of enormous importance. As soon as you sense that you are beginning to overact—relax, and instantly you will feel as refreshed as if you had had a cold shower, and will return to the truthfulness of what you are doing on the stage."

All these things flash in fragmentary fashion through your head when you are trying to calm yourself before going onstage, to collect your attention and feel that you are in control of it. When your head is clear, when you distinctly remember what you need to do, when you are vividly aware of everything you see and hear around you, then you gain confidence in your own powers. You need that for Onegin. I am not in the least distracted from this state of self-confidence and superiority over other people when the singer who plays Lenski says: "Come on, time to go." I answer him with my eyes and a self-confident smile. As I step onto the stage with my first chord, unhurried, in time with the orchestra, I am just drawing the glove from my right hand. It must be admitted here that this self-confidence came very gradually, and the first time I entered I was incapable of walking even two steps up to the terrace to kiss Madame Larina's hand. My legs failed me and I still recall that terrible sensation of being crippled.

But we must go back to the irresistibly logical directorial art of Stanislavski. From the instant when the figure of Onegin emerges from the wings everyone on the stage and in the auditorium has eyes only for him: Lenski, who with pride awaits the extraordinary impression to be made by this famous person; Madame Larina, who hides her secret tremors behind her well-bred smile of greeting; Olga, with her scarcely-veiled, childlike curiosity; and, finally, Tatiana, who is chilled to the marrow by her inner rapture and fear of the destiny that may be in store for her. All this is easily read by the audience from the singers' facial expressions, because Onegin himself, at whom everyone is looking, has walked toward the terrace steps to stand in front of Madame Larina, with his back still turned to the auditorium. What does he look like? The audience has not yet seen his face and this further heightens the interest in him.

This is how Stanislavski prepared Onegin's entrance—yet there is nothing arbitrarily calculated in it. It is all perfectly natural, as is the whole course of events. To be sure, Onegin must now justify this heightened interest in his person. He must not disenchant the audience when at last they have a clear view of him.

Now the music of Onegin's entrance has faded and he is motionless for a moment; as he bows to Madame Larina the last chord strikes. After a pause Lenski begins his introduction: "Mesdames, I have taken the liberty of bringing along a friend. . . ."

"Oh dear!" calls Stanislavski from the auditorium. "Why are you making an aria out of that? Why are you trying to show off your voice to us? You have a lot more singing ahead of you and we shall readily discover what kind of a voice you have. At this juncture Onegin is the principal figure, not you. All you have to do is introduce him. Therefore without thinking about how this word or that will sound keep your mind on only *what* you have to say. If you break down the phrase in order to understand the meaning of each word, you must first press down on all the words and then leave the weight on only those which are significant in meaning. Which are the important words in your phrases: 'Mesdames, I have taken the liberty of bringing along a friend. Let me present my neighbour, Onegin'? In the first place this form of address has its own logical accent. Therefore 'mesdames' is an important word. After that is it of consequence or not that you have 'taken the liberty'? What of the words 'bringing along'? After all we have seen that for ourselves. Then we come to the word 'friend'—that is indeed significant; you want to emphasize what an interesting fellow your friend is. He is a credit to you. Then comes the key word 'Onegin'. Thus the chief words are: 'Mesdames', 'friend', 'Onegin'. Incidentally Chaikovski has correctly and clearly indicated the emphasis on these words. But it does sometimes occur that composers slip up in such matters and neither by rhythm nor by melody emphasize the principal words. You started off singing all of the words with equal force. This makes the phrase boring, flat, and above all incomprehensible."

Remembering the different lessons we had on diction and singing, I, as Onegin, tried to use the softest possible intonation: "I am very happy," with a slight accent on the first syllable of the last word and a soft ending. Stanislavski always required his singers to go right to the end of each word, to pronounce all final consonants.

When I come to my second phrase: "I am very, *very* glad", I can sing it with more freedom and resonance. With repeated words it is necessary to use increasing accent. The second "very" calls for a full tone and besides I am singing to the two young ladies and it is up to me to make a favourable impression on them. I may even hint at flirting with them, but then I must immediately return to my self-restraint and slightly mocking attitude of being unapproachable.

"There is constantly a touch of mockery inside you," suggested Stanislavski. "It is because of this that Madame Larina is so embarrassed and everything she says is in such a breathless and distracted way: 'You are welcome . . . (pause) . . . we are glad to have you come . . . (pause) . . . do take a seat.' You say to yourself: 'What does she mean? Sit down where? How? The old lady is quite nonsensical.' Yet you smile politely to show you are pleased with everything. 'Sit down? Oh please don't bother. These are your daughters? How charming! Go inside? Please, whatever you say, you are so kind!' All this is parroted, spoken mechanically, but tactfully. After all, whom have you come to see? The daughters—you must look them over. That is your main purpose now. Otherwise I shall not believe what you say in the quartet in which you describe Olga and Tatiana in detail. Now let me see how you can do it. This is your main objective.

"And you, Lenski," Stanislavski asks, "tell me, to whom are you singing the words: 'It is so charming here. I love this secluded, shady park'?"

"I am replying to Madame Larina and her invitation to go into the house."

"Yes, that is what the text indicates. But in addition to that there is one of the most important factors in our work—the *sub-text,* which enables you to *feel* what the text says in words. Therefore sing to Olga, the object of your love, the flower that has blossomed in this friendly garden. You are a poet. Let Olga feel that after all it was to see her that you have come. I must be able to see the quick, covert exchange of glances between you two. That is the substance of your sub-text and your through-line of action. Never forget that for a moment all during your role."

Now that Lenski has spoken, Madame Larina has collected herself. Her expressions are smoother and calmer: "Splendid . . . [looks amiably at her guests]. I shall now go about my household affairs, and you [a very strict glance at her daughters] entertain our guests . . . [smiles again amiably at the guests]. I must go. . . ."

"At this point make a suggestion of a curtsey and then sweep into the house in a dignified manner. The young people—the guests and the daughters—remain on the terrace. Incidentally you, Lenski, should accompany Madame Larina into the house and leave Onegin for several moments alone with the girls," suggested Stanislavski.

So there I am, Onegin, standing and waiting with curiosity to see how the young ladies will undertake to entertain me. This is a very agreeable situation to be in on the stage. All I have to do is to look around and, especially, study the girls. I can see how embarrassed and awkward they feel under the impact of my unmannerly gaze. Yet I came here to be distracted.

"Look them over as you would horses at a fair and amuse yourself with their embarrassment," Stanislavski once said to me at a rehearsal.

Disconcerted by my look the girls, instead of attempting to entertain me, begin to hide behind the columns. At this point Lenski emerges from the house and comes straight over to me. In his eyes I read happy expectation as he asks: "Well, how do you like it here? Isn't it wonderful?"

The orchestra continues to play a light accompaniment to this rather domestic chatter. Then suddenly a French horn sounds a long-drawn-out, dying note which seems to give the signal for a complete standstill of all action. On the stage everyone is motionless. The atmosphere is that of people who have become absorbed in their own thoughts. This a point when we literally seem to be able to read the thoughts of the principal characters.

Then comes the quartet which is one of the most poetic moments of this first scene. It became an absolutely virtuosic piece of subtle work in the way Stanislavski put it together.

The position on the stage of the characters, from the point of view of ordinary reality, is not convenient, indeed it is even contradictory to elementary logic. The young ladies of the house, instead of following the rules of polite society on how to entertain their guests and make themselves amiable to them, draw off to one side and begin to talk with each other in secret.

But the music and the merging of the actors onstage with it produces a miracle.

"You cannot do this in a play, but in opera it is very easy if you follow the music attentively," Stanislavski taught us. "Sing the whole quartet without moving at all, sing only with your lips and your eyes. Let us call this the 'secret'. In real life such a scene would last two or three seconds, but in opera the music infuses it with the larger span of several minutes."

I remember that at the first rehearsal with music Stanislavski listened to us and then remarked:

"Why do you sing this quartet so loudly? After all it is a secret, a mystery."

"The composer indicates this passage as sung *piano* and that is what we are doing."

"Is there then such a thing as an absolutely fixed *piano*? How would you define it? No, that is a mistaken idea. *Piano* and *forte* indicate only relative strengths of sound. It is up to us to define their limits each time after taking into account the situation which we wish to convey.

"Take this quartet. All the liveliness on stage has died down, all is whispers, so as not to frighten away feelings, the expression of the subconscious. This is a most delicate kind of tracery in watercolours. A *piano* in watercolours will be quite different from one painted in oils.

"Here we are painting the subtlest kind of picture in sounds. Call it what you like—triple *piano*, quintuple *piano*—I do not care. But the auditorium must be hushed and the audience bate its breath until the quartet is over."

That is the sort of thing Stanislavski worked to produce in this scene. And one cannot say it was achieved without a tremendous amount of effort. When most of us, including the music directors, thought we had practically reached the summit, we would hear Stanislavski's "No, no." He could see the beginning of achieving the goal and was determined to reach the top.

The quartet was indeed magical in its effect, yet every syllable of this "musical whispering" could be heard throughout the auditorium. The same was true of that other most subtly refined and polished piece, the duet "Enemies", of which Stanislavski was so proud. He felt that there the technique of pronouncing musical words reached an exemplary degree.

In the quartet each character has his own clear line of inner activity. Onegin, who has instantly sensed the charm of Tatiana, slyly pokes fun at Lenski. Lenski flares up and indicates their tastes are different. Tatiana, who feels that the long-awaited man of whom she has dreamed day and night has come, cries: "This is he!" And finally there is practical Olga, who already guesses what the result of this meeting may be.

The immobility of the picture is held to the last C-major chord. Then with the first note of the bassoon introducing a new scene, the characters come out of their meditative states. The next scene begins with Lenski's "How happy. . ." Onegin has just been ironic about Lenski's attachment to Olga so that he cannot show his feelings too openly in the presence of the others, but Lenski feels compelled at any cost to show her how he feels. This then is a rather intimate scene. How can it be done onstage?

"Do what any clever young people in love do in such circumstances. They are very inventive." So Stanislavski suggests a mise-en-scène that will contrive to keep the scene intimate while putting the actors down in the front of the stage.

"You and Lenski want to get together," Stanislavski says to Olga, "so you take your fiancé to one side but do it in a way to deceive Onegin."

From the first note of the bassoon Olga comes away from the column where she was standing while singing the quartet, and unexpectedly looks at her shoes, then throws a quick glance at Lenski and walks over to the very edge of the terrace, down to the footlights. She suggests that she might be going for a walk, or that something out in the park (in the auditorium) particularly interests her. Lenski, looking around with seeming indifference, becomes likewise interested. And then they find themselves together down front. We see their faces clearly, but Onegin can see only the backs of their heads. And the back of a head is a noncommittal spot. Now the game these two play involves their looking in different directions while in reality conversing, energetically but in quiet tones. Lenski has his eyes glued on a spot to his left in the auditorium but his singing is accented with excitement. "How happy, how happy am I to see you once again." Here Stanislavski suggested that Lenski dwell on the word "happy". But Olga, looking in the opposite direction, makes pretty little faces as she replies: "It seems to me 'twas only yesterday we were together," and so on.

"Don't sing an aria to him, just tease him with words and sounds. You joke and play with him all the time. That is your main course of action. Later this will lead to tragedy."

Despite the boldness of the two singers coming straight down to the front of the stage, the playful poetry of the scene was sustained by their capacity for subtle acting and the convincing underlying logic of this staging. To begin with, the actors themselves were fascinated by this game of hide-and-seek with Onegin, and Stanislavski was able to draw forth from the actors the mischievousness of Olga and the languishing happiness of Lenski. At the height of his powers at that time, Stanislavski convinced his singers by both his logic and his own acting-out of nearly every moment in the opera. This lent special force and a most infectious quality to his work with them.

One can say many good and intelligent words about the art of acting, but seeing one good example of it is more forceful than words. "Example clarifies understanding," said S.T. Aksakov (a popular mid-19th-century writer).

In pointing out the difficult problem of two actors standing right in front of the audience, Stanislavski warned them against the danger of being "enslaved by the public". That is a time when an actor's sense of his own personal being takes over and he is likely to lose the main thread of his role. That is why he needs a powerful grip on an object on which to centre all his attention, to preserve the unbroken course of action in the living of his part.

The scene ends with Olga agreeing to go off, apparently into the park offstage, and Lenski quickly following her. Just before she disappears Olga looks back at Onegin and then trips off, evidently having decided that the game of deception is over and there is no need for further pretense. Lenski follows suit. This is a tiny scene (made up of six phrases in all) but it leaves an impression of a poetic but playful little prank.

In the following scene Onegin is standing behind an armchair between the columns, from which position he has observed with irony Olga and Lenski and their touchingly naïve little pretenses. At the same time Tatiana, who has been trying to conceal herself behind one of the columns, has finally, in desperation, decided to run after Olga and thus avoid conversation with Onegin. But his words "Pray tell me. . ." stop her halfway across the terrace.

"Be amused by her embarrassment. Yet be courteous. Your social polish is demonstrated by the very politeness with which you make impertinent remarks to her," said Stanislavski.

Onegin begins with a comment on the boredom of life down in the country. The melody of his phrases is almost continuous, there are no noticeable pauses, and it is made up of light undulating rises and falls. It is very easy here to drop into a monotonous pattern when all the words roll along and merge with one another. Stanislavski was adamant in making Onegin feel free in his singing while maintaining strict time.

"Special mastery over the sung word derives from the singer's keeping within the exact framework of the musical rhythm while at the same time he plays with his words by almost imperceptibly holding, speeding up, or expanding them. When he does that each phrase seems to come to life, to breathe and be a whole entity. If these words could be measured by a super-metronome of microscopic discrimination, the quarter notes would show up as being uneven: some would be longer and others shorter. Infinitesimal pauses would be revealed yet the singing would coincide with the orchestral beat. But this calls for very special refinement, an almost flaunting sparkle. Onegin needs this capacity. It conveys a light quality of foppishness."

To Onegin's self-assured phrases Tatiana replies at first with bewilderment: "I read a lot . . . I dream sometimes as I wander through the park." But when Onegin pins her down with his supercilious question: "And what, pray, do you dream about?" (Onegin has to underscore his ironical enunciation of the word "dream")—then she has to rebuff him. She has been hurt in a most tender spot and suddenly she looks at Onegin in such a way that he is slightly taken aback. After Onegin's words there is a slight rise in the music, almost like a sigh, and Stanislavski pointed it out with special attention: "It is very significant," he said, "and perhaps one could expand it a little, accent it. I feel in it a wave of protest in Tatiana's soul."

The musicians agreed that it was possible to hold the phrase slightly, and it coincided perfectly with the questioning look Tatiana gives Onegin as she defends her dreams. From this moment Tatiana grows in importance; she has recovered from her earlier embarrassment. She sings in a serious, almost didactic vein to Onegin: "Reflection has been my companion since my infancy." Meantime she quietly moves away, leaving the possibility to Onegin of following her.

They go into the park together, but in another direction from the one taken by Olga and Lenski.

Twilight dims and it is dark inside the house. The next scene begins with Olga dashing in; she runs up onto the terrace and hides, crouching on the ground behind the balustrade. We guess that in the park she and Lenski have been playing tag and now he runs, pursuing her. When he finds her by the balustrade he immediately begins his aria: "Olga, I love you." Thus the declaration of his love is made in an atmosphere of playfulness. In the way Stanislavski planned this scene you can see the liberties he took in order to get away from the usual, mannered, self-conscious sentimentality of the tenor's love song. He sought colours that would emphasize the special quality of his declaration of love and he set it in a frame of half-childlike friendship, the exciting, still unclear stirrings of love and finally the seriousness of the impending moment.

"Find the transition from playfulness through presentiment to the sense of something new and mysterious—then to the earnest, serious, thrilling emotion of love." Olga here plays no lesser role than Lenski as she *listens* to his confession of love. The way in which she receives this confession is the key to the scene. There is no need to say that Lenski here is faced with many special challenges, but he must eschew the usual ardent declaration "in general terms", and this should help him find the right tone for his aria.

"Don't forget," said Stanislavski, "that the whole scene, all of Lenski's ardent declaration, is going on right under the windows of the house and Madame Larina might hear you. Therefore Olga's first wish is that Lenski should not speak so loudly. But still she wants to hear him. So she must be sure the house is empty. She can tiptoe up to the windows, listen, and then sit down comfortably on the steps of the terrace."

The whole scene ends on a quiet note. The two lovebirds are sitting side by side on the steps and dreaming: "In the shelter of a peaceful country life we two have lived. . . ."

"Remember," said Stanislavski to Lenski, "there is no embrace. Even to hold her hand in yours is a great event. So cautiously take Olga by the hand, so that you do not frighten her," he added with a smile, "or else she's likely to flutter away like a little pheasant. Those were the manners of the times. It was an epoch when women were held in reverence."

Olga's line of action in this scene is: first she wants to stop Lenski, then it is fun to listen to him, finally, she is awed—What eyes he has! And then I would be Madame Lenski!

"True poetry need not at all be put in a sentimental, wishy-washy tone, with the cloying sweetness which some tenors use to show their sensibilities," said Stanislavski. "In order to avoid any 'generalization' of your emotions, sing your whole aria in terms of your thoughts. At first the thought is perfectly distinct and then it is followed by feelings. Read me the words of the text."

At such times singers often lapse into embarrassment. While singing they say the words mechanically and fluently, but when called upon to read them without the music they are in trouble. They immediately forget their lines and it is rare indeed that a singer can speak them as intelligibly as he sings them.

"Do you appreciate the charm of the verses and the depth of thought in them quite apart from the music?" asked Stanislavski. "Af-

terwards the melody, the music, will enable you to enhance the expressiveness of the words, the poetry—there lies the direction of your
work.

"Let us establish the fact that there are three main moments, three
units, in the aria. The first is the confession of love: 'I love you as the
frenzied soul of a poet is condemned to love'. . . . This is the centre of
Lenski's life at this point. The second unit is the history of his love. A
broad solemn melody accompanies this theme: 'When still a boy I was
enthralled by you . . . I was a suppliant from afar. . . .' Finally the third
theme: 'Ah, how I love thee and . . . nothing, not an hour, can separate
us. . . .'—this is his vow of eternal love.

"Now make these three thoughts distinct, as you sing they must be
differentiated. You use various colours. It is one thing to recall your love
from boyhood on: 'When still a boy. . . .' But it is something quite
different when you are making your vow. Seek out the colours and the
right enunciation for the emphasis on these thoughts.

*"You must love words and know how to interweave them with the
music. An actor is creative only when he uses sound to paint an image he
visualizes. Make it a rule not to sing a single word without a purpose.
Unless there is an organic relationship which binds the words to the
music there is no art in opera."*

Night falls. The whole duet has taken place in semidarkness, without the usual banal moonlight. Inside the house lamps are being lighted
and the music indicates quite clearly when and at what window each
light is seen.

At the very end of this poetic scene, inside the house, one glimpses
Madame Larina and the Nurse preparing for evening tea. The moon
casts a very pale light now on the top of the house but the lovers are left
in the shadows. The tranquil, happy love of Olga and Lenski is but-
tressed by the coziness of the interior scene and the poetry of evening
light; it makes one feel the promise of future happiness "predestined for
them by their fathers."

The duet of the lovers ends with a long-drawn-out, soft, major
chord. Then, in contrast, the music takes on a completely different
character. There is a sharp contrast and one hears the worried voice of
Madame Larina: "Ah, there you are, but what has become of Tatiana?"

Through this exclamation from Madame Larina one feels at once
the whole change of mood. Stanislavski used this to the full and took the
tone for the ensuing scene from the motif of Madame Larina's deep
concern: She is worried for fear that her daughters are not behaving as
they should with a guest come down from the big city.

"This is a scene that must really be acted out," he said and he put
himself in Madame Larina's place.

Holding her lorgnon in his hand, he comes to the doorway as the music of the duet ends and looks out into the park. No sign of the girls. Then he quietly walks along the terrace down front on the stage, takes one step downwards, and stumbles on Olga and Lenski sitting there in the dark. That happens in consonance with the sharp chord announcing the beginning of a new scene. As Madame Larina he is distinctly worried. Olga and Lenski, so suddenly discovered, flutter up in great embarrassment. He then puts on a severely solemn expression and sings, as suggested by the music: "Please go indoors." When Lenski, confused, says: "After you," Stanislavski uses Madame Larina's lorgnon to point to the door and Olga obediently goes in. Embarrassed, Lenski follows her. And after them sweeps the imperious Mama. The scene this way acquires a touch of comedy while retaining some of its intimacy.

The Nurse hurries off into the wings to look for Tatiana. The image of Madame Larina now acquires a new feature: she is rather like a distracted hen with young chicks. This all points up the mainstream of life in the Larin household: a sense of peace, tranquility, order, ease—which Onegin later on is destined to destroy.

When Onegin emerges from the wings with Tatiana and is telling her about his "uncle of most sterling principles", Madame Larina, Olga, and Lenski are already seated at the table in the dining room. Pausing for a moment to complete his phrase, Onegin then follows Tatiana into the house. They had been walking side by side with Tatiana looking at him with unconcealed delight—so quickly has he enthralled her in the course of their short stroll.

"Walk in but do not take your eyes off his face," Stanislavski told Tatiana.

Now the Larin family and guests are visible to the audience through the open doorway. The scene ends with the Nurse, out of breath, coming back, settling herself on the terrace steps and singing: "Oh my darling, lay your little head. . . ."

"From your words and the tenderness with which you speak of her it is obvious that Tatiana is nearer and dearer to you than she is to her mother. You have already noticed everything, have read in her face that this new gentleman has caught her fancy."

Stanislavski was most anxious to have the finale of the scene so lifelike it would stick in the public's memory. During the last eight measures we see the melting moonlight bathe the house and the columns in the calm night air, and through the open doors we glimpse Madame Larina, her daughters, and their guests sitting around a tea table in the cozy light cast on them by a lamp. "Let us watch them closely and only as the last chord is struck let the curtain slowly, very slowly, close, keeping time with the music. . . ."

Scene Two: The Letter

It would be difficult to find in any Russian opera or indeed any opera anywhere a scene of such profound, passionate feeling and tenderness, one with such rich musical colouring, so penetrating in the revelation of the whole gamut of thoughts, feelings, doubts, sufferings and joys of a young girl's first love, as this Scene of The Letter in *Eugene Onegin*.

It is a gem of classical opera and a brilliant example of Russian dramatic music in the realistic vein, in which musical means are used to penetrate the inner world of a human being, the world "of simple, everyday, universal emotions". This was how Chaikovski himself described it. The composer's aesthetic point of departure was defined exhaustively in a letter to S.N. Taneyev (a fellow composer and pianist) just after finishing *Eugene Onegin:* "You may very well be right when you say that my opera is not stageable. But my answer is that I do not care about its stageworthiness. The fact that I do not possess a drop of theatricality is long since well-known, and I do not distress myself about it anymore. If it can't be staged it won't be produced! [Ed. note: Chaikovski used strong language because he was highly sensitive and his feelings were lacerated by the public's lack of understanding of his aesthetic principles.] I wrote this opera because one fine day I was seized by an indescribable urge to put to music what in *Onegin* calls aloud for musical expression. I did it to the best of my ability. I worked with indescribable fervour and satisfaction, thinking little about movement, effects and such. And, after all, what are so-called effects? If you find them, for example, in something like *Aïda*, I can assure you that no riches in the world could persuade me to write an opera on such a subject, for I need people, not dolls; yet I would gladly undertake to compose any opera, whether or not it contained powerful and startling effects, if it were made up of human beings, like me, having emotional experiences which I too have had and understand."

The Scene of The Letter, in its musical and dramatic structure, is a most perfect expression of Chaikovski's principles as a composer, as set forth in his letter to Taneyev.

In analyzing the structure of this scene, the proportions and finish of its component parts, one must note the well-thought-out and polished libretto of K. Shilovski, which is made up almost entirely of the verse of Pushkin. The perfection of content and form of the Pushkin original no doubt helped Chaikovski to create his operatic masterpiece. Incidentally, this he also mentioned in writing to Taneyev. His thoughts are so highly significant and useful to anyone working in the theatre that the letter, written three weeks later than the one cited above, is worth quoting: ". . . I shall not argue with you further on whether or not my *Onegin* is stageworthy. I could point out that your assertion is not quite just when you say that the characters of Tatiana and Olga are not clarified by actions but rather by means of the soliloquies and dialogues. To be sure, their actions are very simple, nontheatrical, part of every-day life, yet each one acts to the extent his capacities allow. . . . And by the way if, as you assert, *opera is action* and that is lacking in my *Onegin,* then I am ready not to call it an opera but anything else you like: scenes, scenic presentation, a poem, whatever . . . and I am likewise prepared to accept all the consequences from my well-known non-comprehension of the stage and inability to choose proper subjects. It seems to me that all the scenic incongruities are redeemed by the charm of Pushkin's verse. . . . As for the music, I can tell you that if ever any music was composed with sincere passion, with love for the subject and its leading characters, it is the music of *Onegin.*"

The text is indeed nearly all Pushkin. The first words of the Nurse in the second scene are: "Well, I run on and on, but now it's time for bed, Tanya." They are very simple, convincing, and do not contradict the actual Pushkin lines: "I cannot sleep, Nanny, it is so stuffy here, do open a window and sit down near me." There is a variation in the aria where Pushkin speaking of Tatiana says:

> You will be lost, my dear, but ere that time
> In the blinding light of hope
> You will call forth your darkling destiny
> And know the joy of life. . . .

But Chaikovski's libretto says:

> I may be lost, but ere that time
> In the blinding light of hope. . . .

Again a change has been made but with great tact; Pushkin's thought has not been impaired.

But now we come to the collision between the free theatrical fantasy of a singer and the mechanical routine of an opera conductor. Pushkin says:

> In the darkness Tatiana does not sleep
> But talks in low tones with the Nurse.

In these two lines there is an enormous area for the imagination of a singer. Yet in the libretto there are such a lot of wordy "props" that no room is left in which imagination can move. There is a full complement

of scenery and theatrical properties but none of the essential fact—or
poetry.

In the list of standard properties kept in State Theatres one of the
last items is "one classical white nightgown for Tatiana". Of course! She
has to move about on the stage. Pushkin never thought of that! But
Pushkin's Tatiana shall have a proper white nightgown! What an epi-
gram he would have written on that subject!

Then there is the stage direction: "She gets up in a lazy manner and
the Nurse caresses her", or "She remains for some time in a reflective
mood". Finally she is directed to "come downstage" when she sings the
words "My brain falters. . . ."

Such stage directions were inserted in the libretto either by Shilovski, an actor from the Maly Theatre, who helped Chaikovski make
the libretto, or by the first producer of *Onegin*, Samarin, who staged it
at the Conservatory of Music. Such directions are understandable if one
takes into consideration the acting technique of singers and the level of
opera production in those days. But the creative quality of opera has
risen very high in the more than ninety years since *Onegin* was written.
And, of course, Stanislavski's directorial comments which stemmed
from his production of *Onegin* are of incomparably greater artistic
significance than those in the printed libretto. His artistic approach
towards the beginning of the Letter Scene was altogether based on the
music and one of Pushkin's lines:

> In the darkness Tatiana does not sleep
> But talks in low tones with the Nurse.

In *My Life in Art* Stanislavski wrote: "In this second scene, Tatiana
plays throughout in bed without coming down to the footlights or
making operatic gestures as is usually done. This remaining fixed in her
bed required a great amount of work and stamina from the singer. It
also carried the focus of the audience's attention from external acting to
the inner motives activating the scene. There were no extraneous
movements of her arms, legs or body; all this was replaced by facial
expression and small gestures. This delicacy of pattern combined with
that of the music reproduced the subtle polish of the styles of Pushkin
and Chaikovski."

We know well enough what a stern and exacting artist Stanislavski
was in judging acting in general and his own in particular, so we are
bound to believe what he says. As we studied this second scene step by
step we became convinced that the laconic simplicity he achieved in it
(and which fills with alarm the partisans of gorgeousness in operatic
style) was indeed worthy of Pushkin and Chaikovski. The name of

Stanislavski has every right to stand beside their names as a co-creator of the opera.

With the first tense, restless chord, like a heavy sigh which comes from the strings, the curtain swiftly opens and we see Tatiana's bedroom, lighted by a single candle. The white columns of the permanent set provide a cozy alcove in which is placed Tatiana's bed under a tulle canopy. To the right is the shadow of a window with a semicircular top, Tatiana's little dressing table with a mirror, candle holders and boxes on it, and in front of it an easy chair. Over the head of the bed beyond the columns one sees a blinking watch light in front of an ikon. The corners and the upper part of this small room are veiled in darkness. The one candle throws its light only on Tatiana, who lies in the bed, and the Nurse, who is drowsing as she sits at her feet, leaning against the footboard. It is late at night.

The prelude to any scene is usually played with the curtain still closed and is often accompanied by the coughs of a still-inattentive public. But Stanislavski, whenever the music made it possible, had the introduction played with the curtain open, thus enhancing the auditory impression of the prelude by adding the visual impression of the stage.

In this case we penetrate the atmosphere in which Tatiana is living long before we hear her first words. She cannot sleep, she sighs, and, as a sleepless person, she keeps shifting her position to find a comfortable place.

All this is done in time with the music without any special emphasis on the beat. Naturally, the fluent expressiveness of the music requires the singer to act with most subtle shadings.

Muted strings sound like the sighs of an aching heart. The restless triplets among the strings' chords mirror her disturbed emotions and we feel at once why she cannot sleep. After these chords comes the theme of Tatiana's reflections, her deep concentration. The melody is somehow overwhelmed by descending sequences, almost as though she seems to sense what her future is to be. As if speaking for Tatiana and voicing her hopes and fears, there comes an outburst and a painful sighing of the strings, followed by the cello pattern of uneasy thoughts; they surge higher and higher with great feeling, then drop spasmodically as if in despair until we hear the calming chords of the Nurse and her words: "I have been running on and on. . . ." This brings to an end the disturbing music of what is in Tatiana's soul.

The drowsiness of the Nurse is completely justified by the fact that there is as yet no music affecting her. She is practically absent and in this way the distress and solitude of Tatiana is underlined. Stanislavski's interpretation of this scene, with its logic and its close bond with the music, contrasts strikingly with the stage directions given in the printed libretto: "Tatiana is sitting in front of her mirror. She is very pensive. The Nurse stands beside her."

So then, when the curtain opens, we see Tatiana attempting to sleep and the Nurse drowsing. The only light on them is from the single candle which stands on a little mahogany table near the bed. The light of the candle is screened from the audience by a small green shade.

Through the window the diffused light of late evening is visible. As the last soft chord of the prelude is played, the Nurse's head has fallen forward on her chest. Then she wakes up, straightens herself slightly as she says slowly: "Well, I have been running on and on. It's time to settle down, Tanya. I'll wake you early to go to church, now quickly go to sleep." The flutes and clarinets echo the Nurse's caressing tones, "now quickly go to sleep." These are followed by serene triplets which rise higher and higher as if to embrace Tatiana with their gentle sounds. The libretto says: "The Nurse caresses her."

"How to express that caress?" Stanislavski asked the Nurse. "In most theatres they give a massage along the back or up an arm. But you cover her up to the sound of those triplets, the way a mother would cover a child with a blanket."

The Nurse straightens the blanket and covers Tatiana with it, lays her cheek against hers. Then she goes to the ikon, trims the watch light for the night, and bows several times to it. Meanwhile the strings are again beginning to play the theme of Tatiana's reflections. This is the music played in the overture to the opera, the melody which accompanies the words: "Oh mother, how this story of the heartache of these two lovers thrills me. . ." from the first scene in the opera.

Татьяна: Да как же, ма-ма, по-весть мук сердеч-ных...

The violins have sung the passionate "story of the heartache of these two lovers" and faded away. Only then Tatiana, with a sigh, pronounces her first phrase: "Nanny, I cannot sleep! It is so suffocating here, open the window and come sit down near me. . . I am so ill at ease, let us talk about old times." Chaikovski found such wonderfully gentle and lifelike intonations for this *recitativo* that all the singer needs to do is sing it in the right tempo, and all her emotional experiences, her innermost thoughts come through with perfect clarity. One is forcibly reminded of Stanislavski's words: "How lucky you are, you opera singers. The composer gives you everything: the rhythm for your feelings, the right intonations for each word, and a melody which is the pattern of your emotions. All you have to do is find a true basis for the notes given to you and make them your own. How much easier this is for you than for us dramatic actors, who have to create our own rhythms, compose the music of our spoken words, and provide true feelings out in the vacuum of the stage.

"All that is required of the singer playing the Nurse is modest simplicity of sound and manner. God forbid that she will let out her full voice here. That will come later!"

Tatiana's first words are broken into short phrases and the orchestra interrupts her three times with the same plaintive phrases, until it comes to the Nurse's words. Then the whole orchestra assumes a calmly moderate, almost solemn tone as if she were about to recite an old ballad; when she begins her story: "It must have been that God ordained it so. My Vanya, bless him, was younger in years than I."

Note that Tatiana says her first words without raising her head from her pillow. Like all singers training under Stanislavski, she is obliged to sing in many different positions and not just stiffly upright. She is obliged to be highly skilled in singing but also in the control of every movement of her head, arms, her whole body. The eyes of the audience are fixed on her head—that is the whole area in which the singer-actress will perform. Any foreshortening of her body must be carefully planned as it would be by a painter.

The Nurse, after trimming the watch light, having said her prayers before the ikon, responds to Tatiana's call, comes out of the dark corner, and stands by the head of her bed: "What is the matter, Tanya?" She opens the window as requested and hears Tatiana's reply: "I am so ill at ease, let's talk about old times."

"The Nurse's words about how she used to know many interesting stories but now, in her old age, she has forgotten them, can all be said as you move around doing routine things, opening the window, straightening the curtain, moving the candle. But when you come to the words: 'Then bad times came and gave me a hard knock!' sit down again on the bed at Tatiana's feet.

"Above all stick to the rhythm of your own music. It will easily suggest to you a slow, almost crooning beat. Old people have that kind of rhythm, unhurried but melodious, which goes straight along. One phrase smoothly merges with the next and forms a sort of unbroken line of life. The rhythm of the young is always more accented. All your accents are very gentle and serene."

The Nurse is now seated once more at Tatiana's feet. Again the violins begin Tatiana's theme but set in different harmonies, and again we have the impetuous "Tell me, Nanny. . . ." followed by a pause. Here the muted violins lightly touch on the insistently recurring thought ". . .about your bygone years. . . ." A careful chord played by the strings and then comes the all-important phrase, long on Tatiana's lips: "And were you in love then?"

This phrase has to be made clear. It is the key to the whole scene. Tatiana has dared to say aloud the awesome words "in love".

"Chaikovski handled this phrase very delicately," said Stanislavski. "In music and rhythm it is in keeping with the earlier lines of the Nurse—Tatiana would seem to be carrying on the conversation in the Nurse's tone when speaking of her youth. That is for the Nurse, but what about us? The sub-text comes out here in full force. It is well-nigh impossible for Tatiana to bring out those words. And she must not do it overtly. Try to find the inner tremor but continue with the calm external expression. Here the whole point lies in your inner rhythm."

Stanislavski, turning his attention to the Nurse and her reply to Tatiana: "Why, Tatiana, in our time we never even heard of love," went on to remind her that there was no need to underscore the meaning of those words by "ramming them down" or "thrusting out one's chin defiantly". They used to do that sort of thing because singers often thought it was more effective, especially if they wagged their heads as well. Then in the phrase: "My late mother-in-law would have chased me out of this world", after the long high note "cha-a-sed" there was the feeling that "out of this wo-o-rld" should be accented too. That seemed to emphasize the Nurse's sad lot. Here Stanislavski pointed out to the Nurse: "But your attitude towards all that is good-natured, free of spite. Altogether it is not at all in your character to be angry, indignant, spiteful."

Now, again, before Tatiana puts her question, the orchestra repeats the theme with which the opera begins and this time it ends on a note of enquiry. Here Stanislavski remarked:

"Do not be indifferent to the constantly recurring theme. These are the questions that you, as Tatiana, put to life. Each time try to find a fresh response to what the orchestra is saying to you. During this part of the music you are probably scanning the Nurse's face closely and trying to understand how one can *marry* without love. For you, to be 'in love' and 'marry' are indivisible words. Prepare yourself inwardly, as a kind of prelude, and then ask: 'How was it, Nanny, that you married?' You will find the right intonation for this through your own innner impulses. Be very niggardly with your movements. But when you come to, 'How was it, Nanny, that you married?' raise yourself a little on your pillow and afterwards lie back again and listen to the Nurse's story. This story runs along in calm, unhurried tones, it flows like a gurgling brook."

The tale does indeed *flow*, without a pause or jerk. As a piece of music, rich in thought, significant in design as a painting, yet concise and accurate as a short story, it is a faultless masterpiece. Sometimes the singers who have this role wish to branch out and overcolour some places, underscore the comic bits such as: "I was thirteen at the time," or they put in resentful intonations to suggest the injustice of the times and the bitter lot of women then. Stanislavski restrained his singers from that sort of thing.

"Don't try to emphasize or chew on anything. Your spectators are not fools. You put forward your thoughts clearly in the character of your objectives, and we'll understand them. All you have to do is remember your past life, visualize a sort of 'moving picture' of that life. And that is all! Therefore the most important thing is to immerse yourself in your memories. Your music is serious, and at the end when you speak of your wedding it is really solemn—as solemn as 'Lord have mercy'. You have become so absorbed in recalling your past that you do not notice the change that comes over Tatiana, into what sad thoughts she has fallen while listening to your story.

"In the first phrase of the Nurse's tale Chaikovski made a slip. To one musical phrase there are two verbal phrases: 'It was no doubt God's will. My Vanya. . . .' But after the word 'will' there must be a break to set that off from the succeeding phrase. In such cases a singer has to know how to compensate for such slips on the part of the composer.

"'I wept so bitterly from fright and, still weeping, my braid was unplaited, they took me to the church. . . .' the Nurse sings and the tempo of her story slows down as she sinks deeper into her thoughts until the final, meaningful phrase: 'And so—they took me into a family of strangers'. At this the music changes to a harsh *sforzando*, and the bows come down hard on the strings, interrupting the smooth, flowing narrative. Here Tatiana, who has held back her feelings for so long, lets her sadness boil up and her passionate plaint suddenly flows out with force in a new broad melody tense with emotion: 'Oh, Nanny, Nanny, I am suffering, I am full of yearning. . . .' For the first time we hear this theme burst forth—the passionate melody. It will then be repeated by the cellos when Tatiana says: 'I am ready to weep.'

"Here you should gather up all the force you can muster so that there will be a real outburst from your soul. You should have an enormous reserve of temperament. Remember, you are not at all a

weakling, you are a strong girl. You are performing deeds of heroism. You are taking your life into your own hands. You are unhappy, distracted, full of doubts. But in order not to fall into sentimentality, keep seeking out your strong and decisive qualities. Throw yourself on the Nurse's shoulder, embrace her so that she will really be startled, and having sung your phrase with all the strength you have in you, throw yourself back with equal force onto your pillow and hide your face in it."

Then Stanislavski made suggestions to the singer with the role of the Nurse.

"You, Nurse, after a first moment of bewilderment rush over to the ikon for some holy water. As you go feel Tatiana's forehead so that you can say: 'You are all on fire'. Then returning with the holy water you try to sprinkle it on Tatiana, who says: 'Leave me alone, leave me alone'. The last words are: "I am in love', and that bowls you over, you plump down on the foot of the bed as you say: 'How can this be?'

"As always after a high point of great tension a reaction sets in, so there is now a moment of calm. Tatiana is very quiet, her rhythm changes, there is a sense of deep concentration, as if she were looking into her own soul and then calmly but firmly she sings: 'Go! Leave me alone. But, Nanny, first give me a pen and paper, and move the table over. I shall soon lie down'.

"We see Tatiana's face. She is half reclining with her arm under one cheek. Her eyes are fixed on something far away, beyond her candle. We read in her eyes an intensity of thought. We sense that in her thoughts she is far away. The Nurse feels this too as she cautiously pushes the table over to the bed, takes a portfolio and paper from a drawer, gives them to Tatiana and quietly goes away.

"You realize, Nurse, that this is no time to bother Tatiana with your fussing over her, and as you go out do not, please, shake your head and sigh like a tenderhearted old woman. This is a highly serious moment on the stage," Stanislavski said in a quiet and austere tone. When we came to any powerful scene both at rehearsals and during performances his manner was one of austere concern as if something tragic had happened personally to him. He might well become your enemy for life if at such times he noticed indifference on your part, or worse yet if he saw laughter in your eyes. That would forfeit forever any friendly interest he might take in you.

Tatiana is alone. The orchestra repeats for the third time and develops the theme of her passionate confession.

A melody in a major key played by the violins is resolved into nervous pulsation of all the strings. This is followed by an impetuous

flight of short chords which seem to convey the increased beating of Tatiana's heart. The nervous tension fades unresolved in a chord that seems to hang in the air. Tatiana has pulled herself up into a kneeling position, throwing off her blanket. She is full of determination and poetic inspiration: "E'en though I may be lost. . . ." she begins her avowal and her pledge. The melody so long restrained in the orchestra now flows broadly and freely. The accompaniment to Tatiana's voice is light, airy. The agonizing tenseness of the whole scene is now resolved.

"The fact that you have now risen to a kneeling position is tantamount to a real move since up to this point you have scarcely stirred," said Stanislavski. "Don't blur your sculptured pose by any small movements of your arms. Remain motionless throughout your aria."

After this Tatiana settles herself cross-legged on her bed, takes the portfolio from the table, and lays it on her knees. Then she begins to write. This pose is incomparably closer to the real image of Tatiana than the way most actresses dream of looking on the stage.

The cut of Tatiana's nightdress was the object of close study when it was being made. Stanislavski insisted that it should be of the simplest pattern, cut like the nightdresses of the country girls and landowners' daughters for countless generations. The neckline was gathered on a little cord and the short sleeves that covered her shoulders came down a short distance on her arms. There were none of the fancy belts usually worn by stage Tatianas to hold in their white amorphous robes. This nightdress was loose so that it did not impede her movements.

It was necessary to have separate and detailed rehearsals for what one might call the technique of the changes in Tatiana's poses. Nothing was left to chance that a tangled fold of nightdress or blanket might ruin the pattern of the scene.

Tatiana begins to write her letter.

"Now every slightest movement," said Stanislavski, "is important. This is the most subtle part of your acting. Everything depends on your facial expression and the movements of your hand. Make the most of them! It is extremely important *how you look* at the table where the writing materials for your letter are, *how you take* the paper up, *how you reach* for the pen, *how you dip* the pen in the inkwell. Do not leave out anything, do nothing mechanically. By the way you will carry out these customary actions I shall understand what is impelling you at this moment. For all of us this is almost a sacred rite."

The orchestra again plays the first theme of the opera, the chromatic melody of reflection about the "story of the heartache" of lovers. Chaikovski gives this irresolute, moving melody to Tatiana in the most delicate way. There is none of the clearness and delight which rang just now in her words: "I may be lost. . . ." It is still not clear to Tatiana

what to write—as unclear as all the romantic dreams in the books which up to now so filled her thoughts.

The melody slackens, seems to die away, is suddenly broken off by a *sforzando* major chord, a decisive chord after which come tumbling the words: "No, that's not it at all, I must begin again. . . . Oh, what is happening to me. I'm all on fire. I do not know how to begin."

Chaikovski expresses in the music the crushing and tearing up of what she has written, the fluttering off of bits of paper as if driven by a wind.

After the words: "Oh, what is happening to me. I'm all on fire. I do not know how to begin", we suddenly hear the beginning of a quietly intimate and enchantingly transparent melody which like the shepherd's pipe accompanies Tatiana's letter and almost seems to dictate the words to her.

This whole musical interlude preparatory to the writing of the letter consists of ten measures and is made up of the interplay of singing phrases between the oboes, of short responses from the flute and clarinet with chords played on the harp. This all takes place against the background of nervous syncopation of the strings. The chords from the harp come in on the last eighth note of the measure and are quite distinct in their resonance.

When Stanislavski called attention to them he said that one musical critic (N.D. Kashkin), who was a friend of Chaikovski's, asserted that it was the intention of the composer to have these splashing harp sounds represent the dipping of Tatiana's pen into the inkwell. This rhythmic feature is observed by all Tatianas. But it does not jibe with the directions in the libretto, where the actual words of Tatiana are: "I do not know how to begin", and the indication is: "She writes". And then in the middle of this musical phrase the libretto says: "She stops and reads over what she has written."

After listening to the music Stanislavski said:

"It cannot be that you, having just said 'I do not know how to begin' can, with the delay of a second's reflection, start reeling off the letter. It is only in 'opera' that such things can be done. But if you really do not know how to begin then listen carefully to the music. It is written in order to let you know when you are to begin the letter. The stage directions in the libretto were written without the slightest regard for the music. You begin to write only when you frame the words: 'I write you', that is to say you write and at the same time say what you are writing—as one does so often in real life."

Tatiana sitting motionless and listening to the music is one of the finest pieces of staging in the Letter Scene. Complete immobility combined with intense concentration—the sort of thing most opera

singers dread—proved to us what a powerful impression can be achieved on the stage when one is not acting anything. Tatiana, with her forgotten pen held motionless in her fingers, listening to both the music of the orchestra and her own soul, is an unforgettable image of profound poetic feelings. After this prolonged moment of concentration it is quite natural for her to commence to write, quietly at first and then with increasing speed as she is carried away by her letter.

The principal singer in the role of Tatiana, after those who sang the part in the Studio production, was Maya Meltser. Her great vocal and dramatic gifts enabled her to create a most poetic and lifelike Tatiana. Above all she made a most penetrating impression in her rendering of the Letter Scene. She wrote down her recollection of working with Stanislavski on this scene:

> My first rehearsal with Stanislavski was devoted to work on words and the conveying of the thoughts they contained. He called this "massaging a phrase". In the course of this work he was particularly absorbed by and gave very careful consideration to the music. Here is an example of his "massage of a phrase": Of the three possible logical accents on the first phrase of Tatiana's letter "I write you" Stanislavski chose the one on "write" because that is also where the accent falls in the music.
>
> "But don't try to *squeeze* out an intonation. As soon as you begin to think about it that intonation will be wrong and unnatural. All preparations are superfluous. You must fix your attention on a single object and know positively to whom and for what reason you will say 'I may be lost. . .' for this is a solemn vow she is taking for all her life. All this is expressed with particular conviction in Tatiana's letter and the blazing words must convince the paper on which she writes, as if it were Onegin himself."
>
> Beginning with the words: "Yet should you towards my hapless fate feel but a drop of pity. . ." Tatiana's speech becomes nervous, jerky until she comes to the word "never", which stops her for a moment of reflection. After the words: "I vow that I will keep within my soul this my confession of ardent, reckless passion" she alters her position. She puts the paper on the table and through her tears she groans pitifully: "Alas, I lack the strength to restrain my own soul."
>
> "'Choose for this situation a comfortable but at the same time an expressive pose. Here you are having a moment of hesitation. You will have to find some action to convey your state of distraction so that then you can return to writing in an affirmative way. . . . Perhaps you will lean your elbow on the table, perhaps throw your arms down weakly or hang your head. Anything will be right if it is based on inner motivation, but never check these movements of yours in the mirror—that is a dangerous thing to do."
>
> Tatiana drops her hand holding the letter and her pen onto the table. She lets her other arm drop down and bows her head. She sings: "Alas, I lack

the strength to restrain my own soul." This phrase is sung in a broad *adagio*. Here Stanislavski proposed:

"Do not alter your pose until you have finished the phrase. Let those words be an integral part of your visual image of your pose. They complement each other. The essence of art in opera lies in the finish of each phrase and the fluency of expression. Move your shoulders, spread your arms—and the whole effect is lost. 'Let come what may to me. To him I do confess.' A chord, she glances at the letter—another chord, then takes the letter and puts it back in her lap: 'Take heart, let him know all'.

"When you say 'him' look at the letter as if it were his portrait and after that you continue to speak to him in the form of the letter. You do all this, never lagging behind the music but rather keeping very slightly ahead of it; you must create the feeling that the music is following you and not you it."

After four introductory measures Tatiana goes on with her writing: "Why, oh why, did you come here to visit?" The melody changes; it tends to build in still unclear outlines toward the flood of orchestral sound which accompanies: "Who art thou? My guardian angel?" and later with especial force and passion, at the end of the letter: "Imagine I am here alone. . . ."

The music here is still plaintive and full of resignation. Yet all the second part of the letter beginning with the words: "I should never have known you, never known bitter pain. My inexperienced heart in time would have been reconciled, how can I tell, I might have found another friend and been a true wife and virtuous mother"—all this shows firmness, self-confidence. Yet the plaintiveness is still there, a passionate and insistent plaintiveness.

Stanislavski used to say: "If you have two phrases that are more or less equal as to music and to thought, the second one must be given more force than the first, when it is a question of affirmation, or desire, or insistence.

"You must give evidence of greater energy during the second part of the letter. The whole scene moves in waves, flood and ebb tides, and after each receding movement the next wave of emotion should come on with greater force than the preceding one. Chaikovski understood this extremely well and gave expression to it in his music."

Tatiana writes the following part of her letter sitting in almost the same position except for a slight turn of her body. Yet even this small shift in pose together with a new character of her performance creates the impression of a new bit of staging. With the words about her heart becoming reconciled in time, the rhythm increases in speed and force until at the end five full chords of the orchestra break in on Tatiana's thoughts at the word "another". At these chords the letter is again put down. It lies on the table. Here there is a complete change of focus and thus a change in the staging.

"Now you will begin to talk with *him*. You see him in a dream. Let the centre of your focus, i.e. Onegin, be over there, to the left of your bed. Find comfortable positions for yourself," said Stanislavski to the singer.

The next throbbing phrases: "No, to no other in the world would I yield up my heart, by the ruling of all the high powers, by the will of heaven, I am thine", and up to the words: "To my grave, my guardian angel, thou", are accompanied in the Chaikovski score by tremulous triplets. This leads to the most intimate revelation of Tatiana's soul. With courageous simplicity she shows us the very depths of her heart.

"Let us study," said Stanislavski, "all the shadings of your thoughts so that we can set them in perspective, reaching to the high point in this scene. This will begin when you sing: 'Imagine I am here alone, no one can know what is in my heart. . . .' Then comes the culmination.

"The orchestra here repeats your theme with thunderous power. But you must come to this point with great caution, and lay your colours on with skill. Your emotions are all in line with the through-line of action of the whole and you abandon yourself completely to them. But the controller, the master artist who lives inside you and guides you, will decide the right perspective for you to choose from the point of view of distributing your colours. But always bear in mind that when there is a rise it is followed by a slight reaction, then another stronger rise, again a slight recession—until you reach the highest, the culminating point."

To begin with, the character of the music is reflective, calming; it is played against a background of long-drawn-out chords on the strings rising slightly to merge with the flutes and clarinets. But when the moment comes for the recollection of Tatiana's first meeting with Onegin, the theme and the accompaniment surge and move towards the triumphant: "This is he! This is he!" This is followed by tumultuous, thrilling music which swells to a great wave of feeling and sound up to the words: "With consolation and with love"—then suddenly there is complete quiet and only the voice of Tatiana is heard as she sings: "His words have whispered hope". This means that she does have "hope"; it is the most important point in this part of the scene.

In the following bit the words are preceded by an interlude of reflective music. An oboe most expressively leads to the final, triumphant statement of Tatiana's emotions. There is a mournful note of yearning in the words: "It may be all is in vain"—and then finally comes the point of irrevocable decision:

> So be it. Now my fate
> I put into thy hands.
> To thee I offer my tears
> And beg for thy protection.

The impetuous tempo, Tatiana's rhythmically-throbbing words, accompanied by the palpitating sixteenth notes of the violins, very quickly reach the climax of the whole scene, the most powerful surge of Tatiana's feelings.

> I now await thee. Await thee. . .
> One word of hope from thee
> Will revive my heart—
> Unless thou break this oppressive dream,
> Alas, by the rebuke I so deserve.

Here the triumphant theme of Tatiana, which started earlier with the sound of a single oboe, merges with her voice together with all the strings. As she pronounces the last words ("Alas, by the rebuke I so deserve") the whole orchestra turns into a tempest of sound.

The passionate theme ("I am alone") now passes to the brass instruments. Their all-conquering notes soar above the flood tides of the orchestra as a whole. What power lies in the breast of a modest, shy young girl! For the first time during the whole scene she stands up, leans against one of the columns and her eyes look out into the darkness of the auditorium as she listens to what is going on in her own heart. Then, as if recovering herself, Tatiana turns quickly to her letter and adds the last, the most important words under the inspiration of the powerful impact of her emotions. Now the letter is finished!

The accent of the whole orchestra falls on: "I boldly throw myself upon thy honour." This is followed by two culminating chords which lend a solemn touch to the end of the letter. The pause which follows still maintains that moment of solemnity. No one can remain indifferent to such a scene. The growing power and tension are such that one is struck and at the same time made happy by being a witness and participant in the expression of such exalted and wholehearted feelings.

"When you play," Stanislavski said to the orchestra, "think of Tatiana, of her emotions, and play for her. This affects especially the oboe. After all, you are the one who dictates the letter to her," he said to the oboist. "Watch the rehearsals, see how she acts, and perform your role on the oboe in a duet with her. Help her to act out her life on the stage. Besides, in order that the whole orchestra may be well-acquainted with this scene, we shall give a full dress-rehearsal to the accompaniment of a piano for the benefit of the members of the orchestra."

Such rehearsals of impending productions became a fixed part of Stanislavski's opera work. This rule served, first of all, to make all the musicians of the orchestra an integral part of the stage production and, in the second place, it reinforced the basic concept of collective creativeness: Each member of the orchestra was convinced that he was an indispensable factor in the overall production.

"The musicians may tell us," said Stanislavski, "that in the concept of the composer there are no small divisions in, say, the Letter Scene such as we have made. But remember that we are now analyzing all these components of the aria to enrich their content; we do not wish to lose a syllable of the precious Pushkin words but rather to reach down into their very depths. In the moment of their performance on the stage all these small fragments of the aria will be reconstituted into one flowing line of action: Tatiana's effort to open her own heart. We reach this point of synthesis by means of painstaking and profound analysis."

Stanislavski went far beyond the stage directions in the libretto such as "falls into reflective mood", "stands up suddenly", "with great feeling", "paces back and forth in state of meditation." He even went beyond the notations in the score such as *"piano, forte, ritenuto"*, etc. His actress was obliged to know how to pass through "twenty thousand steps of human emotions and all the shadings", to traverse the whole gamut from grief to joy, hope to despair, love to hate, and he pointed out to her that the most interesting part of creativeness is the very *process* of action, not its final result. The whole Letter Scene must be performed with utmost concentration on the text, the inner vision of the "unrolling film of one's life", and completely free of all gestures.

"Each little piece we have marked out in your role will either slip by me unnoticed, without touching my comprehension, or, if you fill each one with rich content, I shall remember it all my life. That is the reason for the existence of theatre. If your heart is empty and cold, so will be the auditorium. I cannot go on forever just admiring the timbre of your voice. You must offer me something more, some food for thought; then I, the audience, to the extent of my capabilities, will leave the theatre enriched, thrilled, lifted clear of the daily, dusty round of life. Either you will give your whole self, all your capacities, to the noble endeavour of enlarging the spirit of the audience, or you came to the theatre to parade your good looks on the stage, flirt with your acquaintances in the audience, and thrill your eighteen-year-old admirers with your voice and your charms.

"Do remember that even the most inept actors have their admirers and therefore examine carefully the quality of your applause. That is one of the first skills an actor must learn: not to be hooked on applause. Pushkin and Chaikovski have entrusted to you their favourite, most beloved characters and the feelings closest to their hearts. Prove yourself worthy of their trust."

When Stanislavski talked this way to this actors they were filled with pride, but at the same time they were made to think in terms of responsibility.

"How to plan to make an impression in this scene?" Stanislavski continued. "First of all through your penetration and understanding of the words you sing. To this end you must have completely mobilized all your consonants to make each word resonant, outstanding. Sloppy consonants are of no effect. You will pronounce the phrase: '. . .by the Will of God I am thine. . .' in such a way that each word is pregnant with a fateful meaning. And what sound will you give to: '. . .To my grave, my guardian angel thou. . . .'? This is, after all, a vow made for life. One cannot babble such words, or half swallow them, *especially their endings*. If you do not sense the special quality of certain words, make them seem to be freshly-minted, inform them with loving kindness, warmth, tenderness—then all the meaning of these splendid lines is lost. The melody of the music remains; it is beautiful but it is bereft of heart. Yet Chaikovski gave special care to every one of the words. They are all very melodious and extremely expressive.

"Another most important point is your focus, the object on which your attention is fixed. To whom are you singing, to whom are you addressing yourself? Your object is always 'he'. But 'he' may be far from you. You are reaching out to him through a wide space of separation and you imagine him to be sitting in his home. Or you envision him as having come to you now and standing beside your bed, or else you are communing with yourself, as in a colloquy between your head and your heart. Then your focal point is inside yourself. That fixed object will define all that you do in the half dozen small units into which you have broken your actions. For one you will sit, in the next you will lean back, in the third you rise to a kneeling position, in the fourth you lie down in a state of profound reflection, your head bowed forward, and then, having reached your decision, you straighten up. Finally at the climactic point and singing your highest note, you are carried away by a surge of feeling, you jump out of your bed to go to him at once, then you stand and listen to the promptings of the orchestra. This culmination of your feelings will also be the moment of your broadcast external actions. You have stood up, you have taken two steps yet these two steps will be memorable moments because up to now the whole scene has depended only on your facial expression."

When Tatiana hears her theme, performed this time by the horns in the orchestra, she writes the last lines of her letter with feverish haste and sings: "I have finished. . . . I dare not read it over." With the last chord in the orchestra she lays down her pen, sits down on her bed, and fixes her gaze on the white sheets of paper.

"Let us have the chance to remember this picture," said Stanislavski to the conductor. "Make a pause of at least five seconds. After such high tension there must be a moment of reaction."

By now this night, so all-important in Tatiana's life, is almost over. From the lower registers of the bassoons, the cellos, gathering up gradually the whole orchestra, there comes a slow swell of sound. At the end there is a clear C-major chord and with it appears the first beam of sunlight. In another second we hear the rippling notes from the harps and then the sun itself strikes the tops of the columns on the stage, envelops the white canopy over the bed and Tatiana herself.

Through the open window a shepherd's horn is heard. Sunlight, quiet, a shepherd's song, a cool breeze through the window—all bespeaks tranquility.

"Oh, the night has passed, all are awake, and the sun is rising," sings Tatiana as she snuffs out her candle.

"A calm morning has begun," said Stanislavski, "all nature is awaking. It is that 'imperturbable nature' which 'shines with everlasting beauty', yet, from contemplating it, your heart grows heavier and more restless. That is why your exclamation: 'But as for me!' and especially this phrase repeated a second time, sounds almost like a suppressed sob. In the libretto the stage direction reads: 'She is pensive'. After such an emotionally upsetting experience can one be merely pensive? Listen to the cello. It clearly speaks of suffering, sighs, tears. And according to the logic of feelings that is as it should be. After a state of great exaltation there must come the reaction of a sense of weakness. And this you must now convey by your behaviour.

"Logically too the cellos repeat the first theme: 'Oh, Nanny, I am suffering. . . .' Note how delicately Chaikovski suggests here what is going on in your heart after your powerful emotional exertion. Finally the motif of the Nurse begins: 'It was the will of God. . . .' And with it we hear her calm voice: 'It's time, my child, get up!' Tatiana is sitting, bent over the table with her head in her arms. We can see her shoulders heaving and we know that she is weeping. But as she hears the Nurse's step she quickly slips her bare feet in her slippers, she grabs the letter, hurriedly folds and seals it (they had no envelopes, as we know them, at that time), and makes haste to sit down at her dressing table by the window and begin to comb her hair as a girl might do had she been awake some time. Here in the music we have the sense of urgency, the notes tumbling after each other, and then the exclamation of the Nurse: 'Why you, my pretty one, are up already! Oh, my little early bird. . . .' She must find Tatiana quietly seated before the mirror of her dressing table, having slipped the letter under the candlestick.

"The Nurse's cue: 'Why you, my pretty one. . .' clearly indicates that she has not seen Tatiana yet. Be careful here to avoid the kind of awkward situation on the stage when an actor looks markedly off in some other direction while waiting for his partner's reply."

Stanislavski solved this very simply by saying to the Nurse: "You told her: 'I shall call you early in time to go to church', so you bring in her freshly-ironed dress. Hang it carefully over the back of a chair near the door. That will prove that you have not really looked at Tatiana and seen that she is already at her dressing table.

"What is the point of the ensuing scene? The Nurse must be reassured that Tatiana is not ill and Tatiana must dispatch the Nurse as quickly as possible with the letter while keeping her face, which is flaming with blushes, well-averted.

"Be sure to avoid the mistake often made on the stage of not following the line of logical thinking. How did you, the Nurse, leave Tatiana? In your mind she was in a dangerous state: do you remember how she talked to you? How did you sleep yourself? Why, you never closed your eyes, you were so concerned about Tatiana. Now decide: How will you enter her room, how will you look at her to see if she is ill or has recovered? This will all go to show your love for Tatiana. You don't just pat her on the back. In most theatres the Nurse usually is frightfully upset with worry about her survival in one act, then in the next that is all forgotten and she shows no concern whatever. You must always stick to the line of logical actions."

Chaikovski accompanies the Nurse's cues with a calm rhythm containing echoes of her theme when she told about her early life, so that there can be no question here of nervous tension on her part. But Stanislavski always taught us that the outward rhythm of our behaviour, the rhythm of our moving about, does not necessarily correspond to our inner rhythm. They can be in complete contrast, and it is in the realization of this that one can see the art of the actor.

Beginning with Tatiana's words: "Oh, Nanny, please do me a favour", that is to say from the start of the duet, the music reflects Tatiana's restless state. The first violins clearly emphasize this with their nervous sixteenth notes.

The duet takes place with Tatiana at her dressing table, hiding her flaming face from the Nurse while the Nurse tries to look into Tatiana's eyes and calm her.

"Push the Nurse over to the door," Stanislavski said to Tatiana, "or else she will stand there forever chatting and saying how glad she is you are well. And you," Stanislavski spoke here to the singer with the role of the Nurse, "pay no attention to the long stage directions in the libretto where it says that you stop at the doorway, delay, come back, and then, looking at the letter in your hand, shake your puzzled head in the usual manner of an old nurse. Once you grasp what you are to do with the letter, go and take it with you quite simply, without any silly doings."

In the fourteenth measure of the music, in which the bassoons and the French horns seem to echo Tatiana's sighs against the background of emotional waves of sound from the lower registers of the cellos, everything seems to fade away, to subside into serenity. Tatiana stands beside one of the columns past which the Nurse has just disappeared. Her head is bowed.

Suddenly there is a sharp *sforzando* in the orchestra which causes Tatiana to come to herself, raise her head, and listen. . . .

Out of the elemental depth of some far-off sound slowly comes once more (for the nth time!) Tatiana's theme, recalling the moment in the beginning of the scene when she threw herself on her Nurse's neck and cried: "Oh, Nanny, Nanny, I am suffering. . . ."

"Why is this theme renewed here?" asked Stanislavski. "After all, Tatiana has already made her decision, we have already heard the majestic theme of her love. Why then do we have again the suffering and the doubts? Why does this theme so insistently pervade the orchestra? Has the terrible wound in her heart reopened? What is Tatiana to do faced by the suffering prompted by the orchestra? Follow the logic of life. What can come into your mind when, after your long struggles, you have taken a decisive step? Do you wonder if you did the right thing? Listen carefully to the music. It is all there. First the slow awakening of suspicion, then consternation, followed by fear and finally despair because of what you have done. Finally all is resolved in a light, discreet *pianissimo*. It is now too late to alter anything. The letter has been dispatched. It cannot be retrieved. Now translate all that into action. What would you do if placed in such circumstances?"

This is what the actress must resolve at the end of the scene, when, in accordance with usually-accepted operatic practice, all the acting is already finished. Yet how to reflect on the stage what the music is saying, giving full value to every measure? The curtain will close only at the very end of the *pizzicato* in the strings where Chaikovski put a *piano-pianissimo*.

In the Letter Scene many long rehearsals brought to fruition the following: Tatiana raises her head, listens to the importuning theme of her doubts, then, when the flutes sharply renew the beginning of the theme, she turns as if to hurry after the Nurse, to get back the letter; after several measures, at the point where the oboe takes up the theme, she runs across the stage to the window; we sense that she hopes to see the Nurse and call her back; then after some indecision, she sinks down on the edge of her bed. To the barely audible sound of the strings the curtain slowly closes.

Third Scene: The Meeting

Stanislavski made it the rule, and dinned it into producers and scene designers, that the sets for any scene must serve the purposes of the essential theme of a production and must not distract the attention of the public from the action onstage.

Does this brief scene, which consists only of a few phrases for Tatiana and a comparatively short aria for Onegin, call for a full setting? Stanislavski decided that all that was needed was an arbor, because of all the lyric scenes in this opera this one was the most concise. Any richness of landscape would only detract from its laconic simplicity.

On what should our attention be focused? Onegin makes a "confession" to Tatiana: in reply to her ardent outpourings he gives her a coldly civil refusal. It is not enough just to sing the aria intelligibly and to end on an ostentatiously high note—an "effect" invented by a famous singer.

In this scene what Stanislavski undertook to do was to reveal the character of a young man in the Pushkin epoch of the early nineteenth century.

"First let us see the man with whom Tatiana fell in love rather than you, the baritone. After all she did not fall in love with you because of your singing voice," he said facetiously, "although the voice should be a help in painting the portrait of a hero of those days.

"What must Onegin have? Above all he must have breeding, impeccable social manners, charm and the finesse of an aristocrat. Secondly he must be able to enunciate his words when singing so that we feel the brilliant cultivation of his speech. If we have the Letter Scene as the key to Tatiana's essential quality, we have the Scene of the Meeting to reveal Onegin," said Stanislavski. "This is the whole character of Onegin. Here you, with all your easy exquisiteness, sign the act of indictment that will spell catastrophe for your own life.

"What really is Onegin? A poseur, an egotist—but a well-mannered one—even a 'good fellow'. Above all he is a poseur, the man playing the role of a contemporary hero. You must handle your Byronic attitude, which infected the gilded youth of those times, with great subtlety. You are a man who has experienced everything; there is nothing more in life to interest you or enliven you. Death is of no importance. Onegin would like to fall in love, but he is disillusioned on that score. He plays the part of a profoundly disenchanted man. You long to live and love but you are unable to do so. You are full of tenderest feelings for Tatiana, you are most attentive, but the seal of death is on you. 'My burden is unbearable, yet what can I do?'

"He has taken in many women with this pose and he is amused because they all fall in love with him. So he jests, makes ironical fun of himself and others. And he came here, to the Larins', to make fun, show off his graces, flirt, for his own adulation. Your purpose should be to make Tatiana feel sorry for you, so that she will long to save you from your disillusion, to put life and buoyancy into you.

"But it's not a matter of playing at passion or of presenting an image, you will fall into cliché routines unless you go into action. It will be up to you to translate into action all that we have been saying about Onegin. How can you and how should you act so that Tatiana can believe that you are really suffering? What steps should you take to make her realize this?

"Your goal in this Scene of the Meeting is to show us through your acting how a disillusioned young man will behave.

"A sixteen-year-old girl faced with a Shalyapin—that is the essence of the situation when you and Tatiana meet. She is awkward, even absurd. She is just a frightened girl. And what you have to undertake is to make her see how noble you are. You should have at your command a whole arsenal of Byronic attitudes. These are the poses of a world-weary man, indifferent to everything. At the big society balls such young men would stand about alone, leaning against columns in the most contrived poses. One arm thrust in your coat à la Napoleon, your head all but concealed inside a high collar, languishing eyes, feet pointing outwards, nothing overdone yet all calculated to make an impression."

Here Stanislavski himself leaned against one of the columns on the stage, his head bent down onto his shoulder, his arms crossed in martyr-like fashion over his breast. His pose was strikingly "poetic" yet rather comic. He had an expression of utter exhaustion and restrained suffering on his face.

"Now find a basis for the most outrageous Byronic poses and make them natural. Your social polish is such that you, as the hero of the piece, are allowed to do anything; you can find yourself completely at ease in any attitude. Therefore your undertaking is 1) to play a Byronic gentleman, 2) to comfort and cheer up Tatiana, 3) to speak of your despair, 4) to consult with her and warn her, all in a friendly fashion.

"You need a certain statuesque quality, and restraint. Whatever you start, carry it through. If you straighten your cravat, lay down your hat, make a gesture of invitation to Tatiana to sit down, you must do it with complete calm and self-control. In each action, even the most insignificant, there is a focal point, just as in photography."

When the curtain opens the audience sees the arbor framed by the columns and flanked with trellises of greenery. Through the openings between the columns of the arbor there are glimpses of fields stretching out into the far distance. The set is a very modest one and focuses all the attention of the audience on the two leading characters.

The stage is flooded with light from the setting sun. It may be pointed out here that in the construction of this set and the colours used, as well as the lighting for them, Stanislavski broke away from the usual operatic banalities used to accompany or stress Tatiana's saddened mood: an autumnal landscape with melancholy leaves falling to the ground.

The scene opens with a women's chorus ("Beautiful maidens") written in a bright A-major key, lively in tempo. This chorus sets a mood of village life, simple, idyllic, which is in calculated contrast to Tatiana's emotional state. The libretto stage directions read: "The household maids are seen picking berries among the bushes." But such picturesque glimpses of life on a country estate have no further purpose than entertainment. They are not woven into the pattern of action; therefore Stanislavski left the chorus offstage, using it only as background against which the action on the stage unfolds. The chorus is heard again at the end of the scene, where even in the libretto it says: "The household girls do not appear on the stage".

To Tatiana's hurried entrance Chaikovski devotes eight measures of restlessly pulsating music on the strings which convey at the same time Tatiana's uneven breathing, from having hurried, and her rapid movements. When the music begins we see Tatiana running forward toward the arbor from upstage. She dashes like the wind from one side of the stage to the other; the tulle scarf laid around her shoulders floats out after her, further emphasizing the impetuousness of her haste. In a second or two we see her running back and as the whole orchestra plays a strong *fortissimo* she dashes into the arbor and, breathless, leans against one of the columns. It is from here that we hear her first words, gasped out with emotion: "Can he be here, Eugene here? Oh, God! Oh, God! What will he have thought! What will he say?"

Her impetuous haste across the stage, her attempt to hide in the arbor, her figure pressed against the column—all convey vividly Tatiana's confusion and create the tenseness of rhythm in which the whole scene will develop. This outward, physical rhythm will of necessity evoke a corresponding inner rhythm of feelings, sensations.

"You can work from the inner to the outer rhythm, or vice versa," Stanislavski reminded us. "In this case the outer rhythm of running is of great help to the actress in feeling what she is going through. But you will not achieve this inner rhythm if all you do is dash in and plunk yourself down on a bench."

Of course there were objections from the singer: "But I have to sing, so how can I run? I get all out of breath."

"When you have done it fifty times you'll be in good training," was Stanislavski's reply. Then he went on:

"Really, some serious training in running will teach your whole organism to adapt itself with speed to such a situation. It is, however, a fact that most singers are lazy about undergoing such training. At such a juncture the *actress* should prove stronger than the *singer* and make the latter submit to training."

After the first gasping ejaculation of "Can he be here!" there is a moment of some calm and we see Tatiana seated limply by the balustrade and hear her sing her brief, sad little arietta: "Oh, why is my sore heart so overcome with mourning. . . ." The French horn responds to Tatiana's voice and expresses her heartache.

At one dress rehearsal in the Art Theatre there was a memorable incident: Stanislavski suddenly jumped up from his usual seat in the sixth row and, running down to the railing around the orchestra, spoke to the musician playing the French horn:

"No, you are not playing the right thing at all. You are playing as if you were wholly unconcerned with what is happening on the stage. You should be playing only for Tatiana. This is something she is going through. Look at her. She is weeping, there are tears in her eyes. But you are busy with your own tune, many miles away from her. You must penetrate to the depths of her heart with your instrument. Weep with her. That's the kind of an orchestra we must have. Is it only the people on the stage who feel what they are doing, while you in the orchestra are just a lot of unfeeling journeymen? No! In the orchestra you are all artists too and each one has his role to play. The whole orchestra is the prompter for the emotions of an operatic artist."

I cannot tell whether it was autosuggestion on my part or not, but Stanislavski's words had such a magical power that after this incident I never heard that French horn solo, while waiting for my entrance (as Onegin), without being so moved I had to make a great effort to get back to the condescending attitude with which I was to meet my victim.

Tatiana sits with her head bowed, sighing, and singing: "Dear God, how hapless am I, how pitiful", and the strings play delicately-pulsing chords as if seconding her mood. There is an immense satisfaction for any opera singer to be in complete unison with the music, when he hears and understands every sigh, every phrase coming from the orchestra, when he is so merged with it that without even looking at the conductor, he senses that some seventy musicians are out there backing him up with their artistry. How greatly this enhances his power and also makes everything onstage seem so clear and understandable. And with what subtlety Stanislavski comprehended this! "Competition in the art of opera," he said, "should not be based on the power of a voice but rather on its expressiveness."

As the strings surge upwards for a whole octave, they hint to Tatiana that someone is coming.

"Steps?" She lifts her head. The strings go an octave higher—she jumps up: "They come closer." Another spurt in the orchestra: "Yes, it is he!"—and she starts to run out of the arbor.

But before she can get away, on the threshold, she sees Onegin; she dashes back into the arbor and leaning close against a column she thinks that perhaps he will pass by without glimpsing her. The audience sides with Tatiana and wishes that this meeting need not take place, because we have the foreboding—we hear it in the orchestra—of untoward things to come. The strings, together with Tatiana, fall silent on a high note of fear and tense expectation. When we try to visualize what is happening on the stage we must always remember that what Stanislavski was always striving for was a total synthesis of each gesture, each move, each step taken, with the music. If the violins suddenly ceased, breaking off on a high note, then Tatiana too ceased to move.

With broad, graceful, light changes of rhythm, suggesting completely rhythmic freedom, the melody of Onegin now pours out as he with gliding steps enters the scene, quietly looking around on all sides.

"You must know how to carry your whole weight on the spring of your legs, like a thoroughbred racing horse," Stanislavski taught us. Having already passed the arbor, Onegin glimpses the edge of a dress behind one of the columns. A light smile crosses his lips. At the moment when the melody ends in a quiet A-major chord, the meeting takes place. Tatiana, who had hoped to slip away unnoticed, is met on the

Allegro moderato

threshold of the arbor by Onegin, who makes a slight, civil but condescending bow to her.

"What are you doing? Why are you trying to frighten the girl with
such loud tones, especially when the words of your cue are: 'Do not
avoid me!'" said Stanislavski stopping Onegin. "Pull all your social
graces together. Your words are extremely delicate: 'The confessions of
a confiding soul, the outpourings of innocent love. . . . Your sincerity is
dear to me. . . .' It is only with the words: 'It roused in me emotions that
long since were silent' that, because of your pretended emotion, you
may raise your voice slightly. But up to this point you must act as the
most tender of friends, like the family doctor.

"Then from the words: 'But I do not choose to flatter you, I shall
return your sincerity in kind. . .' begin to speak very earnestly and in a
way to make the last words: '. . .by a confession *also without any art*'
sound like a solemn promise. . . . 'I well realize the import of this
moment, I value deeply this precious confession and I shall reply to it
with equal, if not greater frankness', and stress the words: 'Also without
any art'".

The opening *recitativo* ends with the most significant words: "Accept this my confession, I give myself over to your judgement."

"Sing that phrase so that it sounds as if you were giving your whole
self, and make the point with a symbolic gesture as though to draw your
heart from your breast and hand it to Tatiana. Not as a gesture but an
act!

"You should put your hat down on the bench, throw your gloves
into it; by the way, take the glove only from your right hand. While you
are doing this with deliberation, Tatiana sings to herself: 'Dear God,
how insulting and how painful!'

"You must invite Tatiana to sit down. Your conversation is to be a
long and very serious one. This is all clearly indicated by Onegin's face;
he quite obviously prepares to gather his thoughts. There is a shade of
'Byronic' pose in this.

"Your right hand here must be used with a perfect grace. As you see,
Tatiana is standing before you like a schoolgirl, with her head hanging.

Cheer her up! Your music provides you with a soft but distinct chord after Tatiana's plaintive words. This chord marks a line of division, as it were, between Tatiana's distress and Onegin's aria. On that chord you make a gesture with your right hand inviting Tatiana to sit down. Your fingers are spread open, but do not on any account move your elbow. As the cellos play a descending melody she sits down carefully, but is too fearful to raise her head. Now comes the first moment of your aria. Here as well as later on all your thoughts, external movements, your poses must be calculated in strict observance to the music. Opera singers think that only their vocal performance is related to the notes, only their singing, and that all the rest—the words, their facial expression, their appearance—must be left to providence and has nothing to do with the music! You must have a score for all your inner and outer movements. The point is that an artist, who sings in accordance with his music and acts in accordance with it, is thereby released from it. Shalyapin proved that and showed everyone how to make use of this fact. Unfortunately we are lazy and unenterprising, as Pushkin said, and we do not take advantage of Shalyapin's experience; we fall back on the old excuse that he, after all, was a genius and we are just ordinary mortals."

The aria, "If life within the family circle", is very difficult for the singer, but not because there are many high notes or because it takes enormous physical effort to sustain the necessary breath as in Verdi roles. This aria is very comfortably arranged from the point of view of breathing. And the *tessitura* is written in notes that are most congenial to a baritone voice, so that just to produce the notes as written is not at all a problem. But to convey the *character* of the aria, its exquisite diction, the airiness with which its melodic pattern glides over the words of the text, the effortless two-quarter rhythm against an orchestral background of three-quarter-note rhythm, is extraordinarily difficult, and requires great vocal refinement. If the aria is sung mechanically it sounds monotonous. Two-thirds of it is based on one and the same melodic turn of the first phrase ("If life within the family circle"). Beginning with a rather high note for a baritone the melody flows downwards and then rises again. This undulating, swing-like movement runs through the entire aria. Towards the end ("Dreams and years can never be brought back") this effect is even heightened. Then the melody swings up as high as high F.

It is very easy for a singer, if he is unskilled in handling such delicate music, to turn the whole aria into a thumping of notes and lose altogether its logical and melodic points. The insidious beginning of each phrase is likely to tempt a singer to place emphases where they should not be. Therefore in this aria a singer does well to heed Stanislavski's saying: "The words are the *theme* for your creativeness and the melody is the *emotion* with which you accompany it. Here there is always the one approach: First grasp quite clearly *what* you are singing and, second, *how* you are going to sing it.

"First of all tell me the principal thoughts which you wish to convey to Tatiana," suggested Stanislavski. Here most singers begin to recall the words, excerpting them from the music, but Stanislavski stopped that. "Those words are accidentally on the tip of your tongue and they will slip off it of their own accord, regardless of your will. So tell me the thoughts they contain in your own words. What is the first? The second? Plan out the various stages of your aria and then you will look for the right inner and outer expression for those thoughts. Both I and Tatiana must see what you are singing about. To understand anything we have to visualize it in our imaginations. So paint us a picture in words, sounds, and, where necessary, gestures."

After careful examination of each phrase it was clear that the whole aria fell into four parts, each containing an objective to be achieved:

1. The compliment—you are a most wonderful fiancée for a man.
2. But I am not worthy of you—I am doomed to a solitary life.
3. My life is already a matter of the past.
4. The exhortation—be sensible and prudent.

All these thoughts must be conveyed and, especially, they must not be blurred. They must be carried out to a fine point of precision. In addition to the effect of the words together with their music, their clarity must be enhanced by the way you set them.

In the first part: ". . .if within the family circle. . ." you are in the calm pose of a man making a most polite compliment. The courtesy is underscored by the graceful remark to Tatiana: "I could not find another such fiancée".

In the second part: We have the beginning of the "Byronic Pose" —"But I am not destined to see bliss." The arms are crossed, the head slightly inclined to one side, as Onegin leans against one of the columns and seems to be withdrawn into himself—yet all is being done for the purpose of getting Tatiana to look at him.

In the third part: "Dreams and years cannot be brought back"— here the Byronic pathos is at its peak. Onegin is a tortured Prometheus! One hand is on the column, the other is pressed to his desolate breast (all done in time to the music). Hapless sufferer!

The fourth part has to do with the words: "Oh, listen to me!" (he speaks as a brother). He sits down beside Tatiana on the bench and assumes a friendly pose as he comforts the girl, speaking as an experienced preceptor in the ways of life. "A young girl many times will replace her dreams with others." This, really, is not very respectful and even a bit insolent, so Onegin here must bear himself with especial delicacy and warmth.

In order to avoid the usual operatic effect when most singers in this role come to the last word and address it to the public, Stanislavski had Onegin sit facing Tatiana so that it was addressed directly to her. As he was showing us this bit of staging, Stanislavski drew a pattern in the air which, to the accompaniment of light quick tones from the clarinets, suggested all the imaginary airiness and vagaries of a young girl's fancy.

But this exquisitely irresponsible gesture which ended the aria with such a dainty flourish was one that I could not successfully make, so I never dared to try it.

What kind of man then is Onegin as the result of these considerations? Which is he: a cold egotist or a responsive, kind person; a haughty, distrait aristocrat or an intelligent observer? Is he really himself suffering under certain subjective or objective circumstances of life? How should one play Onegin? These are the sorts of questions which impatient young artists put to the directors of the production.

"One should not act an image," was the categorical reply Stanislavski always gave. "Carry out all your planned actions correctly, penetrate into and sense all the thoughts contained in your role while you are on the stage, analyze your attitude towards Tatiana. As the result of all that, you will achieve an image. Don't force yourself into any schematic form on the stage. Learn how to act logically as an artist in planning the perspectives in your role."

One well-known opera analyst wrote very justly about Onegin when he said:

". . . It is not true that he is insincere in his moralistic attitude toward Tatiana. On the contrary, the tenor of what he says to her is not only sincere but also sympathetic. In his words all we really hear is the one motif: What can I do since I am bereft of feelings? . . ."

Yes, he is indeed sincere in his role of mentor; it seems to him that he is acting nobly; nor is he capable of the slightest baseness, nor of misleading the sincere feelings of the young girl. Yet his habit of pleasing, of taking poses, does not leave him; he pronounces the words ". . .dreams and years cannot be recalled. . . ." with egotistical enjoyment on his part without ever noticing that Tatiana is quietly weeping.

"However, let the audience decide for itself what sort of a person Onegin is, and Tatiana too," said Stanislavski. "It is up to you, Onegin, to proceed along your own through-line of action or, to be more exact, your counteraction since you maintain an ironical attitude towards your own feelings. And while your heart is still dormant, without being aware of it, you commit many brutal acts and reach involuntarily the point of actual crime."

The finale of the aria melts away on a few light chords. In the silence that follows Tatiana and Onegin sit there without speaking, each thinking about what has been said and what has happened. Onegin looks at Tatiana with a patronizing smile. Tatiana sits with her head deeply bowed. She is afraid now even to look at him. "Give this pause full value. Do not hurry the transition to the next music," said Stanislavski to the conductor. "This is a period at the end of the aria, even a row of periods."

Then the French horns introduce a new episode. Oboes and flutes respond almost like a hunting halloo, and the chorus of the house maids is renewed. The atmosphere of solitude is shattered. The meeting is over. To this lively rhythm of the musical phrase Onegin stands up with resolution; Tatiana with her head still bowed gets up slowly.

"Here a different, more impersonal atmosphere is created," said Stanislavski. "We see something on the order of a professor of mathematics with a student who has failed. Now read her your lecture: 'Learn to control yourself. Not every man will understand you as I do (and emphasize *as I do*). Inexperience leads to disaster.' His words are dry and cruel. And such is the Onegin music that accompanies them against the background of the gay, friendly chorus of the peasant girls. All sentimentality has been done away with; teach her how to take a sober view of life. The words 'inexperience leads only to disaster' call for clipped, rhythmic enunciation. Remember that in the last scene of the opera Tatiana will say: 'Dear God, how cold my blood runs when I recall that chilling look and the sermon preached. . . .' Well, this is that cold-blooded moralistic homily which made her blood run cold for all her life."

Having made his pronouncement Onegin makes a deep bow, letting Tatiana understand that he has nothing more to say.

After this point Stanislavski's directorial instructions are at complete variance with those in the libretto, which read: "Onegin holds out his arm to Tatiana, who looks at him with pleading eyes, then gets up like an automaton and, leaning on his arm, quietly goes out." Stanislavski, however, underlines the meaning of the events occurring on the stage and follows the line of logic of actions as well as the laws of the stage. He does not undertake to illustrate individual lines in this romance. Chaikovski's *Eugene Onegin* is not at all a photographic reproduction of Pushkin's *Eugene Onegin*. For the purposes of the libretto only a very small part of the novel in verse has been retained. Through the absence of various cantos at this point a quite different colouring is given to the whole episode of The Meeting.

That is why in thinking about Tatiana, her state of mind, her fate, her whole line of action through the opera, Stanislavski cut out the printed direction, according to which Tatiana goes out on Onegin's arm. In order not to cancel out the death-dealing impression made on her by Onegin's "confession", and also to maintain the sense of her loneliness and bitter destiny, Stanislavski has her go back to her home alone and not on Onegin's arm.

Eugene Onegin, Act I, Scene 3 (from the 1926 production): Tatiana and Onegin, played by Rumyantsev, meet in the arbor.

When two people leave the stage arm in arm it looks as though they have been reconciled, if there has previously been a quarrel; we sense that they will come to an understanding even if they did not do so while on the stage. That is an inevitable theatrical effect. To have this couple leave the stage arm in arm is an illogical ending to a meeting which set them at variance with one another.

"As they arrived on the stage from different directions in the beginning of the scene, they should also go their different ways at the end," said Stanislavski. "We need to keep to the logic of events and not stick to any customary manners drawn from the novel."

The staging of the end of the scene then had the following pattern: When Onegin rose from the bench Tatiana, without raising her eyes, also stood up, made a curtsey, and like an automaton walked out of the arbor. As she went down the steps she suddenly turned around. In her face and her movements it was clear that she intended to explain something, make some reply, some request, but on seeing Onegin's calm and slighly quizzical look she turned again, almost in despair, and dashed headlong off the stage. Onegin seemed almost to move as if to hold her back, but then stood and looked for some time after her. Then putting on his hat with a decided gesture and pulling on his gloves he walked away in the opposite direction. His departure coincided with the last sounds of the chorus, and the curtain closed immediately.

The imperturbable irony of the "Byronic hero" was thus carried to a logical finish. It was through this interpretation that Stanislavski prepared Onegin for his remorse at the end of the opera, his despair and helplessness in the face of an irreparable mistake.

Scene Four: The Larin Ball

The scene of the Larin Ball is an absolutely perfect example of Chaikovski's musical dramaturgy and, at the same time, of Stanislavski's directorial capacities in relation to music.

Stanislavski was inexorable in the demands he made on his own creative work and his remarks about this production are memorable:

"Not long ago I staged a large crowd scene from an opera. The participants in it were not only singers and members of the chorus but also simple apprentices and more or less experienced supernumeraries. They all were trained in tempo-rhythm. If one compared individual artists, extras, and others with those of our own company (i.e. The Moscow Art Theatre), not one of the Opera Company could even compete with them as exponents of acting. The singers were so much inferior to the actors. However I must confess that in the end the opera artists quite outperformed us, who had seemed the stronger competitors. And this was accomplished with incomparably fewer rehearsals than we have in the Moscow Art Theatre.

"The crowd scene in the opera, from the point of view of sheer dramatic impact, was something we never have been able to achieve in our theatre despite our greatly superior company and more careful preparation.

"What is the secret of this success?

"Tempo-rhythm provided the acting of the singers with splendid clarity, fluency, finish, plasticity, and harmony.

"Tempo-rhythm helped the singers, who are still not very expert in psychotechnique, to find the right inner meanings and emotions for their roles. . . ."

In the footnotes to Stanislavski's collected writings, set down by G.V. Kristi, this statement was attributed to the production of *Eugene Onegin* although no direct mention of this scene is made in the text. Yet there can be no doubt whatsoever that what is referred to is the Larin Ball. No scene like the Larin Ball was ever staged later on by Stanislavski although he did produce several mob scenes which were exemplary, such as those in *The Tsar's Bride, May Night, Boris Godunov,* and *The Golden Cockerel.*

The musical introduction to the scene of the Larin Ball begins with the shimmering melody based on Tatiana's phrase in her letter to

Onegin: "Who art thou, my guardian angel?" Here this melody is closely interwoven with our conception of Tatiana's feelings of love. Then comes the development of the theme of Tatiana's dreams, which are broken in upon by harsh chords. Against that background Tatiana's theme is renewed, but now it is played with greater energy, more vividly, as if all obstacles had been overcome. The atmosphere of the music becomes dramatically tense; then, reaching a certain height, it suddenly dissolves, fading away in a long *tremolo* from the violins. Now again, as in the beginning, the flutes sing softly: "Who art thou, my guardian angel?", and the French horns gently take up the melody which thus gradually evaporates. There are a few echoes, and then they seem to sink into a state of serenity. It is only now that one is aware of a far-off, muffled sound of kettledrums, and the theme of a waltz almost diffidently slips in. . . .

All this prelude, which the score calls an "entr'acte", is built on Tatiana's theme, which suggests that during the whole scene (and this is also indicated by Chaikovski) it will be Tatiana's emotions, her inner being, which remain the focal point of all attention, although she herself scarcely sings at all during the course of the scene. Many customary episodes cluster around her; there are lyric and dramatic impacts, bound up with Lenski's love and Olga's frivolity, with Onegin's capriciousness; the mortal quarrel between the two men flames up—that is the high point of the scene. And yet this Larin Ball takes place on St. Tatiana's Day. It is the heroine's name day. It is her fate, the painful crisis which is going on in her heart—this is the most important line of action running through the whole opera and none of the characters should forget it.

That was Stanislavski's point of departure. He taught us that we must always bear in mind the main theme and not allow ourselves to be drawn away from it by anything irrelevant to it. All the dances, the songs, the mazurkas are interesting in themselves but here they serve only as ornaments, to set off what is all-important: Tatiana's drama, her love, and the wounding, cold egotism of Onegin.

The whole effortless atmosphere of the ball in her honour, the congratulations and greetings, should serve only to enhance her suffering and sense of loneliness.

The Larin Ball was the first crowd scene in an opera that Stanislavski worked on, and it became a training school in acting for all the singers. A fundamental principle of Stanislavski's work was that all the soloists of the company were obliged to take part in the crowd scenes, in the choruses, in the dances. Both the Larin and, later, the Gremin balls were excellent proving grounds for prowess in acting and provided the material for improvised sketches centering around the characters in the crowd. This was our first practical application of lessons in the Stanislavski "system" of acting, instruction in plastic movement, rhythmics, dancing, improvisations dealing with all sorts of situations. The comparatively small chorus of forty singers, thoroughly experienced through their training in music and physical movement, created a most lifelike impression at the Larin Ball. Each actor among the dancers did his best to convey the image of a whole character. The credibility of the general picture was made possible because the actors in it were familiar with the fundamental method of Stanislavski and had excellent control of their tempo-rhythm.

But it was only the most painstaking training over a period of two years which made it possible to achieve such towering artistic results. Even that was a comparatively short period of training when one realizes that the majority of the participants in the *Eugene Onegin* production were making their first appearance on the stage.

According to the libretto stage directions the curtain opens on the Larin Ball Scene when a waltz is in full swing, but Stanislavski sought a more interesting beginning by basing it on the music of the prelude.

"Let us imagine what went on before they began to dance the waltz," he said to those who were to participate at one of the early rehearsals. He half closed his grey eyes, took off his pince-nez, and began to weave a fantasy about the goings on in the course of this St. Tatiana's Day.

"The small ballroom in the Larin house is divided into two parts by a portal, just as our studio is. In one part there is the entry, where we are all sitting, and there stands a large table all set for supper. Beyond the columns of the portal is the living room, where people can dance.

"Guests arrived in the afternoon and took their places around the table about six o'clock. They have been dining slowly for three hours, conversing, toasting each other, especially Tatiana. Onegin and Lenski came later than the others. Madame Larina made a place for Onegin beside herself and Lenski, as fiancé, sat next to Olga. There was not enough room at the table for all the young people, so some settled themselves in corners of the dining room, others crowded around the columns of the portal.

"Dinner over, tea was served. A samovar was put on the table and a large cake for Tatiana. The Nurse settled herself beside the samovar and poured the tea. The guests have become a bit subdued as a result of the long and filling repast. Where is Tatiana? She was sitting at the opposite end of the table from Madame Larina, but when Onegin arrived she slipped away unnoticed into the living room. This happens often at the end of a dinner party: when all the toasts have been proposed they forget about the guest of honour, each one absorbed in his own conversation. Lenski has gone over, just with Olga, to one corner of the room, near the big Dutch stove. Onegin has grown bored looking over all the faces of the guests and he answers Madame Larina's remarks in an absentminded way. The elderly guests are already nodding. Tatiana is stealing glances at Onegin from behind one of the columns. Now the conversation subsides . . . in a moment or two all will be dozing. . . .

"This is the moment—when there is a lull in the celebrations, a slight sense of fatigue and drowsiness on the part of the guests—when we shall begin to play this scene. In this way the coming back to consciousness, the rising liveliness of a ball in full swing will all happen in the full view of the public together with their hearing the music."

The curtain opens as the "entr'acte" is ending, just as the Tatiana theme is again appearing. For the fifty musical measures that are played before the waltz begins, the crowd scene is played in pantomime; at first there is little movement but the liveliness of the scene grows in intensity as does the tempo-rhythm of the orchestra.

Now comes the first, almost timid, faraway hint of bits of a waltz and everyone at table sits up.

The growing liveliness of the orchestra is reflected on the stage by the actors, who subject or rather attune all their movements to the sounds of the instruments. Stanislavski had them change from their rather sluggish, slow movements to more distinct, sharper actions winding up in the fluency of dancing. Step by step the whole scene is drawn into the vortex of the waltz rhythm. Out of a brief musical interlude he evolved a convincing, rhythmically contrived crowd scene with a characteristic colouring.

Every participant of the Larin Ball had a separate, independent role to play. Sometimes this might be almost imperceptible to the public because most of it was acted out beyond the columns in the living room, and it might be only for a moment that an insignificant player would appear downstage to invite a lady to dance with him, as part of the stage director's plan.

But even such a slight appearance downstage would be trimmed with details bearing on the pattern of the whole, so that despite the brevity, the role had its own responsible place in the scheme and was emotionally stirring for the performer of it.

In directing *Eugene Onegin* Stanislavski was assisted by Zinaïda Sokolova and Varvara V. Zalesskaya, a long-time associate of his in the theatre. Under the supervision of Madame Sokolova she prepared short "biographies" for all those who took part in the Larin Ball. In working with the participating actors she created a whole gallery of characters. They were drawn from images painted by Pushkin but they were also filled out by the actors themselves together with the directors. The first to play these parts became so well-known in them that later on when the roles were taken over by others they were known by the names of those who had created the parts. There were in all some forty-five of them.

There were groups of women: young girls, friends of Olga's and Tatiana's; young ladies and some not so young; old women, gossips, hangers-on of various kinds. Each personage in such a group had to have both inner and outer traits to correspond with the given character. The traits were worked out by the actors themselves and were based on the following factors: 1) past life, 2) character, habits, tendencies, 3) social position, 4) relationship to the others at the Ball, 5) purpose in life, 6) external appearance, 7) age.

This resulted, more or less, in characteristic patterns which were then embroidered in detail onstage.

Take the lady landowner Madame Dondysh (the name of the actress). She lived mostly in Moscow and on a rather elaborate scale. After living in Moscow she had come down to stay on her estate for two years to straighten out her affairs. She has a niece who is her heir. She is being brought up by Monsieur Finemouche. She hides from her niece the reason for living in the country, says it's because of her health. Her husband stays on in Moscow.

Madame Dondysh's first love was Uncle Vasya. He is now an old man, a landowner, who is also at the Ball. She likes to play at cards and at flirting. She's not serious about the latter, but she likes to be admired. She cannot live without society; she corresponds with her women friends in Moscow so that she is able to pass on all the gossip from there. She is critical of everything about Madame Larina, but she is very civil to her even if cool. She considers everyone else her inferiors. Particularly she dislikes Madame Kharlikova, who is at the Ball. Madame Dondysh wants to marry off her niece. The niece (played by Madame Gherardi) is known as one of the "graces of Moscow" and she is an enviable "catch". She has grown up in her aunt's home in the country but has lived for two years in Moscow, although without going much into society. She's a spoiled girl, is proud of being a Muscovite, considers herself the equal of Onegin. She is gay, a bit affected, a coquette. The young ladies of the countryside swarm around her. She is critical of everything and is said to be a most stylish young woman. Mademoiselle Pustyakova is very jealous of her. With the exception of Onegin, Petushkov is her favourite partner in dancing.

Here is a personage (played by Madame Kuznetsova) from a different social level, a village deacon's widow, church worker, poor, lives beside the church. She is hardworking, is very aware of her dependence on others, a toady, rather sanctimonious. She is accustomed to scrounging money, presents. Loves sweets, is interested in how people dress. Makes all her own clothes. Enjoys matchmaking. At the time of the Ball she is trying to arrange a marriage between Mademoiselle Pustyakova and Petushkov. (They are both at the Ball). She is particularly interested in Onegin as a "good catch" matrimonially. But how to get at him—after all, he's a city sophisticate!

Present at the Ball are also a local belle, Mademoiselle Naibova, fiancée of Miznichkov, and Madame Durina, a young widow thirty-five years old. She is on the lookout for a husband, loves bright-coloured clothes. There is the young bride Madame Devikler who is embarrassed by her own marital bliss, tries to hide it, always wants to be with her husband; and the daughter of a deacon who is only fifteen, has never been to a ball before, is the youngest person there; the ward of a rich lady landowner, twenty-five years old, a placid, timid girl, attracted to Tatiana; an old maid, stingy, a gossip; a young widow, eager, a pert coquette; the wife of Dr. Uspenski, madly in love with her husband and madly jealous of him, shy but blossoms when she falls in with the old gossips. Madame Kharlikova is a skinny shrew. Her daughter, aged twenty-five, is also at the Ball, together with two of her former prospective husbands who "got away". Madame Pustyakova lives happily with her husband, raises hogs, is fond of cats. Her mother, Madame Skotinina, is a well-preserved, fair-skinned widow, who moves slowly, placidly. One daughter, Dunya, is twenty-seven, irritable, arrogant, a spoiled flirt. Her younger sister is fourteen, a tomboy, ill-mannered, has grown up with boys. There is a grandmother (no name given) aged seventy-five, who is a friend of Madame Larina's, in fact her godmother. Her granddaughter is Olga's closest friend, a forthright, friendly, very lively girl. Madame Larina's goddaughter, Mademoiselle Pykhtina, is already the housekeeper in her home, also a friend of Olga's and devoted to her godmother.

In writing about the Ball, Madame M.L. Meltser (who later sang the role of Tatiana for many years) told about this scene in the opera and the training she went through in preparation for it:

"I was given the role of a young widow at the Larin Ball. I was confronted with all sorts of questions concerning the past and the present life of my character when I began work on it: who was I, where did I come from, where do I live, what is my connection with the Larins, with Olga, Tatiana, Onegin, Lenski, and my relation to the events that transpire at the Ball. . . . My imagination suggested a whole series of circumstances germane to my part. I recall a few of them: I was a nearby neighbour of the Larins as our estates were close together, but I had only come to live in the neighbourhood recently, after the death of my husband. That is how I acquired the ways of a provincial lady with a city background who could indulge in careless mockery of her countrified acquaintances. It was only lack of money that kept me in the country while all the time I was crazy to go back to town. This circumstance obliged me to hunt even more assiduously for a husband and therefore be interested in the men at the Larin Ball. I share my impressions with women friends to whom I can' trust my feelings and thoughts. And since the most brilliant 'prospects'—Onegin and Lenski—are already assigned by public opinion to Tatiana and Olga, I am seized with feelings of ill will towards the two girls—a mixture of irony and jealousy."

The roles of the members of the chorus as well as male actors were worked out in the same way. Here are some of them: Grozdin, a "splendid master", the owner of poverty-stricken peasants; the village gossip; a hanger-on of uncertain age, rather deaf; his twenty-four-year-old, feebleminded son; Feyanov, a retired councillor; the village Beau Brummel, Petushkov; his cousin; Miznichkov, fiancé of the Naibova girl, soon to be married; Durin-Ivashkov, a young fellow of some twenty-seven years of age, the "young one" who beams, is in love, well brought up; Uncle Vasya, sixty, a general favourite; the local doctor, fifty, a great lady's man; Kharlikov, a rich landowner, keeps a French tutor in the house; his son aged twenty-four, engaged to be married; "fat Pustyakov", a lazy, good-natured wag; the Skotinins, grey-haired parents with children of all ages, from thirty down to two years old (he is about sixty but a sturdy, powerful old man, full of life and energy, narrow-minded, a rather coarse serf-owner; he is also the owner of remarkable kennels; his twenty-five-year-old son is looked upon by the family as being a failure for hating country life and estate management); a grandfather in his seventies, a rickety old man dating back to Catherine the Great's day; his grandson, aged eighteen, who has been away in boarding school and now has come to his first ball; Pykhtin, an army man of about fifty-five, has kept his military bearing and wears enormous moustaches (he is a widower, lives with his housekeeper, who rules him with a rod of iron).

Each one of those mentioned had much more detailed biographies and developed stage characteristics attached to them. These biographies were not brilliant, perhaps, from a literary or artistic point of view but this was the first time in any opera house that the faceless chorus was turned into living, individual personalities.

Stanislavski established a new order of things in opera under which a member of the chorus became a true artist, and not just a person bereft of all individuality who always played the same part throughout his life—that of "anonymous member of the chorus".

When the curtain opened the audience saw all the guests at the Larin Ball placed around the stage in a definite scheme, and the exact position of each person was strictly maintained so that the impact of the

Eugene Onegin, Act I, Scene 4 (from the 1926 production): Dinner guests at the Larin Ball.

scene was like that of a painting. The supper table was set up almost beside the curtain and therefore the characters in moving around the table were obliged to come out onto the forestage and were therefore clearly visible to the public.

Stanislavski told his assistant directors to "plan the scene so that the actors who moved out onto the forestage did so in accordance with the logic of the life they were leading onstage; they did it because it was necessary for them to do so at a given moment and not because they stepped out of the mise-en-scène and moved to the footlights as if on a concert platform."

When the orchestra lets itself go completely as it pours out the theme of the waltz, all the young people in waltz rhythm push into the living room and couples are soon whirling around. The older folks, keeping the rhythm with their feet, also turn to the living room beyond the columns. There remain at the table only Madame Larina and some old cronies whom no one invites to dance. Now Onegin is clearly visible to the audience. He looks through his lorgnon at the dancing couples. Everyone is excited, good-naturedly enjoying the occasion; there is no stiffness, genuine gaiety is in full swing. The imperturbably calm figure of Onegin in his black evening clothes stands out as a fixed point against a background of whirling couples in a kaleidoscope of coloured clothing.

At the moment when the chorus begins to sing, some young people from the living room crowd around the table to say to their hostess: "What a lovely surprise! We did not expect it." They are expressing their astonishment and gratitude to the lady of the house. That was the very simple way to solve the technical problem of throwing the sound of their voices out front. The individual phrases of various groups in the chorus were scattered haphazardly in the score by the composer: "We have not been invited to such a party for a long time", "A first-rate party", and so on. These phrases are tossed back and forth by groups of singers with various kinds of voices as they pass by: a group of sopranos, having sung their phrase, dashes off to the living room, and they are met by another group, say of tenors, singing their theme and coming out in the opposite direction. This gay movement back and forth created a rhythm of heightened liveliness. Throughout the whole course of the waltz there were a number of episodes involving both members of the chorus and the soloists. The first episode is a solo of bass voices, a group of elderly landowners addicted to hunting. With the words: "In our neck of the woods we seldom see the gay brilliance of such a ball", this group of provincial eccentrics go over to Madame Larina to thank her for the entertainment and then lumber off across the forestage and on into the living room, where they disappear. In the pauses between their cues they assume picturesquely comic poses and they keep their eyes peeled on the girls dancing around. At the same time as this group of elderly landowners is going by, the old ladies at the table form into a group and begin their alto melody: "What they call a good time is spending the whole day tearing through thickets, across fields and marshes. . . ." Their mocking eyes follow the hunters. They have just finished making fun of the old men when the hero of the evening looms between the columns of the entry into the living room: he is the Captain and crowding around him is a group of women and girls full of pleasure and gratitude for the military music he has provided. They all move towards Madame Larina, downstage, replacing the departing landowners moving in the opposite direction. The appearance of the Captain is synchronized with his cue: "Enough, enough, I am only too happy", at which point he is in the centre of the stage. With the dash of a guards officer he swings around to the ladies following him and sings: "I too have every intention . . . to dance". Whereupon he executes another dashing turn, stamps his heels vigorously, and with all the flourish of which a provincial idol is capable, he bows in front of Madame Larina. She is overcome, delightedly takes his arm, and they go off into the living room to dance.

Tatiana has come in with the girls surrounding the Captain and when they run back to the living room she remains in a corner of the stage near a sofa. After the Captain and her mother have passed into the

living room, only the old lady gossips and Onegin are left about the supper table. This is a moment of meeting between the two principals in the opera. Slipping gracefully into the forestage, Onegin firmly takes Tatiana by the arm and quickly pilots her up the steps into the living room, where he whirls her around in a waltz. All this happens in an instant but it is very apparent to the audience. The faces of the old ladies at the table are instantly on the alert and flash with curiosity. They are all but overwhelmed by the tide of excitement: "Look! look! the dandy is dancing! High time too. . . ." Some of the old cronies sit with their backs to the auditorium and others face it but one clearly hears their voices and can keep track of the expressions on their faces.

Now that Onegin has gone off with Tatiana, they draw together in a huddle and gossip away at full bent. But Onegin and Tatiana dance only once around the room and then stand by the entrance to the living room with their backs to the audience. He overhears the last words of the gossips: "He's a Freemason. . . . He drinks only red wine and by the glassful. . . ."

He comes quickly down to the forestage and as he moves he sings irritably: "That's a fine opinion of me. I have heard my fill of spiteful gossip. . . ."

While he is singing this brief soliloquy, Olga, flushed with excitement and dancing, flutters out from the dancing room. Lenski is hot on her trail. Evidently she is playing some sort of game with him. With a laugh she sits down at the table beside one of the old ladies and whispers something in her ear, while Lenski tries to stop her. The audience has been aware of the happy young lovers from the beginning of the ball scene because the director put them off in a corner together where they could whisper to each other. Now we see them for the second time. At one side of the stage is Onegin, annoyed, and on the other the happy engaged couple.

What happens next proceeds with lightning speed. Onegin turns his head and sees Olga, only a few feet away, glancing slyly at Lenski. Whereupon he quickly slips over to her with the words: "May I? . . ." In turning to him Olga is now in the middle between Lenski and Onegin. All this is instantaneous. The waltz music is going on at a furious pace. Before Olga can throw a questioning glance at Lenski, Onegin takes her firmly by the arm. In answer to Lenski's words: "You promised this dance to me", Onegin says carelessly over his shoulder, as he leads Olga into the living room: "You must have been wrong". Olga, flattered by Onegin's marked attention, runs on ahead of him. Onegin whirls Olga around while Lenski, at first taken aback by the unexpected turn of affairs, starts to follow Onegin but then remains motionless on the steps leading into the living room: "Oh, what is this? I cannot believe my eyes! Olga! Good God! What is the matter with me?"

This scene occurs more rapidly than one can describe it in words, and neither we, the audience, nor the old ladies at the table have time to realize as yet what a portentous event has taken place: the spark of jealousy has been struck and nothing will quench it.

Immediately after this scene the chorus begins the song: "A glorious feast. . . ." At the entrance into the living room we see a number of guests and with them, embarrassed but delighted, Madame Larina. She has been the recipient of so much gratitude and praise that she comes back to the dining room, advancing downstage to hide her embarrassment, but the whole chorus follows her: "It has been so long since we were asked to such a party. . . . What pleasure!" Madame Larina, quite overcome, kisses her old friends and everyone begins to applaud her. She is very pleased but in a slightly arch manner she waves aside further demonstrations and returns to the living room, followed by her applauding guests. With this little celebration of Madame Larina the waltz music ends and the second half of the scene begins.

The dining room (forestage) is empty. Only Olga remains behind when all the others go out. She pours herself some tea. In the living room the guests, flushed from constant waltzing, are walking around. The old ladies are seated against the walls, watching the young people and the bored Onegin through their lorgnons. Olga's jealous fiancé, Lenski, partly concealed, stands near the columns.

There is a short musical interlude, and then three emphatic chords which herald the scene of explanation between Olga and Lenski. "Can it be that I deserved such mockery from you? . . ."

"This phrase is given to you so that you can come forward from the columns and approach the table to catch Olga's attention," Stanislavski said to Lenski. "But the point is not only to be rhythmically correct but at the same time to convey the character of your feelings for Olga. There should be nothing heavy-handed here. This is not a vulgar domestic quarrel. It is a matter of coquetry and childish jealousy."

Stanislavski's objective in this scene of "explanation" between Lenski and Olga was to have his actors show the emotional resentment and ill-concealed hurt on his part, and her slyly-wicked enjoyment from her successful flirtation with Onegin, yet keep it all simple, pleasant, calculated to evoke warmth and tenderness.

One of Stanislavski's main endeavours in this scene, and in working on the whole role of Lenski, was to make him manly and clear away all the usual sticky sentimentality connected with it. And indeed it took an enormous amount of effort to get Lenski to the point of singing: "Oh, Olga, you do not love me. . . ." without teary feelings of self-pity, but relying only on the action of the words.

"Express your thought clearly," said Stanislavski as he constantly interrupted Lenski. "Stop trying to paint a picture of emotion. The

music does all that for you. It is the prompter of your feelings and of ours as well. All you have to do is go into *action*. Seek out her eyes so that you may read in them the answer to your words, and fathom whether she is just being playful or is in earnest. That is your simple, your only objective." Then turning to Olga he said: "But you, by contrast, try to do something so that your eyes will be hidden from him, because you have 'deviltry' in them. That is why you come all around the table with the words: 'This is all nonsense and raving; you have no cause for jealousy. . . .' And, by the way, the cream pitcher is at the other end of the table and you appear to be preparing to pour some cream into your tea. But that is all a game. You are enjoying Lenski's jealousy, and, since you have that naughtiness inside, you want to do everything to inflame his love. If he is jealous he must love you. But do everything—take your cup, stir your tea, walk around the table and pour the cream—all in perfect rhythm, with evident enjoyment."

The brief scene of misunderstanding between Olga and Lenski is on the point of ending in reconciliation, just before the cotillion is to begin. Now Lenski, shifting from reproaches to caresses, sits down in a very friendly way beside Olga, puts his hand over hers and says, trustfully: "You are dancing the cotillion with me?" In another moment all will be happily settled, but at this point from behind the columns, where he has been watching the scene, comes Onegin's voice: "No, with me! Isn't it so, you promised it to me?" The music for this phrase is dry, peremptory, harsh. Onegin ruthlessly continues his persecution of Lenski. And Olga is again caught up in her thoughtless flirtation with Onegin. Softly withdrawing her hand from Lenski's she slips away with the words: "There! That's your punishment for being jealous!" and runs off to where Onegin is, beside one of the columns. They have a brief chat about the French tutor, in order to tease Lenski. This is Onegin's main line of action—to tease everyone, ridicule them all, until the time comes when he himself will be punished.

At the back of the stage, in the living room, a crowd has gathered around the French tutor; Lenski remains alone in the empty dining room. He seems so lonely, so removed from contact with everything. None of the guests pays the slightest attention to him. This was one of Stanislavski's most expressive directorial strokes. Such things appear to be extremely simple and unpremeditated: everything seems to flow from the surrounding circumstances as if the stage director had had no hand in the design. Actually that is real art, when there are no traces of the director and everything transpires on the stage in accordance with the logic of events.

A lively group of people now comes from the living room to fill the dining room. But where is Tatiana? A surprise for her has been prepared and the principal figure is not there. Her name-day celebration

has for some time been clouded over; she has gone to her room because she cannot bear to see Onegin courting Olga. This is an important point in the main direction of Tatiana's role. They search for her. They find her in a nearby room, everyone looks in that direction, and finally they drag her back. She is embarrassed, shy, and not at all lighthearted.

Once more the action is centered around the dining table. At the head, in Madame Larina's place, is Tatiana. The French tutor is in the centre and all around are the guests. Onegin and Olga are at the other side of the dining room, opposite Tatiana. He is standing behind Olga's chair, leans over it, whispers something which makes her laugh. While the French tutor is singing some verses in her honour, Tatiana tries hard to listen to his jingle but at the same time is trying unobtrusively to look through the crowd of guests to see Onegin and Olga and try to guess from their faces what it is they are chattering about so merrily. In this fashion the director shows that the line of the inner pattern of the main actors is maintained intact even when they are not taking part in the musical ensemble. We sense all the time what a difficult and bitter day this is for Tatiana.

The guests who have listened to the French tutor's verse applaud him with the words: "Bravo! Bravo, monsieur!" This applause was rehearsed group by group and in different rhythms which correspond with the age and temperaments of the guests.

"A soft smile should accompany the whole of the Larin Ball," said Stanislavski. "What we need is a simple, kindly, country atmosphere provided by rather eccentric but good-natured people. Remember that you are playing Pushkin, not Gogol. There are no scamps here (as in *Dead Souls*), no misers, bullies, fatuous fools, no pompous stuffed shirts. Pushkin and Chaikovski do not ridicule their characters no matter how funny and eccentric they may be. Let all the guests, whether landowners, old gossips, young girls, bear in mind as they act the general atmosphere in which their lives down in the provinces are passed."

Now the old French tutor has sung his piece and he ceremoniously advances on the forestage towards Tatiana to deliver his verses, carefully rolled up and tied with a pink ribbon. As he does this he elaborately sinks onto one knee. But he is unable to rise from this position, so Tatiana, who has received his scroll with a curtsey, now helps the old gentleman to his feet and leads him to an armchair.

From the living room come sounds of drums and the triumphant Captain announces the beginning of the cotillion. The girls make themselves look as pretty as possible and sit down. Then to each lady comes a partner to invite her to dance. Stanislavski, as usual, made a large formal scene of this as the climax of the Larin Ball.

Around the dining table there is a lot of excitement in anticipation of the dancing. There in the middle of the gay and colourful scene is one

solitary figure who does not move, takes no part in the general jollity, who has for some time attracted attention by his downcast appearance. This is Lenski, who has remained rooted to the spot where he and Olga had their quarrel. His figure, clad in black amid the gay clothes of the provincial guests (an effect carefully planned by Stanislavski), is evidence of the fact that all is not well although none of the guests at the Ball are as yet aware of this.

In inviting a lady to dance each one of the men had to invent his own most effective approach. It all looked like some sort of competition among the provincial beaux, vying with each other as to agility and light playfulness, even when some of the entries were rather awkward, albeit respectable, old gentlemen. This scene was the high note of gaiety which each guest was supposed to have reached by degrees.

The Captain, dancing forward, offers his arm to Tatiana—so says the libretto. But in Stanislavski's version Tatiana does not dance. She is in no mood to dance and that is in clear keeping with her line of action. She would have danced had Onegin invited her to be his partner, but Onegin is dancing with Olga. This is another blow to her pride.

The bubbling, gushing music of the mazurka called for equally effervescent action on the stage, but, of course, this was no ballet mazurka performed by professional dancers in the traditional opera fashion, but instead a mazurka as would have been danced by real guests.

Stanislavski staged this gaiety of action in three ways. The first was the stream of gentlemen coming to invite the ladies to dance; the second was the movement of the couples hurrying off to the living room to dance the mazurka; the third was the swirling movement of the mazurka itself glimpsed through the columns. As all of these streams were in flux at the same time, the stage was filled with a pattern of crosscurrents of gaiety.

Each musical phrase of the mazurka—there are eight of them—was pointed up by two or three couples in different parts of the stage. It was only in the first phrase that the Captain with a young lady in a pink dress stood out. And in the second, Onegin and Olga.

This scene of boisterously dancing guests required a great deal of rehearsing. Every movement was directed so that each actor knew exactly in what musical phrase, in what pattern of rhythm, on which side of the dining table he was to pass and to what lady he was to offer his invitations and lead off into the ballroom to dance. But that was not all. Each actor had to find the means by which he would express his own degree of enjoyment of the occasion. And to be really gay on the stage is much more difficult than to play serious, dramatic scenes.

To those who distinguished themselves in lighthearted inventiveness in their invitation to the ladies to dance in the cotillion Stanislavski offered a humourous prize of a piece of silver. What he was trying to achieve was not technical excellence in dancing the mazurka (although that skill was definitely important) but to get an actor to give the best show of a person who might go to a dance perhaps twice a year on some special holiday occasion. These were trials of acting virtuosity. But when the actors let themselves go too far, he would remind them:

"Be careful. It is very dangerous to slip into buffoonery and try to make the audience laugh. You must, under all circumstances, hew to the line of old-time proprieties. If you attempt to wring laughs out of the audience you will be distorting Pushkin and Chaikovski and giving an entirely false impression of them.

"You," said Stanislavski to the chorus, "are a group of landowners who have never had a proper opportunity to learn ballroom dancing. So you go about it with great effort and some awkwardness. But this is both pleasant and amusing to all. There is no need here for Gogol's barbs. The old ladies are not witches, what they like best to do is gossip. They study Onegin carefully with the feelings of people who are naively simple, who live way out in the country. So you stick to the line of 'naive rustics'. The orchestra plays martial music. Well, they have never heard anything like that. What goings on! What a pile of sound! And jollity! Then suddenly—the quarrel! After all the naive, childlike fun they are faced almost with death. Those are the colours which will lend credence to the music. If you proceed along this path, following the logic of your own feelings and the music, and keep the whole play in perspective that is all that is needed. Bear this in mind."

Gradually the dining room is emptied as more and more of the guests are drawn towards the living room by the bravura of the mazurka music. At the end of the mazurka only one person is left at the table—the motionless figure of Lenski. Tatiana, who had not danced with anyone, was the last to leave and at the entrance to the living room she ran into Onegin. He politely stepped aside to let her pass but did not ask her to dance with him. With the last chord of the music Onegin is standing between the columns leading into the living room, looking at Lenski sitting at the table. This is supposedly the end of the first part of the mazurka. Onegin looks cheerful, pleased with his revenge, and is in a mood of condescension and reconciliation.

Now comes the dénouement of the Larin Ball and Lenski is the principal figure.

With the second part of the mazurka comes the quarrel between him and Onegin. At first the tone is restrained but then the tension mounts.

With easy and careless grace, to the accompaniment of soft violin music, Onegin comes down to Lenski and, stopping behind his chair, casually says: "You're not dancing, Lenski?"

The beginning of this scene is built on the condescending ridicule of the one and the restrained irritation of the other. In the living room, at the beginning of this conversation and in keeping with the soft tones of the music, there are only two couples dancing the mazurka.

"Wait a bit before giving way to your resentment, keep yourself in hand, as long as you can you should remain outwardly calm. Beware of hysterics, be manly, and don't turn into a crybaby," said Stanislavski in various ways, over and over, to Lenski. He sat down at the table himself and went through the whole scene with complete external calm, while only his eyes and the corners of his mouth revealed how Lenski must have been boiling with inner rage. Then suddenly came the explosion: "Onegin, you are no longer a friend of mine. . ." which brings to an end the artificial quiet of their talk. The music changes. So does the staging. Lenski is unwilling to sit beside Onegin any longer. The conversation takes a sharp tone and attracts the attention of the guests, who gradually crowd around the living-room door.

"And you," said Stanislavski to Onegin, "try to keep to your line of poking fun and not understanding what Lenski is so hot under the collar about. But when you see that people are beginning to notice what is going on then you make a genuine effort to persuade Lenski to calm down. You do this very seriously and with concern. More than anything else you fear public attention and to be placed in a ridiculous position because of this quarrel."

After Lenski's words: "I despise you!" he leaves Onegin and angrily goes to the other side of the stage, turns a chair around and sits down with his back to him.

By now the people who have been dancing upstage realize that a quarrel is brewing and they comment: "Now *there* is a surprise. It is no laughing matter any longer."

They begin to trickle out of the ballroom and stand around the columns watching the quarrel. They remain at the top of the steps and do not come into the dining room, in which, therefore, there are only the two men. Yet Lenski feels the need of sympathetic witnesses, since he considers himself as having been insulted. He does not care who thinks what about the transpiring event, whereas Onegin, on the contrary, is pained by the other guests' participation and tries to snuff out the quarrel at any price. Therefore he comes quickly and firmly out onto the forestage, picking up a chair on the way, and sits down beside Lenski. He sings to him, almost secretly: "Listen, Lenski, you are mistaken!" This is his last attempt to keep peace. All the guests are now listening to their conversation and Lenski, seeing this, becomes even more excited and almost hysterically showers Onegin with one question after another. (Chaikovski's music expresses it beautifully as with each word the musical accents are intensified): "Then why did you squeeze her *hand?* *Whisper* something in her ear? She *blushed,* and laughed. *What, what* did you say to her?—What, what?" Lenski all but screams.

Onegin's reply is scornful: "Listen, this is all silly, there are people all around us", and that finally drives poor Lenski beyond control. He cries out with passionate vehemence: ". . .I demand satisfaction!" With these words he quickly walks away from Onegin. The full chorus sings: "What's the matter? Tell us, what has happened?" The quarrel has now assumed such proportions that Lenski is no longer able to restrain his lacerated feelings. He utters the final, decisive words: "And I ask you to receive my challenge." As he pronounces these words which are so terrifying to hear in this peaceful home, Madame Larina appears, coming through the crowd of her guests. She has come too late to stop the quarrel and does not altogether realize what has happened in her absence. She is shocked, alarmed, bewildered, and with the words: "Dear Lord! Have pity! On our home, have pity!" collapses into the nearest chair.

Madame Larina sits weeping at the table, Tatiana is clinging to one of the columns. And on the other side of her, frightened, stand Olga and the Nurse. Lenski is in the centre of the stage with the guests, and Onegin, estranged from everyone, stands on the forestage.

Everything subsides—on the stage, in the auditorium—until complete silence reigns.

"In your home. . ." sings Lenski in a low voice, and repeats: "In your home. . . ."

"This is where you must see with strong impact an inner picture of what these words mean to you. At this time all your life in this home must pass before your inner vision, especially what happened here in the dining room. After all, you have been coming to this house ever since you were a child. How many memories surge into your mind now! The more of them you see in your imagination the truer will be your expression. As you pronounce these words, the more significance, the more fresh colour will go into your voice. Forget right now that you are a lyric tenor. Your voice must be pregnant with drama. You must win me not by the power of your voice but the expressiveness of the way you say those words, by the emotional colouration you give to them. For this purpose you must above all bear in mind the logic of their meaning: 'In your home', 'your home'."

"The whole figure of a character on the stage, his carriage, his arms, his legs, must be expressive. He must feel with his whole body, assess his relation to the space surrounding him, to some point in the stage set—in this case a column. At this moment everything is important; a turn of your head, a movement of your hands. The actor should look upon himself as an artist painting his own figure within the framework of the whole scene." Stanislavski constantly reminded us of this. That is why he so often took materials for comparison from the colours of a painter, the skill of an artist in composing and arranging figures in space.

"Wait! Wait," he called to Lenski, who was already beginning to take in his breath to go on singing: ". . .in your house, like golden dreams. . . ." "Now all this is in the hands of your emotions. Make use of the fact, do not hurry, give us a chance to concentrate on the thoughts in your mind. Do not be in a rush to *sing*, hold on to your emotions, to your focus of attention. Restraint is the prime quality of a good actor."

The whole musical ensemble which starts with the words: "In your home", and is called by Chaikovski the finale, was staged as a tableau with complete external immobility, occasioned by the concentration of each person on his own thoughts. Here again the principle of intonation was at the fore, which made clear the especially important words of Lenski, Onegin, Tatiana, and Olga.

Incidentally, it is now that Tatiana utters her first words in this entire act, and they are grief-stricken: "Ah, anguish tears at my heart, it holds me in its painful clutches. . . ."

And we must hear Onegin's words as well: "I am angry at myself, I rashly went too far. . . ."

In the external plan for this scene, when everyone is motionless, it is only Lenski, as the leading character, who does not remain in one spot.

The chorus is placed among the columns leading into the living room and well within sight of the auditorium, since the living room is three steps higher than the dining room. All the guests who followed the quarrel and are sympathetic to Lenski now heighten the dramatic impact of the scene by their reactions.

At the words: "But today I learned . . . that life is not a novel", Lenski leans over to Madame Larina, seated at the table, as if he were speaking to his mother and complaining of his bitter fate.

Having poured out his grief and pain, he leaves the table, casts a look at Olga, and says cruelly: "Like a demon, crafty and evil. . ." and turns to leave. He has nothing more to say and is indifferent to everything. Up to this moment Lenski has been in the centre of the picture. Now comes a new development in the conflict which could be called The Two Enemies.

As Lenski turns to leave in a direction opposite from Onegin, the latter firmly steps forward, wishing to put an end to the quarrel which has been so drawn out. After a short outburst of the chorus (cuts were made here so as not to delay the action), there is a strongly accented *tremolo* in the violins and Onegin, harshly bearing down on each syllable, hammering out his consonants, exclaims to Lenski: "I am at your service. Enough! I have heard you out. . . . You are a madman. You need a lesson to make you mend your ways."

"No need to throw down any gauntlets," said Stanislavski. "You threaten him with your finger as if to say you will show the naughty boy how to behave."

Now the table stands between the two enemies.

After Lenski's words: "You are a dishonourable seducer", the two adversaries come together on the forestage in front of the table, ready to rush at one another. I remember how Stanislavski showed the two singers how to play this outburst of rage. At the words: "Be silent, or I shall kill you," he, his lips white with anger, grabbed a chair to throw at Lenski. This chair had to be kept in Onegin's hands by the Captain, who hurried forward. This turn was most unexpected and powerful. But we actors were not capable of executing this and had to abandon it. Incidentally, whenever he demonstrated for us any moments in our parts he always made a point of repeating:

"Don't follow what I *do* at this point or any other, but observe only the logic of my feelings, the consecutiveness of the action taken." He never insisted that his actors should copy his directorial demonstrations.

After the encounter of the two antagonists down in the front of the stage, Onegin looks fixedly at Lenski, straight in the eye; then he pulls himself together and turns away as if to say: "You're lucky that I restrained myself." Then he slowly goes around the table, makes a slight bow to Madame Larina, and finds his way through the crowd of guests, who step aside as if he carried the plague. He walks deliberately, as if he senses that behind him there is a raging storm of resentment and hatred.

During this time Lenski is taking a despairing farewell from Olga, bending over her hand with tears and saying: "Farewell forever."

"This is not just a high note to be sung," said Stanislavski. "Any well-placed and produced high note directed into the auditorium could serve to convey your grief and presentiment of death. And this is what we want to feel."

Olga runs after Lenski and falls in a faint. She is laid on a chair near the very place where so recently she was chatting with her fiancé. Lenski pushes his way through the guests who crowd around him and urge him to cool off, while expressing their sympathy for him. Some guests move towards Olga, still others towards Madame Larina. Tatiana stands alone to one side looking with despair at the way her name-day party has ended. With the last chord of music there is a tableau with Olga lying in a dead faint in the centre. The curtain closes out the turmoil of the scene. When the curtain opens again in response to applause the tableau remains unchanged.

Fifth Scene: The Duel

The lights are dimmed in the auditorium. The plaintive, tense moaning of the trombones is shut out by a thumping march; the heart is gripped by a premonition of the fate of young Lenski.

At the beginning of this scene Stanislavski departed from his usual rule of letting the audience see what the characters on the stage were doing from the very beginning of the introductory music. In the prelude to the Duel Scene we hear not only Lenski's theme at the time when he was forced to abandon the dreams of his youth, but also the grief of Chaikovski himself, who foresees the doom of his beloved hero. This is not music depicting the past, nor what happened before the action begins on stage, as in the case of the Letter Scene. This music is about the coming tragedy to which the implacable logic of events will lead.

After the cellos have played the whole theme of Lenski's thoughts, the funereal sounds of the trombones again break in heavily on the meditative mood. It is then that the curtains open with a rush. The atmosphere is nervously intense, although externally quiet.

For this scene the gleaming white columns have been sheathed to look like the snow-covered trunks of trees. Other tree trunks, branches, bending over or half fallen to the ground, do away with the symmetry of the columns; white cotton mats looking like snow drifts and a panorama of a snow-covered open space with a wooded area in the background suggest the ruin of a forest. Through the trees there are glimpses of a broad winter landscape.

With skillfully and carefully arranged lighting this small area gave the full impression of a bit of winter landscape. The half-light of early dawn, formed by the gleams of rose-coloured lights playing on the branches and trunks of the trees as the sun rose, made an expressive contrast between the poetic tenderness of nature and the brutality of human nature.

In the foreground, leaning against a tree and looking over to the forest (in the direction of the auditorium), is Lenski. From his pose it is evident that he has been sunk deeply for a long time in his thoughts.

"This is how to listen to the introductory music: Although the curtain has not yet opened, your life on the stage began with the first chord of the music. Therefore regardless of whether the curtain was there or not you nonetheless had already begun to live your part," said Stanislavski to the tenor who was getting ready to sing his aria.

At the beginning of the scene there is no one onstage except Lenski. There are quite separate chords, clearly expressing movement, to prepare for the appearance of his second, Zaretski. Their peremptory character is sharply distinct from Lenski's elegiac music, so that there can be no doubt about who is coming: a rather stupid, coarse fellow who is to act as second. "Well, what's this? Your adversary does not seem to have turned up?" he grumbles. The character of fussy, busy-body Zaretski is so distinctly outlined in the music that all an actor has to do is to be led by it and he will be the stupid man who is to act as Lenski's second.

Lenski brushes off his officious friend with: "He will be here any moment", and remains withdrawn into his own thoughts which are the source of his aria.

The presence of Zaretski, of course, interferes with Lenski's concentration, but one does not argue, as the libretto says, with a miller about the shape of his grindstone.

The music of Lenski's aria is certainly more powerful than the naive, highflown verses of the young poet and Chaikovski extracted a "sub-text" from them that is far more profound and meaningful than the words which are full of lover's nonsense.

"We are playing a scene here which is to end in death," said Stanislavski, "therefore we should start out with quite contrasting tones. It is not right, as many directors propose, to advise actors to create from the beginning a gloomy, depressing picture to reflect the mood of the characters involved. Nature is likely not to take into consideration the moods and preoccupations of people. Therefore take away all the snowflakes falling on Lenski!

"We cannot create the kind of snowstorm envisioned by Pushkin, one which gleams and swirls, therefore let us stick to what is most important: the cheerful, fresh, clear aspect of nature on this particular morning.

"And you," he said turning to Lenski, "must work out very subtly the whole gamut of your emotions while remaining void of all poses, all attitudes of false sentimentality, of doom and sugariness, all those things which can drag this aria down to the level of a soggy elegy.

"Why does a tenor so often slide off into sentimentally plaintive tones? Because he begins to over-portray feelings without any regard for the thoughts behind them. The minor tonality of the aria can almost at once throw a singer off the right track and bury him; he will begin to pity himself, complain over his sad fate. At the same time, he will use his sufferings as a means to flirt with his public.

"Above all be manly. There is nothing more repulsive on the stage than a droopy, saccharine, effeminate tenor. Can there really be any room for sentimental self-pity in the spirit of the hot-headed, impulsive, proud young poet Lenski? Why do I say so much about this? Because I want to plant in you an aversion to this kind of sentimentality, to the toying with the public affected by so many tenors nowadays. . . . Listen to the records of Sobinov. They cannot fully convey the skill, the poetic charm of that artist's singing, but even so there does shine through the quite comprehensible sadness of a courageous character of strength. . . . Tell me," said Stanislavski to the conductor of the orchestra, "what tempi are indicated here by the composer?"

"Chaikovski wrote *andante*, that is to say a calm but not a drawling tempo. Later there is the *adagio*."

"Now then, why the *adagio*? Is that to make it more sensitive? Let us work that out in action on the stage. How does it always have to begin?"

At our rehearsals a pause usually ensued there, since we all knew that Stanislavski would answer his own question. And his answer would always be unexpected. So it was in this case, as he looked over all the serious, slightly embarrassed Lenskis-to-be.

"From some focal point—an object. Where is that object? At the beginning of the aria and especially before it, on what is your attention fixedly concentrated?"

"To begin with, on the brief exchange with Zaretski," said one Lenski.

"Then sing that, please. . . . The notes are all correct but they have no character as yet. And you," said Stanislavski to the man singing the part of Zaretski, "still do not have anything of the needed obtrusiveness, the boring growl, the fussiness. You do not push yourself at Lenski enough. He wants to concentrate and you interfere, you question him quite openly: 'Well, where is your adversary?' You are intent on playing the part of managing everything and nothing is in order yet. You are an old retired captain and are playing a general. And why did you, Lenski, turn a few simple words: 'He will be here directly' into a whole aria?" Here Stanislavski kept needling Lenski, whose lips were pursed, whose head was hanging: "Why so funereal so soon? Zaretski is a chatterbox. Give him a simple and serious answer so that you do not need to talk about this anymore. But you are already beginning to act sad. You should simply concentrate on your serious thoughts and start from there. And in order to think about serious things, which concern life and death, and think about them calmly and deeply, you have to have courage and maturity of mind. That is what you absolutely must possess. Think about something very serious. You will need to recall the *process* of such a state in your own life. I can help you with the first word you need—an *object*. What does a person do when he thinks about, or rather sets about, writing some verse? You are now composing verses. Perhaps you were composing them while the orchestra was playing the prelude, while you were listening to such a musical theme before the curtain opened. A person in such a state seems to be looking at a 'moving picture' of his life which is unrolling before us right here." At this Stanislavski raised his hand to the back of his head. "You appear to be looking inside yourself, your eyes are fixed on some distant point and you are not aware of what is around you but only of what is going on inside your own head. I will sense that and see that whole moving picture of your life passing in review as you do. Perhaps you will see it differently from the way I do. But you have to know and have to be able to produce inside yourself this process of review and meditation on your past.

"These things you must know as a human being living on the stage in accordance with the laws of nature, the laws of being. Now you must select what of all this, and in what form, you will include in your aria and what the meaning of it is," said Stanislavski.

Stanislavski was confident in saying this because by that time he had finally distilled the proposition that all aspects of creative human endeavour are subject to the immutable laws which condition all human nature.

If actor-singers had the perfect control over their creative natures such as Shalyapin had, if they developed their artistic gifts in all directions, each performance in an opera would be infinitely richer in the portrayal of human emotions than any in a theatre of drama. Yet on the road to that perfection there was always the obstacle of that "pretty tone" which, according to Stanislavski, was as difficult to root out of singers as amateurishness in actors.

Singers, whose capital is in their throats, are possessed of a singular sort of psychology. They feel that they are the chosen ones, unique, indispensable, and this results in their having an inflated estimate of their own artistic worth.

That "capital" with which nature endowed a singer brings in dividends after he has had technical training and instruction. It is on arriving at this first stage of vocal achievement that singers often stop, having decided that they have reached the summit of their art.

In the libretto, before Lenski sings: "If I fall pierced by an arrow", it says: "Lenski gets up and *moves downstage*". Whoever wrote that did a great disservice to the singer because he thereby plunged him at once into the bog of operatic cliché acting.

"On the stage you can move only in the direction of some real or imagined focal point. Here in your aria you have two such points: The first is your past life, and the second, Olga, your beloved. Now you can make some move towards her if you see her clearly in your imagination, but this is something of which you must convince us. Above all do not place the focus of your attention in the auditorium—that is forbidden to you for five years—you may place it no farther than the frame of the proscenium, either to the right or to the left. Now you have two *objects*, which is to say two actions to stage. A change in staging is always bound up with a shift in one's object of attention. That does not signify that you will remain in two unchanging poses. These are two situations. The first is for the purpose of an inner survey of your life. Near the tree there is a stump. You may sit down on it or lean against it. But for your second action move to the right, facing the sun, and finish your aria there. But under no circumstances are you to come downstage, to face the public.

"Now begin the action inherent in the words, for your whole aria is based on verbal action. Of what points does it consist, from both the musical and the acting points of view?

"1. What awaits me—is uncertain, but all will be well; I will face with courage whatever fate has prepared for me (I am taking myself in hand).

"2. When *tomorrow* comes, I shall be no more (here you have the contrast).

"3. But you... Tell me: will you come, will you remember me (dialogue with Olga).

"4. Belovèd friend—come! (an appeal).

"5. Conclusion: My springtime, my youth, has gone. ... (the farewell).

"We break up the role into component units. Each one contains some vision, some objective. For you to see your life in your mind's eye, to see Olga, you must possess both a vivid imagination and an ardent desire. You can never do this if you are weakened by self-pity. The whole aria should be performed with expressiveness, with special feeling for every word, every bit of verse. You cannot question your fate with wilted words or diluted emotions.

"Remember that this is Pushkin," said Stanislavski. "He is not panic-stricken in the face of destiny, and Lenski, even while thinking about the secrets of the grave, maintains a courageous calm."

Lenski stands leaning against a tree and watching the sky turn rosy with the dawn. This blends harmoniously with his words: "The glint of early morning heralds the coming of brilliant day. ..." By the time he finishes the aria the reddish disc of a winter sun has risen above the horizon.

Abrupt, quasi-marchlike chords bring Zaretski back onstage. He had been impatiently looking for the arrival of Onegin and Guillot. The carefree, unconcerned melody of Onegin quite changes the atmosphere of the duel, striking an entirely different note from that of Lenski's aria.

This melody and indeed the whole condut of Onegin, who has arrived late and brought along his French valet, clearly reveals his characteristic attitude that the duel is a trifling incident. His whole conversation with Zaretski is carried on in the rude tone of a joke in bad taste and his introduction of Guillot, his valet, as his second is also quite outside the bounds of decent behaviour.

Here Stanislavski incited the performers to carry each situation on the stage to the point of utmost sharpness.

"In order to make the situation understandable," he said to Onegin, "it is not enough for you to be simply unconcerned in your manner. That suggests only that you may be out of sorts, or unwell, and therefore behave badly. You have to act a farce. Play up the comic overtones of your first entrance to the limit, look at this whole business as a bit of circus. Ridicule Zaretski. It is only then that the difference between your attitude and that of Lenski's toward this duel will be clarified. We have just heard Lenski's aria. This contrast will emphasize the whole absurdity of the tragic outcome.

"So now you introduce your valet Guillot. That is a whole comic scene in itself. The rickety little Frenchman all but curtsies to Zaretski. He wears tight-fitting, pale-coloured pants, an almost effeminate cloak with wide sleeves and fur trimmings. He has a top hat on his head and his shoes are of patent leather. . . ." Stanislavski proceeded to demonstrate amusingly how the Frenchman would stamp his freezing feet while trying to keep an agreeable smile on his face which was already blue with the cold.

Onegin takes the crookedly smiling face by the chin and points it in the direction of Zaretski, the way you make a pointer turn toward game. Zaretski's bulging eyes show to what extent he is shocked and indignant.

After carrying on his conversation in a careful tone with Zaretski and introducing Guillot, Onegin then turns to Lenski and says half jokingly: "Well, shall we begin?" But now the music accompanies his phrase with heavy bass chords to indicate that the fooling is over and the serious time has begun.

Lenski's reply: "Let us begin, why not?" alters the mood of the scene. Stanislavski laid great stress on every turn, every vowel, every consonant in these two short phrases.

"Weigh these words. You can sing them in twenty different ways. With Onegin the word 'begin' should sound like the end of a phrase. *What* are they to begin: a comedy, some foolishness, some meaningless enterprise, or is it something ominous, in deadly earnest? In the logic of your actions as you put the question there is something inconclusive. But Lenski's reply: 'Let us begin, why not?' has the sound of broad confirmation. Don't slip into any hesitant, pitiful tone; it is not in keeping with your character to be hesitant in the face of your opponent. After all, he is the offender.

"The slightest alteration in the colour of a vowel in a word already alters the character of the emotions it stirs, so be sure to remain in complete control in this."

After the decisive words: "Let us begin. . ." the orchestra embarks with great force on the foreboding theme: "What the coming day. . . ." At this juncture the melody is carried in the bass register in gloomy tones, and the wind instruments also playing in lower tones add dark colours.

Acting as Onegin, Stanislavski made a broad gesture during this phrase: "I have done all I could. Now let things be as you will." After a long pause there begins a scarcely audible *pizzicato* to accompany the duet, which is sung almost in a whisper.

As in the quartet in the first scene of the opera this duet is performed with the most exquisitely distinct enunciation of each word and in a most delicate *pianissimo.*

The adversaries stand at either extremity of the stage. Lenski is still where he stood while singing his aria, whereas Onegin, after putting his question, has gone off to the opposite side.

In this duet there is a moment of musical exaltation arising from the question: "Should we not rather laugh before dipping our hands in blood?" Here the two men, in response to an inner impulse and to the prompting of the music, turn toward each other with a tentative question in their eyes . . . but after that comes the "No . . . no. . . ." Here Stanislavski proposed that whereas Lenski's "no" should be firm, that of Onegin's might sound rather questioning.

The music now proceeds in an *allegro,* followed by a *vivace.* The main action now ensues. First Zaretski hands the pistol to Onegin and points to a place offstage where he is to stand. This was made necessary by the dimensions of the stage, which rendered it impossible for the adversaries to stand at the required distance from each other and still be in the sight of the public.

"This is also necessary," Stanislavski decided, "because at the sound of the shot we should see only Lenski—we cannot have our eyes on both men at once. Then after the death of Lenski our interest will be centred on seeing Onegin." After Onegin has gone offstage Guillot with an exquisite bow hands a pistol to Lenski.

"How will you take the pistol?" Stanislavski asked Lenski. "You are not simply taking a weapon into your hand. It is death. Accept it with the utmost seriousness."

Lenski also goes into the wings. Zaretski remains alone onstage to give the signal to fire. Having performed his duty and looked without flinching first at one and then at the other, Zaretski cautiously ("as if performing a religious rite," suggested Stanislavski) withdraws to a position upstage behind a tree. Now Lenski emerges on the forestage at his appointed place to stand. The inner tenseness of this moment is clearly conveyed by all the strings in the orchestra, but Lenski is extremely calm and deliberate in his movements. He does not have the time to raise his pistol to the level of his eyes when a shot is heard. Lenski slowly slips to the ground.

(We were specially trained in how to fall by exchanging quick broad movements for small, very slow ones in order to gain the full sensation of falling.)

A great deal of action was packed into the two *fermata* pauses.

"Are you really satisfied that Lenski has been killed? Don't just be operatic about it. Feel his heart to see if it is still beating," Stanislavski told Zaretski, "and after Onegin's muffled question: 'Is he dead?' do not hurry with your reply. First take your cap off slowly, then look significantly at Onegin, turn away from him, and then say 'He is dead.'

"And you," said Stanislavski turning to Onegin, "of course, do not 'hold your head in your hands' as the libretto tells you to do; but very slowly remove your fur hat and stand still. That is probably how he stood, transfixed, for some twenty minutes beside his friend whom he had killed."

This is the motionless tableau with which the scene ends, while the orchestra plays out the mournful finale in the course of which the familiar theme "What the coming day. . ." sweeps over all the instruments in turn.

The sun has come up. The picture is one of nature in winter, its quiet solace in contrast to the drama of death.

Scene Six: The Gremin Ball

Beginning with the Gremin Ball the opera takes on quite another life; new people appear. The scene is laid in St. Petersburg. With their transfer from the backwaters of life in the provinces Tatiana and Olga are now so changed that the actors are called upon to play quite new parts.

To us young performers it seemed that after playing the scene of the Larin Ball more or less successfully it would be very simple to do any other, including the Gremin Ball. Right here we ran into the challenges of Stanislavski. All who have ever worked with him are well aware of the fact that no matter how splendidly they had prepared their roles, when it came to actual performance on the stage he always found unfinished places that still had to be perfected.

When he inspected this sixth scene which had been prepared by his assistants, he said that it would have to be done all over again from the beginning. We must learn all over again how to walk, dance, sit down, invite a lady to dance, converse with her—and do this until we could reproduce the manners of high society in St. Petersburg: as ministers of state, ambassadors, officers of the guard, officials, generals, countesses, princesses, and so on. In brief we had to learn the social graces of the world of high society in which the action would now take place.

We began to have lessons in the manners of the early 19th century. Stanislavski gave us a series of improvisations or sketches which he performed along with us: the men had to learn how to offer their arm to ladies, promenade with them, take them back to their places after a dance, chatting with them along the way, bowing. Incidentally, the military had one kind of etiquette and the civilians another. Special training was given to the actors playing the parts of adjutants, who were supposed always to be unnoticed but at hand for their generals, without being in their way. Stanislavski insisted on our acquiring an easy and simple carriage, quite in tone with an official ball in high society, and this required a lot of work, many exercises.

This work began with our learning how to use our arms and especially our hands. The men had solid rolls of newspapers placed in their armpits so that they became accustomed to a military stance. All were required to stand against a doorjamb, their backs and heads pressed flat. This exercise was given for the purpose of producing a straight figure, and a correct placing of the head.

When he was checking on our exercises Stanislavski would go over to one of the live "caryatids", as we conceived ourselves to be, and try to put his fingers in between his back and the doorjamb. If the back was not "glued" against the jamb, he would say:

"You're not a courtier yet, not a guards officer. It's too soon for you to be invited to the ball."

The women were scolded if their elbows and shoulders were too angular, or if their heads were not well-placed. Stanislavski assumed, as he used to say, the role of governess. Sharp elbows used to get sharp raps from a ruler. One of the more difficult graces to acquire was that of the light, fleeting bow of a modish young man (a civilian). Stanislavski's own large body was so flexible that as he glided lightly over the parquet floor and made an undulating bow before one of the ladies, he seemed almost suspended in air and gave the impression of being winged. This sort of thing was very difficult for the actors to achieve, as was the handling of the fan for the actresses, who had to learn to use it as a sort of prolongation of their hands. It was with such movement exercises that we prepared ourselves for the Gremin Ball. The Ball opened with a stately polonaise. For this type of dance-promenade there should be a great number of dancing couples and a large space. That is why this scene is usually played all over the full extent of the stage. For the ballroom dancing that is, of course, appropriate, but not for the more intimate scenes such as the meeting of Tatiana with Onegin and Gremin's aria. Since Stanislavski had foremost in his mind the through-line of action of the whole opera, he arranged his setting mainly for these personal encounters. Besides, the dimensions of our studio stage were such that there was no possibility of making a large ballroom out of it. Stanislavski's reasoning ran like this:

"We will show a part of the ballroom. One of the sides with places to sit. Take as an example a reception at the Governor General's, whom we shall call Gremin, in St. Petersburg. We shall handle the polonaise as a sort of programmed movement. It will not be just a promenade of couples but a gathering of all the guests from all the reception rooms who will come here to be received by their host, the Governor General. At this same time Onegin will arrive belatedly at the Ball. After their meeting with Gremin all the guests will go in.couples, as in the polonaise, back to where they came from."

Stanislavski, who was a sensitive musician, heard a minor theme in the middle of the polonaise coming from the cellos and casting a melancholy shadow on the brilliance of the first and last parts of the dance. While this melody was being played he brought all dance movement to a standstill; the guests made deep bows to General Gremin, and Onegin, in a broad manner, paced up and down on the forestage.

In this way Stanislavski broke the monotony of the polonaise and also singled out his hero from the crowd. The sad, languid music which accompanies Onegin's appearance so blends with his character and mood at this moment that Chaikovski probably wrote this middle passage in the polonaise especially for him, inwardly desolate and depressed by melancholy memories as he was.

The four, columned pillars now were covered with handsome ivory and gold ornamentation. Three official portraits hung in the background: Empress Catherine II, Alexander I, and Nicholas I nearer the front. They were original paintings made by artists of the period, which lent a genuine palatial touch to the modest Studio interior. The costume designer (Matruni) made a careful choice of colour for the costumes of the ladies and officers to blend with the muted tones of the paintings. There was nothing loud or vivid in the scene such as there usually is in those opera or ballet décors which pass for being picturesque.

The dances were produced by A.A. Pospekhin, who taught body movement for many years in the Stanislavski Studio.

In the original production of the opera on the Studio stage, the couples dancing the polonaise came in from the public vestibule of the auditorium and proceeded through the audience onto the stage.

After their presentation to Governor General Gremin they came out again the same way.

Generally speaking the *Eugene Onegin* production on the Studio stage was characterized by this very close relationship between the actors and the audience, yet it never impinged upon our complete freedom in creativeness. Stanislavski taught us so thoroughly to attend to our own work on the stage that we never lost that sense of what is called, in his system of acting, "public solitude".

When this opera was produced later on the large stage, the polonaise promenade moved forward from the depths of the set and went back there.

After the stately polonaise, which filled the whole stage with parallel lines of couples, the scene was emptied and in the foreground, to the right, only the solitary figure of Onegin remained, standing under the portrait of the Emperor. He had been standing there for some time but was not visible because of the movement on the stage.

After the guests had gone off to rest after the dance, the gloomy figure of Onegin suddenly recalled to the audience his unhappy fate. Stanislavski worked for a long time with the various singers being trained for this role, teaching them a new rhythm for his state of mind in which, after the disillusion of his fruitless wanderings, he now appears at the Gremin Ball.

"Act as though you were seriously ill and yet are concealing the fact. There is something in your body that never ceases to ache, it gives you no respite. Try to find this sensation in your back. Let the long-drawn-out melody of the polonaise flow down your spine, like a never-ending, wracking pain. You must convey a sense of spiritual oppression. Look for it in your body, in the physical rhythm of the way you walk, the way you let yourself down into a chair. In other words, seek out this feeling of weight through your physical being.

"But remember that you are not merely expressing bodily indisposition but 'soul-wearying nostalgia'. Usually this nostalgic yearning is demonstrated by gloomy brows, the biting of lips and a tense face. But you must keep your face always free of tension so that it can at all times be ready to express any and all of your feelings of nostalgic weariness and sadness; find the rhythm for it in the way you bear yourself. Try to recall how you behave physically when you are sad or upset. That is exactly how you will act when you are spiritually exhausted. So look for Onegin's deep boredom with life not in your eyebrows but in your back."

"Here too I feel so bored. . . ." This is the start of Onegin's brief soliloquy after the noise of the dancing has died away and the guests have dispersed around or behind the columns at the top of the steps and are absorbed in their own conversations.

Onegin throws himself into an armchair, leaning over one side of it and placing his limp hands on the arms: this is another Childe Harold pose expressive of extreme apathy, the loss of all interest in life. Stanislavski gave a wonderful demonstration of this, resting his elbows on a delicately gilded little table near his armchair. He was so full of inner yearning that he made us grieve for him. The phrase: ". . .where that forever-bloodstained shade comes every day before my eyes", shows how he is tortured by the nightmare memory of the friend he killed, how he looks around, turns as if the ghost of Lenski were behind his back! After this (there are three sharp, tense chords in the music) he wearily leans against the back of the chair, like an invalid who has just suffered some kind of severe attack.

"But please don't drag out that C endlessly in 'from the ship straight to the ball'. Baritones love to pull out all the stops on that note quite forgetting Onegin's grievous state."

Immediately after this the very lively music for the schottische begins. It is a wild rhythm, a whirl of dancing figures, and this further depresses Onegin. He has risen, to be sure, and pushed away the armchair, to put it out of the way of the dancers, but their unnatural movements and artificial facial expressions irritate him further and he deliberately turns away from them to use his lorgnon to examine the portrait of the Emperor. He is still doing this when the schottische is over and all the ladies have dropped deep curtseys to their bowing escorts.

There is a brief pause after which the chorus suddenly begins to sing: "Princess Gremin, look, look. . . ." She is still not visible, she is at the far end of the rows of guests but all attention is now drawn to her.

Now we shall see Tatiana. And Onegin will see her too.

This will be a great test for him. That is why Stanislavski stressed so particularly the apathy, the melancholy in everything Onegin said and did, so that when he sees Tatiana he can be recalled anew to life, can be resurrected within the very sight of the audience.

But he must not be resurrected in an operatic way (is dying, and then jumps up and dances), but in a very human fashion, going from step to step in his recovery as he gazes on this new Tatiana.

For Tatiana's appearance Chaikovski wrote some brightly serene music in quasi-waltz rhythm, in which a clarinet carries an exquisite melody against a background of strings. With calm stateliness she comes forward with Gremin, acknowledging the bows and compliments of the gathered guests. This entry of Tatiana and Gremin required many preparatory exercises and much skill so that it would not turn into a simple march. They had to move freely, rhythmically to the accompaniment of two- and three-quarter-note measures which produce a sense of calm and dignity.

Tatiana stops at the top of the steps near the columns and turns to the guests. The ladies greet her in turn. She receives each one in a friendly and dignified way. This staging of the scene emphasizes the new role of Tatiana, "the easy grace of a reigning hostess". Onegin has ample opportunity to watch and study "that girl" to whom he once read such an admonitory sermon.

"At first look at her quite calmly as though. . . 'Can it really be Tatiana?' No, no, you must be mistaken. . . . Then begin to take a really good look at her. 'Yes, it is she! Oh, no, it really cannot be!' It is only then that you begin to be excited. And the longer you look at her the more excited you become. Here is an objective for you to reach in the short space from 'Can it really be Tatiana?' up to 'This queenly hostess seems to be she!'

"From this instant, after passing through various stages—your conversation with Gremin, listening to his aria, and, finally, to your meeting with Tatiana—you gradually move toward the point of explosion, to the arousing of your 'cold and sluggish soul', and you yourself become an entirely different person by the time you come to your aria: 'Alas, there is no doubt'. That is the main line of action through your part. Follow it and carefully distribute your tone coloration.

"In this opera you practically have two roles," said Stanislavski at rehearsals. "First you have the bored egotist who looks at everyone around him like toys to be played with. This is the part of a man with a cold heart and sluggish soul. Then the other is the role of a man reborn in the instant when the flame of love is lighted in him. It was not without purpose that Chaikovski gave you that passionate melody, the same that he gave to Tatiana when she too clearly felt love in her own heart. Now your soul has come to life and will fight desperately to save the happiness slipping from your grasp. This will be the goal of your life. . . . Up to now you have lived without purpose, without effort.

"In your soul as an artist there should be two different human beings, two parts to play: first you put on the world-weary attitude of soul, and now you will become really *young;* at first all was pose and now you will be a sincere and ardent young man.

"Unless you play both contrasting roles, the bored poseur and egotist and the passionate, fiery man in love—there will be no Onegin and the image of Tatiana too will fade. The finale of the Gremin Ball and the last scene have to be played with the power of a Hamlet."

While Onegin is watching Princess Gremin she is surrounded at the top of the steps by officers with whom she is chatting. At the same time Prince Gremin espies Onegin and comes to greet him. They stand off to the right (from the audience) and shake hands cordially, not having seen each other for a long time.

"But do not shake hands in the present-day fashion. Simply take each other by the hand, do not raise them, stand quite still. Do not whisper in each other's ear and pretend to be conversing. Speak to each other only with your eyes.

"You, Onegin, are trying to find a way to behave. You are interested in the person you are talking to but at the same time you are anxious not to lose sight of Tatiana. Here the focus of your attention is doubled; you keep an eye on her and for that reason begin to speak of her: 'Tell me, Prince. . . .' "

Stanislavski was particularly preoccupied with Gremin's aria.

"It is necessary to avoid the unpleasant impression which so often is produced by this aria when it is sung as if a general has come to an aristocratic gathering and is saying in a loud voice for all to hear that he is in love with a young woman and has married her."

What Stanislavski aimed at was to create an atmosphere of intimacy for this conversation, so he helped Gremin enunciate with great
delicacy and become skillful enough to give the impression of "secret"
song.

"That does not mean that the whole aria should be sung *pianissimo*.
Later, when you will need a *forte* to express your thoughts and feelings,
you can let out your voice, but in the beginning you need to have the
sense of an intimate conversation so that when I too, as a listener, get
that feeling it will remain with me even when you increase the volume
of your voice. . . . What is the point of the aria? If you show off your
self-satisfaction it will result in a rather noisy exhibition of boastfulness,
whereas if you appear slightly embarrassed by your position as the
husband of a very young woman, if you try to justify yourself to Onegin,
and especially if you read in his face and deduce from his questions that
here is some kind of a secret, perhaps a past love, then your aria will
acquire an extremely delicate character and your praise of Tatiana will
sound like so much respectful admiration of her."

All this is part of the through-line of action for the whole opera.
Gremin's aria further wounds Onegin's self-esteem and tortures him. It
begins as a prolongation of the preceding conversation—there is no
external change or preparation for it. Just before the middle of the aria,
when the tempo is heightened, Gremin makes a sign to Onegin inviting
him to sit down. They seat themselves in armchairs at either side of a
small table and Gremin finishes his aria in that position. This gives a
quality of intimacy to the whole episode. As he sits in the foreground
Onegin sometimes listens attentively to Gremin and sometimes his
thoughts wander off into his memories; his feelings throughout the aria
are those of remorse and regret. Gremin's quiet dignity and gentle
nobility shine through the whole aria and his tone in talking with
Onegin is very considerate and confidential. In drawing the character
of Gremin Chaikovski diverges from Pushkin, who describes Tatiana's
husband as a fat, important general who is "superior to all and turns up
his nose and raises his shoulders"; he did not even give him a name but
designated him only by the name of "Prince".

In consonance with the laws of the stage Chaikovski acted with
great sensibility in giving Gremin such a warmhearted aria because it is
a reflection of Tatiana, her pure, moral outlook, her spiritual beauty.
What Onegin overlooked in Tatiana is now brought home to him by
Gremin.

After the aria there is a long pause during which the two men sit,
each deep in his own thoughts; they are interrupted by a chord which
apparently brings them back to reality. They both stand up: "And so let
us go and I shall present you to her". And Gremin walks firmly towards
Tatiana who is to be seen at the top of the steps, between the columns.

By means of short phrases, the orchestra admirably conveys Onegin's inner turmoil, his agitation as he goes to this meeting.

The moment when his eyes meet those of Tatiana is underscored by a sharp, throbbing *sforzando*. This is immediately followed by the love theme which was so tempestuously developed at the end of the Letter Scene. But now it sounds like the echo of a far-off memory. Externally both Tatiana and Onegin are quite calm. Tatiana's phrase of greeting is smooth: "I am pleased to see you, we have met before"—these are all even notes. But Onegin's inner trepidation and embarrassment are very well conveyed by the jerky pauses: "In the country" (pause), "Yes!" (pause), "Long ago!" (silence). . . .

At the end of this dialogue the exquisite theme is renewed which heralded Tatiana's entrance and now accompanies her as she leaves, after a polite bow, on her husband's arm. They are followed out by the guests. In the brief eight measures at an increased tempo which precede Onegin's soliloquy the whole stage is emptied. Onegin stands there as if thunderstruck and watches Tatiana depart in the distance. Then he moves up to the top of the steps. This unleashes the tempest in his heart which the actor must now uncover. In this swift-moving, impetuous aria there are in all two questions: "Can this be that same girl? But what has come over me?" And then the answer: "There is no doubt, I am in love."

It was such moments of shock that Stanislavski knew so well how to show. Joyful emotions raged inside him as he turned to "that girl" with the exultant surprise of a man in the grip of feelings that he had never known before. . . . We could only very modestly attempt to copy his brilliant demonstration.

Scene Seven: The Final Scene

This last scene was done in a restrained external pattern. A small round table and two armchairs occupied almost all of the space between the columns, leaving little room for the actors. Therefore there was no pacing up and down the stage here. The actors were left two square yards of room so that the entire attention of the audience would be centred on their faces and eyes. In principle this scene echoed the one of Tatiana's Letter, where the external movements of the actress were so compressed that she was obliged to have an extremely expressive face and complete clarity of word and voice.

As in the Letter Scene the curtain opened with the first chord of the music and the audience saw Tatiana exactly as she was portrayed in Pushkin's novel:

> She sits there, all undone and pale,
> Poring over a letter
> Leaning her hand against her cheek
> And quietly weeping. . . .
> None but would sense her unspoken sorrow
> None but would know again
> Tatiana, poor Tatiana,
> Of many years gone by. . . .

Tatiana was dressed in dark green velvet with a scarf around her shoulders. Stanislavski did not carry out the words "undone" because to show her dishevelled might be considered too naturalistic on the stage. Also he quite ignored the stage directions in the old libretto which read: "Tatiana enters in an elegant morning gown, with a letter in her hand." The important point of the dénouement of the drama is not in the fact of how she is dressed but in her reactions to the letter she has received. The introductory music clearly reveals the inner state of Tatiana.

The sad, slightly monotonous melody of the prelude suggests an importunate recurrent thought, and is repeated when Tatiana sings:

> Onegin, I was younger
> Then, and better too, it seems. . . .

When the opening curtain reveals the bowed figure of Princess Gremin and we hear in the throbbing music the reflection of her heart, it is clear to us that Onegin's letter has brought back to her the memory of her girlhood love and lost hopes. We begin to understand that she has sacrificed herself to duty, but that she is weary at heart, unhappy, and we recognize once more the earlier Tatiana.

Her frank avowal in her soliloquy was foreshadowed in the previous scene and we gain a more profound insight into the soul of Tatiana this way than if she merely emerged from the wings and announced to us that she was that same girl again.

The lyrical episode of Tatiana's avowal is interrupted by a wild *allegro* in the orchestra in which there is a whirlwind of feelings, a presentiment of the oncoming storm. On the wings of this wild *allegro* Onegin bursts onto the stage. He is stopped by a look from Tatiana who, after a moment of helplessness, has taken herself well in hand. This is the beginning of a brief duel between two souls locked in a desperate struggle. At the end of it Onegin, seeing Tatiana's proud reserve, in a state of desperation throws himself at her feet.

"Do not touch Tatiana," whispered Stanislavski to Onegin, as he raised his head to her hand. "Just bow your head in front of her hand, but do not so much as touch her. . . . Try to have your figure, as you kneel on one knee, not be rectangular but rather bowed almost parallel to the floor. Put your weight on your right knee so as not to break the line of the left side of your figure, which is turned towards the audience. In this way your pose suggests action, aspiration towards her."

In the moments of greatest emotion he always taught us to be sure that our bodies remained free and fluent in movement.

"The more powerful the scene, the freer your body must remain, above all your face and your hands," Stanislavski insisted. "This must be a memorable moment so do not blur the picture of it by any insignificant movements. Tatiana stands, an image of cool aloofness. In the dust at her feet is Onegin, in an attitude of remorse, of humility, pitiful, beseeching."

This situation is maintained throughout the encounter between Tatiana and Onegin. Her first words are: "Enough, stand up." And here Stanislavski suggested:

"No, no! Do not stand up yet! You are too guilty, you have not yet been forgiven. . . . With bowed head Onegin listens to Tatiana's bitter words: 'Onegin, do you remember that hour, in the garden, under the trees, when fate threw us together? And how humbly I listened to your exhortation?'

"Only then does Onegin raise his head slightly to sing: 'O, have pity on me. I was so mistaken. I have been so punished.' And then at the end of the phrase, like a period," said Stanislavski, "he bows his head once more.

"You must try to wring from her at least a drop of pity for you, touch her heart with those two phrases: 'I was so mistaken. I have been so punished.' The first phrase is the stronger one and the second tapers off, sinks almost to a whisper. Tatiana must make an involuntary movement of sympathy but immediately restrain herself. After Onegin's words there is a cello solo in the orchestra which seems to be a continuation of Onegin's prayer for forgiveness. It is only in harmony with the cello's phrases that you begin, diffidently, to raise your head and then look at Tatiana and finally, slowly, rise to your feet and lean against a column to listen to what she has to say."

That is the end of the first unit which portrays their meeting. The juxtaposition of the principal characters is the same as in the earlier scene in the garden, except that then Onegin leaned against the column in an arrogant manner and Tatiana sat and wept with bowed head. Now that is reversed. Tatiana sits there with her head high and Onegin standing by the column cuts a pitiful and broken figure.

This remains unchanged during the whole of Tatiana's speech: "Onegin, I was younger then and better too, it seems, and I loved you, but what I found in your heart. . . ."

"Here let the words carry all the action," insisted Stanislavski, "no gestures whatsoever. Put an edge on every word so that it will penetrate Onegin. Enunciate with meaning but let there be no bitterness. Soften everything by the gentle, warm timbre of your voice."

Remorsefully Onegin listens to Tatiana, with full recognition of his guilt. However, now Tatiana's words begin to sound not so much like a reproach as a serious doubt on the honour of his intentions: "Why do you cast your eyes on me? Can it not be that it is because I must now appear in high society, that I am wealthy and well-known?" The melody accompanying these words grows broad and majestic, after which the reproach goes even further. "Can it not be that now my shame would be obvious to all and yet bring you some tempting recognition in society?" Here the orchestra produces harsh chords as if chastising Onegin.

"How are you taking all this? Listen carefully! Heavens! How can she speak this way and so twist things as to suspect you of such baseness? You must convey a sense of almost physical pain from Tatiana's reproaches. You are almost suffocated by resentment. Let us see you experience all this standing by the column, and you must let us read it all in your face. Only then will you really sing the words: 'O God! O, God!' What will the O's sound like? Like the expression of unbearable pain."

The old libretto directions say that when Onegin sings his brief arietta: "Can it be that my humble prayer. . ." he does it "sadly".

"No, no," said Stanislavski. "Cut all that 'sadly'. This is a matter of life and death. Sing with every ounce of despair in you! And you," he added, turning to the conductor, "accompany him in the same way.

"This outburst of Onegin's must be very powerful in order to melt the heart of Tatiana. Later on she sings: 'I weep. . . .' If I am brought to believe that you have made Tatiana weep by the strength of your feelings, then the opera is on the right road and the audience will be moved. But if she only says that because the libretto puts the words in her mouth—and this is usually the way it is sung—then *this is not our way of doing things in our theatre*. It is not worth our while, for the sake of such musical formalities, to add one more to the hundred theatres of operatic claptrap already in existence. I say this because sometimes an actor thinks he has produced all he needs to, whereas Pushkin and Chaikovski have produced it all and the actor has not contributed anything of his own. Yet a tremendous responsibility is laid on him. That is why I keep needling you."

Onegin sings and moves toward the empty armchair, to a point almost behind Tatiana. He cannot as yet speak to her as he used to; he does not even dare approach her.

And Tatiana avoids looking at Onegin, she hides her face from him. With head bowed in desperation Onegin ends his plea, and suddenly Tatiana, touched by his passionate confession, exclaims: "I weep."

As in the case of Onegin we now read the whole gamut of suffering on Tatiana's face, all the shadings from an attitude of sheer impregnability to compassion for Onegin, then pity for his past, to tears.

"There must be a very wide range from zero to fever heat," said Stanislavski.

"An actress cannot live through it all unless she listens with absolute concentration to every word Onegin says, catches every slightest intonation in his voice, and hears every sound in the orchestra. Therefore this is no time to 'rest' after you have sung your phrases and wait for your turn to begin to sing again.

" 'Then weep,' Onegin breaks in, 'for your tears are more precious to me than all the treasures in the world.'

"Now you may cautiously take your place beside her, Onegin, for you see how upset Tatiana is. The setting we then have is of two persons sitting together and gazing into the far past (both of you must look in the same direction, at the same spot) as if you had lost all that was dearest in life. This is a moment of spiritual union, almost of reconciliation. Then sing, without moving: 'Happiness was so near, within our reach.' This is the one moment in the whole opera when Tatiana and Onegin sit close together as two beings dearer to one another than anything in the world. And, of course, this setting is memorable because it so clearly expresses their common love and grief."

The two figures sit close to one another, shoulder to shoulder, oblivious to the present and immersed in happier past days.

"Remember the first scene," Stanislavski proposed. "Then this scene ends with the duet and the words 'so near, so near.' The last 'near' dies away in a long *pianissimo* and affords an intimate and tender harmony to the picture. It takes a sharp chord from the orchestra to make them tear themselves away from dangerous memories. Tatiana is the first to tear herself away from Onegin with the words: 'But my fate is sealed and irrevocable.' She returns to her earlier attitude of cool aloofness. He at once jumps up, making the transition from dreams to painful actuality.

"Say to him now with firm and clear enunciation: *'You must, I beg of you, leave me',*" said Stanislavski to Tatiana. To this Onegin, quite bewildered, replies: "Leave you? Leave you? How can I leave you? I must see you every minute. . . ." and so on. Out of these three repetitions of the word "leave" Stanislavski fashioned an entirely separate scene. He imbued each use of the word with a different shade of meaning. First, Onegin does not take in the word, appears to be hearing it for the first time. Then it sinks in, and finally he says it as a kind of protest to Tatiana.

"Convince her that she does not understand what she has said. How could she pronounce such a word just after you have been sitting together and dreaming of possible happiness."

At this point the sub-text comes through each word and therefore each one must be pregnant with meaning. "Don't just mouth a word mechanically. Make a whole scene out of each thought contained in it."

After the three "terrible" words the orchestra repeats the first Onegin theme—his plea. "I must see you every minute, follow you everywhere. . . ." This theme is just as tumultuous, thrilling, and impetuous in character as the first time it was played ("Can it be that my humble plea. . . .") and it ends on an exultant note with the words: "Only bliss. . . ." But now for the first time the Onegin music turns to a minor key of tender sadness as Tatiana sings: "Onegin, at heart you are a man of pride and unflinching honour," and "Eugene, you must, I beg of you, leave me." Tatiana's tone is now decisive, definite. She is in full possession of herself, and that is why Onegin's replies: "I cannot leave you" and "Oh, have pity" begin to sound so tragic.

All of this section of the music is in D-flat major and ends after Onegin's drawn-out "A-ah!" rather tenderly and without any accompaniment from the orchestra as she says: "I love you."

She pronounces these, for her, all-important words standing straight, a little turned away from Onegin. This confession of Tatiana's is full of power, chastity, and simplicity. Stanislavski laid great stress on this moment. He was such a foe of all sentimentality that he always underscored the restraint and nobility of Tatiana and could of course not accept the directions laid down in the libretto: "Tatiana overwhelmed by her own confession leans against Onegin's breast. He embraces her. Then she, coming to her senses, quickly extricates herself from his clasp." That had for long been routine procedure, and Stanislavski naturally would have none of it. For Tatiana to lean on Onegin's breast is out of the question for anyone who has carefully studied the eighth chapter of Pushkin's novel.

"Don't clutter up such significant moments with pressing hands, pawing each other, embraces. On the contrary Onegin steps away from

Tatiana, thunderstruck by her confession. He must first let it sink in, feel it, absorb it. But in routine theatres they immediately rush into each other's arms. Listen to what the music says," insisted Stanislavski.

Indeed, after Tatiana's avowal the flutes and oboes play the most tender, bright, and pure music while the enraptured Onegin is transfixed in joyous astonishment. She stands there simply, with her head slightly bowed. This state of being rooted to a spot by emotion is far more meaningful than would be their falling on each other's necks and embracing.

"What do I hear?" says Onegin in a scarcely audible voice. "What was the word you spoke? Oh joy!"

"Now here he does rush over to Tatiana, not to catch her up in an embrace but to take her hand," Stanislavski said in directing Onegin as he came to the words: "You are now the Tatiana you used to be."

It is not only Tatiana now who checks Onegin with the words: "No, no"; the orchestra with heart-piercing harmonies forces him to stand still and hear Tatiana's final words: "I am now pledged to another . . . and shall forever be true to him." The whole orchestra blazons forth the ultimate aim of her life.

This is, essentially, the most powerful moment of this whole scene. From then on there is the desperate but hopeless struggle on Onegin's part. And although Chaikovski gives Onegin one more ardent arietta to sing in which he tries with blinding passion once more to persuade Tatiana to join her fate with his ("Do not drive me away. . . . It is I whom you love. . . ."), even using such highflown eloquence as ". . .admit that I am sent to you by God, to be your preserver until death. . . . No other path is open to you. . . .", nothing can alter Tatiana's decision.

"You have lost the ground from under your feet," Stanislavski explained to Onegin, "now you are no longer stayed by conventional manners; seize her hand, lay your face to it, try to convince her she cannot live without you. The more strongly and insanely you try to convince Tatiana, the more unbending and fixed she becomes. And that is the high point of the whole story. You flounder more and more, and Tatiana grows firmer and firmer."

Onegin sings his whole arietta at Tatiana's feet like a child pouring out his despair and weakness, holding her hand as if he fears to lose it forever.

But Tatiana is now deaf to all pleading and is, according to Stanislavski, set on teaching him a hard lesson: "Onegin, I will remain firm. I am given to another by destiny and I shall live with him, and not abandon him."

With these words of Tatiana's we come to the finale which starts with the broad tempo of a stately *andante,* and then moves with an ever-swifter *allegro* until, with the last "forever farewell", all ends with the sombre harmonies of the brasses as if they were underscoring the relationship between Tatiana and Onegin. The whole last section with its turbulent declarations develops into a kind of overt struggle: She tries to leave and Onegin holds her back, refuses to let her go from him.

When Tatiana frees herself and leaves, Onegin remains kneeling for a few seconds, takes account of what has happened, and then, as if coming to his senses, he says in a low voice: "This is my undoing."

"Now you have realized what has happened," said Stanislavski. "Here you must change your focus of attention—to grief. This focal point is inside you. Later, when you sing: 'Oh what a pitiful fate is mine!' your focus will shift again, you will gaze into the future, your word coloration will be altered as your focus changes. All three of your exclamations must be different. So remain where you are, overcome by your thoughts. There is nowhere for you to escape to in the usual operatic fashion. Pay no attention to the directions in the libretto which say: 'Onegin rushes offstage'. What we must do is leave the imprint as Pushkin described it:

> . . . Onegin stands
> There as if thunderstruck
> And what a storm of feelings
> Now rages through his heart."

The curtain closes on Onegin in his state of consternation. Three of the most sonorous *fortes* of which a symphony orchestra is capable bring Onegin's last phrase to an end. The profound minor tones of the last drawn-out chords leave the audience in no doubt whatsoever as to the fate of Onegin.

"So now," said Stanislavski to the assembled cast, "if we cast our eyes back over this last scene, you, Tatiana, will have revealed the key to your whole role, your super-objective: 'Now I am pledged to another and will forever be faithful to him'—that is to say your sense of duty transcends the arguments, the inclinations, the yearnings of your heart. And for Onegin, 'Happiness was so possible, so close. . . .' But you were fascinated by your affectations as a bored poseur, you passed right by your happiness, you took no notice of it, and for that you are punished. Give expression to that outline throughout the whole opera in terms of external and inner activity, and you will reveal for me, the spectator, the prime purpose which runs through the whole performance."

In June, 1922, the first performance of *Eugene Onegin* took place on the premises of the Studio. Tickets were sold through the Moscow Art Theatre box office.

The press comments on the first performance of *Eugene Onegin* said:

"The Studio of the Bolshoi Theatre under the direction of Stanislavski gave a dress rehearsal of *Eugene Onegin* in the tiny hall of the Studio. The stage of this small auditorium was set with primitive homemade decors which gave an atmosphere of cosy intimacy.

"Throughout the performance one was aware of great directorial work. Stanislavski's approach differs widely from the usual hackneyed operatic routine. . . . The singers have a complete control of the principle of *recitativo*, tonal declamation, and have adapted it even to the most complex ensemble singing without infringing in the slightest degree on basic polyphonic performance.

"The work of Stanislavski appears not only as a substantial reform in opera production but is also of profound significance in the training of our young opera singers, who frequently are put on the stage without preparatory training for it. This work harbours within itself the renaissance of Russian opera theatre."

In the autumn of 1922, the whole company went to see their director off on the American and European tour of the Moscow Art Theatre. As his substitute for the term of his absence abroad, Stanislavski left B. M. Sushkevich and gave him the following instructions: "In accordance with your promise I am asking you to take over a part of my functions in the Opera Studio. This is what your obligations will consist of:

"1. The transfer to the larger theatre (the Novy or Fourth Studio) stage of the productions already finished or in preparation; organization of the backstage work and erection of the scenery. You will reproduce the general physical form of the productions so that they will hold together in public showings without altering their basic pattern. After the initial performance of each production you will check it to make sure there is no discrepancy and if there is any you will see to it that it is straightened out.

"2. In giving my full confidence to you and the other directors, who are well aware of my convictions, requirements, and aims, I am sure that you will not pass on any performance that would cause me to blush, and you will not allow my name to appear in connection with any production you do not deem satisfactory."

November 24, 1922, saw the opening of the performances by the Bolshoi Opera Studio in the Novy Theatre of *Eugene Onegin* accompanied by the orchestra of the Bolshoi.

In moving the production to the larger stage Stanislavski requested that the setting with the columns, as in the original performances, be retained without change because this was basic to the molding of the opera. This condition was carefully observed.

The whole shape of the production remained as it had been. All that was added were the costumes of the epoch, in accordance with sketches made earlier by B.A. Matrunin as ordered and approved by Stanislavski the previous spring. The costumes for both men and women were made in the workrooms of the Moscow Art Theatre.

Stanislavski was extremely well-versed in the art of costume design and it was not at all easy to satisfy him with regard to the cut of a collar or sleeve of a man's dress suit. In his exacting requirements he gave proof not only of his knowledge of the costumes of various periods but also how to adapt them for wear on the stage. He himself explicitly explained how a man's collar could be cut so that it lay snugly along the neckline, as well as how Onegin's trousers for the ball should be made.

The women's costumes were made under the supervision of the famous costume artist and dressmaker Madame A.G. Silich. It should be pointed out that Stanislavski did not arbitrarily lay down the law concerning the costume of an actor, as some costume designers do. He usually quite unobtrusively planted the idea in the head of an actor or, especially, of an actress of just what kind of costume was needed for a part that would suit his or her external attributes. He would ask:

"How do you like this set? You see, you live here. Are you comfortable in that chair, or walking around, or in general living in the set? What do you still lack for life here? Do you realize just what clothing you need, because you yourself will order or have it made. . . ."

In this way, he gradually trained the taste of his actors, showed them how to harmonize the inner life of their parts with their external appearance.

The first performances in November, 1922, were conducted by V.P. Bakaleinikov, V.I. Sadovnikov, and later by M.N. Zhukov. After the first-night opening the Moscow Art Theatre Company sent Stanislavski this telegram: "Congratulations on the arrival of a new member of the Art Theatre family."

A.V. Lunacharski, U.S.S.R. Minister of Education, summed up the many reviews of the production:

"We have here a fact not limited to this year, a tremendous fact in the field of theatre quests: this is the musical Studio of Stanislavski. It has produced a most enchanting adaptation of *Eugene Onegin*. Even when it was shown in the house where Stanislavski lives it was the perfection of fragrance. Here we are dealing with the staging of a specific opera, an opera by Chaikovski on a subject on which Pushkin prided himself as an artist of everyday life. It was extraordinarily propelled by Stanislavski in the direction of life as seen and portrayed by the Art Theatre—with great artistic truthfulness. And it turned out that the music of Chaikovski, as applied to many homely scenes of life down on the big country estates, gained enormously by this interpretation which was not at all stilted but entirely lifelike. In addition Comrade Stanislavski, who has the taste of a genius, did not at all take the music as some of the people in the Musical Drama do, which is to say as if no particular stress need be laid on it; let it accompany as it pleases but the stage action should prevail. Comrade Stanislavski made every effort to make the action rhythmic, every effort to have the music rule the stage, moving the bodies and the souls of the people who are performing. There were no artificial dramatics. What he revealed was the balance between the most profound truths of life and the spirit of the music."

3

The Tsar's Bride

WITH THE PRODUCTION OF *The Tsar's Bride*, which opened on November 28, 1926, the young Opera Studio entered a new phase. Its name was changed to The State Opera Studio with the sub-title "Named for Stanislavski." It was given joint occupancy of the Dmitrovski Theatre with Nemirovich-Danchenko's Musical Studio.

This building was not at that time as beautiful as it is now, after the radical renovation of 1935–38. The stage was small and poorly equipped, the auditorium was not comfortable, the backstage and dressing rooms were inconvenient; still it was a real theatre, a professional theatre and not an amateur training studio. The years of 1925 and 1926 saw Stanislavski ardently at work both as a producer-director and also as an administrator and organizer of this new theatre. And he was fully occupied with the choice of a proper repertoire for it.

The young Studio already had three operas in its repertoire: *Eugene Onegin*, Massenet's *Werther*, and *The Secret Marriage* by Cimarosa. They were rehearsing Puccini's *La Bohème*. But the chief interest of Stanislavski lay in Russian classic opera. That is why he prepared *The Tsar's Bride* of Rimski-Korsakov for the opening performance in the new theatre. After that came *May Night* and on the list to be produced were *Boris Godunov* and *The Queen of Spades*.

Side by side with the preparation of the repertoire were the regular classes. In opening a new theatre the Studio needed to have a solidly trained troupe, welded together not only by the inspiration and example of Stanislavski, the drawing power and renown of his name, but also by a working discipline.

The Studio was motivated only by enthusiasm—the students and artists received no material support; they were all students without scholarships. This, naturally, had a negative effect on the course of rehearsals. Therefore the slogan of that time and indeed throughout the period of the Studio's existence was that set forth in Stanislavski's principles: *Art requires sacrifice. An actor must always be healthy; your health is not just your possession, it belongs also to your whole group.*

The Studio is not wealthy enough to maintain understudies for all the singers. The Studio declares itself in a state of martial law.

To Stanislavski the concept of a singer, a human being, devoting himself to art, was inextricably bound up to the highest degree with the cultivation of inner decency, delicacy, and perceptiveness in dealing with people. Unfortunately not all those qualities are innate in artists. There were instances in the Studio of that coarse, arrogant egotism and lax behaviour which are so easily picked up by young singers. Stanislavski laid equal stress on the general tone of their conduct both in and out of the theatre and on their acting and singing capacities. Questions of ethics were on an equal footing for him with questions of artistry.

In those tense times of the Studio's existence the repertoire was prepared, staged, and shaped out of a semiacademic, semiprofessional studio enterprise into a completely rounded theatre. The documents that have been preserved show what a capable and strong-willed organizer Stanislavski proved himself to be in this difficult task. Despite some opinions held about him, he was by no means merely an idealistic leader in the field of art removed from all administrative concerns. He was able to gather around him experienced people who knew how to plan the technical and material sides of the Studio. He asked F.D. Ostrogradski to be his deputy and by energetic efforts Ostrogradski succeeded in buttressing firmly the future of the theatre. It was thanks to his initiative that in the spring of 1925 the Society of Friends of the Opera Studio was founded for the purposes of establishing the Studio and providing financial support. The members were drawn from the most outstanding leaders in the world of art and Soviet public life. They elected N.A. Semashko as president.

One of the principal events in this period was the accession of V.I. Suk as our musical director. The coming together of two such masters as Stanislavski and Suk opened up wide perspectives for the development and establishment of new bases for creative opera—the union of vocal and dramatic art. To have Suk, the great musical authority and at that time head of the Bolshoi Theatre, comprehend and accept Stanislavski's ideas for opera was a great reinforcement for his plans. And if within the narrow circle of opera leaders Stanislavski found opposition to his ideas, then in Suk he found an ardent defender who gave tremendous help to the young theatre not only by the authority of his name, but also by his day-to-day musical training of the company and by his activity as a conductor.

The Tsar's Bride was studied and staged by Stanislavski with the active participation and under the musical supervision of Suk.

During the preparatory work on the production Stanislavski established a special order of work which is rarely used in theatres.

He introduced a logbook of daily accomplishments. As in a mirror, the whole current of the theatre's life was reflected—what was achieved, what was lacking. The duty of keeping this record was assigned to an assistant who was both a stage director and an administrator.

In accordance with Stanislavski's principle of collective responsibility for the theatre, he organized an executive committee, confirmed by the appropriate branch of the Commissariat of Public Education, to which two representatives of the company were elected. In addition, a large group of young singers was initiated into the work of shaping the theatre. This again was an implementation of one of the most important tenets of Stanislavski's way of working.

All November was filled with work at fever heat as we accustomed ourselves to the new building, and began molding our young opera company, which now had its own symphonic orchestra, many members of which became true enthusiasts for what Stanislavski was doing.

A dress rehearsal on November 19, 1926, was made memorable by a comic incident which, however, nearly ended in tragedy. The theatre building, which had formerly been a merchants' clubhouse, was very old and had not been repaired for a very long time. In order to get the season started such practical repairs were made as were required by the fire department, which had pointed out the dangerous state of the attic.

At the most thrilling and solemn moment of this rehearsal, when the first act was scarcely under way, a large chunk of plaster fell from the ceiling over the orchestra, followed by a cloud of dust. It was a bolt out of the blue. Everyone scattered in fright. The members of the orchestra scrambled under the stage. The cast dashed offstage and the people in the audience who were seated in the first rows rushed up the aisles towards the exits. Stanislavski, who sat in the front row, covered his head with his hands and, bending over, also scooted up the nearest aisle. It seemed as though the whole building might collapse. At the same time, from the opening in the ceiling, a quantity of sawdust fell with a thud on the footlights, further adding to the alarm. To top it all we now saw a pair of legs encased in boots dangling from the gaping black hole overhead.

It looked as though a man must crash down at any instant through the ceiling into the orchestra pit. But after the first few moments of panic had passed, rescue operations were begun.

A canvas fly was instantly taken from the wings and stretched over the orchestra pit. One end was held up by actors on the stage and the other by members of the audience. Cries were heard: "Hold on! Hold tight! Just a minute!" Then when all was ready they yelled: "Now jump! Don't be afraid!" But the booted legs, dangling in the air, suddenly were drawn up and disappeared. The fright and tension of the people below was dissipated by roars of laughter and jokes. It turned out that one of the firemen, checking on the condition of the attic, had stepped on a rotten floor beam. It broke under his weight and precipitated the whole incident.

Stanislavski stated that this was an omen of good luck, and by the next day everything was repaired and the rehearsals went on at their usual pace. After six run-throughs the public dress rehearsal was held on November 26th with great success.

The logbook carried the comment: "The audience present at this rehearsal . . . gave Stanislavski an ovation. . . . Much applauded were also the conductor Zhukov and the assistant stage directors S.F. Alexeyev and Zinaïda Sokolova (Stanislavski's brother and sister). . . ."

Finally on Sunday, November 28, 1926, Stanislavski's Opera Theatre was officially opened with *The Tsar's Bride*.

The record book states: "The performance went exceptionally well. The tickets were all sold. The crowd scene in the first act with the revels of Ivan the Terrible's guardsmen was punctuated by applause. At the end of the first act the audience gave a prolonged ovation to Stanislavski. After the second and third acts they also applauded and after the fourth there was another ovation for Stanislavski, his assistants, the conductor, and the whole cast. Huge baskets of flowers were brought onto the stage and presented to them.

"After the end of the performance everyone connected with the production in any capacity and the distinguished guests as well were invited to a modest supper. Stanislavski announced to the assembled company that he had received a ribbon from the famous actress Ermolova (of the Maly Theatre) with her name on it and that this ribbon would serve as a guarantee of our future success, provided we maintained the same pure attitude towards our art as Madame Ermolova had towards hers all through her life.

"Very warm thanks were expressed to N.A. Semashko, President of the Friends of the Studio, and he replied with a witty speech in which he compared our undertaking to a military operation.

"Stanislavski then thanked everyone concerned with our theatre, each person, each group, with an expression of full appreciation of the work done by them. He stressed the significance of the training of our group of stagehands and the necessity of their work being praised with that of the artists.

"The occasion ended with dancing and broke up after 3 a.m."

Act One

The Tsar's Bride of Rimski-Korsakov is painted on a broad historical canvas and reproduces the living spirit of the 16th century with vivid colouring and that sweep and temperament which we get in the best works of literature and painting. The libretto is drawn from a play with the same title by L.A. Mei which is a model of this genre.

The music of *The Tsar's Bride* is one of the most sincere and exciting of Rimski-Korsakov's compositions. He delves more deeply here than in his other works down to the elemental sources of Russian songs and paints more profoundly true images, in terms of music and drama, of the Russian people. To get inside and reach the essence of these images and then show them on the stage requires great historical perceptiveness on the part of the director of the opera and also of the conductor. Only then does the whole extent of the imagined life acquire tension and maintain a high degree of credibility. It was back at the time of the founding of the Moscow Art Theatre, of their first production—which was *Tsar Fyodor*—that Stanislavski made a deep study of the spirit and the life of the 16th century. He knew how our ancestors spent their daily lives in great hewn-log houses in the merchants' quarters, or in the Kremlin palaces; how they stood all night in the churches at masses, or got up early in the morning to attend them; how they ate and drank, how they were dressed indoors and out-of-doors. Stanislavski knew how the tenor of family and social life affected the psychology and conduct of the Russian people; how their clothing, with sleeves so long that they came down over their fingers, determined their gestures; how their special collars and two-foot-high hats made the boyars seem important. He also knew the conditions of life at that time, and it was not any hand-me-down theatrical knowledge; he knew that beggars waited in the entries to the houses of the devout; how people feel when they emerge from the semidark, incense-clouded interior of a cathedral into the clear outside air, how they look up at the gilded cupolas—in a word he knew the prose and the poetry of history that combined to create the intangible spirit of the time, something one senses as being familiar, close, dear, a past truly divined.

"From the moment the roles are assigned to you—those of Gryaznoy, Marfa, Lyubasha," said Stanislavski, "they no longer exist apart as roles—they become you, placed in the same circumstances of life into which the author, the composer, the librettist put them. Find the logical line of your conduct inside those circumstances, the logic of your thoughts and feelings, the logic of your external bearing. What knowledge do you need for this? Where do you live? What do you need to know, for example, Gryaznoy, in order to receive guests? You are the host; recall what you do in ordinary life when you receive guests, how you offer them a place to sit, how you entertain them.

"Where will you seat them? How many of them will there be? Where will you put Malyuta—he who is the deputy of the Tsar, his right-hand man? Where does Lyubasha live? Where are all your courtmaiden singers? You may perhaps have to invite them too. Where will they perform their dance in a ring while they sing? Will it not be necessary to move the tables so that there will be more open space? All these questions serve logically to produce the needed background of where you, Gryaznoy, live."

Of course, Stanislavski had planned out all the staging and sets in which the actors were to perform.

But he roused their imaginations before they even began to study their parts. Stanislavski was no longer the "despot-director", as he called himself when he was young in the introduction to his directorial plan for *The Sea Gull*. His rich and fertile experience had taught him how to get the actor, without his knowing it, not only to accept but also to enjoy the setting in which he was to perform—indeed the actor would come to consider that it was the only possible one for him and that he had participated in its creation. An actor's liking for the setting, the surroundings in which he is to perform, for the costumes, were factors Stanislavski considered necessary in order to produce a solid, growing, and long-lived production.

All the company were entranced with the scenery models made by Simov. The model for the first act which shows a chamber in the house of Gryaznoy was an immediate introduction to the everyday atmosphere of a wealthy household of the 16th century.

The architecture of the house of Gryaznoy—with its projections and nooks, its staircases, the sense of closeness more than snugness, together with that feeling of coziness which is still preserved in the ancient chapels of the Old Believers in Northern Russia and on the Kerzhenets River—was all reflected in the Simov set.

The guardsmen were all clothed in red and black kaftans trimmed with sheepskin; the household of Gryaznoy, the maids, were all in hemp dresses and bast sandals.

"The first act," said Stanislavski, "is a simple canvas, the third act at the merchant Sobakin's home is a piece of brightly printed cloth, and the last act in the palace is gold brocade."

Again Stanislavski conducted his great work of preparation, of establishing the inner line of the performance, of molding the characters and revealing the music, on the rehearsal stage in the building where he lived. The whole opera had to be performed in this rehearsal hall and only then was it transferred to the stage of the theatre. This was his usual practice.

The most difficult problems to solve as the action developed into an unbroken line of movement lay in the ensembles—the duets, trios, and so on. At these points the action usually slowed down or stopped entirely as the actor-singers seemed to become unrelated to one another and attempted to convey their thoughts only by their singing.

All the ensembles in the opera were handled as unbroken links in a chain of logical action of each character. This method made it possible to produce an operatic whole, a performance of musically dramatic integrity.

But the ability of each singer to justify his conduct as a participant in an ensemble and to carry the line of his inner actions throughout the whole opera was not all. The audience had to understand the meaning of the words: Every single word in an ensemble, when various lines are being sung at the same time, cannot, of course, possibly be understood. This was where the technique of word reading, which had already been worked out in *Eugene Onegin*, came to the rescue. But we still had to do a lot of work on it because the ensembles in *The Tsar's Bride* are much longer than those in *Eugene Onegin*.

At the last chord of the overture the curtains opened. One saw a chamber arranged on the following plan:

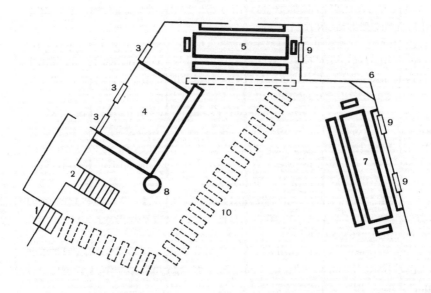

1. To the left was a door leading into an entryway. It was through this that the guests entered.

2. A staircase leading up to the women's quarters.

3. Windows (interior ones) looking down from the women's quarters into the chamber below. At first they are curtained. That is where Lyubasha lives and it is from here that the maids come down.

4. A large Dutch stove decorated with coloured tiles flanked with two large flat spaces on which to recline. On top of the stove are boxes, pitchers, and various household vessels. Hanging on the wall near the stove are swords, arquebuses, lances.

5. Beyond the stove, upstage, on a platform one step above the floor across the edge of the chamber, is a window to the right as seen from the

auditorium. In this angle is a table set for guests, with lighted candles on it. This was a supplementary table.

6. In a corner on the right a shelf trimmed with embroidered towels with an ikon and a watch light.

7. The main table, also laid for guests. Loaves of bread, cucumbers in bowls, goblets for wine. Lighted candles, pitchers of wine.

8. A cask of wine and a ladle above it.

9. Windows.

10. There are colourful, long mats on the floor.

In the chamber Gryaznoy, with his back half-turned to the audience, is seated in a mood of gloomy reflection with his unseeing eyes fixed on the large stove.

"You have been drinking continuously for two weeks," Stanislavski said to the singer playing the part. "You are bloated from drunkenness, but you can get no rest. You don't want to see anyone, not guests, not Lyubasha. All you need is Bomeley with his mysterious powders and herbs. Try to recall from your own past what it is like to live with only the thought of some unrelenting desire, going through your everyday life mechanically; what it means to get 'hooked' by this one thought, to stop in the middle of something you are doing, and give yourself up to reflection. This is the point of departure for your role. But before you can begin it you must construct a past leading up to it."

Gryaznoy's aria starts with a theme marked *moderato assai* and *un poco pesante.*

"Try to feel this heavy theme going all through you and realize that you can find no respite," said Stanislavski. "Then your every movement will be as heavy, as inflexible, as this whole phrase. Let it, as it were, penetrate your whole body. Then every turn you make will be musically rhythmic.

"But the music and its character only shows you the *how*, first you must determine the *what*, that is to say what your action is to be. You must know how your whole day unfolds. A singer on the stage is usually in a static state. To get rid of this he has to find various forms of physical action based on living human behaviour, meshed in with the inner line of action running through his entire role. If you have a great deal to do on the stage you will have no time to turn your attention to the audience.

"You should find inside yourself and inside this chamber a whole series of imaginary objectives so that you will avoid that 'static' state. Let us say you are looking out the window, into the dark—what do you see? Glance at your weapons on the wall—they should be polished. There's a saddle—what needs to be done to it? There's the table prepared for guests—cast a host's eyes over it. Yet all the time Gryaznoy's thoughts are really on Marfa, therefore beware of freezing up into immobility by holding just to that thought. Then remember that your head aches from all your carousing. Wine no longer has any effect on you. You have been drinking for two weeks on end. When you come to the point of using words to draw a picture, to make comparisons between what you used to be and what you now are, keep away from operatic gestures. There will be no gestures at all, only the movements that life imposes. Try to go through the whole scene dramatically but using only a pattern of physical actions."

In this way the singer portraying Gryaznoy learns how to act the whole scene without singing, merely pronouncing the words. This gives him a real sense of being alive on the stage.

"Now sing the words, just as you spoke them," said Stanislavski.

In this way the singer's bearing on the stage became quite simple, unforced, and the words when sung became unbelievably expressive. His voice took on fresh colour, in keeping with the mood and thought contained in this phrase.

However this simplicity once found, this conduct and mood so right for the part, quickly evaporates unless it is nailed down by frequent repetition which produces a conscious "technique" in order, in turn, to create the right inner creative state.

That is why Stanislavski, at every rehearsal, never let up on his demands and indeed kept requiring more and more from his singer as an actor. These requirements applied to various aspects of his acting:

"The phrase: Begin with the thought contained in the key word. Learn to mold the phrase into an image you can possess. Understand clearly what you are saying, don't use accents in a merely mechanical way. Don't whine when you say: 'Where has my former prowess gone?' but rather try to discover what has come over you and act it out. Each word enunciated should have a relationship to the whole phrase. When you slur your diction you will take the edge off the word, you will lose the aroma of the phrase. After you have clarified the phrase, grasped it, sing it first without words, just with sounds. And convey in this manner the whole sub-text of the phrase. What we need even more than the words is your relationship to them."

Gryaznoy's first phrase is: "I cannot rid my mind of her beauty. . . ." Here Stanislavski at once interrupted:

"Where is the focus of your attention? I do not see it. Where is this beautiful woman who is out of sight? Don't remain a single second out of focus. Otherwise 'operatic gestures' will take over. 'I told the merchant to answer straight'—do you visualize that merchant? You quarrel with him. And now about your rival, Lykov, he is on the other side—do you see him?" Stanislavski pursued his questioning. "Then look at yourself. Throw a glance back over your own life. That means stick always to an object of attention which will evoke the required emotions; then the music will add force to your feelings."

Gryaznoy sang the first part of his aria seated. Before the middle part he went over to the cask of wine, filled the ladle full, and gulped it down, thus adding a flourish to the more lively section of the aria as he felt the effect of the wine coursing through his veins.

"When you come to the climax and the high note at the end: 'All is gone', justify it by wanting to smash up everything. Bang your fist on the table—but not literally, of course," suggested Stanislavski.

The guests arrive. A first group of four push their way in: hilarious, puffing guardsmen. Their first words sung in chorus are: "Greetings, Grisha!" Stanislavski arranged it this way to avoid the sudden irruption of the whole mass of the chorus as is usually done.

"Greet each other in friendly fashion. Comrades in arms slap each other on the back, give vigorous nudges in the ribs. But this should all be done lightly without any show of physical strength."

The host must greet each group of guests as they appear with goblets of wine.

Malyuta enters on his theme, which is *allegro no troppo.*

"He must be met with great honour, as if he were the Tsar. No familiarity of manner. Take his staff and tall hat with great respect, as if he were a high priest. . . ."

With the arrival of the guardsmen and Malyuta a large crowd scene begins. Such scenes were handled with particular care by Stanislavski, whose main purpose was to keep things alive on the stage.

"The actors should be intent on amusing each other, not themselves. *The main thing is always not to play for yourselves, not to play for the audience but to play for your partner onstage,"* said Stanislavski. "Your true focal point is on the stage. You can choose the most common object for your attention, provided it is *not across the footlights:* it can be your partner or anything else *onstage.*

"*An actor must not cater to his own wishes,* he must always act," said Stanislavski looking at us all severely. "A member of the chorus," he added, "has to figure out a character for himself which has a mutual relationship with his partners; he should make a pattern for the past and future of his role and be involved in the present surrounding circumstances. If there is no life from which the actor comes to us, if there is nothing behind his role, if he has imagined nothing—then there is nothing for him to do when he is onstage. Do not forget the 'Magic If' formula," Stanislavski kept reminding us. "What setting are you in?" he asked all of us who were in the first act. To this he himself gave an answer: "The music tells you. Follow it. You must immerse yourself in the sound of it and then interpret it in terms of each character. An actor should be able to grasp its essence and act on it in accordance with his own inner vision without waiting to be directed, because then he would just be copying the director. . . . What is the setting? This act is in dark tones. This is a centre of vice, debauchery, evil passions. There are the guardsmen, spies, libelers, beasts. Complete abandon. Gryaznoy is a wild beast in a cage, he is prowling around like a tiger.

"The ceilings are low. It is evening. Nighttime. They have come to Grisha's to drink, to amuse themselves. The top man is here. Malyuta is treated like an archpriest. He must fill up as much room as possible, puff himself up, spread himself out! The more impressive Malyuta makes himself the more offhand is his manner. Malyuta wallows in the rhythm of majesty and imperturbability. He sits there like a swine! The guardsmen are coarse brutes. Suddenly a quasi-German appears among them: Lykov, who has come from Germany, where he studied at a university. What sort of a place has he happened into? Accompanying him is Bomeley, a bootlicker, toadying to everyone, as if to say: Please, don't throw me out. He is a voluptuary like Malyuta. In this setting we see Lykov, who has grown away from these barbaric manners, and captive Lyubasha, who continues to love her tyrant Gryaznoy.

"Now act in this atmosphere, define your objectives, find your focal points of attention, keep to an inner line of action. First: you have come to Grisha, you can joke with him. Second: The top man has arrived. Take Malyuta for the object of your attention but add respect to your manner (as if he were the conductor of the orchestra, Suk). Do this all very naively, without theorizing. Third: Everyone drinks mead to the health of the host. Each one does this differently and in accordance with his position or closeness to Gryaznoy. Then, take Lykov—he's a bit of a foreigner! Treat him with curiosity, as if he were an actor rehearsing with you for the first time. He has just come from abroad, no one knows him. Well then, use your own personal experience, impressions, reactions, and translate them into the language and circumstances of the play. . . .

"Tempo-rhythm is an all-important factor in opera. You must study it, and come to know it so well that it becomes part of your flesh and blood and you do not have to think about it. When you go into action you cannot think any longer about the music, or else you will not be able to create anything. This is what you will have to work out: as in life words are used to define various objectives, actions, expressions, so in music the melody and your voice should serve the same purpose. You have been taught the right approach to singing. You may not sing a single note that is unrelated to your inner course of action without having prepared for these sounds a sort of prelude composed of your relationship to them. The feelings are in the music, they do not listen to the sound of a voice. . . . You must understand the music because it is the expression of your own feelings. You must know why this or that note, this or that rhythm, this or that timbre, has been assigned to you and what it suggests to you. Music is the guide to all your conduct on the stage."

When Gryaznoy says: "Ho! there, the mead! And quickly!", two servants with large beakers on trays enter from an inner apartment. At the same time a whole noisy gang of guardsmen push their way into the chamber to an impetuous rhythm in the music which leads up to the phrase of the chorus: "Well, here's to your health!"

All the guardsmen who have burst in hurl their hats onto the benches, and grab beakers of wine.

"You must drink with great earnestness and 'Bottoms up!' And then shake your empty goblets upside down as if to show that you drank every last drop to his health." At a last chord the guardsmen form a group in a fixed staging.

Stanislavski worked with great strictness to maintain a clear, well-finished pattern in a crowd scene. He worked with as complete authority as a conductor who insists on purity of sound in the orchestra. It was forbidden to move during the pause after the last chord ("Don't clutter!" yelled Stanislavski) nor yet were the actors allowed to freeze automatically in a pose. They had to find some basis for their temporary immobility by means of inner activity and not allow it to be arbitrary.

"There is the same pause in action on the stage as there is in the music, in the orchestra. But it must not be a vacuum. There can never be a lifeless pause on the stage. You stop because you are looking at your host and are waiting to hear what he will say. Therefore keep close watch over him. If a person is very attentive to anyone or anything he has no reason to move. Movement will only distract his attention," said Stanislavski.

After Gryaznoy's phrase: "Thanks to you for your kind words", the orchestra begins to play the theme of Lykov and the alchemist Bomeley. Here is the rival of Gryaznoy, Lykov, the betrothed of Marfa.

"The audience must understand clearly who it is that has arrived. This meeting should be made pregnant with meaning. The audience should remember it," said Stanislavski, "because it will be the cause of the whole drama."

If this meeting is to be impressive it must be carefully prepared. Stanislavski himself showed how to do this. He came onstage as Gryaznoy, bowed to Malyuta, who was drinking wine seated at the angle of the big table, and was on the point of making some joking remark. There was a roguish and gay expression on his face. Then with the introduction of the new theme in the orchestra the door opened and Lykov appeared on the threshold. At that Stanislavski quietly turned his face to the door and stood there motionless. We saw his smile fade and be gradually replaced by a dark expression. He still remained in exactly the same pose as when he was talking to Malyuta: leaning over with his hand on the table. After his face had undergone a complete transformation he slowly straightened up, turned to Lykov and moved over towards him. By now his face had only a searching look in it, the gloom had gone from it. On the contrary, an expression of satisfaction dawned on it. Gryaznoy was studying his opponent. What will the outcome of this tense encounter be, what will occur to the mind of this unbridled guardsman?

"Welcome to you!" sang Stanislavski with a wide grin, showing all his teeth, and pronouncing each consonant with the ultraclear beat of Shalyapin, while in his face one could clearly read the sub-text of the phrase: "Oh what a puppy you are! We shall see, we shall see who will win out!" Each movement in his face throughout this scene was closely bound up with the music.

This kind of an encounter not only defined the special quality of the relationship between the two leading characters, it also singled Lykov out from among all the other guests. Stanislavski emphasized the particularity of Lykov by having him wear an elegant rose-coloured kaftan, which stood out as a bright spot from the dark red hues used in the other costumes.

After this, when Gryaznoy sings: "Pray be seated, but do not be too exacting. . . ." the choral fugue begins.

"Never stress words with feelings, or emotional colours: do not try to sugar sweetness with a smile, or underscore gloom with a gloomy face and knitted brows. On the contrary, sweetish words should be sprinkled with a little pepper," said Stanislavski in commenting on the words: "Sweeter than honey is a caressing word." The movements on stage were now organized by him in the form of a fugue. Each introduction of the tenors, the baritones, or the bassos was marked by their change of place.

"How many musical units are vividly expressed in this piece?" Stanislavski asked the conductor. "Eight? Very well, that means we shall have eight groups. Each group will move to a spot indicated for its phrase. It is only Malyuta who will remain seated after Gryaznoy has ceremoniously conducted him to his place after wiping off the bench with the skirt of his kaftan."

At the end of the chorus all the guardsmen are in their places at table. Only Lykov has to sit by himself near the stove. But then Gryaznoy pulls himself together and with marked civility invites him to take a seat of honour at the main table.

Lykov's aria-tale "All is different" is begun from where he was sitting. He needs only to stand up to be seen by everyone. This singer must have good diction so that he can paint a picture of what he saw while abroad. When Lykov sings that Germans "parade their women finely dressed and do not keep them cooped up as we do here" the guardsmen roar with laughter. They listen with curiosity, occasionally with bewilderment, as they hear about these foreign customs. Only Gryaznoy is absorbed in his own thoughts. He is again caught up in his idea and from time to time he looks searchingly at Bomeley, seated opposite him. When at the end of his aria, Lykov proposes a toast to the Tsar, they all stand up, drink it in silence during a pause.

After Malyuta says to Gryaznoy: "Why don't you have your psaltery players come and extol the Tsar", the music begins the ceremonious glorification of the Tsar.

The very old psaltery players come in, cross themselves before the ikons, bow to Malyuta and Gryaznoy, and then sit down on the benches beside the stove. Some girls appear at the inside windows, several come out at the top of the stairs.

All this chorus is arranged by Stanislavski in terms of movement, from the ceremonious "gloria" to the Tsar to the parade past Malyuta who, as it were, accepts the salute.

He stands at the centre of one side of the table, with the guardsmen in groups according to their voices—each group has its entrance—and they pass four in a row. The first, according to the musical theme, are the bassos; they place themselves at the opposite end of the stage from Malyuta, thus forming the back row of the paraders. All the others follow after them and come around the forestage in order to take their places in front of the bassos. This produces a continuing flow of movement on the stage which makes the impression of a quasi-military manoeuvre.

The chorus, thus accompanied by the constant movement, is powerful in effect. Malyuta climbs up onto a bench, the guardsmen flank him. He turns to them and sings: "How right the Tsar to fasten brooms to your saddles, O Boyars. We will sweep all filth out of our holy Russia." These words so inspire the guardsmen that one is terrified by the fanatical determination in their faces. They gallop around the stage yelling, waving their arms as if lashing around with whips, and altogether they create an impression of savage and menacing revelry. Lykov, who has taken refuge near a window, looks on with bewilderment, and Bomeley, who has all but hidden himself under a bench, is pushed over by one of the rioting guardsmen. The girls who had watched the rather solemn procession with curiosity now are terrified and run away. The old psaltery players crowd into corners near the stove.

Malyuta is delighted and now asks for dance music. The feast moves forward to its climax.

The prelude to the "Yar Khmel" drinking song serves as a step in the direction of the next mise-en-scène. The guardsmen carry the large dining table and benches right out onto the forestage in order to free more space in the centre of the chamber for the dancing. The girls come down the stairs from the women's quarters to get ready for the round dance (khorovod). Everything is done in rhythm with the music.

"There is a kind of 'fade-out' just before the singing resumes," remarked Stanislavski with regard to the pause before the chorus begins. "This is reasonable because a moment of immobility is needed before new action can be initiated.... There should be no moving about during this pause. Do not blur the pattern," he continued.

It is one of the most deeply rooted traditions in opera that there should be dances in the first act. Usually during the drinking song chorus the ballerinas do a Russian dance in colourful sarafan dresses while the chorus stands to one side and sings.

"Something has to be done to get away from the old ballet routine," he said at one of the first rehearsals. "It has to be made more varied, molded into a scene to introduce the round dance. . . .

"What is the idea of this scene? The girls and the peasant women have come. They have to be provided with characteristic features. The hands of the peasant women are little developed, they are like trowels. Their arms are straight, all movement is from the shoulder, like ram-rods. There can be no question of graceful ballet forms here. Hands are deformed with hard work. Noses are wiped on the soft end of the palm!

"What is your psychological line? It cannot bear any resemblance to the abandon of those girls in Moscow's gypsy restaurants. You see, it is not often that you are made to dance. You can flirt a bit with modesty, but act as if you were in a cage with tigers. Here are these devils surrounding you and you are Christians. Malyuta has a diabolic look as he watches the women and chooses the one he will rake in.

"Part One: Come out in two groups, cling together, hide behind one another. Be embarrassed. Then push some one of you at Malyuta. And you [speaking to the actress who is put forward] try to save yourself from his paws, escape, and run quickly back to the others.

"Part Two: 'I am coming, little one. . . .' They try to dance, but still shyly, are embarrassed. The round dance is formed.

"Part Three: 'I will invite a guest, a guest dear to me. . . .' They ask Malyuta to join in, they pull him into the round dance. One group grabs him, the other tries to pull him away. He lumbers around like a bear.

"Part Four: Now drag in 'the old woman' [the aged housekeeper sitting on the steps of the stair]. Let her be Malyuta's partner in the dance. Push her over to him. Now form a ring around them. Everyone roars with laughter and Malyuta is pleased.

"Part Five: Now the real round dance begins with the introductory steps. The girls are bolder now and do a little fooling. Let them coax the guardsmen into the ring. Invite Lykov—he's so shy! Lykov tries in every way to refuse and slip away unnoticed. Now everything sweeps to a wild end. They riot around. The peasant women put on the guards-men's hats, the guardsmen tie on the women's kerchieves. The round dance breaks up into groups.

"With the song 'My darling will be. . .' the dancing reaches its high point—in fact they are no longer dancing but leaping wildly around. With the last chord of the music they all collapse: some throw them-selves on the floor, others on the flat surfaces at the side of the stove, and still others onto the benches.

"As they yell the chamber looks almost like a field of mock battle at which Gryaznoy, who has been deeply preoccupied with his thoughts, now looks with amused bewilderment. He has been sitting with his back to his guests and therefore his face has been in full view of the audience.

"Don't be playing suffering," Stanislavski reminded him. "Just be reflecting about something. The point about your present situation is that you cannot withdraw to be alone with your thoughts. You do not need to act anything. The whole mise-en-scène will do the acting for you. Incidentally don't forget the law of our kind of theatre, and please make a note of it in red ink: Do not just 'act'; just follow the line of simple physical actions and the rest will come of itself."

And indeed, the solitary, immobile figure, set in the middle of an action-picked picture, is in such sharp contrast to the general jollity that the attention of the audience is inevitably drawn to this main character and impelled to follow the trend of his inner life.

The way Stanislavski staged this crowd scene can serve as a model of directorial skill in combining mass movements with an unbroken line, clearly visible to the audience, of the lives of the principal characters. Their roles not only do not cease to develop during the ballet or choral interludes, they even become more powerfully explicit.

"What is your main objective during such a scene?" Stanislavski asked the actors. "To amuse each other, not yourselves. Try to jolly your partner and never mind the audience."

At the end of the dancing Malyuta sits down on the bench next to Gryaznoy; he has a girl on either knee.

"Ah, wine has banished from my memory. . . ." Malyuta is speaking about Lyubasha. At the mention of her name all the girls prick up their ears. They are afraid of her. Here Bomeley comes into action. He is to play such a large part in her fate. He has been sitting all the while at the end of the table on the forestage. Now three of the principal characters are all at the table. It is natural for Malyuta, as he rests after dancing, to tell Bomeley about Lyubasha. "She sings like a little bird. Her brows are arched, her eyes like sparks, and her braid of hair reaches to her heels."

"Savour every word," said Stanislavski, showing the actor how to do it. "Malyuta is a voluptuous old fellow. . . ." In the orchestra accompaniment to Malyuta's tale about Lyubasha the strings have several quick runs. The girls who are to run off are divided into groups and each group dashes offstage to its own run of notes, after tearing themselves from the embraces of the guardsmen. The men sprawling on the floor near the door grab at the skirts of the girls as they run past.

This madly riotous, hilariously drunken bacchanalia stops on an unresolved chord in the orchestra, after which there is an expectant pause.

During this pause Lyubasha emerges on the upper landing (to the left from the auditorium) of the stairs leading to the women's quarters. She looks over the whole stage and especially at Gryaznoy and then she calmly walks down the stairs. With her first downward step the orchestra comes in with an accompaniment to her dignified entrance.

Lyubasha halts at the next to last step. She towers over the whole crowd of guardsmen on all sides of her. Drunken Malyuta rises to his feet to salute her: "Good health to you, Goddaughter! Good health!"

"Sing the word 'Goddaughter' with enjoyment, stressing the meaning of it which is not altogether usual. Kiss each other, not in a theatrical manner, but quite naturally on the cheek. Then a deep bow from the waist," Stanislavski added in prompting the action. "Now think," he said turning to Lyubasha, "what it means for you to enter this chamber, for you as a woman, whose husband does not send for her for days, weeks, a month at a time. May you show your suffering here, in public? On the contrary. Your objective is to please, be unaffected, not betray any feelings of suffering, and not be at all flirtatious. You must feel 'I am beautiful' but not do anything about it. The consciousness of your beauty—that gives the general tone to your conduct. 'I possess the right to have everything, all will be well.' Give one quick glance at Gryaznoy to see what humour he is in. No need to make any to-do about that glance, we shall in any case notice it.

"And you, guardsmen, what is the general tone, the rhythm, of this scene for you?

"A mare from a remarkable English breed has been trotted out, everyone is studying her, and she looks at them all as a mare would do. You look over Lyubasha as experts in prize horseflesh. A notable beauty has come in. Each of you feels a very hot inner rhythm. Only Gryaznoy looks on with indifference. Of course he must be flattered by the fact that everyone likes Lyubasha. Several of the guardsmen give him broad winks to show that they are experts.

"While the conversation between Lyubasha and Malyuta is taking place there must be no distracting movement, because this apparently insignificant little talk ('Your little eyes look drowsy', 'I was not asleep, my head ached', 'Sing us a song', 'Which one?') must be very important. You are about to sing a song, not so much for the guests as for Gryaznoy. After Malyuta's words: 'I beg you to listen, my Goddaughter will sing for us!' you throw another quick glance at Gryaznoy and it is only then that there is a distinct change in the setting. At the next musical phrase and before the beginning of the song 'Get me ready quickly. . .' the guardsmen, in rhythm with the music, move the benches and arrange them so that they can sit and listen to the 'concert'. Meantime they help Lyubasha to climb up onto the flat space next to the stove where she will stand while singing."

The figure of Lyubasha, dressed in a dark-coloured sarafan, stands out against the white tiles of the Dutch stove in the dimly lighted chamber where some of the candles have burnt out. The guardsmen sit facing her, with their backs to the audience. Only Gryaznoy remains seated where he was, at the first table, and in the same pose. He is not touched in any way by Lyubasha—he may even be slightly irritated by her. Almost next to Lyubasha, near the stove, is Bomeley. His eyes are fixed on her. Although there are a number of people onstage the audience sees the faces only of Lyubasha, Gryaznoy, and Bomeley and can read there the inner life of these three. This disposition of the main characters is just one more example of the artistic finesse with which Stanislavski knew how to subject a situation to the pattern of the through-line of action.

"Your song is very pathetic and tragic, therefore you must sing it with sentiment and tragedy. Be courageous in your grief. Whining and snivelling will get you nowhere with Gryaznoy, in fact it will only irritate him more. Both Gryaznoy and Lyubasha are strong characters and courageous by nature," was Stanislavski's reminder.

In the musical interlude between two verses there is a slight movement on the stage as the listeners alter their poses and, perhaps, only Gryaznoy slowly turns and looks at Lyubasha. Otherwise, during her song, everything on the stage is quiescent.

A sharp chord breaks the spell. The tense atmosphere during the singing is replaced by boisterous, drunken enthusiasm. "Oh, how she sings! It makes your heart melt quite away!" Stanislavski told Malyuta to beat his chest with his fist in his excitement. "Drunken people react very boisterously."

Despite all the uproar Malyuta does not forget his job: "Perhaps the Tsar himself may already be awake. . . ." This cue has a sobering effect on everyone. A new picture now emerges on the stage. All the guardsmen, with Malyuta at their head, begin to put on black robes, preparing to go to church. The half-lighted chamber is now full of black-clad figures waving their long sleeves about like wings (the robes have been brought in without being noticed by the audience). The lone figure of Lyubasha stands out amid the dark, milling mass, and seems more doomed and tragic than ever. With uncertain gait, their legs catching in their long robes, the guests stumble out.

Only Bomeley, his eyes still fixed on Lyubasha, remains behind. He senses her loneliness and makes predatory plans to get at this beautiful woman. While the guardsmen are crowding around the doors and taking leave of Gryaznoy, and he with careful concern is holding up the lurching Malyuta, Lyubasha goes up the stairs and hurriedly disappears into the women's quarters. Bomeley, that avid hunter of women, tries to hold her back but Lyubasha, aware of his intent, pushes him aside with distaste. Stanislavski pointed out this brief encounter, which establishes some kind of tie between them. Having seen his guests out Gryaznoy now begins his long-awaited conversation with Bomeley, not suspecting that Lyubasha from a window above sees and hears everything.

"Now for the first time in the whole act you can breathe freely," said Stanislavski to Gryaznoy. "You now have hope, and therefore life lies ahead. From this moment on your role moves in a new direction. Now you have only one objective—to get that potion from Bomeley and give it to Marfa to drink. Afterwards you will see that there are in all only three or four objectives in your role. And eventually there will turn out to be only one main objective. But that will not be for some time.

"Remember," Stanislavski kept repeating at rehearsals, "that this trio, Gryaznoy, Bomeley, and Lyubasha, represents a terrible secret, indeed a most dangerous one; it is practically treason to the state. Here we must have the subtlest *piano* and most delicate diction so that each word of each of the three characters wil be entirely distinct."

After the trio, in the course of which the secret scheme is consummated, Gryaznoy happily escorts Bomeley out of the chamber. Lyubasha cautiously comes downstairs and quickly hides behind the stove when she hears Gryaznoy returning. All this was worked out in a rhythmic pattern down to the last quarter note and was perfectly executed with grace by the actress playing Lyubasha. Exhausted but happy Gryaznoy returns and stretches himself in the doorway. The moment has come when he can be alone with his hopes. But then, to the sound of a soft E-major chord, Lyubasha cautiously emerges. Gryaznoy is no longer alone in the chamber and instantly his face hardens, turns cold. A seemingly unimportant talk takes place about early morning mass.

"Your head," said Stanislavski to Gryaznoy, "is aching badly, you haven't had any sleep for a long time, and here's your nuisance of a wife."

Tired, Gryaznoy stretches himself out on a bench and tries to avoid any conversation by pretending he wants to go to sleep.

All the ensuing duet is based on Lyubasha's desire to catch Gryaznoy's eye, sit beside him, talk quietly with him—and on his eluding all conversation. The moves in this duet flow logically from one to the next and are planned around the table standing on the forestage. The singers are in the most favourable position from the point of view of projecting sounds and also of being seen by the audience.

The duet consists of four musical units to which the four positions of the actors carefully correspond.

The first unit is planned as follows. Gryaznoy is stretched out on the bench in front of the table, on the forestage. Lyubasha approaches the

The Tsar's Bride, Act I (from the 1926 production): Lyubasha reproaches Gryaznoy.

table cautiously and asks: "Why are you angry at me?" She is standing almost behind Gryaznoy's back and comes cautiously closer to see his face. With his "Leave me alone!" to the accompaniment of a loud chord, Gryaznoy jumps up and seats himself at the table.

"You cannot bear these mild reproaches, they drive you mad. But you have jumped up and sat down and now pull yourself together. To Lyubasha's next cue: 'Is there another, a better, more winning one?' you reply as quietly as you can, holding yourself in: 'Go to bed, Lyubasha.' But keep your face hidden from her. That is not difficult as you are seated with your back to her."

Next comes the musical prelude to the actual duet. At this time Lyubasha cautiously moves around the table to sit down beside Gryaznoy.

"You, Lyubasha," said Stanislavski, "have four musical phrases. Reckon your movements, as you walk around the table, approach Gryaznoy, so that at the end of the last phrase. 'Ah, you have fallen out of love with me' you will sit down beside him and cautiously touch him with your hand."

Even this slight touch is unbearable to irascible Gryaznoy; it gives him an excuse to jump up and go to another place farther away from Lyubasha. At the end of the next musical phrase Gryaznoy goes and sits down at the other side of the table.

Lyubasha remains alone on the bench out in front. It is in this setting that the second part of the duet is performed. Gryaznoy sings his cues with his head turned away from Lyubasha and looking out the window.

"Try to convince yourself that you are not to blame in any way. . . ." Just at this point a faint light of dawn comes through the window. The night is almost over.

With the words: "No, it cannot be that you will abandon me," Lyubasha rushes over and stands in front of him. He instantly turns away. She sings with great emotion: "No doubt you have taken another to your heart, oh leave her. . . ." Stanislavski said here: "The music tells you that your scene is built on contrasts, so try to sing quietly and lovingly until your emotions break through. You are seized with despair, but immediately you regain control of yourself. The more you restrain yourself the higher the tide of emotions will rise. 'For I am the only one who really loves you'—and then go on again with great restraint."

Lyubasha once more cautiously comes closer to Gryaznoy and sits down.

"But do not lay a finger on him or he will jump up again," whispered Stanislavski to Lyubasha. "You do not need your hands, use your words."

Gryaznoy, who is tortured with remorse, sits still, his face averted, listens to her suppressed sobs, looks at a forgotten pitcher of wine standing on the table, while next to him, bowed over the table, Lyubasha bemoans her bitter fate. The explosion of her heart's agony reaches its greatest height in the music when she sings: "I gave you everything." Unable to bear the tension any longer Gryaznoy gulps down a goblet of wine, tears himself away from Lyubasha, and rapidly goes out, leaving her alone.

"You act," said Stanislavski, "firmly, brutally, like a man stubbornly pursuing his goal, but do not overdo in making him too one-sided as is so often done on the stage. Tears and well-founded reproaches cannot but affect even the coldest heart. How you will react to them is another matter: you smother all these human chords inside you, you drown them in wine."

Lyubasha's last phrase is: ". . .you will abandon me!" The descending tones in the music press down the weeping Lyubasha. She is a solitary, pathetic figure . . . while the rosy light of dawn is cheerfully reflected on the gleaming tiles of the Dutch stove.

There is the sound of church bells. The hour of early mass. Gryaznoy has hurriedly slipped into his black robe and as he rushes out can throw back a "farewell" over his shoulder.

After hesitating for a while a desperate resolution comes over the forlorn woman. To the sounds of impetuous music she runs to the windows and, looking out, sings: "His eyes may be on her, but he will never possess her." Then she dashes to the staircase, determined to "exorcise" the witch; she goes up the steps to the women's quarters and as the curtain closes we see her slipping into a fur coat to follow Gryaznoy.

The sun now brilliantly floods the chamber strewn with the signs of the night's carousing.

It was very easy for the singers to perform in this setting. The lifelikeness of the décor in which the leading characters lived, the staging, the logically rather than theatrically impelled effects, all helped them in moving about on the stage. The actors and the audience too had the sense of being in an atmosphere of actual life.

Act Two

The Simov sets for the second act exuded the soft warmth of a Russian autumn. The basic structure of the set was the wall of a monastery, the gateway with a watch light over it; the wooden house of Sobakin on a high foundation, with steps leading to a high platform; Sobakin's courtyard enclosed with a palisade, and in a corner of the enclosure a gate. A well-stoop with a watch light and ikon over it is almost on the forestage. In the distance there is a glimpse of autumn fields; a high sky over all is painted on the rear panorama which imparts a gentle warmth to the scene.

The first act contained the knotting of irreconcilable conflicts among the principal characters of the opera: Gryaznoy, Lykov, Lyubasha, and Bomeley. In contrast to the gloomy colours of the first act, the second act begins bright and clear. The peaceful, hearty atmosphere of life in the Alexandrovski quarter of Moscow is broken in on by the appearance of Ivan the Terrible's guardsmen and later, at the end of the act, by Lyubasha.

To the left, at the very edge of the stage is a tall monastery tower where Bomeley has his chemical laboratory. At first Stanislavski had thought to place this in the cellar under the tower so that Bomeley would crawl up from there and later drag Lyubasha down there, but the stage arrangements were such that this could not be done. At the beginning of the act the tower does not in any way reveal the evil purpose it harbours.

The action begins late in the day, after vespers, as the devout parishioners come out of the monastery. The rhythm of the movements of tired people is well conveyed by the transparent music of Rimski-Korsakov, with a touch of bells ringing in the overtones. The unhurried chatting of the women who sit down to rest after standing all through the vesper service. . . . The air is full of Indian summer sunshine. . . . Stanislavski insisted that the chorus be limited in number. Among the peasants one glimpses a few outstanding faces. Typical of 16th-century Russia, as the curtain opens one sees the beggars at the gates of the monastery, the deformed and crippled people on crutches. The devout congregation comes out in groups of two, three, four, who move over to the well and drink water from a dipper. To them it is holy water; then they settle down near the fence to rest, gossip and munch their buns which have been blessed in church. They talk about the weather, the Tsar's prospective bride. This peaceful picture is broken in on by a raiding party of the Tsar's guardsmen. Everyone tries to hide, some behind the well, some under the Sobakin terrace, others behind the wall of the monastery, in the garden, behind the hedge. Frightened faces can be seen all over.

The Tsar's Bride, Act II (from the 1926 production): Beggars and parishioners outside the monastery.

This episode of the guardsmen singing the chorus: "All, it would seem, have been forewarned", required, according to Stanislavski, some kind of basis for their remaining on the scene. They could not just stop in front of the conductor to sing their piece.

"This should be a moment of consultation," said Stanislavski. "You must try to figure out all the factors. First, do you all know where you are to go, where Prince Gvozdev lives? Actors must always know their geography very clearly. Next, are you all gathered, can there be some latecomers who will not know what to do? Explain it to them. There's a foretaste of fine booty for you hunters, tell them about this. Probably there is a chief among you. Rouse your imagination."

All these questions resulted in making the singers act inwardly: the raid on and the looting of Prince Gvozdev's manor may have been a matter for the Tsar, but every member of his guard was personally interested.

"Like swift falcons we will swoop down on his estate, and there will be no getting away, no mercy from us!"—that was how they spoke to themselves.

When the people who had hidden from them begin to crawl out from under benches, behind hedges and palisades, whether they are beggars or the inhabitants of the quarter they say: "They are in a gang; it is going to be tough for someone." They then clarify their own attitude towards the guards with the last phrase of the chorus: "They call themselves the servants of the Tsar, but they are worse than wild dogs."

A small scene, the emergence of a young man from Bomeley's tower and the conversation of the crowd with him, was worked out with great care by Stanislavski.

A naive, long-haired young fellow comes out of the tower entrance walking backwards and bowing very low. The innocent replies the youth makes about the German inspire in the crowd fear and loathing. Thus he becomes quite bewildered and throws onto the ground the herbs he was trying to hide in his hat. The whole chorus is supposed to react to his "magic herbs" as they would to a poisonous snake. They take the bewildered youth over to the well to have him bathe himself in holy water, pouring it over his head and making him drink it.

The slight excitement of this scene is replaced by a quiet rhythm in the music during which the crowd slowly disperses. The stage is almost empty. The only people who remain are the beggars at the gate. Accompanied by her theme Marfa emerges from the monastery, followed by her friend Dunyasha.

They are two young daughters of merchants, all dressed up. They seat themselves on a bench at the very front of the forestage to wait for Marfa's father. This gives Marfa the most favourable situation in which to sing her aria. Youthful merriment, unaffected manners, shyness— these are the essential inner constituents of this scene. A peaceful life flowed under the walls of the monastery.

"First of all you two must be playful," Stanislavski said, "before you begin to be confidential and make your secret confessions. You are two young rascals with terrifying inner ardor. Your eyes flash: 'Oh, how I love him! Oh, he has gone away! Oh, he has come back!' Work yourselves up. Invent a whole lot of nonsense, foolishness; let the music give you ideas for this. Think up twenty-five silly things to do, poke each other in the stomach. . . . What else can you do? In such spots as the two breaks in your aria, especially before the words: 'How many lovely days. . . !' (sixteen measures) you should have a whole reservoir of little playful things to do, many attitudes—for your secrets, for lyrical moments, for fooling. But all this must be woven into an unbroken strand. There must be no blank spaces. You must carry on the continuing line of your roles and plan it in all kinds of ways. Find the fertile spots on which you can build the moods in your parts. It can be that something untoward had happened, suppose you have knocked your foreheads together, but then some silly prank rights everything and after that the whole role runs along 'in the groove'. Later one of you silly girls is put into a gilded cage and then poisoned. But for now your insouciance is complete! You are in such a state of bliss you scarcely know what to do with yourselves. You are both dancing on air—and you can dance sitting down too."

Here Stanislavski used his middle fingers to rap out a dance on the table. They performed all sorts of tricks and created the complete illusion of dancing.

Dunyasha has to abide by the same rhythm as Marfa, even though she is not yet in love. But in five minutes she will be.

"When you sing: 'How many lovely days we spent. . .' do not go off by yourself into your memories but take Dunyasha along with you. Paint the picture for her. You see the garden. You must visualize every tree, every branch, every little path. Imagine every bush, walk along those paths so that as soon as you recall them, all the other memories will come flooding in and your feelings with them of their own accord. You can create in your imagination any garden you please, as long as the memory of it is tied to your own life. And never repeat an earlier rehearsal or performance. Renew each time the 'given circumstances' and then you will fulfill the requirement of Pushkin that you reach a state of sincerity of emotions. Always forget what you said and did earlier, and begin all over again as you do in real life."

An actress sometimes used to say to him at the start of rehearsal:

"I would do so and so."

"Do not merely say that, *do* it," insisted Stanislavski. "Put yourself fully into the given circumstances of your role and go into action. To say 'I would do' is a piece of dry reasoning, it's not action. . . . In this part of your role you are constantly alternating between two states: you are moving about, walking, or you are engaged in a dialogue, where your diction must be crystal clear and you move as little as possible. You must develop the habit of keeping the sound bound to the word. You must speak in terms of 'What do I see with my *inner eye*'. Before you begin each phrase it is imperative to be prepared with a whole process of inner vision. 'Let us walk along Tverskaya Street,' I say to my neighbour, and instantly I visualize without fail that particular street. Singers tend to think about a sound, a note, and not about the essential meaning of what they are singing.

"Your whole tale, everything that has been happening to you, is summed up in: 'I am an affianced bride. God has brought me together again with Vanya.' That is the main theme of your role."

Here the orchestra renews the theme of glory to the Tsar. Beginning very softly in the bassoons, then bringing in the other instruments, it broadens and swells. Now two guardsmen emerge from the monastery and stand at either side of the portal. There is a quick run of sixteenth notes in the orchestra and the impression is created of speed, people running about. Six nuns dash out of the monastery portal and fall to their knees in front of it. Again comes the glory to the Tsar theme but now from the brasses and it develops to a mighty pitch. At the same time a tall black-clad monk, with a conical velvet cap on his head, a staff in his hand, appears in the portal. Over his black habit he wears a rich fur coat thrown around his shoulders and a huge silver cross on his chest. He walks like a sinner laden with chains. Paying no attention to the nuns he moves towards the well and devoutly crosses himself. A sharp chord comes from the orchestra and he stops short, having glimpsed, beyond the ikon over the well, a young girl thoughtfully looking up to the sky. Under the insistent gaze of the monk she turns abruptly towards him and is transfixed.

"Suddenly towering over you," said Stanislavski to Marfa, "you see a horrible face, a mask, a fateful figure. You see your future as you look deep into his eyes. And you," this to the actor playing Ivan the Terrible, "first study the ikon and then are aware of Marfa. . . . The moment should be drawn in various shades: first your hand is frozen in midair as you cross yourself, then you are full of admiration, which passes on into the smile of a tiger as you let your arm down mechanically . . . until, finally, you give a relieved sigh, as much as to say 'She belongs to me!' "

Meantime Marfa, frozen with fear, sings: "Ah, why does the blood run cold in my heart?" Ivan moves over to the expectant Malyuta and says something to him, indicating Marfa with a glance. The audience can guess what Ivan is saying. We realize that Marfa's fate is being sealed. She herself does not, of course, recognize the Tsar in the person of this terrifying monk, who forgot the ikon and the holy water as soon as his hawk-like eyes fell on her. Having whispered to Malyuta the Tsar rapidly goes away. The nuns remain on their knees until he has disappeared.

Despite the fleeting quality of this meeting Stanislavski built it into the central point of the opera. Actually the whole stage setting of this second act was constructed for the sake of this meeting between Marfa

The Tsar's Bride, Act II (from the 1926 production): Malyuta, Ivan in monk's disguise, and Marfa.

and the Tsar at the holy well. Rimski-Korsakov devoted only eight measures to this whole scene of the appearance of the Tsar and his meeting with Marfa, yet despite its brevity the episode is pregnant with musical content.

For Marfa this ill-boding meeting with Ivan the Terrible passes like a dark cloud on a bright day. Her momentary qualms quickly melt away when her father returns, bringing with him her fiancé, Lykov.

The meeting between the prospective bride and groom begins with the rather courtly greeting of Lykov.

"Sing it very simply," was Stanislavski's advice to the singer in the part of Lykov. "Rimski-Korsakov has put a rather rich bit of old Russian style in it."

Before Marfa begins to sing there are two measures.

"Do you sense," asked Stanislavski, "that there is a quality of playfulness here? Prove this by showing that you still treat your fiancé in a childish way. During these measures run and hide behind Dunyasha and sing your lines over her shoulder. Sing a phrase, hide again, then come out again and look at him. This is all evidence of your shyness overlaid by a little prankishness.

"Your fiancé is also very embarrassed," Stanislavski went on, "but he is the one to put on a brave face."

The quartet that follows, like other ensemble singing in the opera, was plotted by Stanislavski to be an active episode, reflecting the life of each of the characters involved. The father pushes the embarrassed fiancé towards the bench where he has already settled his daughter, as if to afford an opportunity for the young couple to talk to one another. After the father's first phrase: "Wait but a little, my dear daughter, and he will be yours forever", he, Sobakin, takes Dunyasha by the arm and goes up the steps to the platform above, leaving the betrothed couple alone together. For this scene it would almost seem as though Rimski-Korsakov had guessed what Stanislavski's idea might be, for he left four measures during which Sobakin and Dunyasha do not sing.

In this way, the inner line of action results in converting the quartet into two duets of the principals: one for Dunyasha and Sobakin, the other for Marfa and Lykov. The staging of the scene was vertical in effect with Sobakin and Dunyasha on a level above the place where Marfa and Lykov are sitting. This enabled the public to sense the intimacy of the conversation between the betrothed couple while not destroying the structure of the quartet, since the singers were in effect within close range of each other. The betrothed couple are at first shy and turn away from one another; then gradually they grow bolder, until by the end of the quartet they are sitting quite close together and Lykov cautiously lays his hand on Marfa's.

The quietly triumphant C-major chords at the finale of the quartet set a living picture: the young couple in an intimate pose down below and Marfa's father and friend above looking down lovingly on them.

A brief exchange between Sobakin and his daughter and an invitation to Lykov to come into the house ends with twelve measures of music.

Stanislavski, who was in a high degree aware of each musical phrase, insisted that his actors find a precise inner basis for the music. For him not a measure, not a note or even a rest, could be allowed to pass unnoticed, not to be reflected in the actor's conduct on the stage.

He insisted that special attention be given to the music which was the culmination of any significant happening in the drama being enacted.

Marfa's theme and aria, which for the first three measures are in a major key, gradually change their aspect when they move into a minor key and then end up in bright, serene chords. It is to this music that Marfa and her affianced husband move up the steps into the house.

They do not want to take leave of each other at once. They walk slowly and try to be alone together as long as possible. Their mutual feelings of tenderness show in the shy way they look at each other and cautiously touch hands. Then Marfa leads her fiancé into her house.

In *The Tsar's Bride* there are few gently lyrical places but where they do exist they should be played to the full so that the dramatic clash will stand out in higher relief.

The darkening landscape is brightened by spots of light from windows in the house, from the watch lights over the monastery portal and under the ikon over the well. At the same time as an intermezzo is being played, a figure muffled in a big fur coat, either a man or woman, appears in the background coming from around the corner by the Sobakin courtyard. This mysterious figure glides along the monastery wall, reaches the well, looks up and recognizes the house, then steals through the wicket gate and moves up the staircase to the entrance.

This whole long transit of Lyubasha is shaped on the melody of the intermezzo where the *pizzicati* of the strings suggest cautious steps. All her movements, her stopping and looking around, fit exactly to the music.

This rhythmic movement of his actor-singers was something on which Stanislavski laid particular stress in his theory of operatic art. In a press interview he gave just before the opening of *The Tsar's Bride* he expressed in brief form what he believed was the most important objective in the producing of an opera: ". . . .The action on the stage must be so completely blended with the music that it takes place in identical rhythm with the music. But this is not rhythm for rhythm's sake, as we often see practiced. I want to see a confluence of physical rhythm with the music quite imperceptible to the public: the words so blended with the music that they are produced as an integral part of it. There must be an indistinguishable *identity of movement and rhythm with the music.*

"What is your objective here?" Stanislavski asked the singer in the part of Lyubasha. "First of all you have the simple physical objective of finding the right address amid the extremely difficult given circumstances. You have to seek out a strange house and see your rival with your own eyes. It is dark, it is dangerous for a lone woman to walk along the empty lanes, and besides you are not sure exactly where the house is. That is the line of your physical objective and parallel with it runs that of your inner emotions. What spring must you press to release the appropriate feelings, how to rouse them to action? There is no direct approach to them. You can affect them only through your thoughts, or your actions, or the rhythm of a given feeling.

"First of all you must be thoroughly familiar with the music so that you will not be aware of the score. You must not think about the music or there will be nothing creative in what you do. You must work out inside yourself the same relationship with the music that we have with the spoken word in ordinary life. Not a single sound should be sung, not even your 'a-a-a' in vocalizing, without preparing a proper prelude for it. This is something some singers quite neglect when they are practicing. Your 'a' sound means approval, astonishment, or bewilderment, but it is not just a nice little sound.

"The same applies to action on the stage. You must learn how to understand music in terms of action, develop your musical sense. Always ask yourself the why and wherefore of this or that sound, this or that rhythm. For example, tap out on the palm of your hand whole, half, quarter, or eighth notes and see what different moods they induce. Rhythm has a spontaneous effect on feelings. And the other way around: if there is a change of emotions inside you, it will instantly alter your rhythm correspondingly. You will be truly aware of rhythm only when you are in the grip of feelings. Therefore forced rhythm is no rhythm at all. If you act incorrectly you will move about the stage in an incorrect rhythm. Which means that the right objectives of your role must be welded to the rhythm of the music and then true feelings will emerge.

"Now compose all your actions: your steps, your looking around, your stops, your investigating, your hearkening—and do it so that they will all coincide with the melody. If you are right in how you combine the musical rhythm with the rhythm of your movements, then all the accents of the music will correspond to the accents of your actions.

"You cannot tie emphatic actions to wilted notes. *Rhythm is a certain quantity of objectives packed into a given unit of time.* On the street, at home, keep developing rhythm by means of exercises. Keep on watching your rhythm. Without it you are no actor. Rhythm has a terrific power and opera singers make no use of it. Only Shalyapin understood this."

The actress-singer playing Lyubasha went on with her part.

She cautiously threaded her way through the shadows, trying to slip unnoticed past spots of light, often, at places so indicated by the music, stopping short and standing motionless like a frightened animal.

In the thirty-sixth measure the intermezzo ends on a plaintive, long-drawn-out note and when that stops Lyubasha is already standing motionless in the courtyard of Sobakin, listening to the sounds inside the house. A sharp chord, *sforzando,* from the orchestra, and she breathes a sigh of relief: "So I have found her, this is the nest of the little dove! I shall have a glimpse now of your beauty!" During the next four measures, a creeping theme from the strings seems to lift Lyubasha up the steps to the entrance and a window. Her abrupt, perfunctory lines: "Yes, she's not bad-looking, all pink and white, and languishing eyes" are sung against a background of gradually diminishing brasses which soothe Lyubasha. Her words: "My heart is lightened, he will soon tire of her..." are again sung against a background of an undulating theme played by the strings. Then Stanislavski said: "Now go back, you have calmed down...." Lyubasha had taken Dunyasha for Marfa.

When she has gone halfway down the steps she stops, hesitates; perhaps she should take one more look so as to be completely relieved.

"I'll look once more," she decides and mounts the steps again. Now her figure is lighted by the moon which has risen. Her sheepskin coat, her pale face, and her man's fur cap on her head stand out against the dark timbers of the Sobakin house. One more quick glance through the window and Lyubasha cries out in despair. For the first time she has seen Marfa: "There, that is she, Lyubasha's evil spirit. . . ." Her frightened, fluttering hand reveal the tumult in her soul, her panic and terror at the sight of her victorious rival. The orchestra is filled with panic and terror. Her consternation drives her down the steps, across the courtyard, to the tower where the pagan Bomeley lives.

There is a flurry of sounds in the orchestra culminating in sharp chords. The brasses ring out. This is Lyubasha beating at the heavy door to the tower, banging at Bomeley's door. A shutter is opened at a narrow window and Bomeley's head appears, lighted from behind by the light of a blazing fire.

"Bomeley," said Stanislavski to the singer playing this role, "is occupied with his chemistry. He is boiling various medications over a fire that fitfully lights up his laboratory. He can be dressed in simple working clothes, with an apron full of holes made by acids and sparks from his fire."

Lyubasha offers him a ring and a necklace through the window. Bomeley examines them carefully and returns them. "My powders are not for sale." "Very precious, are they not?" "Yes, precious indeed!"

Lyubasha is sick at heart and tortured with jealousy. She does not grasp the meaning of his words: 'What do you want, a pledge?'

"Say this very simply, you still do not understand anything. Usually an actor knows in advance what his partner's lines will be," said Stanislavski. "When Lyubasha hears the reply about a kiss, she is vehemently indignant and starts to run off."

Without thinking what she is doing she enters the courtyard of Sobakin. Then realizing her mistake she turns towards the well on the forestage. Here she is stopped by Bomeley, who has dashed out like a hunting dog and bars her path. There is a short struggle between them in front of the well. She tears herself away from him but finds her retreat cut off by his threat to tell Gryaznoy all about her—that completely undoes her. She sinks wearily onto that same bench where Marfa sat so recently and sang about her happiness. Lyubasha is the prey of her own passion and jealousy. She implores Bomeley to give her the terrible poison powder to destroy her rival. Bomeley now feels his grip over her and brazenly embraces the bowed-down, powerless Lyubasha. The laughter and gay singing emanating from the Sobakin house alarms them. Lyubasha hides behind the well and Bomeley withdraws into the shadow of the tower.

Caught between the hammer and the anvil, Lyubasha now dashes about between these two terrifying buildings: the dark tower of Bomeley and the happy house of Sobakin.

The laughter in the Sobakin house stops. Standing in front of the well, barely visible in the weak gleam of the watch light, Lyubasha, with bowed head, agrees to Bomeley's price for the precious philtre.

Bomeley, delighted, rushes back into his tower. Lyubasha, left alone, sinks to her knees in front of the ikon over the well. The spot where Ivan the Terrible saw Marfa is now for Lyubasha a place for prayer and confession. Bowed to the ground, she bemoans her fate and reproaches Gryaznoy with: "To what have you brought me, Grigori? . . ."

"This is an extremely important part of your role," said Stanislavski at one of the rehearsals. "The whole situation makes you a pitiful figure evoking sympathy. The music clearly expresses your suffering. All this may tempt you to overact your emotions, your passion. You can easily, given your beautiful voice, the enchantment of the music, and the dramatic situation, fall into self-pity, play up your tearfulness and sentimentality. That is very dangerous and can easily lead you to making a show of yourself for the audience and toying with them by means of your feminine charm.

"But what is the main direction of your role? You wish to return to Gryaznoy, win back his love. Do everything from this point of view. Then the image of your part will emerge. But right now do not play the avenging woman or the hapless, abandoned victim. Do nothing but try to find a solid basis for your actions. After all, you are preparing to poison your rival. How can you justify such an act? Only by the powerful love you feel for Gryaznoy. Therefore the underlying content of your aria ('The Lord will be your judge') is your justification, the proof of your love. When a person is in a difficult situation he always tries to find external reasons for it, he looks for others to blame. Who is to blame in all this, do you think? Of course, Marfa is, in the first instance, although she cannot possibly love as deeply as you do, and then there is Gryaznoy who does not appreciate your love. You are seeking justification before yourself and before God. Therefore what you need here is above all action and not states of feeling."

The last notes of Lyubasha's aria melt away. She has curled herself up in a heap, is quite motionless. There is a long pause followed by the sound of a gay dancing song. This frightens her and she hides behind the well.

The door of the Sobakin house opens at the first bars of the music. At the entryway of the house are Marfa and her father. They are saying good-bye to Lykov, who quickly runs down the steps.

"Come tomorrow and bring Gryaznoy," sings Sobakin, leaning over the railing of the staircase. Beside him stands his beaming daughter. They are bathed in friendly light coming from inside the house. The picture is one of peaceful domesticity. Stopping for an instant near the well Lykov replies: "We'll come, we'll come!" None of them has the slightest suspicion of the impending disaster.

Naturally all this is included in the libretto of the opera and Stanislavski did not invent anything. But what the libretto actually says is, for example: "Lykov and Sobakin open the wicket gate", or "Bomeley comes out through his wicket gate and steals over to Lyubasha", or "Sobakin goes back into his house."

Stanislavski's art lay in his skill in plotting scenes and introducing the most subtle logic into all actions—this not only clarified each situation, it also endowed each one with great depth of meaning.

Next there follows an agitated *tremolo* in the music, accompanying the words: "So Grigori will come here tomorrow? Oh, why does that wretched man not come?" Then on the poison theme with its descending sequences, Bomeley creeps down the stairs.

It is quite dark on the stage now. At the well Bomeley gives Lyubasha the poison powder.

"Make the transfer as secret as possible, like thieves hiding near the well. It is clear that all you are doing is handing over a white envelope. *It* is playing the scene, not your face."

After this Lyubasha turns in the direction of Marfa: "Do not complain to me, my pretty one. I have paid for your beauty."

"Now stand up, you need hide no longer. Handle the powder with great care. Hold it up in Marfa's direction; lift it as if it were something weighty, After all, it is Marfa's life. . . ." After the words: "Take me to your lair, you German", Bomeley wraps the tottering Lyubasha in her fur coat, holds her firmly, and drags her into his tower. The light goes out in Bomeley's tower and also in the Sobakin house.

In the complete darkness the guardsmen return from their raid on Prince Gvozdev's home. They are hilarious, boisterous, and drunk. As they sing: "Eagles that gather in the heavens. . ." they dance a bit. They carry lanterns on their pikes which cast an uncertain light on the dark outlines of their figures.

The song swells, the drunken dancing of the dark figures grows more violent, creating an atmosphere of agitation and uneasiness for the end of the second act.

Act Three

In contrast to the chamber at Gryaznoy's with its picturesque angles, galleries and staircases, the bare, timbered walls of Sobakin's are very simple. The only furniture is the large tiled stove in the centre of one wall, benches at a table and along the sides of the room, and a spinning wheel with a stool beside the stove. There is a sideboard, and a painted chest near the door.

"They have everything stowed away in storerooms in chests," said Stanislavski. "On the surface they live very parsimoniously, they rather stress the simplicity of their circumstances. . . . Therefore the contrast will be all the greater for Marfa when she is taken out of this timbered cottage to the gilded chambers of the Tsar's palace."

Through a small square window covered with a sheet of mica the setting sun sends in a few sparse rays, throwing light on Sobakin and his two guests—Lykov and his friend Gryaznoy, who has the secret powder in his coat.

"Think how you feel," said Stanislavski when he was rehearsing Gryaznoy, "as you, with the fatal magic powder on your person. look at Marfa's affianced husband, and at her father, who rejected your suit for his daughter's hand. What an absurd fool this happy Lykov now appears in your eyes. You have only to drop the powder into the wine as soon as you find a suitable moment. That's why you are sitting here and listening to all the excitement and joys of this young man who has asked your advice. You do not have to *act* anything; all you have to do is see Marfa, put the powder into her wine. During the betrothal it will be even easier to do this, so the ceremony does not in the least disturb you. In any case the marriage will not take place."

The act begins with a big trio: Sobakin is seated under the ikons in the corner, Lykov is on his right and Gryaznoy, his left. Marfa is in the Parade of Maidens, from which the Tsar will pick his bride, so they will have to wait for the betrothal ceremony. Lykov, naturally, is upset by this, as is Gryaznoy. They both put their hopes on the fact that there are twelve maidens in the review, and not just Marfa. However, they are obliged to wait for the results.

"You have to be loosened up," said Stanislavski. "You are not at home on the stage. You keep wanting to project something. But what you should be is just yourself, as you are when you are at home alone, without even your wife about. Try to reach that state and stop thinking altogether about the audience. You have to get to a sense of truth such as you feel in ordinary life, but you keep pursuing some theatrical objective instead of one true to life. When you come onstage you instantly wind up some kind of coil in your back. With that you will always move on springs like a mannequin. But if you can succeed in feeling quite at home on the stage, even more at ease than in your own house, you will acquire a real sense of bliss. In that state you will wish to go on and on acting, whereas when you feel you are in a false position you want to escape from it as quickly as you can.

"Now what is your immediate objective?" asked Stanislavski, turning to Sobakin. "You have to cheer up Lykov. Try to sing to this end.

Lykov is merely thoughtful. Don't put on an aspect of sadness, or suffering. It is up to you, Sobakin, to convince Lykov—but this is a double game you are playing. You are, after all, a merchant, never forget that. On the one hand is Lykov, but on the other—the Tsar. You are not yet sure how things will turn out."

The rehearsal went on.

"No," interupted Stanislavski, "you are not giving out anything but sounds. You do not as yet need such large sounds for your feelings. Singing is beautiful only when it is natural and expresses something. But singing made up only of pretty sounds is anti-artistic because it is not sparked by inner feelings. You have a voice, a living organ which better than any instrument can express emotion, and you treat it like a trombone [Stanislavski was speaking here to the basso who sang the role of Sobakin]. This is unnatural and therefore you cannot speak expressively as in real life. The audience, which has come to the theatre and has never heard *The Tsar's Bride,* will have no idea of what it is about because with that kind of singing it is impossible to hear the words or know what they signify."

Then he got up and went over to Lykov.

"Right now I am Sobakin. Why don't you sing for *me?* You are intent on singing for the audience and you have turned your left shoulder to me. But your whole purpose is to 'get to' Sobakin, you have to find ways of reaching him so that you can marry Marfa. A voice is a very delicate instrument. Right now there was a tone of demand in it, a bit brazen. You should be more diplomatic in asking for your bride. . . ." (Here Lykov sang at Stanislavski.)

"No, you should sing with *modesty,* but don't just put on a show of modesty. As you are singing now, you might be asking Sobakin to give you a cat or a dog, but not a bride. The quality of your tone must convince me. It is all there in the music. What you have to do is to make the colorations in the music your very own.

"There, this time I believe you, you have achieved a tone quality that is yours, not just a mechanical one. If Chekhov could only be here he would go out of his mind with joy to hear how easily music prompts you to do what it takes years to learn how to do in a play. You took the quality of the tone from live feelings and did not just hammer it out."

Sobakin then sings: "Time was when I have sat at table one of twelve. . . ."

"Now paint me a picture with those sounds," said Stanislavski, "tell me how you liked to be one of twelve at table, how dignified you felt. Make full use of every phrase, as Shalyapin did. A tone may be metallic but it must have colour. And you cannot use the same coloration to sing about joy, worry, or a shrewd move. You should develop this technique of sound until it is automatic. But devote only fifteen percent of your attention to it, not ninety, as most opera singers do.

"Gryaznoy is gay and sarcastic. He is a member of the Tsar's guard, he represents power. With wicked calm he waits for developments; that is all he has to do. 'I proposed myself to be your friend,' Gryaznoy sings to Lykov. Do you feel that careless arrogance which should ring through those words?" Then, turning to Sobakin, Stanislavski said: "There is an operatic cliché for a nice little old man. He has a womanish smile. If he is angry he knits his brows. It isn't so in real life or in modern painting; tones are a combination of many colours. Goodness is not of just one size, it comes in various measurements. It is necessary to lay on a variety of colours for feelings too. You must quite cold-bloodedly weigh the advantages of being a father-in-law to the one or to the other. You are a shrewd business man and you like your bottle."

So it was that with the aid of many repetitions of sounds, words, thoughts, psychological shadings, physical relaxation, facial expressions and gestures, Stanislavski succeeded in achieving a finished performance of expressive simplicity for this small bit of the opera.

The anticipation of the results of the Tsar's review affected Lykov most of all. Then when Sobakin, who was not without inner agitation over the idea that he might become the Tsar's father-in-law, goes down to the cellar to fetch some mead, the two aspirants to the love of Marfa remain alone and a taut conversation between them takes place.

Lykov paces up and down the chamber (there are ten measures of music to express his uncertainty and doubts before his *recitative* begins). Gryaznoy remains in the same place covertly watching Lykov. Lykov sits down beside the stove and asks: "Tell me, Boyar, if you were, as I have been, accepted as the suitor of a girl whom you love, what would you do?" To ask such a question of Gryaznoy about his promised wife is the extreme of naïve blindness.

"Can you hear how diabolically arrogant Gryaznoy sounds in the music?"

Here Stanislavski threw himself full-length on the bench by the table, stretching out his long legs, wiggling his feet in a dance rhythm, almost clowning with them, thus showing Gryaznoy what his attitude should be.

"There are many tones in your reply: serious, ironical, agreeing— but no one can say whether you are speaking the truth or not."

Gryaznoy became self-assured, powerful, full of scorn for such a simpleton as Lykov, who when he is with him is more helpless than ever. Sobakin carries in the mead and three goblets. The three men are just lifting the wine to their lips when a deafening, warning chord stops them. Four measures of music send the men scurrying across the stage to the window, their quick movements clearly indicating the tenseness of the anticipation they all feel regardless of their superficial calm.

"The music hurries but you walk," said Stanislavski to the actress singing the part of Domna Saburova, as she enters.

The whole aria of Domna Saburova, who has just run over from the Tsar's review, is written in jerky form, conveying her physical state —she is out of breath, nervously excited: "Oh, goodness, let me catch my breath. . . ." Sobakin asks: "But where are the girls?" Domna: "They went to the dressing room . . . to take off their finery. . . . Oh goodness . . . what happiness . . . the Lord has sent me. . . ."

"No, your breathlessness is not right. 'I cannot look at anyone, I can only talk'. A person out of breath does not run, she tries to move as little as possible, she wants only to rest. You are not only out of breath, you are near fainting. You show no desire to catch your breath. You will have to work out a technique for breathlessness. Perhaps if you swallow it may help?" The actress insists it does not help.

"If it does not help, then I was wrong. Forget about it. Or else some of you will be saying that I told you to do so and so in this or that way. But I do not recall what I said. Evidently I made a mistake. When one is out of breath one tries to ejaculate a phrase as quickly as possible, then straightens up and tries to draw a breath. One may not even breathe in but just wag one's head. The point is, the pauses must not be those of ordinary speech. . . ."

Stanislavski suggested that Sobakin and Lykov sit Domna down at the table and pour her some mead, while Gryaznoy remains alone beyond the stove as a stranger separated from the family conversation about the wedding. Gryaznoy, however, can scarcely conceal his agitation. Like a beast of prey preparing to pounce, he follows every detail of the account of the Tsar's Parade of the Maidens.

To simple-minded Domna it seemed that when the Tsar talked and joked with her daughter Dunyasha he was so enchanted with her he would make her his wife. There was only one phrase in her story which related to Marfa: "But at your daughter," she said to Sobakin, "he looked with a searching eye." Those listening are immediately tense and keep their eyes glued on Domna's face as if there they could read their fate; Gryaznoy can scarcely breathe. But the foolish woman runs on and on about her own Dunyasha. She is positive she will become a Tsaritsa. Each one of the men concludes for reasons of his own that Marfa did not please the Tsar. Sobakin's face shows clearly that he is disappointed by her failure. Lykov's face brightens. Gryaznoy draws a deep breath and, stretching himself, strolls over to the window. He is not in the least interested in the delight of Domna.

The dark cloud has passed. All has happened for the best. Sobakin betrays some regret as he says: "Then, I suppose, the review is over?" But the confident manner of Domna makes the question seem superfluous. The weight of uncertainty has been dispelled. Everything now goes back, in the Sobakin house, to normal life. They can now begin to prepare for Marfa's betrothal to Lykov. As Sobakin leaves the room, following the still breathless and happy Domna, he says with a significant look: "I too am going. I have certain things to get out."

The two rivals are left together on the stage. Daylight has faded from the window, only a few red gleams from the setting sun are reflected on the tiled stove and the ikons in the darkened chamber. Now Lykov is again overcome with joy, while Gryaznoy is preparing the love potion for Marfa.

After Sobakin's parting words Rimski-Korsakov wrote eight measures in the score before the *recitative* of Lykov begins.

Stanislavski used this small space of time to create a scene crammed with inner activity. The soft, soothing melody induces Lykov to breathe freely once more. He turns his face to the ikons with a prayer of thankfulness and hope, crosses himself in a wide gesture, and stands motionless. Gryaznoy watches him, puts his hands behind his back and rocks on his heels. "Go ahead and pray—a lot of good that will do you", his self-confident figure seems to be saying.

All the following scene—Lykov's *recitative* and aria—is aimed at Gryaznoy, to whom Lykov trustingly confides his happiness.

Before the beginning of the aria there is a long prelude in a melodious, quasi-dance rhythm. Stanislavski, who designed definitely colourful patterns for every individual unit of a role, made Lykov almost dance with joy in accordance with the logic of his emotions. Gryaznoy idly looks on as he lolls on a bench near the stove. Stanislavski then has Lykov, so confident of his joy, go over and sit beside Gryaznoy as if he were a close friend. He sings to him about his agitation, he strokes Gryaznoy's leg carelessly stretched out along the bench and does not even notice the derision on his face.

The fixed, heavy look of Gryaznoy as he watches Lykov disport himself so childishly is far more powerful in effect than any stormy, temperamental actor's performance, because the significance of his look is quite clear. After his quiet reply to Lykov: "But I told you, did I not, that there was no need to grieve and groan in advance", and while he is saying: "At your wedding I shall get drunk", he throws one leg over Lykov's knee and says nonchalantly: "So I'll drink to you now. There is some mead."

"Keep looking at Lykov," said Stanislavski, "and be thinking all the while—'Oh what a little idiot you are'."

Lykov proposes to pour out the wine himself but Gryaznoy quickly intercepts him, saying: "See how dark it has grown!", and quietly takes a tray from the table with two goblets and a pot of wine. With cat-like steps he hurriedly carries it across the stage to the lighted window. This action proceeds to the accompaniment of the "poison theme" with which we have become familiar, and fixes the attention of the audience on Gryaznoy.

In the dark chamber illuminated only by a beam of light from the window Gryaznoy cautiously drops the powder into one of the goblets while standing with his back to Lykov, who is now seated at the table. Gryaznoy has no special need to hide anything from Lykov because the position of the table and the window at opposite sides of the stage was planned from the beginning just for this most important moment in the act. After carefully swishing the wine around so that the powder will dissolve more quickly, Gryaznoy slyly wipes his hands on the skirts of his kaftan. This further stresses the sinister and secret act he has committed.

A long pause ensues. Both men await developments: Lykov sits at the table immersed in thought, Grayznoy sways back and forth on his feet, looking at Lykov with derision.

The betrothal rite between Lykov and Marfa is about to take place. This is the finale of the act. Each person is waiting for the ceremony with external calm but inner agitation. They are placed at opposite ends of the stage.

The broad *andante* of the ceremonial music for the betrothal determines the movements of the participants. A bright A-major theme for all the strings pours in a great wave over everything and lends a festive, joyous air to the occasion.

The orchestra prelude runs for sixteen measures so that it is quite long enough to arrange for the stately entrance of the betrothal guests in keeping with the sedate manners of the ancient Russian rites.

"Everything must be in ritual order, just the way the priest reads the liturgy," said Stanislavski at the first rehearsals. "You must study the rite very carefully so that physically it will be part of you. Everything is done in pairs, the guests walk as they do in the procession of the Cross, quite solemnly, shoulder to shoulder as if they were bound together."

At the first sounds of the music for this scene a young girl appears on the threshold of the doorway carrying two candelabra with five lighted tapers in each. After the preceding dimness, the chamber is now lighted and assumes a festive atmosphere. After the girl with the candles comes Petrovna carrying a bearskin. This will be laid in the foreground in front of the table for the betrothed couple to stand on as they receive congratulations. Then Sobakin, father of the bride, enters together with Domna Saburova, who will serve as the proxy mother in the ceremony. They carry an ikon and a loaf of bread. After them comes the bride, accompanied by Dunyasha and other friends as bridesmaids.

As Marfa appears in the doorway Gryaznoy with friendly ceremony puts his arm around Lykov's shoulders and leads him over to her. Gryaznoy is the master of ceremonies now.

The bridesmaids come in all dressed in gaily-coloured printed linen sarafans. The bride and groom first make a low bow to Marfa's father, then to Domna Saburova, and kiss the ikon and the bread. As this ceremony ends Gryaznoy comes from behind the bridesmaids with the two glasses he has taken from the recess by the window and carries them to the young couple. This coincides exactly with the last chord of the processional music.

"The larger glass for the bridegroom," says Gryaznoy as he makes a sweeping bow to Lykov. Lykov firmly grasps his glass and looks questioningly at Marfa. "And less for the bride. . . ." This phrase is composed with high *tessitura* for the baritone, and as Gryaznoy sings it, it contains a tone of command. As if to say: "In this glass there is not only wine but happiness!" Meanwhile, looking deep into Marfa's eyes he offers her the other glass on the tray. This is the beginning of a most important moment, not only in this act but in the whole opera. Marfa drinks the wine—which seals her doom.

Such moments of wide significance Stanislavski polished to jewel-like perfection. Now the slightest gesture, or glance of an eye, was of great importance.

An agitated musical theme is heard six times before the moment when Marfa drinks the fateful potion. Gryaznoy has put into her drink the poison which Lyubasha obtained from Bomeley, but he believes that this is a love philtre which, with each drop she swallows, will confirm in her an overwhelming passion for him.

Lykov drains his glass in one gulp and puts it back empty on the tray.

"Pay no attention to that," said Stanislavski to Gryaznoy, "do not let your eyes leave Marfa's face. . . . And you, Marfa, have a chance to play with the glass."

Marfa hesitates, her glass is very large; she takes a swallow, then a little apologetically suggests she cannot drink it all; besides, the wine has a rather strange taste, yet she decides to drink some more and finally hands back to Gryaznoy the only partially-emptied glass. This gesture should coincide with the last chord of the music, and at the same time Gryaznoy brusquely moves the tray aside. Marfa's hand is still out-stretched as Gryaznoy sings: "The ancient custom is to drink it to the bottom."

"There is a dramatic pause here," said Stanislavski.

The music reveals everything to the actors: how to move, what the rhythm is, the kinds of emotions. Yet at this point the score says there is a pause—*fermata*. So the actors have to be guided both outwardly and inwardly by their own rhythm, and in accordance with what they do it will be immediately evident: Do they continue to be alive or does all life on the stage come to a standstill?

At this point the librettist puts in the directions for Marfa: "She drinks the whole glass of wine and bows." "Yet this particular scene is dominated by Gryaznoy, not by Marfa," said Stanislavski. "Her role is a passive one."

Stanislavski himself showed what to do in the pause. As the music stops he firmly goes to Marfa ("Gryaznoy is not conforming to the marriage ritual now," said he as he walked to her). He takes her glass, which she was raising irresolutely to her lips, and practically forces the wine down her throat the way one obliges a sick child to take his medicine. He tips the glass up, higher and higher, not giving her a chance to breathe, and then when it would seem it was completely drained he snatches it from her, looks into it (he is worried for fear some of the powder might be left in the bottom), heaves a sigh of relief, and with a satisfied smile puts it back on the tray. Then he returns to where he was standing and by his look shows that the ceremony will now go on. He bows serenely and begins to sing: "God grant that your house may always enjoy abundance. . . ." Marfa, bewildered, smiles; the guests are all happy—the bride drank the full measure of wine and therefore her life will be full and happy. Then come the congratula-tions. The ceremony continues against the background of a complicat-ed sextet and a chorus of women's voices.

The young couple is ceremoniously led beyond the table to the ikon corner. Those close to them—Sobakin, Domna Saburova, Dunyasha, Gryaznoy—stand around the table, forming a family group. The bridesmaids are at a distance. Deep bows are made. The couple bow to all of their friends. The whole sextet of congratulations is repeated twice, thus affording all the participants the opportunity to present their felicitations.

Stanislavski had each person presenting congratulations bow and kiss the groom, as the men did, or the bride, as the women did. At first it seems almost impossible to sing, kiss, and bow.

"What's the problem of giving a kiss when you are singing?" asked Stanislavski. "A group of actor-singers has the power to do anything. All you need to do is to be carried away by your possibilities. If you don't know how to do this, you must learn. Just choose the appropriate moment while you are singing. Make breathing pauses for yourself. Rimski-Korsakov would not have objected, provided they are put to artistic use."

With the last, long-drawn-out chord of the sextet everyone sits down on the benches around the chamber. There is a brief pause.

A sharp run of sixteenth notes from the orchestra galvanizes the scene. Everyone is on the alert. "It is time to Enjoin the Betrothed," says Domna Saburova, rising and beckoning the bridesmaids, "you support me." She moves to the centre stage in front of the table.

"Greet this proposal enthusiastically," said Stanislavski to the young women, who preen themselves a bit. "We don't need to know about the ethnological origins of the ceremony of Enjoining the Betrothed," he continued. "All we need to take is the essence of all the existing rites of this sort. We must have action, for without it the ritual would only be a bore. What would take in ordinary circumstances a half hour we must convey in one minute. Action on the stage must not be allowed to stagnate, but at the same time this should not be turned into a divertissement, an extraneous number."

This whole scene of Enjoining the Betrothed is very brief in Stanislavski's handling of it, especially in contrast to the preceding ceremonial. It is necessary to push the joyousness of the occasion to its culminating point because the tragic dénouement is close at hand. He developed the action gradually but with unrelenting and increasing speed, converting it into a dance as with every four measures, that is to say with each repetition of a sung phrase, more and more young women were added to the movement.

When the words addressed to Lykov are sung, Stanislavski instructed Gryaznoy to "go in and dance in place of the groom. You can do this with unbridled joy."

This singles out Gryaznoy on the forestage. First slowly, gracefully, then ever faster and with increasing abandon his figure in its red kaftan whirls wildly in and out of the groups of young women. This enhances the general liveliness of the atmosphere and heightens the tension still further.

Suddenly the singing is interrupted as the orchestra goes into a C-major *tremolo* which then moves, after Petrovna's words: "Boyars are here with a message from the Tsar", into a minor key. Against the background of this *tremolo* the ponderous Malyuta theme emerges.

Everyone who has been dancing is now rooted to the spot in attitudes of expectancy. Only the betrothed couple, absorbed in each other, remain seated at the table, not noticing as yet anything that is transpiring. "You will be the last to sense intuitively that a calamity has befallen you," said Stanislavski to them.

As Malyuta appears his sinister theme sounds. He suddenly fills the doorway like some predatory animal. He slowly crosses the threshold, bowing his head and tall hat to enter. He is followed by two ladies from the court, boyarinas, dressed in gorgeous gowns of gold tissue and wearing unusually high headdresses all decked with jewels. They place themselves on either side of Malyuta, a little to the rear of him, like two witnesses. Their aspect is forbiddingly official. Here all the young women run away from Malyuta towards the forestage where, with their backs to the audience, they drop to their knees and bow to the ground before him.

Over their forms Malyuta and the boyarinas are clearly visible to the audience. It is only now that Malyuta's first word is heard: "Vassili!" (as he addresses Sobakin).

He pronounces the word very deliberately as if enjoying the terror and anxiety which his fierce, penetrating look inspires. It is only now that Marfa and Lykov become aware of Malyuta and of what has happened.

Malyuta begins to speak, heavily stressing each syllable: "Our great Sovereign, Tsar and Grand Duke, Ivan Vassilievich. . . ." As he begins to speak Sobakin and all who have been standing sink to their knees, while Marfa and Lykov slowly rise and listen to the Tsar's ukase.

This great scene which is so stunning in every detail was planned by Stanislavski in place of the meagre directions in the libretto which read: "Enter Malyuta with boyars. Sobakin and the others bow low to him."

"Malyuta," said Stanislavski to the singer in that role, "you are promulgating a manifesto from the Tsar and every syllable is like a stone."

The Malyuta theme gradually swells. It sounds rather like a gospel reading in a church. Marfa and Lykov seem prisoners on trial who with horror begin to realize that these terrifying words have to do with them. "And will take unto himself as spouse your daughter Marfa. . ." concludes the announcement made by Malyuta, as he hands the document with the Tsar's seal to Sobakin.

At these final words Marfa rushes out from behind the table over to Malyuta, looking at him with horror, and then, turning away from him as if she had seen a ghost, she throws herself sobbing on her father's neck. Now the two boyarinas step forward. With fixed expressions on their faces they gently but firmly pull Marfa away from her father, and holding her by the arms lead her toward the door. Malyuta makes a deep bow to her. But at the door Marfa tears herself from the hands of the boyarinas and again rushes towards her father. The boyarinas once more take hold of her and lead her away, now broken in spirit and gazing back over her shoulder at her father and Lykov.

Sobakin makes the sign of the cross over her as she departs. Lykov rushes around looking for help to save her, support her, but no one can do anything for him.

Gryaznoy stands transfixed by the terrible blow.

Act Four

"The Gilded Cage" is what Stanislavski called this fourth act of *The Tsar's Bride*. The space is a low, vaulted chamber which contains the carved ivory throne of the Tsaritsa, and it has a small door covered in red cloth leading to the inner apartments. There are two narrow, deep-set windows covered with grilles—one looks into the palace proper and the other down a corridor. They throw a wan light onto the gleaming gold of the walls. The floor is covered with red cloth.

"The general mood of this act," said Stanislavski at the first rehearsals, "is that of anxiety, as it is in the house of a person who is dangerously ill, when every sound is listened to as coming from the chamber where someone is struggling to keep alive; when messengers are hurriedly despatched and people talk in whispers, anxiously looking at each other. After all, it is the Tsaritsa who is so ill; this is the palace—what a responsibility for everyone!"

In order to create this atmosphere, Stanislavski had the curtains opened with the first notes of the orchestra. The music for this act begins with a sharp F-minor chord from the brasses like a pitiful cry. This is answered, as if echoing it, by a softer chord from the strings like a heavy sigh. There are four measures of these pitiful exclamations from the brasses and four muted moans from the strings. Then begins an agitated back-and-forth melody between the contrabasses. One is aware of a kind of spasmodic haste in the music, which is played over twice in different tonalities. The special significance of the red door in the

centre of the set, behind which something is going on, is immediately
apparent as soon as the curtains are opened. A young woman, a court
attendant, slips out through the door and softly closes it behind her, and
then lays her ear to it. She is very worried. Another comes out with a
pitcher and quickly but quietly passes on into the corridor. Then a third
runs out, holding a handkerchief to her mouth to cover her sobs. She
leans her head against the frame of the door near the first young woman;
they both weep on each other's shoulders and softly enter the mysterious doorway.

During the last measures of the prelude Sobakin, broken by the
disaster which is befalling him, comes out of the Tsaritsa's inner
apartments. The singer playing this part must be able to express the
grief of a father, before whose very eyes his crazed daughter is dying
while he, utterly helpless, stands by.

Sobakin's aria had to be worked over with painstaking attention. It
is written in a *tessitura* that is so easy for a basso to handle that it offers
a great temptation to show off his voice and enjoy with admiration his
own vocal performance.

"Don't boom so loudly—your daughter is dying in the next room.
Your objective is not to display your voice but to use it as a means to
express your grief," said Stanislavski.

"What is the thread that runs through this scene—will she, or will
she not, die? Why have you appeared here? To seek relief from the sight
of the suffering that is torturing her. The inner course of your actions
will not be felt without a physical pattern. When you find that physical
direction everything else in this act will fall into place and your emotions will surge of their own accord. You can never build the right mood
if your physical basis for it is not right. Moods can take on a variety of
shadings according to your own inner state but the physical direction
remains unaltered and must be followed through any and all moods.
Therefore establish that physical direction first of all. This is particularly important when you have powerful expressions of grief, despair or
suffering because otherwise an actor is tempted to play those passionate
emotions for their own sake.

"If you came onstage just now with a true purpose, sat down for a
true reason, had a true inner vision of what is happening offstage—in
Marfa's room from which you have just emerged—then one action
would of itself follow another. This physical line is something you must
practice constantly, morning and evening. And it is absolutely necessary to know how to follow it in all moods, as your fantasy supplies you
with more and more given circumstances in which to move. From this
will arise the unconscious gesture as a result of 'sincerity of emotion'.
Bear this in mind and enhance what it is that gives rise to its being. If
your physical actions are truly based, your inner line of feelings will

follow. A part becomes ossified if an actor is careless about his gestures. That is why you are not allowed at this point to use any gestures at all. Try to act without moving at all. In this way your gestures will not become threadbare and later on the very gesture you need will be available."

Sobakin sits on a bench in the middle of the stage, facing the audience, and is immersed within the compass of his own thoughts. His deep concentration, meditation, complete obliviousness to all that is going on around him, his profound absorption in his thoughts and the images he is seeing in his mind's eye, make his aria gentle in sound and very expressive in word and feeling.

"If the public listens to this aria in complete quiet, if they remain motionless when it is over, do not even cough—then you will know that you achieved your objective. But if they break into applause that will mean that all you have done is to perform a vocal 'turn'," said Stanislavski in concluding the rehearsal with Sobakin.

Domna Saburova rouses Sobakin from his state of deep meditation, as she cautiously emerges through the mystery-shrouded door and comes over to where he is sitting, with the words: "Do not grieve so, God is merciful."

"You have come out from the Tsaritsa's chamber, but not for the purpose of comforting Sobakin," said Stanislavski to the singer in that role. "You must find a reason for coming out. You had something to do that is related to Marfa. Perhaps you came to get a towel you had forgotten and you will go back with it, but meantime you have seen grieving Sobakin so you seize the occasion to console him and get a brief respite for yourself. But you must not lose track of the main object of your attention which is beyond the wall of the chamber, that is to say: Marfa. She is not onstage yet she is playing the principal role here. This scene is just a brief rest for Sobakin and you."

Onstage are two people overwhelmed with grief, sitting beside each other. One of them tries to comfort the other, without really believing her words of consolation.

"Look at your partner's eyes," said Stanislavski. "No matter what you sing to him you should try to see how he has taken your words. It happens so often on the stage that one actor says something to another but then is not in the least interested in whether or not his partner has understood or accepted what has been said. . . . The fact that you may have stressed each phrase with a determined movement of your chin does not make it expressive. Obviously you are not in the right inner state."

"Alas, it is not so," replies Sobakin to Domna Saburova.

"Be sure to sing the thought which goes with those words—which your imagination prompts you to think. What do you mean by 'it is not so'? You think she will die, will be carried to her grave? That's what should be contained in those words. If you sing about what you yourself envision then I as a spectator will see the same thing. It may not be exactly what you see in your mind but I shall see something of my own, you will make me feel what you feel. Sing to my eyes, not to my ears."

The scene is full of anxious trepidation, fear of a calamity, watchfulness. In this tense atmosphere events now begin to unroll.

There is a rapid run of notes in the orchestra and out from the door, which up to now has been carefully closed, a young woman dashes hurriedly crying: "Boyarina, the Tsaritsa has awakened!" Again the same quick succession of notes in the orchestra and a guardsman rushes in from the corridor with the message: "A boyar is coming with word from the Tsar." The palace is full of confused running hither and thither.

"Don't be in such a hurry to make your entrance," Stavislavski called to the guardsman. "Make a pause of two seconds and then enter in the same rhythm as you will begin to sing. You need this expectant pause to prepare your entrance."

Sobakin looks expectantly into the corridor, at the farther end of which Gryaznoy appears. Accompanying his firm steps the orchestra produces abrupt flourishes in the brasses.

The two boyars now face each other. Gryaznoy is dressed in a ceremonial dark-blue-and-gold kaftan, with a wide rose-coloured belt into which a knife with an elaborately jewelled handle has been stuck.

A formal exchange of greetings takes place. Everything must be done with the utmost propriety in words and bows.

"Great restraint is needed, and elaborate diction. Also great consideration of rank. The two men stand there, filling up as much space as possible. First words are spoken, then a bow is made, and there is a wait until the return greeting has been given before another new one can be begun."

"My great greeting to Boyar Vassili Stepanovich [Sobakin]," sings Gryaznoy, stressing each word, and as he sings the whole phrase he slowly raises his arm, disengaging his hand from the long gold-tissue sleeve, and then slowly lets it fall and, leaning over, touches the tips of his fingers to the floor. After which he slowly stands up straight again.

"The deeper the bow," said Stanislavski, "the greater the worthiness and importance of the person to whom it is made."

"Our great sovereign has entrusted me, his slave, to carry this message," Gryaznoy continues. In demonstrating the manners of the Tsar's ambassador, Stanislavski with great dignity spread his whole hand out on his chest as the words "his slave" were sung to make quite clear what boastful pride was contained in this word "slave". When Sobakin discreetly tries to ask "who is the villain" who has poisoned the Tsaritsa, Gryaznoy stops him with such a forbidding official gesture that Sobakin, all embarrassed, quickly goes out and closes the door.

Gryaznoy remains alone on the stage. Back in the corridor the guardsmen of the palace patrol are sitting where they cannot see Gryaznoy and he can be by himself for a minute. His manner then changes abruptly.

"What is your objective in this last act?" asked Stanislavski. "Follow the pattern of your role. . . . You finished off Lykov. 'Now she is mine. She is the Tsaritsa but no matter—she is mine.' She is ill? For the first time now you hear that someone is weeping. Ah well, that's only the disturbance of love. It must be that Bomeley's philtre is at work and she is pining for you. The Tsar sent you with a message? Well, that was only a pretext to see her. Do not lose track of this sequence, of this complex path which is logical human behaviour—it is the only line of interest the theatre can offer. You will come to complete self-annihilation in this act, therefore the more imperious and self-confident you are at the beginning of the act the more richly effective will be the colours of your palette."

The majestic manners of the Tsar's ambassador vanish instantly when Gryaznoy is left alone. Like a thief, he moves cautiously to Marfa's door. The four measures of music that precede the singing give Gryaznoy the possibility of reaching the door and listening. The tremulous accompaniment of broken triplets convey his inner excitement and joy. Holding his ear to the door and trying to restrain the beating of his heart, Gryaznoy begins to sing to the effect that Marfa's illness is attributable to love and that he would give half an arm just to look at her "if only once more".

Marfa's voice is heard: "Let me go, I want to hear it all myself." This makes Gryaznoy quickly jump away from the door and return to the spot where he was standing before.

Marfa, with tottering steps, enters the scene. Her waiting women hold her up. The stage is quickly filled with the boyarinas who attend her. Near her are Sobakin, Domna Saburova, Dunyasha. The Tsar's ailing bride has appeared.

"There is no reason to feign madness in your role. The moment when you are to pass out of this world to another is that of gradual extinction. First you must find the physical pattern of an invalid, his weakness," said Stanislavski. "At this point a sick person wishes to appear strong. You must know what movements are difficult for you to make, what you are able to do, what you are not. An actor must sense his condition of weakness throughout his own body, except for the muscles which are to be tensed for singing.

"No emotions are necessary at all, just logical physical actions. Then your nature will assert itself and they will come of their own accord. This is extremely important: in order to play a sick or aged person one must find the centre of gravity in one's body, concentrate all attention on one's body so as not to fall. It is very difficult to get up; it is easier to move in a crooked rather than a straight line. Your rhythm is low, it is dangerous to turn, especially. If an abrupt turn is made, you may fall. It is also dangerous to sit down; you may also fall doing that. Always begin by finding some point of support so that you will be able to turn around. Your gait will be that of a slow trotter, almost that of a drunken person. I am giving you the extreme symptoms of your illness. They will have to be reduced later and made to conform to the music.

"Plan the physical side of your role exactly and do not overlook even the briefest interval in it—that is the main objective required of an actor.

"The particular quality of your role as the ailing Marfa lies in the fact that your line of concentration on objects is inconsistent, broken. Your state is made up of images passing through your imagination. As these change you think you see now Gryaznoy, now Lykov. Your memories seem to be your present realities—a dream. You are not aware of the varying degrees as you pass from one image to another as you would be if you were in good health, yet you test each image thoroughly and attentively and in this you are acting like a normal person. You must pay strictest attention to these changing images and remember only that your back and legs are weak. You must never for a moment think of your good looks. If an actress may ever do that it is only when required by her role, but here it would be unbearable."

Now Marfa has come onstage and after her Domna Saburova in a state of alarm with a number of young women (a chorus of women's voices). Marfa has been able to dash through the door and practically collapse on one end of the bench in centre stage. She is surrounded by the young women, who sing: "Bethink yourself, Tsaritsa, it is not good for you to allow yourself to be thus disturbed. . . ." "Let me go, let me go, I tell you. . . ." says Marfa, pushing her way through the ring of young women and forcing herself to walk to the throne, on which she sits down, as if to rest after a great effort. Stumbling triplets in the score imitate very well her uncertain, hurried steps.

Marfa is on the throne, dressed in a heavy raspberry-velvet robe, shot with gold thread, in which her little form is quite submerged. She has a royal crown on her head, with a rim of pearls. Pearls hang in clusters on either side of her head, she has various necklaces on and all these ornaments only serve to make her face seem more exhausted, tortured, ill. Gryaznoy is standing on the threshold of the archway leading into the corridor, feasting his eyes on Marfa.

"Remember that you have not seen Marfa since she was taken away to the palace and all this time you were certain that she was longing for you," said Stanislavski. Marfa's suite are all placed around the throne. Sobakin and Domna Saburova stand on either side of it. All are ready and waiting to hear the message from the Tsar.

"Come close, Boyar, I am listening," sings Marfa. Again the orchestra plays ceremonial flourishes in the course of which Gryaznoy comes forward and kneels before the throne, making a sweeping bow to the ground. Then, having stood up, Gryaznoy sings that the Tsar has ordered enquiries to be made about the Tsaritsa's health.

Marfa's replies are snappish, impatient, agitated. She is even angry and ends with the words: "This is all lies and inventions." Again flourishes are heard—Gryaznoy's theme—but now they are pitched in a minor key. He will now speak of how, with his own hand, he killed the villain Lykov.

"Sing this with great pleasure, hasten to impart the good news to Marfa," said Stanislavski.

Gryaznoy stands facing Marfa. Outwardly he is calm, but one hand plays imperceptibly with the handle of the knife in his belt.

"No gestures! No noise with your feet, no shifting your weight from one to the other. Everything is monumental in size now and all is contained in your eyes and your words. But then you must show us *how* you killed Lykov. Cleave the air with a mighty blow as you sing: 'Straight to the heart I struck him'. You draw the picture with your words and also with a clear gesture so that Marfa will have a real reason for fainting."

Marfa, who has raised herself and leaned forward as she heard the terrible words and saw the dreadful gesture, now falls back on the throne in a dead faint. This is the signal for the beginning of the quintet and chorus: "Our suffering Tsaritsa is undone!"

At first Gryaznoy is quite bewildered. "What is the matter with her?" he asks with dismay of those around him. Marfa's attendants rush to her as she half lies on the throne and carry her over to the bench in the centre of the stage. Stanislavski planned exactly who would carry Marfa and from which side each person would come. Gryaznoy supported her head.

"Carry her with great reverence, carefully, as if she were a sacred relic. At this point the bearing of each person is important. An angelic soul, beloved of all, is about to depart. Each must find his own appropriate action, all must participate. If you do not know what to do," said Stanislavski to the women's chorus, "don't just stand there. Try to think of something helpful to do. . . . You may weep, but you must never show your tears to the audience. On the contrary you must conceal them. That has a much more powerful effect."

Marfa has been carried over to the bench, where she lies stretched out like a corpse. The complicated ensemble of quintet and chorus is sung in low tones, almost in a whisper so as not to disturb the invalid.

At her head are her father and Domna Saburova, at her feet, Gryaznoy and Malyuta.

All the women are at the right of the audience and the men at the left. A crowd of guardsmen is milling around the door leading to the corridor. Recumbent Marfa and Gryaznoy kneeling at her feet are a bond between the two large groups of men and women. During the ensemble singing nearly everyone has been motionless except for cautious attempts to see Marfa.

This ensemble is very difficult from the musical standpoint. The chorus and the soloists come in at different times and in order not to miss a cue the singers usually, quite openly, watch the conductor's baton. But Stanislavski was adamantly opposed to this. He demanded a complete knowledge of the score so that all cues were picked up by ear.

"You may check on yourselves, but you must know how to look at the conductor with side vision and only when absolutely necessary. You will have to work out a basis for any such glances and incorporate them in the score of your role. On the stage now it is necessary to maintain an atmosphere of extremely tense attention concentrated on the dying Marfa. At this point any absentminded looking-around would only destroy the atmosphere. There is not one person here who is indifferent to Marfa's fate. Therefore you have to know the score of the music so well that you do not have to worry about your cues. You must not be consciously thinking about the music or there will be no creativeness onstage."

The Tsaritsa regains consciousness. They raise her up carefully, putting cushions under her head and at her back so that she can sit up. Gryaznoy tries to catch her glance in order to get her attention. Marfa, as if waking from a deep sleep, looks around at everyone in the room with an indifferent gaze. Then suddenly, seeing Gryaznoy, she comes to life, leans toward him and takes his hand.

Gryaznoy, transfixed with joy, carefully takes her little hand in his. Everyone on the stage waits motionless to see what will happen. And suddenly Marfa sings in a caressing tone: "So you are still alive, Ivan Sergeyevich [Lykov]?"

"Draw back as if you have been given a blow," said Stanislavski, "but do not let go of Marfa's hand." A shudder runs through all on the stage and they dare not move. Marfa continues: "Ah, Vanya, Vanya, what dreams come to one's mind. . . ."

Gryaznoy cannot bear to see the look in Marfa's eyes. He has realized not only that he is not loved but also that he is not recognized, but they remain hand in hand and he cannot let go. It is only after his words: "Come to yourself, Tsaritsa!" that Gryaznoy frees his hand. Now we come to the next phase of his emotions. "These disturbances of love" have proved a myth. Gryaznoy must realize that Bomeley has played him false.

"You are obliged to find the cause of this disaster. A person always seeks to find it outside himself, in circumstances, in other people. Right now you think that Bomeley is the cause. You transfer to him all of your hatred rather than blame yourself."

During Marfa's talk Gryaznoy has remained on his knees before her. But when, in his imagination, Gryaznoy is conversing with Bomeley, Stanislavski had him bow down closer to the floor in order to express more powerfully his torturing search for some way out of his intolerable condition.

Then Gryaznoy is caught up in a wave of courage publicly to confess everything. Stanislavski sought to make this moment of confession significant, even with a touch of grandeur, and to this end had the singer spiritually and physically brought as low as possible. Marfa turns her face away, exhausted by her own effort, after the final words: "Then Gryaznoy came to the palace and said that he had murdered you. What a friend! Oh Gryaznoy! You certainly found a way to console a bride." She sings them almost with indifference. She falls once more into a state of apathy. Yet those words of hers, to everyone's astonishment, incite Gryaznoy to make his confession.

"You are coming now to the tragic moment," said Stanislavski. "You are making a public confession of your crime. To act this highly dramatic moment in your role you must first of all relax all muscular tension. The more dramatic your situation, the more it will require of your temperament and powers of expression, thus the freer and more flexible you must be. Therefore as you approach this place, check on your muscles and your whole body. Above all avoid clenched fists. Like corks they will bottle up your whole temperament. Everything gets stuck right in those fists. Concentrate all the power of expression in your eyes and in your words. Be sure there are no tense muscles in your face either.

"Try not to produce strong feelings but rather reinforce the image you hold in your imagination. You will be tempted to *show* 'how I suffered, how I loved, how I am suffering now' but what you must try hard to do is draw a picture of all that happened to you. You must explain to everyone what love it was that brought you and others such pain, and then you yourself will begin to feel that pain. You must pay tremendous attention to the image which rises before your eyes. You must *convince* everyone so that we can comprehend what happened to you."

Gryaznoy resolutely gets to his feet and with the words: "Indeed! Gryaznoy will yet console you. . . ." He moves to the centre of the stage. He looks around at everyone (Stanislavski insisted that Gryaznoy see everyone's eyes and rivet the attention of everyone on himself) and begins his confession: "I am a sinner accursed. I vilified Lykov falsely, I destroyed the bride of the Tsar."

Those present are stunned. All this is so difficult at first to grasp that no one moves. Malyuta, anxious to smother at once a terrible scandal and save his friend while it is still possible, grasps Gryaznoy by the arm: "Grigori, what's the matter with you?" His fellow guardsmen who are thronging around the entrance also try to stop him: "Come to your senses, you are only destroying yourself." But Gryaznoy does not care, he simply waves them away as if they did not understand anything. Marfa's delirium begins again and everyone's attention, so concentrated on Gryaznoy, is diverted briefly to her. "You say that we must not believe in dreams. But it is not a simple one." Marfa's ravings, her pitiful aspect only deepen Gryaznoy's remorse. He moves swiftly to her side and leans over her (there is a movement among her attendants as if to protect her from this madman) and he says: "Oh martyred one, it is I that destroyed you. It was I, I *myself* who gave you the poison."

"Use these words to express how you suffer for her sake," said Stanislavski in prompting Gryaznoy. Now Gryaznoy's confession has gone too far and Malyuta can no longer save him from his guilt.

"Madman! What has he done?" exclaims Malyuta, turning away from him. The word "madman" is taken up by Gryaznoy. This word helps him to explain everything. "Yes, I am a madman, she long ago drove me out of my mind."

"Now, convince everyone, make them understand you so that they cannot forgive you. Sing as if you were not here in a chamber but out on the Red Square. Everyone must hear you. But still remember that volume of sound is not what impresses, you gain power in relation to your expressiveness.

"The great secret here is to keep your body, above all your hands, free from all tenseness. The more powerfully you can play this scene, the more relaxed must be your body, especially your hands. When Salvini suffocated Desdemona his fingers touched her throat without the slightest tenseness and the audience was struck with horror. You must express all the power of your inner compulsion, your emotions, your thoughts by means of your words as you sing them."

Heavy, resolute chords accompany the theme of Gryaznoy's confession. These chords then blend into agitated runs. The swirl of these sounds requires the actors onstage to make broad, firm gestures. Stanislavski said:

"During this music no one may make a shallow gesture. Any gesture must be above the shoulders and over the head. If you cross yourself when you sing: 'God is my witness, I myself was deceived' then do it with a most sweeping firm gesture in rhythm with the music. Don't blur, don't skimp, don't make gestures that look as though you were catching flies.

"Here you have two definite objectives. The first is to explain to everyone that you did not intend to poison her but win her by means of a love philtre. The second is to make a picture of how you love her, 'as the wild wind loves its liberty'. Therefore do not act emotions or suffering here but picture the wild wind in its free course. Imagine that you have wings and are in flight.

"Keep the focal point of attention very high, as high as the dome over the audience, or the sky. If you approach this part of your role in the right way you can move as you please, make any gestures, even exaggerated ones, with your arms, for now I will believe everything you do."

The emotional confession of Gryaznoy is interrupted by the indignant chorus of all those present on the stage. "Be silent, wicked man. How dare you speak thus in the presence of our Tsaritsa. Take him away."

With the last chord of this chorus threatening arms are stretched in the direction of Gryaznoy, standing in the centre of the stage. It is like a tableau. But Stanislavski does not let it become static. Gryaznoy has to be convinced by his own eyes of the menace of the crowd.

"The power of your look should be such that, at first, the threatening arms are lowered and the eyes of the crowd cannot meet yours. Finally they are all turned away from you. All this must be very distinct."

This scene serves as a transition to Marfa's aria. The whole attention of the audience has been fixed on Gryaznoy and the crowd, while Marfa, still sitting where she was, has been forgotten. Stanislavski kept everything focused on Gryaznoy up to the very moment when Marfa begins to sing. Her first words are quite unexpected: "Ivan Sergeyevich, shall we go into the garden?" This is in powerful contrast to the preceding scene and is enhanced further by the facial expressions of everyone on stage.

Now Marfa is the centre of attention: "Do you not wish to catch up with me now?" she asks Gryaznoy.

Stanislavski suggested to her that she run to the corridor, but in considering the logic of her conduct, he asked:

"Can you run, when we have just seen that you walk with difficulty? No. You may take several steps and begin to fall. Gryaznoy, standing nearby, will take hold of you and not let you fall to the ground. Domna Saburova, Petrovna, and Marfa's attendants will rush to her as she totters in her weakness, take her from Gryaznoy, and try to seat her again where she was before, but she, seeing something on the floor near the footlights, will insist on moving forward.

"Marfa will sit down on the floor where she saw a little flower. Petrovna and the young women lift her onto a stool and put cushions around her for her to lean on. She is now in the very foreground and, from the point of view of singing, in a most advantageous position. But Marfa is not able even to sit up. She has to be supported all the time. Therefore, she is surrounded by a group of women, with Domna Saburova in charge, and they watch every movement she makes.

"Recall," said Stanislavski during a rehearsal, "what is done for a seriously ill person, how to help, how to anticipate his slightest desire. But at the same time do not attract the attention of the audience to yourselves. Do everything practically imperceptibly, because it is Marfa who is the chief person in this scene and all attention must be centred on her. She has to sing a difficult aria while at the same time creating the impression of a weak, dying woman. The public must understand how weak, how close to death Marfa is by means of your help to her, your actions."

All the rest of the crowd onstage are motionless, with their eyes fixed on Marfa as she picks up from the floor a wisp of something and handles it as if it were a little flower.

Marfa's last aria consists of a series of "changing images", as Stanislavski called them. A little bell-like flower, an apple tree, the garden she sang about in the second act. From all these dreams she would come back to reality: "Alas, it is a dream, it is a dream," and again would recur the visions of the vault of heaven, a cloud, which to her seemed to resemble a golden bridal crown.

The whole aria is a tale told by Marfa to Lykov who she seems to feel is close beside her. Here Stanislavski made Gryaznoy assume the role of Lykov. Going down on one knee out on the forestage with his profile to the audience, he does not take his eyes off Marfa's face; it is as though he is taking farewell of her. This should enhance the moral torture Gryaznoy is undergoing and prepare him for the words following the aria: "No, it is not to be borne."

Marfa looks once into Gryaznoy's eyes and leans towards him before the words: "Alas, it is a dream." Gryaznoy feels that she is speaking to him in a loving way. But then, when she recognizes Gryaznoy, she screams and hides her head on the breast of her old nurse Petrovna.

"What you need here are very distinct objects of concentration: flowers, a terrible dream, a little cloud, but no suffering, self-pity, or sentimentality. You have to see all these objects in your imagination and vividly reproduce them in the words of your song. I, as a spectator, will understand what they are when you yourself see them and reproduce them in words and sounds."

The climax of Marfa's aria is reached with the words: "See, over

there, a golden crown like a cloud up in the sky." There is an exaltation
here. You hear it in the melody and in the orchestra, and it cannot fail to
affect the conduct of the actress who is experiencing a powerful emotion, who senses a flooding in of spiritual and physical powers.

"This is your strongest point and you cannot remain in a half-re-
cumbent position. The setting must be changed. Yet it would be a false
note if you were to get to your feet now. All you can do is struggle to
your knees and stretch your arms to heaven, but you cannot have the
strength to do more than that if you are to retain your image of being
mortally ill. Indeed you have to play the whole act in a sitting position.
This will be a test of your art as an actress and as a singer. To sing with
his two feet firmly planted on the floor is not such a spectacular
performance for a professional singer," said Stanislavski, with a touch
of ridicule.

The end of the aria tapers off and the last A-flat has a dying sound
like the weakness that follows a strong emotion.

Having sung her aria Marfa leans back against the women who
support her; she is now quite bereft of strength. The audience can see
that her end is near.

During the finale of Marfa's aria and her subsidence, Lyubasha,
chief instigator of what is occurring, is seen carefully threading her way
from the depth of the corridor. She is dressed in a black sarafan, not
unlike the habit of a nun, with a white kerchief on her head. The
monastic austerity of her appearance contrasts sharply with the vivid
colours of the palace apartments.

The final chord of Marfa's aria has died away. All during the aria the
women's chorus, surrounding Marfa, has been weeping. Some watch
her, pressing their handkerchieves to their lips in order not to sob out
loud; others turn away to conceal their tears. Each figure in her own
way is expressive of compassion for Marfa. Here Stanislavski established a plan for the external appearance of each figure, each group
with a variety of poses, turns, and slants.

The tense immobility of the picture is shattered by Gryaznoy's:
"No, it is not to be borne. Lead me, Malyuta, before the dread Tri-
bunal. . . . But first let me settle matters with Bomeley."

"Rush over to Malyuta," said Stanislavski, "beg him, as a friend, to
help." Malyuta is dressed magnificently in a rose-and-gold kaftan,
the colour of which contrasts trenchantly with the implacable
expression on his red-bearded face—he is now unapproachable to
Gryaznoy.

A curt nod from Malyuta and four of the guardsmen lay hold of him.
He is held firmly. He is bewildered, looks around helplessly.

There is a brief pause, during which Lyubasha emerges into the
centre of the stage from behind the crowd of guardsmen surrounding

Gryaznoy. Her entrance is heralded by powerful resonant sounds from the brasses in the orchestra, reminiscent of the beginning of the act. "Settle matters with me whom you have forgotten, my dear."

"The figure of doom has appeared," said Stanislavski, "but beware of playing her as an evil woman. Lyubasha has not come here to avenge but to show her love. Appeal to Gryaznoy's heart, pull out all the stops, do anything to reach him. But when you see that he has completely hardened his heart against you, beg for death," added Stanislavski in directing Lyubasha. By this means he was trying to steer her away from playing the usual hand-me-down figure of an evil woman composed only of the dark tones of rage and revenge.

"The very plot of the play forces you to seek revenge, that is why it is so easy to slip into a cliché character. Look for contrasting tones—that is why I suggest that you show your love for Gryaznoy at this point. 'You destroyed my heart, you had no pity on my tears or prayers', you sing. This hints at revenge and rage, but if you fill those words with love you will make your character more lifelike."

With her last words: "Kill me, you murderer", Lyubasha opens wide her arms, throws her head back, and courageously awaits her death.

"You beg for death when you realize that you are hateful to him."

Gryaznoy tears himself loose from the hands of his guards and with a sweep of his arm plunges his knife into Lyubasha's bosom. Of course it seems like a powerful blow whereas in reality he scarcely touches her. Lyubasha falls at first onto a bench, then with great effort lifts herself with both arms and says: "Thank you, straight to the heart" and softly sinks to the floor, turning over gracefully as she falls.

She lies prone, her arms stretched out, on the threshold of the corridor, with her head towards the public.

Stanislavski paid particular attention to these scenes of falling, dying, fainting.

"The public remembers this sort of thing very well, therefore the technique of its accomplishment must be so perfected that actors know how to perform it all with grace, gently, avoiding all naturalistic and coarse effects."

That is why he taught his actors how to fall by dividing the action into consecutive parts, making it possible for them consciously to control every turn of the body and slowly relax every tension.

At the moment of the stabbing, all onstage turn away with horror, cover their face, and it is only after Lyubasha falls to the ground that they collect themselves and cry: "Heavens, he has killed her." The guards now rush at Gryaznoy but he stops them with a sweep of his knife. He is now a terrifying sight, a violent madman. But when his eyes fall on Marfa, his rage subsides. His words: "Let me say farewell to her" sound like a meek request and he does not even notice one of the guards stealing up behind him and tearing the knife from his hand.

As he approaches Marfa, a ponderous D-minor chord from the orchestra seems to bear down on Gryaznoy, forcing him to his knees.

He kneels near Marfa and his last words are: "Innocent martyr, forgive me. . . ." Then he makes a long bow to the ground in front of her.

Marfa, no longer able to grasp what is going on, answers in transparent, weakly resonant tones: "Come tomorrow, Vanya"—and, leaning back in the arms of her attendants, she dies. Everyone onstage falls onto his knees. Gryaznoy's eyes are fixed on the shining, smiling face of Marfa, who appears to be dreaming. The curtain slowly closes on the tableau.

This production of *The Tsar's Bride*, which opened on November 28, 1926, was proclaimed as an historic event.

Izvestia had this to say: "The day of the premiere . . . of *The Tsar's Bride* is a memorable date in the history of Russian opera. This performance not only brushes aside all the old traditions of opera that made it merely a concert in costumes, it also breaks open new paths, lays the first stone in the edifice of an Opera Art Theatre. . . . The production is cast in the spirit of artistic, psychological realism—a form thoroughly explored in theatres of drama, but opening a new era in opera. . . .

"Of course, it was only with sensitive and flexible young people, not vitiated by the old routines of the operatic stage, that this great and patient teacher and his assistants could accomplish what up to now has been within the reach of only a few highly gifted opera artists. His Studio . . . thus becomes the first school for the training of actors in opera. It is necessary to say that in the cast of *The Tsar's Bride* no one gave evidence of outstanding talent. Nevertheless all of them (there are no smaller or larger roles) maintained the highest level of mastery in acting even if the vocal side of their accomplishment was somewhat weaker.

"In the first place the synthesis achieved of singing, clear enunciation, intelligible recitation, and lively rhythmic movements makes the chorus a living entity on the stage. . . ."

There were many other such reviews in journals of criticism and music. One of them wrote:

"The Opera Studio of Stanislavski carries within itself the pledge of a great future and leads us to believe that its achievement will not only forward the perfecting of operatic art but will as well provide many practical ways of instilling qualities of inner musicianship in many other fields of contemporary theatre."

4

La Bohème

PUCCINI DIED IN 1924, and his opera *La Bohème* was included in Stanislavski's list of productions soon after. The first performance was given on April 12, 1927.

The choice of this opera was not accidental. Puccini rejected traditional operatic forms and his music followed very closely the intent of the text, the development of a subject. He was thus very close to Stanislavski in his creative ideas.

"I look upon Puccini as a composer especially suited to our purposes," said Stanislavski. "He had great feeling for the stage. His music is closely knit with the words, and the combination of them results in a compact unity. Puccini was a profoundly theatrical person and that's what makes his compositions especially valuable."

Stanislavski well understood and appreciated Puccini as a composer who wrote music for action on the stage and who kept this purpose always in the forefront of his mind.

"When he was asked by a friend whether, when he was composing an opera, he first heard the music or envisioned the stage, Puccini replied: 'I see, first of all I see! I see people, the colours, the gestures of the actors. I am a man of the theatre. . . . If I do not succeed in seeing . . . the stage in front of me, I do not write, I cannot write a single note.' "

This reply is evidence of the creative link between Puccini and Stanislavski, who asserted:

"A singer must always see in his mind's eye the thing about which he is singing. The incontrovertibility of such a position is obvious, even though so few singers as yet avail themselves of this powerful means of enhancing their vocal expressiveness."

The whole musical texture of *La Bohème*, which flows uninterruptedly and easily from one mood to another, contrasts sharply with the operas of Puccini's predecessors with their refined, involved musical forms, the special set pieces in the score, the resulting pauses.

Stanislavski and his pupils were now faced with the task of acquiring a whole new style of operatic action on the stage.

The blending in Puccini's music of Italian ardor with French grace, of broadly sad yet tenderly lyric impulses of the heart, provided an atmosphere on the stage completely in contrast to that of the classic Russian operas. So the work on *La Bohème* was devoted to searching for a style, for new methods of singing and action, which would create this new atmosphere in which the singers would live and move.

We had to reproduce the life of the Latin Quarter in Paris, with its students and artists. We had to play demonstrative Frenchmen and learn how to sing in the Italian manner, although the text would be sung in Russian. After *The Tsar's Bride*, in which we represented our 16th-century Muscovite ancestors, phlegmatic or passionate Russians, we had to metamorphose ourselves into contemporary Frenchmen.

Yes, really contemporary Frenchmen, because Stanislavski decided to transfer the action from the 1840's to the beginning of the 20th century. He did not do this in order to go contrary to the author's ideas but to enlarge our understanding of them.

Stanislavski said: "Let us play *La Bohème* as if the action were taking place in the Paris of today. After all, the lot of talented young people in Paris now is the same as it was in the middle of the last century."

In this handling of the plot Stanislavski was not at variance with Henri Murger, author of *Scènes de la vie de Bohème*, who wrote in the preface to his novel: "The Bohemian milieu of the present book has a long history. It is a kind of life that has existed everywhere and in all epochs and may claim noted antecedents. Bohemian life represents a wide field for testing the relationship between art and life; it can lead to the Academy of the Immortals, to the flophouse, or to the morgue."

The carefree life of the main characters of the work is full of warm simplicity, great emotions, profound thoughts. This lends significance to the problems propounded by the play. Incidentally, Stanislavski never chose works that were meaningless and shallow for his productions. He was able to endow every performance with significant and valuable ideals; he knew how to find great thoughts in what appeared to be simple scenes and he always guided each play and all of his actors along the high planes of thought and feeling.

Act One

Two young friends—the one a poet, the other a painter—are living in a mansard apartment looking out over the roofs of Paris. These roofs, lightly powdered with snow, are visible through a huge window in their attic apartment. This window lets light spill into the poverty-stricken quarters of the "future celebrities", as they naturally conceive themselves to be, but also a lot of cold in winter.

In the libretto the setting is described as: "... a table, a small bookcase, a small sideboard, four chairs, an easel, a bed, scattered books, portfolios, two candlesticks, two doors, one in the centre, the other to the left. A fireplace is on the left."

If one followed those directions one might concoct a cozy little room for a young artist. The author of the libretto did not dare point up the "carefree poverty" in its true colours.

For Stanislavski the mantelpiece, sideboard, bed, and bookcase in this mansard room were not acceptable. They would interfere with, becloud, the main idea of the play: that gnawing poverty often lives side by side with carefree openhandedness; that even in a bare, uncomfortable attic room gaiety and humour and even the tenderest love can and do exist.

"That is where the poetry lies," said Stanislavski to the actors and V.A. Simov, the designer of the sets. "A mantelpiece on the stage—that is too hackneyed," he went on. "We have no need of that at all. When you light a fire in it the place instantly becomes warm and cozy. But since we are laying the action in contemporary Paris, in those mansard rooms, as in our attics in Moscow, there would be little iron stoves. Let us exchange our mantelpiece for a three-legged iron stove. . . ."

One of the men usually sleeps on some sort of long packing-case, covered with a blanket, and the other on an old divan. We had to find one which had been thrown out as useless, with some of the springs and stuffing coming through. But the blanket covering it could be a decent one. There is one table in the room, small, delicate, gilded; one wonders how it happens to be here. One leg has come off, and a rough stick has been jammed in to replace it. That is all the furniture. Pictures by the painter in the art nouveau style are on the walls; and the manuscripts of the poet are kept under the divan. Some glasses, plates, and one very simple candlestick are all on the windowsill.

The wall to the right of the audience slopes upwards, as it is part of the mansard roof. For this reason the whole set looks rather like a cross-section of a cardboard doll's house, with a large window through which one can see a panorama of Paris wreathed in smoke. There is a cold sunset sky hanging over the city. It is Christmas Eve.

The two friends are at work. With his legs wrapped in a blanket Rodolphe is sitting on the divan contemplating the roofs of Paris. Several sheets of paper lie in front of him on the table. Marcel, wrapped in a shawl, is standing at the easel with his palette in his hand.

There is no overture in *La Bohème;* the curtain rapidly opens with the first notes from the orchestra. The opera begins with forty measures in a very quick tempo—*allegro vivace*—and in three-eighths time, like a fast waltz. The audience has to have time to take in the setting, so that from the very first words it will understand what is going on onstage.

"Whose music is that," Stanislavski asked, "which is now prompting our feelings and how are you reacting to it?"

The music is conveying some kind of tension, force, agitation. A rapid melody rises with the flutes and strings and persistently repeats part of a scale over and over as if knocking in one and the same place. The hoarse bassoons, together with cellos, interrupt this melody with a kind of shivering which reminds one of the state which prompts the words "Brr . . . but it's cold!"

The question now is how the actors are to respond by their actions to this music.

There are the two characters onstage. Of course the music could apply to both of them. In it one senses the drive, the excitement deriving from work, but also the cold which makes one shiver and almost hop up and down. How can the actors convey this? Stanislavski, in directing an opera, reasoned this way:

"The music presents to you your inner state, the shades of your emotions, thus the inner rhythm of your life. But a driving rhythm is not necessarily expressed in energetic external gestures. A person can be full of drive and inwardly excited while remaining completely motionless.

"In order to help the audience figure out the situation, their attention must not immediately be divided in attempting to keep track of both characters.

"Let us, for the time being ignore Rodolphe, who is externally calm, and turn the music of the beginning of the act in the direction of Marcel," proposed Stanislavski. "With impatience, even a touch of violence, he is applying his chilled paint to his canvas. That accounts for the persistence, the annoying repetitions of the melody. You keep painting over the same place and you still cannot get it right! There is a strong draught coming from the window, your feet are freezing, and your fingers stiff with cold. The poet has an easy row to hoe—he can sit there on a divan with his legs wrapped in a blanket and ponder his verses while looking out over the roofs of Paris. But you, Marcel, have to mix your paints, which have thickened with the cold, and blow on your stiff fingers. So go ahead and do that in the rhythm prompted by the music. There can be no apathy here. Don't forget that you have to finish and deliver your painting today, so that you can have money for a good old Christmas party. That also steps up your tone. There is also the spur to you of painting a tropical sea, hot weather, something that looks like a beach under a burning sun—and you are doing it in a freezing attic. Puccini, of course, rather makes your situation more acute by forcing you to paint merciless heat when you are frozen.

"So try out the fantasy of your actions in a hundred different shades and then choose those that are the most interesting and expressive. But do everything along with the music, drawing only on it. Otherwise you will lapse into naturalism. All live action on the opera stage which is not filtered through the music, ennobled by it, becomes immediately coarse and vulgar."

So, before he began to sing the baritone who played Marcel had to undergo all sorts of training in order to pass his examination first as a painter with palette and brushes properly held as an artist would handle them, then as an actor executing every slightest movement in the rhythm of the music. What we then beheld was a Marcel, a jolly, not too refined type (to be in contrast with the poetic and gentle Rodolphe), in a long smock, sporting an artist's beard, hopping up and down, stamping his feet, and boldly sweeping his brushes across his canvas. The music even seemed to suggest to him how to mix his colours, when to lay them on, when to rest, stand back and screw up his eyes to consider his work, while blowing on his fingers. "However, you have to try, you must finish it," he sings to himself in a voice trembling with cold. But after a few measures, unable to stand the cold any longer ("Let old Pharaoh be drowned in his chariot") he hurls his palette and brushes into a box underneath the easel and with two jumps lands under Rodolphe's blanket. Now there is a change and Rodolphe is the focal point. We see what appears to be one huge body wrapped in a blanket but with two heads sticking out of it. This mise-en-scène is most unexpected because of its originality; it has no operatic grace but it is very logical and succeeds extremely well in conveying the cold from which both men are suffering.

"What are you doing?" Marcel asks as he wraps himself up in the blanket with Rodolphe, who does not move. There are several spasmodic phrases from the strings which jolt the poet out of his meditations. Rodolphe begins to sing a lightly rising, exquisite melody which is an abrupt change from the preceding rather rough music.

"I am fascinated by seeing how all the chimneys are wreathing Paris in smoke. It is only our own chimney which is too lazy to do so. Like a lazy lord it obviously has no concern for us." This lilting phrase will be repeated later as the *leitmotiv* of his poetic nature. The words are playfully humourous and contrast with the delicacy of the melody.

"He is not willing to warm your serene highness without firewood," says Marcel nodding his head in the direction of the empty grate.

"The insatiable creature is simply beastly," concludes Rodolphe.

"Here everything depends on your diction," said Stanislavski at rehearsal. "What is the essence of this scene which opens the opera? There are two young Frenchmen freezing, up in their attic room, but it does not break their spirit, they can even talk of love. What should you, as actors, be able to do now? Sit without moving and talk with each other. This is complicated by the fact that it is very cold. You must warm yourselves. How do you keep warm inside a blanket? First of all by not moving so that no cold air can get under it. Make sure there is no draught. When the music calls for action, fall in with it: straighten your blanket, pull it up over your backs. This must all be done very distinctly. For example: four measures of shivering, four measures of rubbing yourselves, four measures of shaking. I am speaking, of course, in approximations. If your actions are clear the audience will understand and get the feel of the music.

"It is necessary to have the audience live in terms of the composer.

"It is easy and simple to carry out all these physical actions together with the music. What you have to find is the rhythm of young and ardent human beings. First of all you must realize the limited truth of your situation: the thermometer stands only a few degrees above freezing in your room on the stage and you are going to have to spend the day there. How does a person act in such a case? He must warm himself. He must do this energetically but without a lot of fuss. You are there under a blanket and if you begin to fling your arms about you will interfere with your enunciation. You do not have the proper restraint as yet. Say to yourselves: now I will do this much, then I will do that.

"Your second objective is to learn how to converse meantime in an expressive way through your singing. *Your singing is an expression of what your life is right now—it is not a thing apart.*

"Carry all this over into the substance of your conversation. Bear in mind the technique of a dialogue. You must pick up your partner's cue and hand him your own in such a way that the ball is kept in the air. And each phrase should have its own design. Any phrase without that is terribly dull.

"So now you are singing about the grate," said Stanislavski to Rodolphe, "but you do this in words, without any action. You have a melodious accompaniment but your words are full of sarcasm. This is no place for sentimental complaints, you have to vent your resentment on the grate in stinging words: a lazy lord taking his ease.

"Here is a lighthearted young Frenchman who amuses himself by poking fun even at the drama he is writing, which he will burn presently in the stove in order to get a little warmth. This is no occasion for dull chitchat.

"One cannot sing of passion in a limp condition. All your words are full of energetic action, radiantly so. There is no other reason for an actor to appear on the stage. And any actor who wanders through his role without a compass in his hand, in a haphazard way, under arbitrary external impulse, cannot possibly impress.

"Lightness is the germinal quality of this opera-play. What is its principal line? These people cannot be got down by anything. Everything constitutes a pleasure to them."

Under the impact of immutable logic and of Stanislavski's requirement of precision, the singers gradually shed their usual methods of acting which had been inculcated in them in music schools or which they had acquired by imitation. Operatic performers quickly learn how to make a declaration of love, to suffer, to meditate, to die, and so on, and they repeat these forms in all analogous situations that they happen to be in. These are well-known, rubber-stamp effects. Nearly everyone knows them all, and speaks of them scornfully, yet . . . a majority of singers go right on using them.

That is why Stanislavski laid down the law: Every new role, in all of its physical actions and objectives, must be studied afresh as if it were one's first part.

"You know very well," he said to his actors, "what to do in real life if you are cold and have to warm yourself. You do this almost subconsciously because of previously established and often repeated conditioned reflexes. Unerringly you instantly and precisely react to real cold. But on the stage all this is imaginary, there is no real cold. Therefore you must consciously build the logical sequence of your physical actions. Later these proven actions will be incorporated in the score of your role and eventually they will again become, as in real life, unconscious.

"Do not make a big to-do, calm down, do only what is absolutely required for you in your lives as Marcel and Rodolphe."

Stanislavski would then constantly check on the truthfulness of any conduct on the stage; this meant judging also its bond with the music, the logic of the actor's thoughts carried by the coloration of the words sung.

But to begin with he would make Rodolphe sing with expression about "our wretched stove".

"I neither see nor feel how much you hate that stove. Scorch it with your look, annihilate it with your words: 'Insatiable monster, you savage beast, you are simply terrible.'

"Do you sense what forceful diction you need for this?"

Stanislavski himself undertook to reproduce the sibilants until they gleamed. He loved consonants and in his use of them they seemed to acquire a quality of animation. An entirely new impression is made by a phrase when its expressiveness has an edge and its form has a high polish on it. Such a phrase easily wings its way across the orchestra and then one need only see the face and eyes of an actor to understand his whole performance.

The actors are put in a position in this part of the first act where they can be effective only through the expressiveness of their singing and their faces. All the audience sees is their two faces, lighted by the rays of the sunset, above a large shapeless sack. Marcel and Rodolphe sit there almost motionless.

"Yes, it's cold here, repectably so," snaps Rodolphe.

"And my fingers are quite stiff. It seemed all the while that I was holding a lump of ice, which is what Musette has in the place of a heart," Marcel complains sarcastically to Rodolphe.

"Oh love!" replies Rodolphe on a high, ringing note. "Yes, you need a lot of fuel in that grate. . . ."

Here Stanislavski interrupted the singers in an effort to put more colour and flavour in their words and notes.

"Take that 'lump of ice' and even Musette herself, please, and present her in a way that makes it at once clear to us that she has thrown you over but that you still love her. Paint a picture for us of the 'ice maiden'. We shall see her in action shortly and you must spark our interest in her. Good diction is not enough for this—you must shade colours and substance behind the words.

"And you must take up Marcel's wail and begin to make fun of him," said Stanislavski to Rodolphe. "Imitate him when you sing the word 'lo-o-ve' "—which Stanislavski himself proceeded to do. "And the fact that you need a lot of fuel to stoke *that* fire is also a joke. You must needle, tease each other with your words. In this way you will forget the cold for a bit.

"It is quite another matter when singers not only produce their phrases with elaborate diction but also begin to bait each other with gaiety and wit. Their dialogue then acquires a clear meaning and every word is distinctly heard despite the very fast rhythm. Phrases follow each other in a rush, without a pause.

" 'Yes, you need a lot of fuel in *that grate*,' Rodolphe has said with a sly dig, but by stressing 'that grate' it is instantly clear to whose heart he is alluding."

"And forever," agrees Marcel in a tragic tone.

"Men burn in it like faggots," continues Rodolphe.

"They burn to ashes," adds Marcel.

"In horrible torture," puts in Rodolphe with comic agony.

"She never even notices. . ." concludes Marcel with almost tragic breadth of sound. But in the orchestra the bassoons, cellos, and double basses have begun to throb again. The two men return to chill reality.

Their situation remains unchanged; they continue to sit there wrapped to their chins in the one blanket. Their arms are out of sight. Stanislavski allowed them no gesticulation.

Sometimes when a singer did not know what to do with his hands while singing and therefore batted his arms about, Stanislavski would ask him jokingly: "What's the matter—are the flies interfering with your singing?"

To go back to the duet between Rodolphe and Marcel:

"You know one could freeze to death like this," exclaims Rodolphe on a high-pitched note.

"My arms ache," adds Marcel, an octave lower.

"Why weep, why all these martyred intonations?" asked Stanislavski. "Never be so literal. Bad actors colour every single word because they have no psychological perspective. Therefore when they come to a word like 'cold' they instantly begin to show how they shiver, or the word 'hot' and they pretend to pant from the heat. If they come to 'love' they produce a sweet smile. All those are ready-made stencils. Always search out first the inner wellspring of action. What do you have in mind? Are you complaining? To whom? No, you are protesting! You are looking for a way out of your problems.

"So sing as if you were protesting to all Paris against the injustice wreaked on you. You are preparing right now to burn your own writings as the flaming protest of an artist who can write ten other plays as good as this one, but you do not do this out of despair."

How lively and buoyant the atmosphere becomes when the actors take the line of young people who refuse to lose heart, no matter what their circumstances, and who begin to compete with each other in demonstrating the generosity of their extravagant artistic temperaments. Rodolphe begins: "Here is an idea," and he gives voice to it in a broad sweep to the accompaniment of the music embodying the "idea". It is unexpected: "Let our thoughts and talents go up in flames."

"Let us burn up that sea!" says Marcel magnanimously, pointing to his picture. "No, the smell from the paint would be awful," Rodolphe says with a touch of pride. "Better burn the play. Here's a red hot drama. Let's begin with it."

"Do you want to read it?" asks Marcel, astonished. "Oh, how awful!"

"No. The paper will turn to ashes, and my inspiration will fly up the chimney. My work will be lost to posterity. What a loss for the world!"

"What a hero!" concludes Marcel with feigned pathos.

"Do you feel," suggested Stanislavski, "how it is that only now you can change your position, that is to say after you have reached your bold decision? To do this you simply have to fetch out the manuscript from under the divan. And don't forget to put a touch of spice in the words 'red-hot drama'."

What did a change of position mean according to Stanislavski's requirements? It was not that one just walked over there and somebody sat down somewhere else. In the first place all movement had to be made in a definitely prescribed rhythm, inside a definite segment of time and with no superfluous gesture.

"There can be no blurring, no muddiness: A pattern of movement must be absolutely precise as regards the body, arms, and legs onstage. You should develop your own sense of how to mold a situation. In opera you need sculptural precision, enlivened by an inner feeling of truthfulness. Do not forget that the music is playing all of the time and that you are moved inwardly and outwardly in consonance with it." This was something on which Stanislavski rang all the changes in convincing his actors how to perform.

Consequently in Stanislavski's theatre there was none of the meandering around the stage that opera singers love to indulge in, innocently pretending that this represents the freedom of creativeness.

"Think of yourselves always as being an integral part of an overall picture," said Stanislavski. "You have to have a built-in control that observes all your actions yet does not interfere with your life. This control is somewhere in here," and he touched the back of his head. "Tommaso Salvini's expression for this was: 'An actor laughs and weeps and all the while he is watching himself do it.' " Stanislavski often quoted those words of the greatest exponent of the school of "living your part".

A change of the staging signifies a change of inner objective, of action, of mood, and also, as a result, a change in the character of the music. Therefore Stanislavski asked his actors:

"When will you cross the stage from the divan to the stove? Listen to the music; it will tell you everything. When the music changes, your positions change."

Everyone listened attentively to the music, which Stanislavski, incidentally, had played over and over in order to arouse the imagination of his actors. This close listening on the part of the singers bred in them an entirely new relationship with the music, something which a singer who works only on his own role does not usually have, as he devotes the bulk of his attention to learning his own measures, pauses, and cues.

Now we clearly hear how the bravura music is replaced by a lightly throbbing *tremolo* from the strings and harps and against that background a tender flute playing the theme of Rodolphe, the theme of poetic creation. At the beginning of this music (Puccini put in the score *dolcissimo*) Rodolphe and Marcel seat themselves close beside the stove, almost as if they were leaning against it. Any instant now it will warm them up: Rodolphe's manuscript will be burning in it.

"Here's the first act of my drama," sings Rodolphe, giving a handful of sheets to Marcel. "It's done!" exclaims Marcel as a flame leaps up in the stove. Now the figures of the two men are lighted by the fire. Their faces are turned to the stove, and Stanislavski has them remain quietly motionless so that the scene will leave an imprint on the minds of the spectators.

This brief scene and the soft music which accompanies it now end as the orchestra plunges into a powerful *forte* as if reproducing a man's heavy tread by the sounds in the cellos and contrabasses. A third friend enters: This is Colline, a student of philosophy. He is tall, bearded, awkward, makes one think of a bear. He has a bundle of books in his arms—they represent the cash which they had hoped to raise to pay for their supper. But the pawnbroker has refused to accept them as security because it is Christmas Eve. To explain this Colline has two phrases as he enters:

"The Day of Judgement is at hand. At this time no pledges are accepted."

Colline stops at the doorway. He is dressed in a light overcoat and muffler which is wrapped around him to cover his face almost up to his eyes. The orchestra reflects the cold that Colline brings in with him by some sharp chords from all of the instruments, like the ones at the beginning of the act when Rodolphe and Marcel were shivering under their blanket.

Now there are three of them gathered around the stove: Rodolphe and Marcel are seated and Colline stands between them. The conversation immediately takes on the tone of the usual witty banter among these bohemians.

"Where did that come from?" asks Colline, nodding his head towards the fire and rubbing his cold hands.

"Hush, I am putting on a drama," answers the poet.

"In the stove? A rather hot subject. . . . Unfortunately it's a short play," says Colline caustically.

"That, my friend, is its chief charm," parries Rodolphe.

The music now gives an expressive imitation, during this conversation, of the alternately flaring and then flickering flames. The first act of the drama is now burned up.

"Let me have the drama critic's seat," says Colline, settling himself between Rodolphe and Marcel. Now the three are sitting in a row like part of an audience at a play.

"The intermissions are boring and exhausting," says disgusted Marcel.

"Well then, here's the second act," says Rodolphe and hands Marcel another bundle of sheets. There is a long pause (Puccini gives it two measures) during which Marcel lays the pages of the manuscript in the stove. All three sit there with their attention centred on the fire; then at precisely the same time the orchestra and the stove burst into flame. The three figures are illuminated by the dancing flames as they play on their faces and on the walls of the mansard room. It is already dark and the sunset glow is fading outside the window. Twilight. The fire makes the place warm and cozy. The men sitting in front of the stove continue to twit each other.

Colline: "There is power in a thought."

"And depth," breaks in Marcel.

"That sheet burned so brightly! It was a scene between 'him and her'," Rodolphe explains to his audience.

"How it sizzled!" exclaims Colline with exaggerated enthusiasm.

"Look there," says Marcel, carefully pointing at something, "there are kisses."

"Now three acts will be performed simultaneously," says the author to cheer his "audience" as he stuffs another bundle of papers into the stove.

The fire in the stove flares up. "You are illumined by the light of glory," exclaims Colline, and then all three go on to say: "The happiness in the stove is heartwarming to us all." They are all in high spirits despite the fact that they have just burned a precious manuscript.

"Enjoy yourselves as children do," said Stanislavski. "You know, they are sometimes quite cruel in this."

Light, rapid sixteenth notes dash intermittently along in the music. They then go lower and lower until finally they fade away in an almost inaudible *pizzicato*. There is a pause. This is where Stanislavski makes his actors exercise great restraint.

"Remain still for a long while, gazing into the stove. Look for even a small spark, as if you nourished the hope that the fire might flare up again. Life is cold, famished, warmed only by strange accidental happenings and very weak hopes. These people try not to be discouraged and therefore they crack their desperate jokes at their own expense, yet sometimes life seems burdensome and dark—fortunately not for long."

That was the interpretation Stanislavski gave to this pause. This moment of reflection then is resolved in an unexpected burst of clowning. On a high note, "Awa-a-y with him", Marcel and Colline pounce on the "author", Rodolphe, and soon all three grown-up youngsters are on the floor in a scrimmage. This coincides with the entrance of Schaunard, a musician. He comes in with dancing steps, with parcels, a bundle of firewood, his pockets bulging with bottles, and stops in the centre of the stage among his comrades, who are rolling around on the floor like kittens. A new scene begins. Good old Schaunard has come—bringing gaiety and the prospect of full stomachs.

Of course, nothing went quite so smoothly at rehearsals. What I write here describes the result of hard work and innumerable rehearsals and shows how Stanislavski envisaged the scenes, how they came out when the work on them was done.

We see the fellow bohemians sitting on the floor while Schaunard stands in their midst showering them with money and parcels. They scramble for the coins.

"This little scene of collecting and looking at the money should make an impression to be remembered," said Stanislavski. "Pile the coins carefully in a row on the table. They are going to play a game with this money and their landlord Benoit. The audience must see the money."

"Firewood! Cigars! Wine!" they exclaim, one after another, and then with great warmth they all sing: "Fate has decreed that we should expire in the arms of pleasure."

"I committed a crime," says Schaunard, striking the attitude of a proud statue holding high a bottle of champagne. "I robbed a till."

"It's a genuine franc, no doubt about it," his stunned comrades playfully rejoinder, and quickly move over to the table.

Now the action is transferred once more to the table and divan where earlier in the act the shivering poet and painter had taken refuge. But there is no repetition here of the earlier staging. The table now is the centre of festivity with a lighted candle surrounded by food and cakes. Three of them sit at the table, with great gusto putting away the "heaven-sent" viands. Schaunard, standing, relates his adventures. It seems that some Englishman ("a lord or my lord, I do not know") had hired him to teach his parrot music. For large sums of money, of course. For three days he played his horn to the parrot. To rid himself of this ignominious job he had an affair with the maid, who fed the parrot parsley, from which it died.

The spice of this scene lies in how Schaunard with relish describes how he hoodwinked the Englishman, while his famished friends pay no attention to what he is saying because they are enjoying a gorgeous supper.

When Schaunard finishes his tale on a high note with the death of his pestiferous parrot, Colline, with his mouth full of food, imperturbably asks: "Who died?" Carried away by his own story, Schaunard now sees that nearly all the food on the table has been eaten.

"Take all the uneaten bits of food away from them and make a pile on the table," said Stavislavski, smiling at the scene.

Having salvaged the remains of the supper from his comrades Schaunard now goes on with his story.

"These supplies we must save up for a rainy day...."

The glasses are quickly filled with wine. They all stand up, clink glasses across the table but do not have time to raise them to their lips—there is a knock at the door. The music, which has been a dancing melody during all of Schaunard's speech, now strikes a rather lonely, agitated note. They are all transfixed with their glasses in their hands.

"May I come in?" says a voice outside the door.

"Who is it?" Marcel asks with asperity.

"Benoit."

The orchestra goes into a violent *fortissimo*, picturing despair, fear, with, of course, comic overtones. The wail of the music quickly turns into rapid grumbles with triplets on the strings, to show how the young men are trying to recover from their embarrassment.

All of them in their alarm put their untouched glasses on the table and then crawl under it. From there issue jumbled cries of: "Nobody's home!" "We have all gone out!" "The place is closed up!"

"Is it not possible to sing this in some unusual way?" Stanislavski asked Suk. "With some kind of animal noises? After all, it's just a lot of foolery." Suk agreed and after that these phrases were sung with moo-ing, miaowing, and other trick noises.

"Just one word," is heard from outside the door, The friends hold a consultation by an exchange of glances, while the cellos agitatedly gallop around, and Schaunard goes to the door. A long pause. Then a scene in pantomime. To begin with, Schaunard with great caution, as if he were unfastening the cage of a wild beast, opens the door. Then, with equal caution, a head with a black skull cap and spectacles appears in the opening and surveys the premises. Whereupon severely, as if giving a warning, Benoit says, "Just one"—meaning just one word.

The cellos now begin a light, almost apologetic, phrase, as Benoit's face breaks into a smile and he hands a bill to Schaunard, saying very politely: "Rent". Then, as if by magic, the whole mood suddenly changes. The bohemians are delighted, they are terribly happy that their landlord Benoit has come.

"Receive him as a most dear and long-awaited guest," said Stanis-lavski to the actors. "Begin to be hilarious over his arrival."

"Holla! Give him the armchair," sings Marcel most ceremoniously.

"Use these words," said Stanislavski, "as an excuse to move all the furniture around. That will indicate that he is a most cherished guest."

In this way a new arrangement of the staging is achieved. Schau-nard carries the table to the centre of the stage, almost to the footlights, while behind him Rodolphe and Colline drag the divan and set it behind the table. The glasses full of wine are standing, and the piles of money are still lying on the edge of the table. Marcel leads the "dear guest" in state to the table. All of them together, with equal ceremony, invite him to have a drink and offer him a glass—all of which is done, the moving of the furniture and handling of the landlord, in strict accor-dance with the minuet rhythm of the music. The scene is punctuated with brief phrases: "Pray . . .", "Take a seat", "Here's a glass", "To your health", "To the ladies". He is obliged to drink; the young people are so polite, amiable, and insistent and not at all truculent. So they all stand at the table and drink. But then the landlord remembers why he had come up. Having drunk a glass of wine he turns the conversation to his business: "It's time to pay for your room. . . ."

"Why talk about bills?" says Marcel, settling Benoit in the middle of the divan and pointing to the money, but Schaunard again puts wine into his glass and says: "Please ... let us drink ... to you." And then they all in solemn chorus sing: "We drink to your health."

"I came up because you gave me your word. . ." Benoit again reverts to his subject. Marcel interrupts him with a fine sweep of his arm and points at the money. "It's been ready for you for a long time." A look of horror comes over the faces of his comrades but Marcel gives them a sly wink to show that he knows what he is doing. As Benoit reaches out for the money Marcel grabs his hand impulsively, presses it tenderly to his heart. "Do stay and chat with us for a bit. . . . How old are you now, dear Monsieur Benoit?" "How old? What a question!" replies Benoit, who senses a trick behind the words. As indeed there was. His hand, reaching for the money, hangs in midair—the money is no longer where it was. Schaunard in moving around the table was able, unnoticed, to sweep it up into his pocket. Perplexed, Benoit tries to figure out how it happened—the money was there and now it is gone. But the young men do not give him any peace with all their pestering questions.

"Forty or thereabouts," suggests Rodolphe. "Oh no, a lot older," says Benoit brushing them aside. "But no, that's not possible," insists Colline. "Why did you go to the Bal-Mabille?" quizzes Marcel. "Did you meet someone there?"

That is a bait Benoit swallowed. The old reprobate first holds back but then begins to boast: "There was someone . . ." he confesses. "Tell me, is she beautiful?" breaks in Marcel.

"Charming."

Now they bear down on him from all sides: "You rascal, you lady-killer. What taste!"

"Butter him up as hard as you can and each one of you twit him," said Stanislavski, cheering the actors on. "Do it so that you yourselves will get a lot of fun out of it. Only then will the audience be entertained."

The audience sees this picture: Benoit, a short, bald, roundheaded man, is seated behind a small table facing the audience, surrounded by his tenants. Two of them sit beside him on the divan, the other two are behind him, so that as they begin to pelt him from all sides he keeps spinning around to reply.

"You devious old reprobate. . . . You irresistible, terrible lady-killer," Rodolphe sings with great gusto and the others all join in: "You dangerous menace to female hearts." Like the old crow who was caught by the fox's flattery, Benoit succumbs. His Don Juan vanity is aroused and gradually, at first with some modesty, confidentially, he begins really to boast. He describes his conquests. Benoit's tale is vividly illustrated by the music. There are the quick moves in his chase "after her", and the colouring that suggests each "flame". He does not care for the fat ones. He simply cannot abide the skinny, bony ones (you can hear their bones rattle in the orchestra).

> From lanky ladies I always flee
> This I do quite habitually
> Such meagre fare is not the life
> For me. Just cast your eye [significant pause]
> . . . At my own wife.

At this the orchestra thunders with horror, as it did when Benoit came to the door. But then the young bohemians were horrified by his coming and now it is by his depravity. After exchanging preliminary glances they hide themselves with pretended horror in various parts of the room as if they thought Benoit a monster. Benoit is left by himself, quite bewildered, not knowing what has happened.

"Run from him in various directions, as you would from a terrible snake," suggested Stanislavski.

Now the scene on the stage is quite unusual. In the middle of the big divan sits little Benoit by himself, all crumpled up with alarm, while from all corners of the room, like hunters after game, the four men, with pretended injured innocence, mischievously point at him. What comes next is clearly consonant with the music. Each one of the bohemians, beginning with Marcel, has his phrase to sing, such as: "This faithless husband has come here to teach debauchery," or Rodolphe's: "He defiles our honest home with his shameful wickedness", and so on. And each phrase is followed by a general cry from all of them of: "Shame!" As he sings his phrase Marcel moves towards Benoit with firm steps and with the cry of "Shame!" he jumps onto the divan, then the table, as if preparing to crush the life out of this snake. Rodolphe and the others follow suit. Squirming at their feet Benoit can only whimper: "But I . . . but you . . ." "Not a word, not a sound! Clear out of our sight at once!" the pranksters all howl. At the last deafening roar: "Clear out at once!" to the rising tones of the music and a roll of the kettledrums Benoit flees through the door, and the bohemians stand still for an instant at the open door in their "ballet" poses of hot chase. All of which is done in a very clear, musical pattern.

"Well, goodnight, dear Benoit," they all sing with a stress on every syllable as they still stand in their comic poses. Then, laughing, they turn away from the door and go back to their interrupted occupations.

"Go back to everyday life, each one intent on his own affairs, in a new, calm rhythm. In this pause, when you come away from the door, you must already have assumed that calm rhythm in which Schaunard sings the next phrase: 'Now it's time to go down to the Latin Quarter.'"

It must be confessed that the singers in the roles of Marcel, Rodolphe, Schaunard, and Colline had a great deal of trouble with their diction. The tempo of their music is very rapid, and their phrases are frequently interrupted by each other's cues. The full orchestra was playing almost all of the time and the resonance from it, as a rule, was formidable. Usually at rehearsals, with the innumerable repetitions, the words became so familiar to the singers that it was difficult to know whether or not the audience could distinguish them. In such cases Stanislavski recommended that we try ourselves out on a completely new group of listeners who knew nothing at all about the opera.

After Schaunard's cue they get ready to leave for the Café Momus. "Divide up our capital," suggests Schaunard. "Divide, divide, divide," echo the others. Schaunard gives each one his share.

Stanislavski was extremely careful about there being no aimless tramping around on the stage. Each person had his job to do: the following scene had to be prepared. The remnants of supper and the bottles had to be cleared away. There is only one mirror and each one had to look at himself in that. This is where, incidentally, there is talk about Colline's beard. He decides to shave it off and appear at the Café Momus looking much younger.

They are all ready to leave except Rodolphe, who is delayed because he has to finish an article for a magazine. But he will join them presently. The mansard room is otherwise empty. One hears the steps of Colline as he lumbers downstairs—this is clearly reproduced by the orchestra. "Colline, did you get down alive?" calls Rodolphe down the dark staircase. "So far," Colline's voice comes from below. Then silence.

Through the window there is seen a clear, dark blue sky. Rodolphe sits at the table in the centre of the stage. The lighted candle is in front of him. A new scene begins.

But before coming to this Stanislavski had his actors sum up what they had done, so that they could go on to develop their roles without a director.

"What were your objectives during all of the first half of the act?" he asked. "Let us count the units, the scenes: 1. The exposition of the plot—two lighthearted friends are freezing with the cold, they must warm themselves; 2. They burn the manuscript, Colline comes in; 3. Arrival of Schaunard, like Santa Claus, with gifts, a plethora of wealth; 4. The feast and Schaunard's tale about the parrot—all this scene is at the table; 5. Benoit comes to collect the rent. A hilarious roughhouse and, finally; 6. The flight of Benoit and your departure. A total of six units, six objectives, six definite, different stagings. And for each one there was a clear physical objective. No feelings, no emotional experiences! That will all come of its own accord.

"But these six units must not remain divided off, as can happen when pauses simply distinguish one musical number from the next. Gradually all these six units will merge for you into one general, large objective. This will come about if you constantly bear in mind the main theme of action: Keep lighthearted, do not let your spirits slump while you battle with a hard life."

Rodolphe is sitting with his pencil poised over a sheet of paper. His face, which is turned towards the audience, is lighted by the candle. The rest of the stage is dark. He has fallen into a state of meditation. The orchestra plays a rather light, dance-like melody, in a gay rhythm. Rodolphe is obviously in no mood to work. "I'm not in form," he says as he listens to the music. There is a pause. Then suddenly a cautious knock at the door. "Who is there?" asks Rodolphe. "Please excuse me!" "A woman's voice!" Rodolphe is puzzled, goes to the door and opens it. On the threshold is the figure of a young girl in a simple dark blue dress, with an apron.

"Excuse me, but my candle blew out. . . ." "Come in." "No, why should I?" "Don't be embarrassed. Come in." A broad wave of music rises from the orchestra. It rises to a certain height and then begins to recede, almost die away, and ends on a long-drawn-out sigh from a single clarinet. The girl faints.

"You are not well, you are so pale!" exclaims bewildered Rodolphe as he picks up the limp figure which has slipped down to the floor. "Now what am I to do?" he asks, holding the unconscious girl in his arms in the centre of the stage. He carefully lays her on the divan and splashes her face with water. The girl stirs, then sits up with Rodolphe's help, looks around with astonishment, trying to think where she is, how she came there.

"Are you better now?" asks Rodolphe. "Yes." "It's horribly cold here, sit down near the stove. Here, take a swallow of wine." "Thank you. Just a drop for me." She drinks "That's fine," says Rodolphe with satisfaction. Then adds, to himself: "A charming child."

Mimi, as we shall call her, although Rodolphe does not know who she is, gets up from the divan with the words: "Would you let me light my candle? I am better now." "Are you in a hurry?" he asks politely. "Yes."

Rodolphe goes to the door, where Mimi's candlestick fell from her hand, lights her candle from the one on the table and hands it to her. "Thank you. Good night!" says Mimi and moves towards the door. Rodolphe accompanies her to the threshold and softly sings: "Good night!" The door is closed and Rodolphe goes back to the table and sits down. All is silent.

Puccini set five pauses—*fermatas*—for this scene. Stanislavski exploited them to the full because with the help of these pauses he could vastly extend the content of the acting of the singers.

All during this scene the music is very delicate, soft, and careful, if one may use that term. It is all composed of short chords from the strings, and rests. Stanislavski characterized it this way:

"The whole scene is made of thistledown, of careful breathing. At any moment it may fly away. A bird has fluttered in, fallen into Rodolphe's hands. He carries her tenderly. One has to know how to play this. How does he carry her? It's a whole poem in itself. Find the poetry of this meeting. Here the music steals into one's very soul. . . .

"As for you," he said to Mimi, "you were on the stairs, your candle blew out. You are not well, you have had nothing to eat. You do not know or think about your illness. No sign here of the fourth act. All you have to be is famished, overworked, helpless, a poor woman. Alone. 'If I knock at a door, perhaps a woman will open!'

"This is your first meeting, and it is usually over-played. But you do not fall in love at once. How do you express this love? To do so you must find a whole series of physical actions. Look the possibilities over, study carefully what it is that strikes you, choose what you like, weigh it. All during the scene look at him so that you can come to know him, sound him out, study him. That is the direction of your objectives. The capacity to lay out such a through-line of action is something that you hammer out for yourself all during your life as an artist. This is now the point where you set up your principal landmarks. Your further work will be to fill in the spaces between them. For example, what does it mean to open the door into the room of a stranger? To knock without knowing who is behind the door? Study each step of the process, don't overlook an instant, not one degree. You must write this down in every slightest detail in your notebook for your role. Now what are the principal landmarks in this scene?" He answered the question himself:

"1. Darkness. You wish to light your candle. This is an easy objective. 2. What would happen if just then you had a dizzy spell? 3. Act so that he would not notice that your head is swimming. 4. Relax all your muscles to fall. 5. Look at the divan. 6. Note what the room is like. 7. What sort of a young man is this? 8. Study him. This is a whole scene in itself, a whole chapter.

"And you, Rodolphe, what are your objectives?

"1. Hurry to write your article. 2. A knock at the door. Must get rid of any importunate caller. 3. You see her, wish to look at her closely. 4. She faints, she is ill. You must help. You are now a physician, a nurse. 5. Light her candle. Escort her to the door."

Stanislavski suggested that his actors make notes as soon as any scene was sketched out, even roughly. But, as a matter of fact, he had his opera singers do this from the very beginning of a role at the same time as they were being trained vocally for their parts.

"There is no worse way to ossify, to freeze a singer in his acting, than to make him learn his whole role without his knowing what will transpire on the stage and what his share will be in the overall performance."

Parenthetically it should be said quite frankly that the method suggested by Stanislavski is far from being put into practice by our opera theatres even now.

"At the very first rehearsals of *La Bohème*," wrote Madame Sobolevskaya, who sang Mimi, "Stanislavski made this proposal to me: to write down for him the score, as he put it, of the physical actions for all of the first act, from the beginning of my life to the moment when I entered the scene. I was to write in as detailed a manner as possible, giving only the bare facts without any emotional coloration.

" 'When you will have done this,' he said, 'I shall ask you to go farther: under the unbroken line of physical actions to draw an equally unbroken line of *desires* which logically underlie all your action. For example: You sit down, draw your legs under you, bend your head over—those are all physical actions. I wish to sit in a more comfortable position—that is the logical basis for what you do—in order to be closer to Rodolphe, to look at him because I like him—that is the psychological explanation of your desire and your action.'

"I did this work," Sobolevskaya added. "Stanislavski was on the whole pleased with it, although he said: 'You could have put in more details, achieved a finer edge on your objectives, been even more definite. This is a very useful thing to do. Stick to this method, it will be of help to you in the future.' "

Rodolphe is alone on the stage just as we left him when Mimi went out with her lighted candle. The young man's mood has naturally changed. The unexpected visit of an unknown girl, her shyness, her helplessness, her fainting are fresh in his memory. With her appearance the whole room came to life, and now it is all dark again.

Yet Rodolphe has scarcely seated himself at the table and begun to collect his thoughts when again there is a knock at the door and a voice saying: "Oh, forgive me, forgive me. . . ." Immediately the door is partly opened and we see the face of Mimi lighted by her candle: "The key to my room . . . I must have dropped it here." Well, this was quite natural: when Rodolphe picked her up and carried her to the divan her key might easily have dropped out of her hand. But . . . Rodolphe's rhythm undergoes an abrupt change. No yawning now, this is his chance to coax along, to prolong, their acquaintance. But done very delicately, without any slightest sign of aggressiveness. Mimi is genuinely alarmed: "He mustn't get any idea . . ." "Oh, do be careful. The draught through the door is horrid." This sounds almost like an aria for Rodolphe despite the prosaic content of the words. Through it shines a feeling of young happiness. And instantly after he speaks Mimi's candle is blown out. "Oh dear. Now I must light it again. . . ." Mimi's words are a request but—and this was suggested by Stanislavski—when Rodolphe turns to the table he covertly blows out his own candle. "Now see that, my candle blew out too. . . ." he says regretfully. It is quite dark now in the room. The figures of the actors are scarcely visible.

"Soon the moon will be up and we shall give you light but meantime see that your diction is improved," said Stanislavski, "because now it is only words that will carry the action."

"It's dark and cold," replies Rodolphe, "but we'll find your key very soon." "Your neighbour is a nuisance to you." "Nonsense, what are you talking about?" So, as they toss remarks back and forth they get down on their knees and pass their hands over the floor. The movement of their hands is rhythmic and in harmony with the music, in which two melodies seem to be conversing.

In the libretto there are directions to the singers telling them when and how they are to "act". For example, in explaining this scene it says of Rodolphe, "finding himself near the door, he bolts it."

"You are not under any circumstances to do any such thing," said Stanislavski. "That would instantly cheapen the scene, whereas it should be quite pure and chaste." Then there is another stage direction in the libretto: "He looks for the key, shuffling his feet over the floor." Probably this was put that way because it is difficult to get lordly actors, much less opera singers, or above all principal characters, to go down on their knees and feel the floor with their fingers as ordinary people do when they have to find something in the dark. "Shuffling his feet" to find a key—that is simply not a serious way to go about it. How could he, in "shuffling his feet", come across Mimi's hand? Such marvels occur only in nonsensical operatic situations, but they have continued to be tolerated for decades and no one even notices them. Working with Stanislavski young actors really search, sweep their hands over the floor, and crawl around on their knees.

Rodolphe finally finds the key and gives the fact away with his ejaculation: "Ah!" Mimi quickly asks: "Was it the key?" But the poet has quickly secreted it in his pocket and says: "No, it is not here." At a rehearsal Mimi gave him a sly look to show that she had seen what he did.

"No," said Stanislavski, "you do not notice anything or you will blur your image." So they continue their hunt on either side of the table until

Rodolphe touches Mimi's hand under it. Then comes the surprised "Ah!" from Mimi, and a long-drawn-out, dying note from a French horn in the orchestra. Then the aria "Cold little hand" begins.

In his search for unaffected, natural arrangements of actors on the stage, especially when a well-known aria is about to be sung, Stanislavski never allowed his singers to strike a pose in preparation for its performance, as if they were to sing a separate and important number on a program. Each event had to flow naturally into the next. Therefore, while still kneeling on the floor, Rodolphe takes Mimi's cold hand in his and begins:

"The little hand is cold, I must warm it for you. It is so very dark, no use to search any longer." The orchestra repeats his last phrase as if to convince Mimi that this is so. During that music Rodolphe has the opportunity to take Mimi by the arm, help her off the floor, and carefully set her on the divan. Now Mimi is sitting before the table and Rodolphe continues to sing: "Shortly now the beautiful moon will look through our window and caress us."

As he says these words he goes over to Marcel's bed—it is only two steps—and takes a blanket from it. While doing that he sings: "But that need not keep me from telling you briefly who I am, what I do, and how I live. Shall I do it?"

Mimi agrees by nodding her head and settling herself comfortably on the divan. Rodolphe stands behind it, the blanket in his hands, and begins his tale: "Who am I? Who am I? A poor poet. What work do I do? I write. What do I live on? I do not really know." In the pauses between the phrases he quietly and carefully wraps Mimi in the blanket. This is all perfectly natural, it's cold and Mimi has been shivering for a long time. Now the situation between the two assumes the character of a cosy, friendly chat. Rodolphe can go on telling, singing, his history for as long as he likes because Mimi listens in comfort. The blanket and Mimi's cosy pose give a lively and poetic tone to the scene. The position of Rodolphe is very easy for singing. He addresses Mimi who is sitting in front of him and in this way the sound of his voice carries directly to the auditorium.

Rodolphe sings about how "a poet is a carefree beggar": he soars forever in a world of dreams, he can build castles to his heart's desire, be a millionaire in his soul. The aria ends with a compliment quite in the French style: "Yet sometimes I am robbed outright by the beautiful eyes of a Dulcinea to whom without regret I hand over all my riches".

At the end he says: "I have opened all my heart to you in these few words. Now tell me who you are, I beg of you."

What did Stanislavski wish to get from the singer of this famous aria?

"What is your objective?" he asked and answered his own question:

"It is to talk about yourself. You speak as a comrade, openly. And Mimi should reply in kind. You are still not in love, you are just comrades, who speak frankly to one another. Two sweet young faces are smiling at one another. You should sing your story as if it were for the first time.

"The objective is clear: You are to sing and narrate, with the main point being that you do it 'as if it were for the first time.' That is extremely difficult and, to be frank, not everyone can do it. But unless it is done this way the aria turns into an elaborately studied set piece calculated to show off all the charms of a tenor voice."

Undoubtedly the aria has to be learned thoroughly and "sung through" as singers say, which means they have not to bother about the sound. But the creative freedom of a singer about which Stanislavski was speaking (a singer must tell his story as if it were for the *first time*) is impeded by various things. First, frequent repetitions of the learned words cause them to lose all meaning and a singer reproduces them mechanically without thinking about any sense. Second, there is so much powerful enchantment in the Puccini melody itself—so much lightheartedness, warmth, joy, enthusiasm—that it seems one can simply give oneself up to this music and not think at all about the words. This, indeed, is what often happens with extremely good vocalists.

"But that is just speculating with Puccini's music," said Stanislavski. "Since you have come onto the stage I want you to show me the life of a human being, his thoughts, the shadings of his thoughts. If a musician does not act, but just sings notes, what does the action consist of? This is an opera, not a symphony. Yes, and there is action in it because the conductor is painting a picture for me which I can see in my imagination. But if you sing only bare notes, what has my imagination to work on? So you must follow not only the musical line but also the *musico-dramatic* line.

"You sing for me not just a melody, with words which have lost all significance for you, but words whose *meaning you have discovered, reinforced by your imagination and ornamented by the melody.*

"What is the kernel of your aria? It is insouciance. You have one jacket to your name, nothing else, but you can boast. And it is this carefree attitude that Mimi falls in love with. It is not your beautiful voice at all. She has a lovely voice of her own," added Stanislavski jokingly.

After analyzing the aria from the point of view of its intent and from the musical standpoint, we established the fact that it fell into four parts, all different as to meaning and musical colours. 1. This is in the nature of a prelude: you must get warm. Let us wait until the moon rises and meantime I will tell you about myself. 2. I am such and such a person and I do such and such things. 3. Since I am a poet, my imagination makes me wealthy, although I really possess nothing. But women's eyes often rob me of my castles in the air, which vanish like a mist. But I do not regret anything I give those eyes. Then the conclusion: "I have opened all my heart to you" and now it is your turn.

If this is clearly conveyed, then the whole meaning of the aria, the tale of a poet, will be understood. Then all the tender dying-away tones of a tenor voice, all the put-on, cold agitation with which hackneyed singers are wont to dress up this aria, fall away and in their stead we have live emotions and true vocal colouring.

As the last sounds of Rodolphe's aria melt away with his words "I beg of you" on a major chord, immediately, in simplest form, with a single note from the orchestra Mimi begins her reply, her story. There is no need for the singer to alter her position; she begins to sing sitting in the same place. It is only Rodolphe who moves forward and settles himself on the floor at Mimi's feet, in order to listen better—and also so that the audience will have a better view of her, be able to hear her more easily.

Great care was taken in comparing the libretto text with the Italian original. It was so involved and banal that it proved impossible to sing it and still follow Stanislavski's absolute dictum: *The audience must hear every word uttered by a singer. Half of the success of opera comes from perfect diction. . . .*

So we used a much simpler version prepared by Stanislavski's brother Vladimir:

> They call me Mimi
> Although my name is Lucia.
> My life is but a simple one,
> Happy and quite tranquil.
> Silken flowers I embroider,
> Roses, violets, on order—
> I love my work, I adore real flowers.

In these words there is no operatic stuffiness, which so often inverts the meanings of a text.

Mimi is seated, wrapped in a blanket with her legs curled up under her, in a corner of the old divan, and sings the story of her life very simply, with the same very distinct enunciation that the poet used in his song. It is, of course, difficult to sing sitting down but Stanislavski required his singers to perform in all positions and gave them special training to do this.

Mimi's tale consists of two principal parts and each in turn has its subject. To tell this in one's own words—and for Stanislavski this was the necessary first step in starting work, especially on a monologue—the significance of her story was as follows:

Part One: I am so and so. My occupation is such and such. I embroider roses, and violets. I love my work very much because I love flowers and their fragrance. In their tender exhalations I feel springtime. It seems to me that such feeling is called poetry. "Do you agree?" she asks Rodolphe.

"Ye-es," answers the poet who is deeply moved. And indeed this simple, young Parisian girl is endowed with a poetic nature, only she is not aware of this.

Part Two: Here the story is about daily occupations. She prepares her own dinner, she only rarely goes to church, but hastens to add that she does say her prayers. She lives in the same house, on an upper floor, and from her window sees only roofs and the sky. But . . . and here the poetry in her heart begins to speak. She is very happy because in spring the sun sends its first warm rays to her, and on her windowsill she has a real rose which blooms continually, whose fragrance she adores. Her last phrase is tinged with touching sadness and tenderness: "What a shame that the flowers I embroider are quite lacking in all fragrance." Puccini, who was aware of the subtlest shadings in a woman's soul, has very special colours in the music he wrote to reflect these delicate tones. His music, which is at times given to powerful resonance and solemnity, never is out of touch with the emotions being experienced by the characters on the stage. It follows consistently the most delicate nuances of their thoughts.

Mimi's last words: "There is nothing else that I can tell you about myself. I can only ask forgiveness, as a neighbour, for making this accidental visit"—are uttered almost in *recitative*, accompanied by a serene, long chord on the strings.

In the skill of using the *recitative* form, half sung in musical rhythm, half spoken, Stanislavski was an unsurpassed master. He was well-versed in the use of free, musical rhythm on the stage. All the productions of the Moscow Art Theatre were based on this knowledge of his and in it lay their great power.

By now the moon has long been up and bathed the stage in its pale blue beams, which distinctly reveal the figures of Mimi and Rodolphe.

The mansard room seems now transformed in the illumination of the moonlit night. The attractive simplicity of the relationship between Mimi and Rodolphe, as expressed in their arias, has created an atmosphere expectant of happiness. But that is still only a vague feeling merely guessed at by the audience. The actors themselves are not thinking in such terms. Stanislavski obliged them to restrain all intimations of feelings of love.

Mimi's last phrase has just been finished when from below, from a courtyard on the street, hoarse cries are heard: "Hey, Rodolphe, Rodolphe, Rodolphe! You desert anchorite, you verse weaver, sleepyhead." These are from Rodolphe's impatient friends, who are tired of waiting for him. Mimi, naturally, is alarmed, and their quiet talk has been interrupted. "Who is there?" she asks. "Friends of mine," he replied soothingly. He goes to the window and, opening it a crack, he sings down into the street: "I'm not alone, there are two of us here. Go on to Café Momus. Reserve places, wait for us there." From below come the sounds of a comic march: "Momus, Momus, forward march, on the double, on to battle. Poetry advance. . . ."

The sounds of the march fade and onstage there is new movement. The short, joking colloquy with the jolly friends below seems to have opened the eyes of the young couple in the attic. They look at each other differently now and begin to sense the significance of their meeting. This is, of course, prompted by the music coming from the orchestra which paints hot, absorbing emotions. Rodolphe is seized with poetic inspiration and he begins with gradually increasing ardor to make his confession: "Unearthly being! Your image shines with tender, heavenly light! In you I find all my joy, all that I have ever dreamed of! All is enshrined in you alone!"

With Rodolphe's outburst of ardor the orchestra adds greater expressiveness and resonance to the voice of the singer, and Mimi can no longer restrain the feelings that have set her on fire, so that her voice blends with Rodolphe's in a triumphant, joyful melody: "Yes, love has taken me in thrall as well. . . ."

This is the climax of the scene between Mimi and Rodolphe and of all of the first act. Here Stanislavski had this to say to the singers:

"At this point put everything you have into your singing and give out all that is in you—you may even overact. For the moment we must see the flash of those 'sincere emotions' about which Pushkin wrote. If you have prepared everything well and logically before you come to this culminating place, I shall believe in everything you do, even exaggerated gestures which you may be impelled to make."

As Rodolphe sings his short arietta: "Unearthly being . . ." he slowly approaches Mimi, who is listening to him with bated breath. At the last chord of their brief duet, with the words: "Hail, love!" Rodolphe wishes to embrace Mimi.

"No, that's impossible." Mimi turns away. "Your friends are waiting for you." "Are you leaving?" asks Rodolphe anxiously. "I dare not propose it myself . . . but I would go with you," confesses Mimi. The music is tremulous, tender, cautious. "You would, Mimi?" Rodolphe exclaims with enthusiasm, "but would it not be better if you and I stayed here? Would you not be cold out there?" "Near you I will keep warm."

"There's the touch of a woman," suggested Stanislavski. "A Frenchwoman knows how to put it. It is all done lightly and humourously."

All these phrases are meant by Puccini to be conversational in tone, with ordinary intonations, yet at the same time there is a singing quality to them which makes them caressing and meaningful.

"Quickly give me your little hand," sings Rodolphe tenderly and in the same tone Mimi replies: "I cannot refuse it." "But you are mine?" "Yes, yours, yours." They move slowly towards the door and disappear. From offstage we hear their last wards: "Oh love, love!" A bright, triumphant C-major chord from the entire orchestra swallows up their fading voices.

Act Two

The librettist proposed the following settings for the second act: "A square, with small shops on the left. The Café Momus, Christmas Eve. Mixed crowds of people: city dwellers, soldiers, servants, children, students, *grisettes*, policemen, etc. . . ." That is to say, a traditional city square surrounded by houses and, of course, empty in the middle where the main events are to transpire. This is where the joint life of Mimi and Rodolphe is to begin. This too is the scene of the reconciliation between Marcel and Musette and the fresh flaring of their love.

"There are two fundamental elements in this scene," said Stanislavski, "lyric and comic. We must arrange a more intimate setting for the two pairs of lovers than a city square, while keeping the noisy life of Paris in the background."

In eliminating the city square of the libretto, he went on to say:

"Let us carry the action inside the Café Momus. This will enable us to lend an atmosphere of credible intimacy to the scene and yet preserve the general gay holiday tone. Outside the large windows of the café one can glimpse street life. On Christmas Eve it is rather chilly in Paris; therefore it is better to carry on the complicated exchanges between the lovers inside the café rather than out on the square."

Students, soldiers, vendors, *midinettes*—all the inhabitants of the Latin Quarter—who are strolling around the square, according to the libretto, are now centered in the Café Momus. The people at the little tables are gay and noisy. Some pay and leave, others take their places. Flower girls come in to sell their wares, others offer cigarettes, balloons. Waiters push their way among the tables. In the corner to the right

Madame Momus herself is installed behind a row of gleaming bottles and piles of crockery.

As the curtain opens the little tables down nearest the footlights, where the main action will take place, are occupied by other clients. They seem to leave quite casually just before the arrival of the principal characters, thus making room for them.

The entrance to the café is placed in the centre of the wall to the left of the audience, between large glass windows. The doors are three steps up from the floor; therefore each person entering the café is visible to the audience.

The action of the second act begins with as much agitation as the first, with no orchestral prelude. With the first sounds of the music the curtain opens and the audience is instantly plunged into the gay Christmas spirit of the happy-go-lucky Latin Quarter.

"We have very little time to introduce the audience into the café's atmosphere and course of events, therefore we must be extremely precise in all the actions onstage and in the progression of the scenes. The noisier it is on the stage, the more confused, abandoned, casual, the more exact must be the organization of it all. A successful impromptu is one which is thoroughly rehearsed," warned Stanislavski.

Moving the action inside the café occasioned some alteration of the text as well. Originally the crowd milled around the square; now that crowd was inside the café, sitting at small tables, celebrating the holiday, clamouring for food, wine, buying flowers, toys, etc. Whereas in the libretto the first words of the chorus (made up of street vendors) are: "Bananas! Dates! Oranges! Cakes! Tangerines! ..." now the words had to be adapted to the flower girls offering their wares to the people sitting in the café.

After that, instead of the awkward phrases: "Stick together, let's go", "I'm tired of this rabble", the text is more effective and in keeping with what is happening onstage: "Roses! Fresh roses!" And from a group entering the café: "Give us a table where we can all be together." The waiter replies: "Right away! I'll lay your places!" Then the group adds: "It would be cozier for us over here."

There is something I must point out here to the readers of this book and that is the very great and special requirements Stanislavski made of the text of any opera libretto. Everyone is well-aware of the quantity of blank, meaningless words in a libretto, especially of one in translation. Stanislavski was accustomed to giving full value to *every single word* uttered on the stage, never admitting a blank or meaningless one to be sung.

"In the libretto every word is precious," he said. "That is why the characters must be given words that stir them to *action*, not contemplation. Opera suffers for the very reason that one character sings and does not act, while the others onstage just look on."

So here in this crowd scene he insisted that each character know exactly all the actions in progress on the stage at every moment that he was on.

"What is the course of your life on this evening?" was the question Stanislavski put to each participant. "Who are you? What is your name? Did you come here on your own or were you invited? Who are your acquaintances here? What will you do while here? What objectives do you, as an acting participant in the scene, have? Use your fantasy! Without fantasy you are not an actor. You need a good imagination and interesting objectives. To carry them out you will have to choose an appropriate tempo-rhythm which the music will suggest to you. But you will be unable to find the right tempo-rhythm for your life if you are not exactly aware of what you are to *do* on the stage."

He went on to underscore certain points:

"By participating in the chorus in a mass scene an actor-singer has the opportunity to try out small, truthful actions. If you do not train yourselves to proceed from these small truths to larger ones you will only learn to lie, and that is the road to ham acting, routine performance. They speak in the theatre of an 'experienced actor'. That usually connotes a rubber-stamp performer."

In order to coordinate a hilarious holiday scene into a background against which to carry a clear through-line of action for the principal characters, Stanislavski dictated a precise scheme of action:

First moment. Beginning of the act. Thirty-five measures of music before there is a general pause. It is evening. All the café tables are occupied. It is a holiday.

Second moment. The next twenty measures of music. New people keep coming in from outside. They try to find tables. They meet friends (at the tables upstage). Two more groups come in.

Third moment. The next twenty-eight measures. Street vendors, espying newcomers, offer their wares: flowers, candy, etc.

Fourth moment. Enter Schaunard and Colline. They are known to the people seated at two small tables down front. They have a brief conversation. The vendors recognize them as old customers. They exchange remarks.

Fifth moment. Enter Mimi and Rodolphe. "Let's look for a scarf."

Sixth moment. Enter Marcel. Scene with flower girls.

Seventh moment. Return of Mimi and Rodolphe. Everyone looks at the newcomers. "Who is that?" They meet their fellow bohemians.

Eight moment. The cry of Parpignol, a hawker of toys, from outside on the street.

Ninth moment. Introduction of Mimi to the bohemians. All the tables are full.

Tenth moment. Parpignol enters. Everyone wants to buy one of his toys. They beckon to him from all sides. The bohemians buy some too. The toys are talked about by the occupants of the tables. They are the object of general interest.

Eleventh moment. Appearance of Musette. General exultation. Everyone knows her. Some know of her affair with Marcel. Others have heard about the banker in her life.

Twelfth moment. Enter Alcindoro, the banker. The public is interested in him, as are Madame Momus, the waiters, flower girls, other vendors.

Thirteenth moment. Musette upsets a plate. The beginning of a general commotion. They all exchange remarks with one another and watch the ensuing events.

Fourteenth moment. The people at the tables to the left watch Schaunard's manoeuvres, and rush out to see what the row is about.

Fifteenth moment. The people at the tables to the right watch the development of a row and tell the others about it.

Sixteenth moment. A waltz. General excitement, everyone greets Musette. They know what the matter is. They are on her side.

Seventeenth moment. The quarrel. "He bores me." Everyone is on the alert. What will happen now?

Eighteenth moment. Musette screams. Her slipper is too tight. General tumult. When the reason is known, general laughter.

Nineteenth moment. The banker leaves to get Musette other slippers.

Twentieth moment. Reconciliation of Marcel and Musette. They toast Musette.

Twenty-first moment. Soldiers enter. They all want to look around, get the best tables.

Twenty-second moment. The bohemians leave. Their vacated table is immediately occupied.

Twenty-third moment. The banker returns. The bill is handed to him. Everyone is pleased by this outcome and makes fun of Alcindoro.

As we look at the scheme we see that the first three units, or moments, as Stanislavski called them, are devoted to creating a general holiday atmosphere in the Café Momus. But these three units are clearly segregated. The first gives a general picture of the café. All the tables are filled with lively guests who are exchanging remarks back and forth. Waiters are pushing their way around among the tables.

Those who are leaving say good-bye and new guests arrive and greet friends already there. One group enters through the middle door, another through a side entrance. There is a jolly confusion.

The vendors of flowers and candy appear. They move around from table to table. The waiters continue to push their way between the tables and the buffet where Madame Momus readies the drinks and food for them to serve. This provides a noisy holiday atmosphere, into which the principal characters can be injected because by now the audience has had a chance to clarify the general setting.

All the friends—the bohemians—arrive separately at the café so that the audience will get a clear impression of them as they come in. The first to get there is Schaunard, who has his own musical theme. He comes through a side door and crosses the forestage to go directly to Madame Momus. Following him comes Colline. Immediately after them Rodolphe and Mimi enter through the middle door. Mimi, full of life and joy, asks Rodolphe to buy her a scarf. When Rodolphe says: "Keep close to me, let's go" they go back into the street. They just show themselves to us and then disappear. Right after this jolly Marcel comes in, also through a side door, and says: "Here they come and I feel like dancing. Lovely girls. This is love", and he begins a playful game with the flower girls. The girls dodge him, he catches them. All this happens among the little tables on the forestage.

"Not a single superfluous move outside the rhythm of the music," warned Stanislavski. All the planned movements should become second nature and therefore easy and attractive. Everything should be done effortlessly and delicately, in keeping with the style of the music. The girls like to dance and love to play with Marcel. He wants to kiss every one of them. At his word "love" the first one runs up in front of him and instantly a second one comes up from behind. He turns around but the second one has already eluded him. Then a third comes up from behind as if she were going to embrace him, but no sooner has he turned towards her than she escapes between the tables. A fourth girl, near the wall, calls to him but as soon as Marcel comes near her she too escapes. When he sings: "I give you my love" he throws himself at the whole group of them but they run off upstage between the tables. Marcel remains near the main table which has just been vacated.

Stanislavski scrupulously indicated every line in his pattern for the staging. But even though he established an exact design he continued during rehearsals to get his actors to react freshly to each event, to find new adaptations of their relations to what was occuring, which meant putting real pressure on their imaginations.

"Remember the rule," he said, "and at every instant decide what you yourself would do if placed in these circumstances. Find new solutions for today." He ended up by reminding us that "the audience will not listen to anything that is rigidly fixed and forced on them."

So now the three bohemians gather at the main table on the fore-stage. A waiter stands close-by to take their order. They chat about a book Colline has bought, then they ask each other: "Where is Rodolphe?" At this moment Rodolphe appears with Mimi but they do not as yet go to their friends because they are talking to each other—about a scarf, coral beads, and, of course, love and jealousy.

Now it turns out that it is not by accident that one little table on the forestage, to the right of the audience, is separated from the rest of the café by a lattice, making it a little private nook. Later, when Musette arrives, it will play a big part, but now it is excellent as a place for the private conversation between Mimi and Rodolphe. There is a mirror on the wall and, standing in front of it, Mimi tries on the pink scarf she has just been given. The lattice divides the lovers from their companions and makes their private conversation on the forestage possible.

In the score there was a short scene with some children. But since their presence would have no relation to the main action in La Bohème it was decided that this little scene would be transferred to people in the café. A general laugh was scored by a pleasant little old man, who shared a small table in the foreground with an officer, who becoming rather "overloaded" with drink had to be helped out of the café by a waiter. This was just a passing, comic episode.

The officer sitting at the table separated by the lattice from Rodolphe and Mimi overheard and watched them. He was elegant, a bit of a fop, with a small moustache and a monocle. In Stanislavski's crowd scenes there never was anyone onstage who lacked individuality. Even those who had no lines, who acted only in pantomime, were subject to individual attention by the director and made to conform to the overall picture of the given period and situation.

So this elegant officer played his tiny but important part in the general action of the scene.

After the old man was "ushered" out, to the general merriment of the people in the café, a triumphant melody welled up from the orchestra as an accompaniment to Mimi and Rodolphe.

Their conversation begins with his words: "What are you looking at?" Mimi replies: "Are you jealous?" Rodolphe: "Where love is, jealousy is not far off." The libretto explains this exchange by saying: "Mimi is looking at some students." But Stanislavski put a keener edge on the scene by introducing the figure of the officer. He had Rodolphe leave Mimi alone for a while in front of the mirror as he went to Madame Momus at the buffet. This situation is used by the officer at the small table, who has no objection at all to scraping up an acquaintance with a pretty young modiste. This is quite in keeping with the customs of the Quarter. He comes up behind Mimi and looks at her reflection in the mirror, twirls his moustache, and is on the point of speaking to her. Just then Rodolphe appears and his cue: "What are you looking at?" is aimed at the embarrassed officer, who is beating a retreat, and Mimi's reply naturally is quite à propos: "Are you jealous?" Their further conversation is, of course, on themes of mutual assurance and love.

Now the pair of lovers are ready to join their comrades at the table they are occupying. Outside the windows, on the sidewalk where there is a constant stream of people passing by, one hears the cry of "Parpignol!" "Here's Parpignol himself with his toys!"

With that line Rodolphe and Mimi walk hand in hand downstage to their friends' table. Exclamations: "Two more places to be laid!" "At last!" "Well, here we are." Rodolphe introduces Mimi to his friends: "This is Mimi, our neighbour. Let her be an ornament to our feast. She has been sung by me. My lyre celebrates her!" And so on and on in the same elevated poetic style.

Up to this point the keynote of the atmosphere has been that of a jolly Christmas Eve in the Latin Quarter. But with the arrival of Rodolphe and Mimi it reverts to the continuing line of the intimate life of the bohemians, the beginning of which was shown in Act One. Thus the holiday crowds, the café life—all now become a background for that life.

"At the other tables the merrymaking will rise and fall," said Stanislavski. "It will correspond exactly with the central focus of action around the table of the bohemians.

"What is the through-line of action that runs through this act? It is a kind of honeymoon atmosphere. It's like the composition of a family where people come together and then part. But the main point now is—Mimi and her happiness. She carries the burden of the through-line of action, but everyone contributes to this, including the customers in the café.

"And what is Mimi's principal line of action in this act?" asked Stanislavski, turning to the singer with the role of Mimi. "It is that for the moment everything surrounding you gives you pleasure and amusement and you do not want to miss a whit of any of the blessings of life. 'I want a scarf!' and immediately you wish to go and get one. There is impatience in every move you make, you are high-spirited, gay. There are crowds of people around you—that too pleases you. You must look at all of them, some may be friends who are sympathetic. The real emotions of an actor are made up of many strands drawn from life, from one or another that passes through your consciousness.

" 'Does the scarf suit me?' Don't flirt, look at it in earnest. 'Oh, look at those corals!' You say that quite innocently without any concealed thought that Rodolphe would immediately buy them for you. 'Are you jealous?' That would be fine. After being entirely alone you find yourself among friends, in the midst of a new, a joyous life." Stanislavski impressed this on the singer, trying to evoke in her the "thought-feelings" which would lead her to the main direction of her part.

"Only two minutes have elapsed since you arrived here," said Stanislavski, "and you are already quite at ease."

Then turning to the singers he stated: "What is of prime importance is that you are not yet real bohemians. No gaiety! Not enough fancy! In Paris among the artists they roar with laughter. At your table there must be two elements always in play: the jocular and the lyrical. The lyrical, which concerns the new pair of lovers, and the jocular, which has to do with you. Yes, the whole restaurant is just one big joke, a farce. Try to sense what your present situation means: Some Frenchmen have taken into their midst a woman, they show her every attention. Everything is done in the most refined way; bohemians are often very chivalrous. No one can pay court to a woman the way the French can. Prepare a place for her, buy her flowers, toys, joke, chat with her but never seriously, help her to food. The best of everything must be for Mimi. You are all involved with Mimi. Her sweetness is overpowering, in her enjoyment she grasps at everything: flowers, toys, cakes, wine. Try to kiss her hand without letting Rodolphe see you do it. Meantime he keeps jealous guard over you—he knows his comrades.

"You must always have champagne, not cider," interjected Stanislavski. During rehearsals, which were frequently stopped by him, he kept trying for a sharper edge to a word, a richer content to a phrase, by supplying sub-texts with unexpected qualities of lightness. He strove to create the impression of spontaneity in everything that was happening on the stage.

"In the theatre every comic line must have a keen edge so that each movement, even of fingers and eyes, will carry meaning. Hilarity can be that of an actor or that of a person in ordinary life. The latter is aimed at some person or purpose, but the former is aimed at the whole audience. It is usually forced, overplayed, and therefore coarse," said Stanislavski. "Now let us go over once more Mimi's arrival, her introduction to Rodolphe's friends, and Parpignol's entrance with his toys. Look for a carefree tone, get up a stunt party. Forget about the rehearsal room, think of being somewhere down in a jolly rathskeller."

The centre of attention is—Mimi. After she has been introduced with a flourish to his friends by Rodolphe there begins a gay show. First they go through the mock ceremony of blessing the union of the "newlyweds", with a sprinkling of Latin tags, and some drops of wine, all drinking from one loving cup, and other such amusing acts, for the concocting of which Stanislavski was a past master.

"Even when you find the right framework, don't let that satisfy you," urged Stanislavski. "Keep on developing it and try not to repeat yourselves."

With Colline's ceremonially intoned: "I herewith pledge my acceptance" the so-called "wedding" comes to an end and Parpignol, the toy vendor, enters the café. Life in the café, which had been temporarily toned down, now begins to boil up again and mostly in the vicinity of Mimi. To begin with each of the bohemians presents to her his congratulations and a toy, each from a different angle. The same is done by various others in the café. The "bachelors" Schaunard, Colline, and Marcel dash over to the buffet to get some treat or other for Mimi. All this is done at a very lively tempo (the libretto indicates an *allegretto giocoso*). The whole café is set in motion and Mimi, accepting good wishes, clinks glasses with everyone and remains the focus of attention. In the libretto there is again a mention of children buying toys at this point but Stanislavski eliminated them. It was important from his point of view to keep the action focused on Mimi for this is the culminating point of happiness in her short life. The lines for the children, suitably adapted, are given to people in the café. We do not see again such a joyous moment for Mimi and therefore, as it is part of the through-line of action of the opera, it is important to stress it to the full with every possible theatrical means. Besides, the entire composition of the music for this scene calls for this.

Next the action moves to a second couple: Marcel and Musette. Up to now we have seen Marcel always gay and know nothing of his unhappy emotions. Stanislavski purposely kept saying to Marcel during rehearsals: "Above all remain carefree in manner, because under that insouciance, laughter and foolery is hidden a deep wound in your heart."

Puccini was a skilled dramatist, and he knew how to lift the curtain, ever so slightly, on the secret pain in Marcel's heart, letting us glimpse it as he looks on at the happiness of his friend. From Marcel's tone in talking with Mimi one senses that he is a bit ruffled by all the billing and cooing of the lovebirds and is ready to assert that anyone who falls in love deserves to be pitied. To this contention the composer devotes a passage in A-major which heralds the appearance of Musette.

The new scene begins with Marcel's words: "You are well-pleased, Mademoiselle Mimi, with the present of your loving Rodolphe?" Mimi confidingly replies that she had long yearned for such a scarf and that Rodolphe read this desire in her heart because he loved her. Schaunard and Colline pour fuel on the flame and Marcel begins to be slightly annoyed. "Everything in this world is lies, deceit. He is to be pitied whose heart is enthralled by love." Rodolphe aggravates the situation by his reply to Marcel: "Only he is worthy to be a true poet who knows how to love with all his heart."

The lively, rippling music which accompanies this talk lightly flits from one to the other participant as it imperceptibly rises in *tessitura* to indicate the heat generated by the discussion. It ends with the obviously irritated cue of Marcel: "Love is honey, but of a special variety." Here matters almost verge on a quarrel.

"Can it be he is offended?" asks Mimi. Rodolphe replies: "Marcel is merely out of sorts." Schaunard proposes a toast. They all, including Marcel, join in: "It is better to drink wine! Here's to wine!" The last word is sung in unison, with a triumphant chord to accompany and signalize their joyful agreement. Then suddenly. . . .

There is an unexpected pause brought about by the appearance on the threshold of the cafe of a beautiful, gorgeously-dressed woman with a look of triumph on her face—this is Musette, who reduces the whole café to stunned immobility. Through the window one glimpses her escort, who has not yet entered, an important-looking, elderly man in a top hat. Stanislavski always insisted on a clear-cut entrance for each new character.

"Please hold that pause," Stanislavski requested. "This is a moment which must be fixed in the mind of the audience."

Sounds have died away in the café. Only Marcel is standing facing Musette as she enters and he with melodramatic emotion cries, "Bring me a goblet of oblivion-inducing wine!" Now it is clear that she is the cause of Marcel's heartache.

Musette, after throwing a glance around the café, seeing her old bohemian comrades, hearing Marcel's cry about oblivion, goes to the little table beyond the lattice. The musical accompaniment is a delicately capricious melody in a sharply rhythmic pattern.

The stunned quiet of the pause is now replaced by a surge of movement all over the café. The first to begin are the bohemians, with "It is she! It is Musette!" She, after all, used to be one of them, their intimate friend. They all greet her except Marcel, who pointedly has seated himself with his back to Musette's table. The whole café is now in an uproar: "Who is it? What is she? Where? Musette? What clothes!" Many stand up to get a better look at her and they question each other.

"You must greet her," said Stanislavski at a rehearsal, "like a famous singer. An extraordinarily attractive creature has appeared in the café. *How* you look at her, what you see, what you think of the arrival of this unknown woman—all that is suggested to you by the rhythm of the music and your own intuition."

Musette passes like a conqueror, brushing Mimi with her brocaded, fur-trimmed wrap on her way to her table down front beyond the lattice. It is only now that Alcindoro comes through the entrance to the café on his cue. You hear his disgruntled objections: "You can't do that. Really, would it not be better over there?" by which he meant some other place, since here in these democratic surroundings his evening dress, silk cape, and top hat attract too much attention.

But brazen Musette treats him as a trainer would a circus dog: "Come, Lulu, come here", and she points to a place at the table for her respectable, bourgeois escort. "You can't use such pet names here in such company", he growls but he sits down where she tells him to.

"You play the exquisite, wild-beast tamer," suggested Stanislavski to the singer in the role of Musette. "But don't make a ballet out of it. Do everything in rhythm but not stressed. We must feel your rhythm in every slightest movement but it must not be noticeable."

The lattice separates the table of the bohemians from Musette. And it is by the lattice that she puts on a show which they, knowing her, are quite prepared for. Schaunard is the first to conclude that it will be fun.

Now all the principal characters are down front on the stage. The director's planning of the sets really *forced* them all down there. This was something that Stanislavski often called to the attention of young stage directors. "Make your layout of the production and build your sets so that the singer *must* be down front, and is not just there because he, with no regard for the scenery, has walked down to the footlights to 'report' his singing to the conductor. The ability to arrange settings which are needed by and comfortable for the actor-singers is one of the important functions of a director of opera—that is if he wants to get the singers to remain alive and active human beings while onstage. ·

"What is going on now along the main through-line of action of this opera?" Stanislavski asked. "Musette must be reconciled with Marcel, she must hoodwink her older escort and return to the familiar world of the bohemians—this scene is a real operetta. The two bachelors, Schaunard and Colline, undertake to bring Musette and Marcel together again. All the while the lovebirds Rodolphe and Mimi are kissing each other and murmuring loving and playfully jealous phrases, but most of the patrons in the café, aware of Schaunard's and Colline's prank and Musette's coquetry, egg them on. Marcel is perched on his chair like an inaccessible demon on a cliff. To develop the action a large ensemble of all the characters is planned and this includes Musette's 'Waltz', in which she openly admits her love for Marcel.

"All your movements," said Stanislavski to the bohemians and Musette, "call for a great deal of invention and hilarity, so that imperceptibly the link is made between the table of the bohemians and that of Musette."

After careful scrutiny of all the individual musical units of the large ensemble it was established that they fell into five principal movements—the changes in the staging would correspond to them:

1. After Musette's entrance, the banker Alcindoro comes in. Everyone eyes him with interest: the general public, Madame Momus, the waiters, the bohemians.

"To cover up his resentment over being in such unaccustomed

surroundings, the banker assiduously studies the menu, as if it were a
serious piece of literature," suggested Stanislavski.

2. Musette drops a plate of food which is being served to her, in
order to attract the attention of the bohemians and Marcel. This is the
beginning of an uproar.

"Kick the plate out of the waiter's hand so that it flies up in the air,"
proposed Stanislavski.

3. Now Schaunard and Colline set their machinations in motion.
The people at the tables around them notice their manoeuvres and
follow the uproar in the making. It is necessary to keep Alcindoro's
attention diverted from Musette so that she will be free to carry out her
own scheme. She wants to be reconciled with Marcel. To distract
Alcindoro's attention, Schaunard goes over to greet him. Colline offers
him a smoke. Now it is time to establish "wireless" communications:
notes passed under the lattice. To begin with they shove a note through
with their feet, then they dangle one on a string, finally Musette pushes
one over in her slipper. Then, hopping on one foot, she approaches
Marcel with the words: "What's the matter with you? Have you
no eyes?" Meantime Alcindoro's attention must be kept elsewhere.

"Alcindoro too can find things for himself to be distracted by,"
Stanislavski pointed out.

Before her "waltz" Musette blows face powder from her compact
into Alcindoro's face. Covered with powder, he is taken over to the
buffet to be brushed off.

"Fasten a toy on his back now," proposed Stanislavski.

4. Musette's "waltz". General excitement. Everyone hails Musette.

"Sing standing on your chair but have a reason to get up on it. It's
difficult to see Marcel because of the lattice," said Stanislavski. "But in
any case do not sing directly at him. You're a very shrewd coquette. You
do nothing in a heavy-handed way. You are always piquante. Stress
your rhythm with one eyebrow or one of your little fingers. Everything
must seem quite accidental."

Against this background of outrageous "goings-on" the lovebirds, as
Stanislavski called them, continue their billing and cooing.

5. Finally everything works out. Marcel succumbs. He had held out
for a long time.

"But don't play heavy, soul-searing, Russian love," Stanislavski
warned him. "Still be quite carefree."

The whole ensemble just described required great precision from all
participants with regard to the use of their voices and also their enunciation. The audience had to understand everything. Consequently
everyone engaged in the scene had to know at every moment who was
carrying the idea forward, whose words must not be overshadowed by

other participants. With Musette's cue: "We must now get rid of the old man", starts the culminating moment of the whole scene.

The orchestra suddenly scatters some quick sixteenth notes and stops. There is a pause of anticipation. Musette lets out a penetrating scream, which makes everyone cringe, transfixes them. During the pause Musette carries on a comic conversation with Alcindoro in the most earnest tones. "It burns, it's unbearable," she keeps repeating. "Where?" asks her bewildered escort, who is dumbfounded by all that is going on. "My foot," answers Musette, holding it up to his face.

At this the general pause breaks up in loud laughter, and now the banker has to go out and find some new footgear for Musette.

The orchestra after a rapid, ascending chromatic scale passes into a triumphant E-major theme during which Marcel emerges and all the others follow him. Schaunard and Colline pick up Musette sitting in her chair and triumphantly carry her over to Marcel, who is standing on his chair and holding out his arms to her—this is the glorification of the reconciliation of the two lovers. "My Marcel!" sings Musette with ardor. "You siren," replies Marcel. They embrace! They stand above all the others; confetti is poured on them from all sides and paper serpentines fly through the air.

Schaunard as the chief architect of the affair addresses the whole café: "This is the finale." Now at their table they have two happy couples. Musette is back with her family. All they have to do now is pay the bill and get away before Alcindoro comes back.

The unpleasant moment arrives. The bill is very big. They pool their resources, but it is obviously not sufficient. Suddenly Musette, who is radiantly happy, helps them out of their difficulties. She takes the two bills, hers and that of the bohemians, and gives the order: "Add them together, into one bill. The gentleman who was sitting with me will pay." General joy. "He will pay for everything." But now they must quickly make their escape. The scene when the bill is presented has the background of a march, which ends the second act. Drums are heard in the distance—the soldiers are coming. The people in the café rush to the windows to cheer them. This enables the bohemiams to play the scene of paying the bill at the front of the stage.

Stanislavski asked the conductor, Suk, whether it was necessary to play the whole of the march and wasn't this sort of procession with a handsome drum major at the head merely an operatic tradition.

"All we are interested in at this point is the banker, Alcindoro, who has been made a fool of by the bohemians," said Stanislavski. "That is to say, we want to see his arrival and the silly situation into which he has been thrust with the presentation of the large bill which, in addition to all the other indignities which have been heaped upon him, he must pay."

That was Stanislavski's line of reasoning: He built his productions by eliminating all that was superfluous in order to emphasize what was important and fundamental. Suk quite agreed with him and cuts were made in the march.

During the gay military march music the bohemians, with Musette hopping on one foot, leave the café.

Just before the curtain closes Alcindoro, with a pair of new slippers for Musette in his hand, enters the side door of the café. He is met not by Musette but by two waiters unrolling a long bill. The bewildered banker looking at the bill through his monocle is the butt of general laughter. On this the second act ends.

Act Three

Up to this point the gay, light side of bohemian life has been painted but now the darker side appears.

"Find your way along the through-line of action now with a magnet in your hands," said Stanislavski. "Everything in the music and the action in your roles will be drawn to the super-objective of the whole performance and all else will fall away.

"In this act the dominating factor is dismay and astonishment at life: It is impossible for the lovers to part from one another yet they cannot go on living together any longer. This is the insoluble problem, the cause of the dismay. In the meeting of Rodolphe and Mimi there was something fateful. With Marcel and Musette it is quite different—it was based on carefree insouciance. This gives the general tone to the act," explained Stanislavski.

How was the action to be developed and where is the scene laid?

The libretto puts it at the Porte d'Orléans and includes a mass of details: there is the gate itself and two boulevards, a guard house, plane trees, and finally a small tavern ("on the left"). The time is dawn, on a misty, snowy day in February.

But Stanislavski was opposed to these details.

"What is of import to us is, above all, the tavern. Practically all the action takes place in it or near it. Marcel and Musette live there. There are nighttime carousers. It is necessary to have a street: working people are on their way to work at dawn, shopkeepers are going to market, idle carousers are leaving for home. We need the impression of a cold, foggy dawn, with street lights still showing along the receding highway, but they will be put out later on. The 'February and snow' of the libretto is incomprehensible. The main goal for Mimi and Rodolphe is to get through the winter. February in Paris is the harbinger of spring, the *end* of winter. Why should they have to part if spring were at hand? What we need for our purposes is, rather, a cold day in late autumn with winter still ahead."

That was Stanislavski's interpretation of the setting in which the developing events would unroll. In keeping with this plan, V.A. Simov designed the set: To the right from the auditorium was the façade of the tavern with a large window and with an entrance from the forestage (with four steps). The building itself is only two stories high and on the left side of the façade there is a second-story balcony to which a stairway leads. Under the balcony is a door into the place where Musette lives. To the left of the tavern is a street which recedes from the auditorium and winds around back of the house. Coming from the wings, to the left of the auditorium, one can see the bars of the city gate and a detachment of police guards. On the curtain over the lighted window in the tavern one can see the shadows of people carousing inside with Musette clinking glasses. Near the entrance to the tavern, by the outside staircase, there is a lattice for a creeping vine. The leaves on it are sere, and red—it is autumn. At the entrance to the tavern, there is a stepladder for Marcel's use in painting the sign above the door. It is only half painted.

Stanislavski was always concerned in the first place with providing a set which would be comfortable for actors, while still bearing in mind the expressiveness of its composition, colours, and, here, the features characteristic of life on the edge of Paris.

After a sharp *forte* the orchestra passes to a melody that sounds like falling raindrops—a *pizzicato* on the strings—and then the curtain opens.

We see the figure of a muffled police guard making his rounds.

Beyond the grille of the city gate (that is, offstage) we hear yells of: "You there! Open up! We've got to get to our jobs!" The guard does not hurry. There are a few more impatient cries and the slouching, yawning guard lets a group of workmen through who quickly disappear around a turn in the street.

"No need to make a theatrical, chorus scene out of this," warned Stanislavski. "There are only a few workmen, eight in all. Don't yell in such deep voices or you will sound like night prowlers, and you will destroy the atmosphere of the scene."

The music paints a picture of pre-dawn dampness, of cold cheer, and lonely lives. From the trees swathed in fog, cold, heavy drops fall to the ground and nature is as dark as the mood of Mimi and Rodolphe. But there is a sense of alertness and agitated expectancy in the abrupt *pizzicato* sounds of the strings, played against a background of monotonously drawn-out parallel fifths from the bass viols.

This guarded despair in the music is now interrupted by a series of carefree, guitar-like chords coming from the tavern. Inside there is a warm, cozy, drunken atmosphere—bohemians are carousing. After that the music from the beginning of the act is repeated.

"What is this music typical of?" asked Stanislavski. "How can one convey the morning mists, the breaking of dawn? Shadows of carousers. These are sleepy drunkards, quite intoxicated, but bearing themselves decently (they are intoxicated by red wine, not hard liquor). The fumes affect their feet, not their heads," insisted Stanislavski. "The police guard makes his rounds along this street all night. He has been chilled through and has muffled his head in his hood. One needs a lamplighter to extinguish the streetlights. The act should begin in a half-asleep mood. Find the rhythm for this in the music. You are all to work on sketches built on this theme in order to find the pauses, the logic of it."

All of the cast, including the principals, went through different exercises based on this descriptive music because they all had to be in character, in the mood and atmosphere of the act.

After the workmen have gone, a group of half-drunken revellers emerges singing from the tavern with Musette at their head. Musette is the toast of the tavern. Standing on the steps by the entrance they sing a ditty about "wine the giver of gaiety". Musette, with some man's top hat on her head, sings a solo: "When you drink with friends around you, you are gay and happy." The men stagger up and kiss her hand re-soundingly and sing: "Tra-la-la, here's to love!" The group, not a large one, is made up of five men and there is one fop who insistently presses his attentions on Musette. We shall see him again later on. Stanislavski singles him out in order to explain why Musette leaves Marcel.

The crowd drifts away. The streetlights are put out. Dawn breaks.

Peasant women selling milk come on the scene. "Cheese and butter! Chickens and eggs!" They call their wares and as they go by the guard they show him what they are carrying. They exchange a few words with each other and then disappear in different directions. There are only a few of them, perhaps five. Again the stage is empty. Now the orchestra takes up again the broad, expressive theme of Mimi, and at the same time we see her thin little figure emerge at the end of a street. She is simply dressed and wrapped in a shawl. She is evidently here for the first time and is looking for someone. Can this really be Mimi? How she has changed! She shyly addresses the policeman: "Can you tell me, is there a painter living in a tavern near here?" "Yes, there," he replies, pointing in the direction of the tavern, and then with calm indifference continues on his beat. This exchange has no musical accompaniment.

"For heaven's sake don't have the *recitativo* here. Restrain yourself. An actor is tested by the pauses he can sustain. You must take in the whole of your surroundings. Approach cautiously and slowly. Re-member, your fate is there," begged Stanislavski.

Immediately the door onto the balcony is opened: a smart maid shakes a napkin out. Mimi addresses her: "Do be kind enough to find a painter for me—his name is Marcel. . . ." But the girl in reply merely purses her lips and disappears. Her first attempt having failed, all Mimi can do is wait.

"Walk off down the little alley and wait for a favourable opportunity," said Stanislavski.

Again comes cautious music from the orchestra but this time in a bright C-major key which defines the dawn more clearly. From some nearby church tower come the thin sounds of a morning bell. Blending with it we hear the intermittent triplets familiar to us from the first act. This is Marcel's theme and immediately we see him coming from a side door in the tavern, scowling and rather shivery from the cold morning. With some pots and brushes he climbs heavily up the stepladder to paint the tavern sign. This musical phrase ends on a cautious *pizzicato* and at the same time Mimi comes hesitantly from around the corner. Four chords *fortissimo*—Mimi rushes over to Marcel. "Mimi!" he exclaims. "It was with the greatest difficulty I found you here," says Mimi. They meet in a very friendly way. Their conversation continues. Mimi begs Marcel for help. He is sitting on the lower steps of his ladder. Mimi stands near him. He tries to think of some way of extricating Mimi from her troubles.

Stanislavski worked with great care over the subtlety of the tone coloration of the singers. "We the audience," he said, "are not interested in a formal rendering of the plot—we want to look into the depths, the wellsprings of your hearts. Your words carry your thoughts and the music carries the feelings behind them.

"You have to confess to Marcel that Rodolphe has abandoned you and you want to get him back. But, if you look at life, that is not so simple. There is a whole kaleidoscope of questions. To begin with you have to find out if he is here. Then to discover whether your parting is final or temporary. Finally, and how are you to explain this most important point to Marcel: who is to blame for it? Perhaps you yourself did something that could have contributed to the quarrel. You have to press Marcel to help you, because something is going out of your life, perhaps forever. Do you still hope that all will end well and you will be reconciled with Rodolphe? Of course you do, and that is what is foremost in your mind.

"You must feed your subconscious with a quantity of such questions and visualize what you are singing about. You must prepare a whole reel of inner images which will reflect everything: your quarrels with Rodolphe, the bright days you have had together, and what you envisage as your future. There must be no generalizations, everything must be concrete. And if you sing exactly what you are seeing here and now—that will be genuinely creative art. You may think that at present you are faced with too many objectives and you have difficulty finding your way around among them. Do not spend too long a time in preparation, do not frighten yourself. The difficult thing to discover is the nature of the problem. Once you find that all else is easy. The important part is in your concentrated attention and in your eyes.

"We are proceeding along the line of both music and drama," continued Stanislavski. "In music, in addition to rhythm and measure, there is a driving force. It expresses itself outwardly in a finished phrase which is both played and also sung. If an actor clearly understands the music and conveys it by act and word, the audience also will feel the music. The spectator must be at one with the composer."

Marcel sits on his stepladder, his feet hanging down, mixes his paints, and listens to Mimi. She is wrapped in a ragged shawl, looks almost like a beggar. At first Marcel pays scant attention to her words, but then a feeling of sympathy springs up in him, although his tone remains insouciant: "Musette has an easy time with me, we lead a gay life. Laughter, singing—that's how life flows by—without sadness."

After Marcel's words about Rodolphe: "He came an hour before dawn and fell asleep on a bench in there," suddenly Mimi has a fit of coughing. Mimi's cough rouses Marcel's suspicions, and it is only then that he puts down his work and climbs down to the sidewalk.

"But don't show your surprise in a theatrical way," Stanislavski warned. "To be surprised you must first be extremely attentive."

Mimi's sad words are accompanied by a transparent E-minor melody: "I am so very tired. . . ." is the end of this duet. Immediately, as a reminder of Rodolphe, the orchestra plays his brief theme from the first act. Marcel hurries to the doorway because he sees that Rodolphe has got up and is coming out. He says to Mimi: "You had better go away from here, Mimi. Really we don't want to have a scene," and leads her behind a hedge.

Rodolphe looks sleepy, rather limp, tousled, and is dressed in some kind of a grey raincoat. He does not in the least resemble the gay and happy creature whom we saw in the last act. He is sad, sullen, abrupt as he comes straight to the point with Marcel: "Marcel, I have thought it all over. . . . We are alone. . . . I have decided to break entirely with Mimi. . . ." For the moment Marcel is patient, condescending: "Again? What's happened now?" As they talk they are standing near the steps entering the tavern.

In this conversation there are three separate moments: 1. Rodolphe's decision to break with Mimi—this to the accompaniment of strong musical phrases, rising to high notes. 2. His justification of himself—he is jealous. "Mimi is at heart a flirt, she merely toys with love." 3. His opinion of the situation: Mimi is hopelessly ill, "her sad end is near at hand."

We can read Mimi's face as she sits close to the greenery, unseen by Rodolphe, and we realize that her hopes have foundered.

The actor-singers are in the fortunate position of being able to make an impression without recourse to the "world of emotions"—all they have to do is preserve the clear line of thought and let Puccini's music "filter through them", as Stanislavski put it.

The scene ends with an ensemble in which Mimi, Rodolphe, and Marcel all join, and although it is written in two-quarter time it is constructed rhythmically on triplets of which Mimi constantly omits the first eighth note in each triplet, thus giving the impression of pulsing, held-in sobs. Mimi sings with sighs: "Oh Lord . . . is he right . . . I am lost . . . can it be . . . I am doomed to die? . . ."

Rodolphe sings: "Mimi is a delicate flower. Poverty destroyed her. My love cannot give back to her either health or strength. . . ." And Marcel repeats: "Poor, poor Mimi."

Rodolphe does not as yet know that Mimi is within hearing. Marcel is in a state of turbulence, he is between two fires; he dare not reveal the fact that Mimi is there, yet she should not be hearing everything they say.

"This is the beginning of the tragedy," said Stanislavski sternly. "You must get ready for a serious ending. We are at the climax of the act now."

After the last chord of the trio fades away, a wave of agitation and heartache begins in the orchestra.

It is related, of course, to Mimi, who gives away her presence by sobbing. Rodolphe rushes over to her: "You have been here and heard everything? Do not pay any attention to what I said. . . ." Embracing the weeping Mimi, he leads her to a bench near the grille, where they will both sit until the end of their duet. Marcel, who is much embarrassed, is drawn away by the sound of Musette's laughter which comes from the tavern. With the words: "Musette is laughing loudly. Who is in there with her? What a flirt! Well, let her wait and see. . . ." he quickly runs up the outside stairs to catch Musette unexpectedly. He no sooner reaches the balcony than the door of the tavern opens and the same foppish young man in a top hat we saw earlier darts out and vanishes around a corner. This brief, ironical scene provides a slight relaxation of the tension which has been building on the stage.

"Every act in real life," said Stanislavski, "has its phases of development. Every so often it is necessary to have a moment of détente. Things boil up, then cool off. This is followed by a reaction and the whole process is renewed. An unbroken line of tension is to be found only in madmen—that is an idée fixe. A normal person is intent on something, then is distracted, then concentrates anew. Moments of reaction are inevitable. This law must be remembered and applied to action on the stage. This scene with Marcel illustrates the process."

Now we come to the episodes of separation. One parting is dramatic, the other is sheer buffoonery.

"Where Musette is—there a comic operetta is always in progress," remarked Stanislavski. "To be sure Murger, with a slightly different colouring, said of her: Musette is an enchanting woman, whose heart is a reception room frequented by outstanding people in the world of art and literature. . . . But in this play there are no such representatives of the arts."

In keeping with the character of these two couples Stanislavski made a plan of staging for the finale of the third act.

For Mimi and Rodolphe, with their deep emotional experiences, memories, and hopes, he arranged a very quiet mise-en-scène. They sit side by side and recall their lives. This is based on subtle psychology, on the shadings of words, intonations, and the use of the eyes. The other pair carry on their dialogue from widely-separated positions. Marcel is on the balcony on the second floor and Musette is down below. Their talk is all excited altercation, with lively ejaculations.

La Bohème, Act III (from the 1927 production): The Separation Quartette. (Photograph reproduced from damaged plate.)

After Musette's gay triplets have dissipated and faded away the orchestra begins a long sustained note on which Mimi begins her speech. Her first words are: "Farewell then." Rodolphe is dismayed: "What do you mean? Are you going away?" Their situation is very

complex and is not immediately understandable. How can Mimi remain alone, and she so ill? Rodolphe should be at her side now.

In this scene Stanislavski had to coach the singers in many ways in
order to ensure their maintaining clarity and subtlety of both thoughts
and feelings.

"Do not miss the main point that all is ended. The sub-text of your
farewell," said he to Mimi, "is: 'I am going away because I am dying.
Although I continue to love Rodolphe, I wish to maintain my self-esteem.'

"And you, Rodolphe, think she is leaving you just because of her
pride and at the very time when you should be at her side to sustain her.
The gravity of this moment lies in the fact that only five minutes ago all
seemed well, and now all is shattered. Your relationship with each other
is now a different one."

In this clarification between them there are three moments which
must be defined:

1. "Alone I shall go along my own old way." "But no sentimentality!" warned Stanislavski, who was the most arrant foe of sentimentality
on the stage.

2. "Send me my belongings, and, by the way, you will find my scarf
under my pillow—if you choose you may keep it in memory of me."
Puccini wrote this phrase for Mimi with the true sense of a dramatist. It
helps the singer to avoid a most dangerous pitfall of sentimentality.
Besides, the scarf will play a big role in the fourth act as a memorable
symbol of their love.

3. This is an *andante con moto* where they say good-bye to each
other and to their life together, its joys, sorrows, reproaches, reconci-
liations. The gleaming melody of their duet lightly passes from one to
the other as if to solace them. There is no sobbing here, and no suffering
is felt. It is as if the consciousness of the sad necessity for them to part
has already diminished the bitterness of their loss.

"Sit there and recall all that was good in your life," suggested
Stanislavski. "You no longer kiss each other, you are already almost
strangers. Your passion has subsided. You feel each other out with your
souls' antennae. This is already a transition to the state of friendly
concern. Yet all the while, in the depths of your hearts the question
keeps welling: 'Should we not remain together?—No, we must part.'"

So the two principal characters sit on a bench near the grille and
their voices weave and blend in their farewell duet. They are completely absorbed in their memories and do not hear at all how, nearby,
right around a corner, another couple is also saying farewell to each
other. As distinct from the principal rendering of the voices of Mimi
and Rodolphe, the others speak in a forceful *recitative*. Musette had
flown out of the tavern door with a shawl around her and a stick with a

bundle hanging from it across her shoulder. She is starting on a journey. Marcel hurls reproaches down at her from the balcony: "Who were you chattering with, and about what? Evidently you were having a good time. When I went in your whole face changed." Musette, never at a loss for words, replies: "He asked me, 'Is it such fun to dance, you sylph? ' And blushing I replied: 'I am only happy when I'm hopping day and night'."

Marcel is angry: "I'll make you dance so you won't forget it if I ever catch him around you again."

"Whoever gave you the right to talk to me as if I were your wife?" laughs Musette.

"You are leaving? So much the better—I'll be that much richer," says Marcel witheringly. Musette teases Marcel with all sorts of shoulder shrugging and dancing around on one foot. Then their conversation becomes tinged with billingsgate: "Oh, you're nothing but a lousy sign painter". She yells this loud enough for the whole street to hear. "You slimy serpent, you toad, you old witch!" is his retort.

This is how Marcel and Musette part company. Yet the tone of it all is almost hilarious.

"She is thinking ahead," said Stanislavski, "about how this evening she will be dancing the cancan in a gay circle of friends."

Now Mimi stands up. The rhythm of her movements is slow. Before their long separation, she and Rodolphe walk awhile with their arms about each other.

Act Four

"We are still in the reckless world of bohemians. Mimi returns to it made wise by her experience. Death comes unawares. They all begin to understand the reality of life." Stanislavski thus summed up the intent of the fourth act before we began to work on it.

Again, as at the very beginning of the opera, a theatrical fanfare opens the action as the quickly-rising curtain reveals the stage. Again we are in the familiar attic room, but outside the window there are no signs of winter. Obviously the time is the end of summer or early autumn. In a niche there is a bouquet of fall flowers. The comrades are in their old places; Rodolphe at the table and Marcel in the embrasure of the window standing before his easel. A number of his sketches have joined the pictures on the wall. The window is open. The two men are trying to work—their thoughts have wandered far away.

At the very beginning the mood of the act is buoyant, carefree, tinged with irony. They are remembering their women friends.

"She was driving by in a carriage?" asks Marcel, continuing their conversation.

"Yes, and with a liveried footman," underscores Rodolphe. " 'Hey, Musette,' I called. 'How's your heart?' 'It doesn't beat, you can't hear it,' answered Musette. 'Too thick a covering of velvet'," Rodolphe added, obviously twitting Marcel.

"Well, her answer was not so bad," said Marcel rather listlessly. Again the music strikes up a loud fanfare, a gay *rondo* and two gay flourishes. "I met *her* too." "Who? Musette?" Rodolphe asks negligently. "No, Mimi." "Really?" This he asks in a worried tone. "She was riding in a carriage and dressed like a queen," Marcel adds with emphasis. "Well, what of that, that's fine," is all Rodolphe can say. "Here's to work," he says with annoyance and the other repeats: "Here's to work." But for the one his "pen refuses to write", while for the other his "brushes are awful" and he cannot make his painting go well. A broad A-flat chord from the orchestra is the introduction to a duet between Rodolphe and Marcel about their past, unforgettable loves. This duet is very important in characterizing these carefree young men who are nonetheless capable of powerful feelings.

"We must at the very beginning of this act be sure to establish ourselves firmly on the right track," said Stanislavski to the actors. "Therefore there is a lot of spadework to be done before we even reach the duet."

The whole exchange between the two about Musette and, particularly, Mimi is of the utmost importance in relation to what follows.

"We must make the audience grasp that the feelings of the two friends have remained unchanged despite the complicated circumstances of their lives, that they are faithful to their beloved ones despite the complex and involved paths taken by them. For each of the men this is a delicate matter and they try to avoid it, especially since the purity of their feelings has remained. Therefore what is the through-line of action for you in this act? 'I am keeping my shining memories, but I hide this fact under an exterior of bravado and irony.' "

The duet begins. Right away, Stanislavski sets before his singers this objective:

"Sing as if you were keeping this a secret from your comrade. Sing the way you did in the quartet in *Eugene Onegin* when it was all done in whispers but was heard throughout the auditorium. This is a place when consonants are all important."

The friends, each unseen by the other, draw something from under their pillows. In Rodolphe's hand we see Mimi's pink scarf and Marcel is holding a picture of Musette. Each in his own corner sings of his own sacred feelings.

Outside the window, twilight is fading. The mansard room is lighted by reflections of the setting sun. This enhances the yearning that has come over them as they recall their memories, and makes each one feel even lonelier. The main thing is, of course, the absorption of their delicate singing in thoughts that are far away from this garret room.

"The minute you lose sight of your objective even for a fraction of a second and your singing turns away from the object of your concentrated attention, you are instantly converted into some kind of provincial opera singer emitting 'pretty sounds'. In order to create life on the stage you must act by means of words. We are trying to achieve a *pianissimo* in your singing but this is not a formal requirement, it evolves out of the depths of your emotions, and not because the notes carry a special indication of a *double piano.*"

Incidentally it was not necessary to remind the conductor, Suk, of this. He himself asked one of the singers: "Why did you suddenly sing *piano* here? I don't understand."

The two men finally succeeded in producing the whole duet in the tones of a delicate watercolour, painted with most tender shadings. And I still remember this duet as if it were a sigh rising from two hearts, like the beating of the heart of each singer.

At the end of the duet the two friends surreptitiously hide their mementos under their pillows and sit in profound absorption, each in his corner.

Finally complete silence reigns. It grows even darker as the twilight fades. Without breaking the general sense of quiet and immobility Rodolphe sings in the same key as the last dying chord of the duet: "It must be quite late." "Yes, it is time for supper, I wonder why Schaunard is not here yet", replies Marcel in the same tone. These simple, trite phrases appear to rouse the friends from the realm of their remembrances, from the world of poetry to the prose of everyday life. Immediately the orchestra takes up the theme of their boisterous, boiling life and Schaunard and Colline enter.

With the lively rhythm of the music the atmosphere of fun returns to the scene and embraces them all.

"Lightness is the key to this play," Stanislavski reminded us, "and indicates the general trend. Nothing can down these people, until a real catastrophe overtakes them. They always can find some basis for their jollity. This is such a moment. There is no special occasion for merriment: for supper all they have is bread and a bit of herring."

Underneath the impact of the music everything is in a state of flux. First of all the table must be set. So they move all the furniture around. Since the dinner will be a formal affair, the setting must be in consonance with it.

Now the men settle themselves around the table in full view of the audience.

"Is that all?" asks Marcel, looking at a large chunk of bread. "Oh no, there is also the dish of Demosthenes—herring," proclaims Colline impressively (he always proclaims rather than just speaks). "And it's pickled," puts in Schaunard.

"Well, we can say grace for such a sumptuous banquet," says Marcel with reviving spirits. "All we need do is to put the champagne on ice." With a flourish Schaunard sets a carafe of water inside his top hat. This is done to the music of a brilliant run of notes, and their boisterous fun continues.

The bohemians play at being in high society and assume titles of counts, princes, etc., as they savagely lampoon the affectations of the aristocracy. "My dear duke, here are the pheasants." "Count, do you not care for the trout?" The "Count", Colline, replies while chewing on a last morsel: "No, thanks, really, I am off to a ball." In this way foolishness lends vivacity to their skimpy meal. All this happens at the very rapid tempo with insidious overtones. This is the time for all sorts of Punch and Judy pranks and they jerk their arms and legs to simulate the movements of puppets.

"Only don't try to entertain the audience with your nonsense. Entertain each other," warned Stanislavski. "Be utterly serious about all sorts of nonsense and interest each other in it. Then the audience will also have its interest engaged by what you are doing. You must now reach out into the auditorium with your foolery; it is the audience which must be caught up in what is happening on the stage. A situation on the stage can entertain and cause laughter only when the actor himself is completely involved and when he does not put on what he supposes to be the mask of comedy. Without sincere, childlike faith in all foolish games the actor cannot create fun on the stage."

Now each one readies his "turn". All this is done in the spirit of improvisation. Look, something is happening to Colline—he is practically bursting with self-importance as he eats the last bit of bread. "I must hurry, the King is waiting for me." His comrades immediately devise a new twist. They start playing at government secrets of highest concern, perhaps even a question of a complot, and some of them retire under the table to conspire. And when Colline unexpectedly blurts out: "His Majesty has offered me a post" there is general rejoicing, and eight legs prance in the air. Now Schaunard wishes to deliver a speech to "this honourable assembly", but the honourable assembly is too far gone in hilarity to be willing to listen to any speeches: "Go to the devil! Nothing doing! *Basta!*" Schaunard quickly changes his tune: "I have just had an idea for a new romantic song." But the company has overflowed its boundaries of tolerance and does not wish to hear of it. "No-no-no", they yell in chorus. But Schaunard persists: "But surely you don't want to do without dancing?" "Now that's a bull's-eye! Right!

Right!" they all yell with delight. The orchestra reflects their lively enthusiasm.

"Pray clear the hall," demands Colline and to the music introducing the dance they move the furniture back into place in ceremonious rhythm, that is to say Rodolphe's divan is put back where it used to stand and the table replaced near the window—this rearrangement prepares the setting for what is to happen later.

Before the dance there is a "general pause" for two measures. "Why? Well, let's fill them," said Stanislavski. "How about a sort of presentation parade of dancers? Let each dancer step into the centre of the room and assume the pose of his dance. You see, there will be an argument shortly about which is the best dance."

In silence, reminiscent of a "danger moment" in the circus, each one proceeds to his place attempting to do so with a brilliant ballet movement. The temperature of the fun rises. This enhancement is, of course, inherent in the Puccini music.

Now the four dancers, in various poses most suited to what they propose to perform, stand before us. First there is Colline—he is for a gavotte and demonstrates how it should be danced. His gracefulness is rather bear-like. Marcel is in favour of a minuet; Rodolphe—a melancholy pavanella and Schaunard is crazy to do a wild fandango.

But in the end they all agree to do a quadrille. "A quadrille is much the best," decides Colline. It is for one thing much easier to dance than a fandango or a minuet.

"Invite your ladies." The "ladies" are Marcel and Rodolphe. Since they are members of high society they are very meticulous and act with the manners of a cook. Schaunard intones a gay air and the quadrille gets off to a successful start. They careen rapturously about, then there is a disagreement. "Balance to corners," calls Colline. "No, it's the ladies' chain," contradicts Schaunard. Now a terrible "riot" is in the making. It begins with his saying: "You nitwit, you boor!" The exchange between the two opponents quickly reaches the stage of hot-blooded expletives: "I'll drink your blood", "Bring on a stretcher", "Carry him to the cemetery." They shake so with fury they can barely stand. The "ladies" faint, come to, and try to pull their partners from each other's throats. Then there is a brief duel during which the "ladies" sing: "While the blows are glancing we can go on dancing," and they hop around the two contestants. The duel is quickly ended. Colline pokes his finger into Schaunard's belly and he keels over instantly onto the floor. They immediately grab the unfortunate man by his arms and legs and tote him around the room as if they were performing some kind of a rite. Suddenly the unexpected happens: Schaunard jumps to his feet and knocks down his opponent in an acrobatic twist which lands them both on the floor. The legs of the one are intertwined with the arms of the other and now a strange animal with two heads and four legs begins to crawl around the stage. Instantly Marcel and Rodolphe climb onto the monster and the procession continues.

In an article which he wrote on *Laws for Opera Performance* Stanislavski described this staging:

"The music indicates the excited state of the young men which reaches its climax in the dance scene. The music thunders and the actors riot noisily. Instead of the usual dance they put together a so-called elephant. One actor lies on the floor stretching up his arms and legs on which a second one extends himself. A third turns a somersault over them. Mimi, now in a dying condition, is carried in. Into this absurd situation she comes to find death. It is by these very contrasts that this scene achieves a most powerful impression."

The dance music and all the foolery to which it is an accompaniment is abruptly stopped by a clap of thunder from the orchestra. Musette stands in the doorway and sees the bunch of youngsters on the floor, who are now transfixed by the unexpected events. After the thunderous effect the orchestra turns to a sudden *pianissimo* (a *tremolo* in the bass viols). Musette announces: "Mimi is here. She has taken a sudden turn for the worse. She did not have the strength to get here by herself." "Where is she? Mimi!" Rodolphe rushes out to the staircase. From being stunned into immobility by this unexpected news, they are now filled with feverish activity. Schaunard and Colline drag Rodolphe's divan to the middle of the stage.

Marcel rushes over to Musette. Now their meeting is a warm one of close friends. There is no trace in her now of the giddiness she had two years earlier in the Café Momus. But after Musette's cue the strings begin a broad melody, full of drama, indicating Mimi's fate. In this phrase every note stands out in clear relief *(marcato)* and the violin solo no longer speaks of sadness and regrets. The character of the music is austere, pitiless, as if calling on one and all to gather their strength. There is no room here at all for sentimental pity—all is deadly earnest.

During this music Mimi enters, but not in the way indicated in the libretto which says: "Rodolphe and Marcel help Mimi to reach the bed."

Instead, as in the first act, Rodolphe carries her in in his arms. Then she was a starved maker of flowers in a plain little dark blue frock; now she is a rich lady in a low-cut gown of luxurious brocade. She is like a bird of paradise who has flown in from goodness knows where, and her figure is in striking contrast to the dark, mean attic room and the modest clothing of its inhabitants.

"Rodolphe, my own, will you take me back?" is her first phrase. With joy and despair Rodolphe sings: "Oh yes, Mimi! This is your home." Tenderly and carefully he places her on the divan.

"The more concern and care you show, the more *painful* it is," said Stanislavski. "Treat her as you would if she had burst an artery."

Her shoulders are uncovered, her arms are bare, she feels cold. Rodolphe covers her with her brocade cape trimmed with fur but it cannot warm her, so on top of the gorgeous dress he lays his old blanket.

"Lay any old thing you can on top of the brocade, in order to warm her," said Stanislavski.

All around her is poverty but at the same time a great deal of human warmth and that is principally what gives her heat. Now she is tired, her mind wanders a little. Meantime Musette has gathered the others, except Rodolphe, and tells them Mimi's sad story. She had left the viscount (he it was who provided the gorgeous clothing) and feeling that death was near she made her way to this place, saying: "My end is at hand. If only I could die near him it would be happiness for me."

All those surrounding Mimi expect her end at any time, but she is happy, she is at home, among friends and beside the man she loves. She ever recalls the happy melodies from the first act. They sound halting

La Bohème, Act IV (from the 1927 production): The death of Mimi.

now, yet she feels new strength, thinks she is well again and expects a renewal of happiness. To be sure she tires quickly, and if only her chilled hands would get warm again. She imagines everything is once more as it used to be; indeed Marcel smiles as brightly as ever, and Schaunard and Colline—Musette too is as kind as ever. In short, she has come here not to suffer but to be calmed and made happy. Her tragedy has now passed over to the others. In the rhythm of their behaviour, the cautious tone of their singing and their conversation—their *recitativo* often sinks to a whisper—in all the attentive, worried glances they throw toward Mimi, we can discern her fate. Schaunard, watching the calm face of Mimi as she dozes, says to Colline: "She has not long to live." This cannot be simply sung, it must be said in a musical *whisper* so that no one on the stage will hear it yet it will reach the whole auditorium.

The atmosphere of watchful waiting is enhanced by the lighting of the stage. On the table in the embrasure of the window there is a single lighted candle with a flickering flame.

It is a tense evening; they all sing or speak in a low voice and walk about on tiptoe.

Marcel and Musette have gone to fetch a muff for Mimi. They both have grown kinder and more reasonable now that they stand before this terrifying experience. Rodolphe's entire attention is focused on Mimi. Only occasionally he goes to the window, stands with his back to the audience, and wipes his eyes with a handkerchief.

At this point the philosopher Colline says good-bye to his faithful friend, his old raincoat: "My ancient coat, most loyal friend, I must part from you. I need your help in the service of another. . . ."

The little arietta is written with great seriousness, without any sentimentality, but . . . standing beside the dying Mimi, can it be sung in the usual bass voice? Every phrase calls for the most subtle possible sound. The score indicates *piano* but, as Stanislavski was always proving, the terms *piano* and *forte* are not of any absolute dimension, they are always relative in size and in this case one has to have a triple *piano*.

After his farewell to his coat, Colline takes Schaunard and they both go out in order to let Rodolphe and Mimi be alone together. Now comes their last duet. For it Puccini wrote music which is so tender, sincere and simple, yet so pregnant with dramatic impact that it has seldom been rivalled.

It starts with a long introduction, a kind of musical reminiscence of their first meeting, when Mimi, in the grip of her first feelings of rapture, sings: "Oh, love has conquered me, my heart is full of joy. . . ." Now, as if resurrecting her past, she sings: "We are here alone. I wanted no one to hear our words, I pretended to be asleep. I have so much to tell you. No, it was only one thing, deeper than any ocean. . . . For you are mine, dearer to me than life. . . ."

And they both sing about the most precious things the human heart can treasure. The singers must put themselves wholly in the power of Puccini, the depth and vividness of his feelings.

Rodolphe compares Mimi to the lovely dawn. She replies simply, humbly, that he is mistaken. He must have meant to say—lovely as the light of the setting sun.

Most touching too is the incident with the scarf, which Rodolphe lays on Mimi's breast. How she revives when she sees his present! Then they begin to recall details of their first meeting, the search for her key. Their exchange becomes playful. All of this is saturated with high poetry and never drops into cheap sentimentality.

This duet of memories of their past is broken off by a suffocating fit of coughing. . . . Mimi has difficulty breathing, but. . . .

"No naturalism, no suffering, tortured expressions of the face," warned Stanislavski. "You," he said to Mimi, "must not allow any external signs of pain. Simply raise yourself a little on your pillow— that's all. But all around you there is agitation. That is what creates the impression of danger."

Schaunard runs in. "What's happened to her?" They put her carefully back on her pillow and pull up the covers. "Keep quiet for a little," begs Rodolphe. "Forgive me, I'll be careful." Mimi lies there quietly and even seems to doze.

To the accompaniment of muted triplets from the orchestra Musette enters with Marcel. Marcel hands Rodolphe some medicine, saying: "I ran for a doctor, asked him to come as quickly as he can. Here's some medicine." Musette is holding a gorgeous white muff. Mimi hears them and asks: "Whose voice is that?" "It is I, Musette," she answers and coming over to Mimi, lays the muff over her hands. "Ah," Mimi exclaims, "how soft it is!" These and the following words "Now my hands will never be cold" are the beginning of the theme of Mimi's passing away. The theme repeats music from the first act—there is the echo of the phrase: "It is very dark, no use to search any farther . . ." and "Such a cold little hand, I must warm it for you. . . ." How far away, almost intangible, are the memories. She falls quietly asleep as if lulled by these short phrases. Just the last one remains suspended for a while in the air—a long-drawn-out, single note which slowly melts away. After that there is a long pause. We sense that this is the moment of Mimi's death.

No matter how strong the emotions of the actors and the spectators, one cannot rely only on feeling. Therefore Stanislavski always analyzed the state of the actors and in this instance he said:

"Mimi is dying. What are the reflexes of a person at this moment? Complete immobility, half-closed eyes, inability to speak—his tongue is tied. Puccini was a subtle expert in his knowledge of human psychology, therefore he wrote Mimi's last words with long pauses in between as if each time she had to gather strength to say the next word. A fleeting smile is also characteristic of such a death," he added, "therefore a long pause is necessary after the fading sounds of the music when Mimi dies."

During this long pause the happily smiling face of Mimi becomes serious and inpenetrable in expression. All the others are wrapped in their own thoughts. Mimi seems to have fallen asleep. They are all waiting for the doctor. Sitting at the head of Mimi's couch Musette begins to pray as best she can: "Oh, Most Sacred Virgin, do not be deaf to her prayer, do not let her die." Suddenly a draft of air from the window nearly extinguishes the candle. Turning to Rodolphe, who is standing at the window, Musette says: "The air will blow the candle out, you must do something to protect it." Rodolphe stands a book on end beside it. Musette goes on with her prayer: "Return her to health, Holy Virgin. I do not deserve forgiveness, but poor Mimi was as pure as an angel."

As Rodolphe heard Musette's prayer he was somewhat comforted and asked her: "Is she better? There is hope, isn't there?" "Of course," replied Musette. Again the law of contrasts comes into play. Hope still lives even when no hope exists any longer. That makes the final blow even heavier.

But Schaunard, who has been standing motionless at the door, his eyes fixed on Mimi, quickly goes to Musette and whispers: "She is already dead." Musette with horror starts back from the head of Mimi's couch and looks at Rodolphe. He is busy with the medicines. Colline slips in noiselessly. He has brought money to pay for a doctor. He moves cautiously over to Rodolphe (in the libretto it says quite illogically "he rushes over" to him) and asks: "How are things?" "As you see," answers Rodolphe, "she is sleeping peacefully." He says these words in a most prosaic voice as one speaks every day. This is something Stanislavski very much insisted on. It is only from the orchestra that one long-drawn-out, melancholy sound comes from the bass viols. Colline and Schaunard whisper surreptitiously. They do not know how to break the news to Rodolphe. "What are you two whispering about?" asks Rodolphe, raising his voice and speaking nervously. In the complete silence all around, this question of Rodolphe makes a shattering impression. "And why do you look at me like that?" Rodolphe cries out. Now they can no longer be silent. Marcel only says: "Pull yourself together." Then come two desperate cries from Rodolphe: "Mimi!" Here the full orchestra comes through (tutta forza) with a reprise of Mimi's last phrase about the love that is deeper than any ocean. All are motionless. The curtain slowly closes.

So it was with *La Bohème*. At the time people reproached Stanislavski for being enthralled with a shallow "petit bourgeois" subject. But . . . in life there are no shallow subjects; there are only myopic eyes and petty capabilities. A hundred thousand people may pass by a landscape or an ordinary everyday situation and not see anything of significance. But let an artist come by and a depressing landscape along a country road is transfigured into a product of high art. All depends on an incisive vision of life.

In conclusion I cannot resist quoting a review written at the time by A. Tsenovski: "The Stanislavski Studio . . . has put on *La Bohème* with great tenderness and remarkable simplicity. There are no exaggerations, special effects, no tricky directorial devices, which would relegate the actors to the background. Here is the touch of a great master, a true artist, whose intent is to fill out, clarify and give shape to the basic idea of the work, without ever having recourse to laming, crippling, or catastrophically mishandling it.

"It was not by chance that Stanislavski put on *The Tsar's Bride* in its entirety and now *La Bohème*. . . . And he has produced it so simply, so 'naturally', so warmly, and so subtly that it comes out as a true work of art. Here is no sentimentality, no sobbing, no extra effects. And it is all done somehow in original and touching tones.

"The question is: In what does Stanislavski's power as a director of opera lie, and what distinguishes his productions from others that attempted to tone down the operatic conventions and turn operas into musical dramas?

"First of all I would say the answer is in the extraordinary *modesty* of his approach. In an opera he sees a *musical creation* and not a drama with music. He most carefully, with utmost caution, lovingly approaches this combination of music and words. He wishes to preserve the whole musical foundation of the chosen work. He does not wish the words to overwhelm the music; he does not wish that our attention should be distracted by purely external impression. He wishes to achieve a *confluence* into a single whole of everything that an opera presents to a spectator."

5

A May Night

THE LAST PRODUCTIONS of Stanislavski dated from the years 1926–1928. One of them was *A May Night* and it merits particular attention as an example of his most mature directorial mastery.

In the autumn of 1928, during the 30th-anniversary celebrations of the Moscow Art Theatre, Stanislavski was taken so ill that he never went on the stage again. He never put on another independent production either in the Art Theatre or in his Opera Theatre. He became principally a teacher and educator, but the work done in the theatres headed by him was based on his ideas and teaching. All he did was to supervise the work of his assistants. The degree of vividness with which the performances were endowed now depended on the capabilities, the talents, of the younger directors.

But the production of *A May Night* was prepared by Stanislavski from beginning to end. The musical direction remained in the hands of V.I. Suk.

The production of *A May Night* was staged by Stanislavski with all the brilliance, the surprises and contrasts with which he always astonished the public. It was the very embodiment of Gogol's *A May Night* with its juicy realism, sly Ukrainian humour, bold fantasies—all the ingredients of a poetic, enchanting spring night in the Ukraine, which is so colourfully revealed in the score by Rimski-Korsakov.

The composer himself, who kept a most restrained chronicle of his creative life, wrote in his *Chronicle of My Life in Music* about his most absorbing work on *A May Night*. This absorption was the result of his studies of folk and ritual songs which laid the foundation for a "whole series of fantastic operas in which worship of the sun and the sun gods was introduced either directly as in *The Snow Maiden* and *Mlada* or obliquely as in *A May Night* and *Christmas Eve*.

"All the choruses in my opera are tinged with ritual or religious customs: The spring games in *Proso*, the Trinity song 'I am winding wreaths', water sprite songs—the long-drawn-out one and also the rapid one in the last act and the round dance of the water sprites. The very action of the opera is tied in by me with Trinity or Water Sprite

Week—called the Green Holidays; besides the drowned girls, according to Gogol, are turned into water sprites. In this way I was able to combine these subjects which I adore with the ritual customs of native life. . . ."

Later on in this same *Chronicle* there are some lines which are pertinent to our understanding of the basic, the inner meaning of this production: "The subject of *A May Night* was for me bound up with memories of the time when my wife became engaged to me, and this opera is dedicated to her."

This means that the opera was written during a happy period in the composer's life and it includes feelings which a person experiences perhaps only once in a lifetime.

Thus the composer himself discloses the sub-text of *A May Night*, and Stanislavski, as a subtle artist, grasped the fact that the important factor in the opera is not the pantheistic-pagan absorption in the cult of the sun (this is merely the background for the development of the action) but the aspiration of youth for happiness and the struggle to obtain it.

Stanislavski sensed in this opera the strong bond with life which is the mark of a true product of art and is what gives it its enduring quality.

A May Night had long attracted him. Even as far back as 1921 we were rehearsing the second act of this opera. At that time there was no intention of putting it on as a whole and the second act was used for instructive purposes because it was a completely independent comic scene. So when we began work on the opera in 1927 one act was practically ready—although it underwent a great deal of reworking then.

A May Night was not just a matter of fascination to Stanislavski as a director. This production also had practical connotations.

"We need to put on something for young people, for students, something in the nature of *The Blue Bird*," said he. "*A May Night*, because of its lyrical purity and humour, is better suited than any other Russian opera to this purpose."

Stanislavski's opinion was amply justified later on: the opera became a great favourite of youngsters still in school.

The opera was produced with singers who now had stage experience. Therefore Stanislavski did not have to have such frequent recourse to demonstrations as he did when the theatre was in its early stages of existence. Now he could demand a more conscious attitude from the actors in relation to the whole performance, and also give them a freer rein in their individual creativeness.

At one of the rehearsals of *A May Night* in 1928 he said:

"Search out the line of action that runs all through the opera, not

Stanislavski at rehearsal, 1927. With him is the singer O. Sobolevskaya.

only while you are preparing it but during all the time that you will be performing in it. Each stage production is valid only when all the words and situations flow into one main current. That is reality.

"*Evenings on a Farm near Dikanka*[1] celebrates youth, the joy of living, the beauties of nature. In *A May Night* life-loving young people are set in opposition to complacent oldsters. So look for that main current of action not only with your minds but also with your feelings, your hearts."

The scenery was designed by M.T. Kurilko, to whom was assigned the job of finding a pictorial solution that would correspond to the gentle lyricism and enchantment of the musical score. Stanislavski always appreciated paintings as sets and was extremely intent on having the artist achieve a genuine kinship between the colours of his paintings and the colours of the music. Painting and music in his theatre must always enhance and complement each other.

"For the spectator who is little trained to hear the music, or hears it only vaguely, we must offer aid more by means of colour," he used to say.

The abstract conventions and schematic sets—the 1920's were the years of flourishing constructivism, bare walls, and the banishment of stage sets—did not find any acceptance from Stanislavski. He held that futuristic innovations and the "laconic" backgrounds stemmed from poverty-stricken fantasy on the part of artists and smacked of something senile.

Act One

The first act of *A May Night* was arranged as follows: In the foreground is Hanna's small yard on the edge of a village, on the shore of a lake which fills the whole panorama. The lake gleams at night, in the moonlight, and on the far shore one can glimpse the ruins of a manor house. The lake plays a great part in the whole play and from the very start Stanislavski keeps it well within the circle of the audience's attention. A rivulet flows out from the lake and there is a small bridge over it which leads to Hanna's house. This small bridge relieves the flatness of the stage as it raises the figures of the people crossing it above the level of the ground.

Hanna's tiny house also stands on a small eminence and this facilitates the arranging of sculptural groups. Near the footlights the ground level of the yard slopes down to where there is a wickerwork cart with sacks and a well. On all sides there are poplar and chestnut trees. On the

1. A collection of stories by Nikolay Gogol in which "A May Night" appears.

right and on the left one can see the roofs of cottages. The scenery is very simple and convenient for the actors. It offers many good places where they can act to advantage and arrange a great variety of situations.

Hanna's house is small but well-built. It has a small stoop under an overhang, two windows which can be raised on the right (of the audience), and one small window on the slope on which the cart is standing. When Levko, after his serenade to Hanna, is to sing his first duet with her, she will sing from the small window and Levko will stand beside the house and lean in the direction of her window.

Stanislavski avoided duets of two singers standing beside each other "like two sticks in a fence".

After the overture, with its images of the mysterious lake of the water sprites, the action begins with a large crowd scene. Preceding it is a thirty-measure comic introduction composed of a folk dance theme. This theme is enlarged and finally turns into a gay, mirthful chorus: "Oh, we sowed the millet, sowed it, sowed it. . . ."

It is evening in the village, the sun is setting. It is May in full bloom, a holiday atmosphere prevails.

In order to make the holiday and the merry games lively and varied, the episodes in the chorus scene had to be worked out in detail. Stanislavski proposed this plan:

1. One village is expecting the visit of another in order to begin the games. The villagers preen themselves, keep on the lookout for their visitors.

2. They meet: they look each other over, they line up for the game, look around, search for acquaintances, search for their sweethearts, bow to people they know.

3. They parley about the game; each player is assigned his post, they get ready.

4. The game is called "Millet": Who will win?

All this plan is carried out during the musical introduction before the singing begins.

This difficult scene with the game took many rehearsals because with such choruses it was not easy to achieve free and easy movements. One chorus as a body moved towards the other and then retreated, while the second moved towards the first. There were many small scamperings and caperings, breaking ranks, all in accordance with the music. Everything was on the move, boiling, mixing, disentangling and then retangling, and it was all done to an exact scheme.

One group boasted about how it sowed the millet. For this Stanislavski needed the invention of some comic feature. So he offered a prize for the best one.

One group sang teasingly: "We will trample the millet. . . ."

"Now show how you are going to trample it," said Stanislavski, "laugh, roar: How can they trample the millet?"

Then the other side comes forward as "horses". They advance in pairs, high-spirited steeds, prancing, tossing their imaginary manes, and trampling the sown millet. The other side, undismayed, says: "We will get your horses." Their girls go out and tame "the wild horses", put "silken reins" over their necks, and lead them, quite submissive now, over to their camp. Now there is confusion among their opponents. The horses must be ransomed, they do not have enough money; then it appears that only a maiden will be accepted as ransom payment. They try to palm off an old woman on the other side—but that fails. They are obliged to hand over a girl.

Triumphantly they carry off Hanna on their shoulders and drive their "horses" back home.

Although this was only a foolish game and despite its apparent confusion and disorderly movements, it was painstakingly organized both rhythmically and dramatically. Stanislavski from the start insisted that each member of the chorus have a distinct line of action and that nothing be done "in general".

"Remember," he said, "what people do when they go to play games: they make acquaintances, look around, choose sweethearts, boast a bit—and this is all done with their eyes, their mutual attitudes. If they come to an agreement—'let's play'—that means that they have an endless thread, a wire which they can bend and give any shape. This is where the creativeness starts. The thought must be developed along a logical line. Some put forward their ideas, others dispute them. There must be argument so that the endless line can be carried along."

Stanislavski had the members of the chorus show as much life in their conduct as the principal characters. Every last person in the chorus was under his eagle eye and the slightest slip or success was immediately mentioned within everyone's hearing.

A *May Night* begins and ends with large crowd scenes. The composer in this way chose to stress the native quality of the opera, the importance of the young participants. Levko and Hanna stand out as characters from the mass of young people, but not as soloists generally do and not in any way set off from the chorus crowd.

Their costumes are exactly the same as those of everyone else. The boys wear wide trousers, the wider the more stylish. Their shirt necks are open, they wear no collars, the backs of their heads are shaven. Their shirts are embroidered with red and dark blue. The girls wear boots and long shirt-like dresses with a hem of a solid colour stitched on. The women wear caps but the girls are bareheaded. They wear kerchieves and aprons over their dresses. Sometimes they have overskirts on. At last the gay crowd of dancing young folk scatters, in groups, in pairs, in different directions. The "hopak" dance music melts away. The sun has almost set by now, its last reflections fall with a warm light on Hanna's cottage. With the last chords of the "hopak" music Hanna herself leaves a group of young men and enters her house. There is a long pause. To a tender melody played on an oboe Levko emerges, cautiously stealing around the corner of the cottage. He wears the customary wide trousers but his "reach almost to the Black Sea"; he is carrying a bandore and he does it so easily it seems almost a part of him. Stanislavski was adamant against aimless strumming by an actor on a balalaïka, guitar, or bandore—he really had to know how to play his instrument.

"You are going to let your instrument express your sentiments," said Stanislavski, "but you are still aware of its being in your way. You must learn to handle it freely and easily."

The scene between Levko and Hanna, his song, their duet, his tale—all was provided with a special character by Stanislavski, to avoid all saccharine banality.

"You, Hanna, ran away from Levko and hid in the cottage. Now you peek out to see if that is not he who is coming. Levko is really looking for her. He is not one to doubt, he is a determined and dashing young man. Their love is sturdy, no sentimentality, all just young and gay. The beginning of the duet is a light game of hide-and-seek. Your objective," said Stanislavski to Levko, "is to lure Hanna out of the house. But Hanna's objective is to draw him hither and then suddenly—look out! Hanna is a Ukrainian Carmen. She embraces, chases away, gets angry—all in one minute. She is unaffected, like a Southerner, cajoles others, like Carmen. All during his first aria ('The sun is low') Levko walks around the cottage, urging Hanna to come out. But Hanna, hiding from him, just peeks through the little window. There are two big pauses in the aria which enable him to look into the windows and search for Hanna. At last the aria is ended, and all was sung in vain, she does not respond. But Levko knows that she is there; 'Can you be sleeping, proud maiden?' he says and, firmly throwing his instrument across his back, he starts to leave. Then a window is opened and he sees the 'proud maiden'. She does not 'come out' as is indicated in the libretto, but her head can be seen in the window."

Her brief *recitative* is accompanied by a single violin. This music can easily entice a singer into making "pretty little sounds", as it is pitched rather high. But Stanislavski from the very start impressed on Hanna that she must give the principal place to the words sung.

"Do everything to provoke a counteraction: There must be a clash, an energetic one. Levko is no soft creature. Your love and his are strong. . . . Tease him. Let him suffer!" Finally he begins to go away and then Hanna is alarmed. He will leave her! She begins to hold him back.

Stanislavski asked the production staff to measure out the whole stage, to make approximate blockings so that the actors would know the exact space available and could regulate their movements in accordance with the music.

When Levko and Hanna begin their duet, Stanislavski said:

"Now the most important thing in your musical score is your focus, the 'object' on which your attention is centred. You must learn your musical and vocal score for the sake of this object. Do away with sentimentality. Take everything in earnest."

The duet "Oh do not be afraid, my little red, red berry" is sung at the window. Hanna leans out and Levko is seated on the banked-up earth by the cottage. Their heads are side by side and the sound of their voices pours straight into the auditorium.

The strings softly end the duet with long, full harmonies. To this caressing music in slow rhythm Levko and Hanna meet at the door of the cottage: Hanna comes out, softly opening the door, and Levko is already at her side.

"No embraces, no squeezing or anything of the sort," prompted Stanislavski. "It is only now that the love story begins. After their capricious conversation Hanna says: 'Wait, Levko. Tell me if you talked with your father and told him you want to marry me. . . .' and then comes the scene with the stars, the terrors, and finally Levko's tale about the drowned girl.

"What is the foundation of Levko's story? It is the idea that you tell your beloved terrifying things so that she will cling closer to you."

Now the lake begins to play its part in Levko's tale and therefore in the opera. This is the abode of water sprites. One must not speak out loud or they will jump at you. At this point the lake begins to glimmer under the light of the moon. The young couple have settled in a corner and covered themselves with a coat. Now and then they look out at the lake. There is a great deal of naiveté and sincerity in this scene of village love. Hanna is captious, the way a child is, but there is an unusual air of simplicity about her.

As he worked on this scene Stanislavski made changes. He had the lovers move from their nook to the cart and Levko's whole tale will be told from there, with Hanna lying beside him listening to his terrifying story.

"But to begin with she will be: 'studying the stars,' as Stanislavski said. "And that is a kind of love game: 'Do look, my dear. Way over there a star has come out.'

"Hanna, however, must listen to Levko with all the seriousness of a child. And Levko must have an inner vision of all that he is singing about. It is very important too that he see it as *now*. He must find new approaches all the time and not stick to one set staging of his tale.

"In his telling about Pannochka, the drowned girl, he should enhance the atmosphere of mystery," Stanislavski added. "This is to prepare for all the pandemonium in the third act. Both Levko and Hanna are naive and mystic. Levko is a daring soul. He is drawn to terrors and deviltry."

Night has fallen, the moon has risen above the poplars and the lake is reflecting its full beams. On the right and on the left little lights have appeared in the cottages. A May night is beginning.

"Now invent the right prelude," said Stanislavski, "the prelude of a game that leads to kissing. The stars, angels, water sprites, terrors—all that is a game, a pretext, for kissing each other. But it must all be done with piquancy and unexpectedness. The kisses, the embraces are all on the sly. Levko is not yet betrothed. He embraces her but immediately he says: 'Oh *excuse* me, I didn't mean to. . . .' Everything is accidental, and delicate. You, Levko," said Stanislavski, "have to steal your hugs and kisses. Your goal is to gain Hanna. This is your continuing line of action."

Levko sits on the piled-up cart and Hanna is half lying across his knees, and, clinging to him, she now and then steals a look at the mysterious lake. She asks him to tell her about the "terrible happening".

Despite her plea: "Tell me, Levko!" he holds back, but he finally begins his tale: "Long, long ago. . . ." To his mysterious air is added the very expressive motif played by the cellos.

"First of all, remember the psychology of the teller of a tale: He always hides what will happen next, whereas you begin to try to frighten me right away," continued Stanislavski.

"When you are rehearsing or playing don't try to get out of your own skin, or slough it off. If you get rid of yourself your show will be dead. You are, after all, supposed to be expressing various human moods. How many are there in the music? Let us say eighty-three of them," said Stanislavski unexpectedly. "It would be anti-artistic if there were no expression for all those moods in this opera, no words, nothing that can be heard distinctly.

"There is an enormous amount of music in words which singers do not really sense. They do not do exercises with them, study the language, learn the *roots* of words, which are their soul. If there is no soul—there is no breath of life. If words do not live, then artistic feelings do not have any life. Why this lack of comprehension? Shalyapin sculpts every phrase, relishes every letter of a word. I do not know how to make you realize that what you are doing is all wrong. For your words now are just a drag on your singing instead of being its chief promoter. You do not have the right artistic consciousness, no real determination."

So Stanislavski persisted in seeing to it that not a single word of Levko's aria was lost, and that the entire tale became mysterious and terrifying for both Hanna and the listeners in the auditorium.

Hanna, horrified by the terrible story of the fate of hapless Pannochka, shyly looks out from behind Levko, closely clinging to him. And we, the audience, look out with them towards the lake as if we expected some terrifying thing to appear. The lake should draw all eyes to itself.

"The mood to be created is: 'There is something here, right beside me'," Stanislavski suggested to his actors. "It is not easy for Hanna to go into her house alone after this nocturnal rendezvous, especially with a water sprite filling her mind."

The pensive absorption which envelops the young couple after the tale is broken by Levko's news that their master intends to set up a distillery in this place and is sending a distiller.

At these words one hears women singing in the distance "I will wind a wreath". The love scene is over. Hanna quickly hides inside her house and Levko slips behind it.

This reference to the Distiller and a distillery is important to the unfolding of the plot. In Gogol the action and counteraction run clearly through the story. The main action consists of popular traditions, spring rites, youth, love. Opposed to this is the line of the distillery, the Distiller, the foolish Headman, the greedy, voluptuary Sister-in-law, the stupid Clerk—all of whom represent the powers that be in the village with whom the young people are fencing.

Here the young girls come in to perform a poetic rite with their woven wreaths which, when morning comes, they will throw into the lake. They also carry birch branches to decorate their cottages.

Rimski-Korsakov has the clarinets in the orchestra repeat over and over a rhythmic phrase which evokes winding and twisting. Stanislavski gave all the girls flowers to carry and had them weave garlands out of them. There is a clarinet solo which marks off the division between each couplet of their song (*moderato quasi allegretto*).

The syncope on the second eighth note and the triplet of sixteenth notes following it provide a feeling of delicate convoluted tracery during the pauses and is very appropriate to the winding of flowers into wreaths.

"The scene then is this," Stanislavski summed up, "the girls have picked special flowers, cut birch branches. They are on their way to appease the water sprites, decorate the cottages, the bridge, the fences. Some weave wreaths, others do the decorating. When they have done all this, in the last act morning will come and the May night will be happily over."

The poetic scene of the so-called water sprites' song is broken in on by drunken Kalenik, who from now on will be wandering around all night, appearing in the most unlikely places and always inopportunely.

Kalenik and the Headman are the principal comic characters in the opera. Up to this time there had not been any really low comedy parts in the repertory of the Studio, except in *The Secret Marriage* and the prologue to *Tsar Saltan*. To play a drunken character, without lapsing into farce and without sacrificing musical quality, is no easy task, but G.M. Bushuyev, the singer with whom Stanislavski worked, became an "exemplary drunkard", if such a term may be used.

"I don't believe you"—how many times was I to hear Stanislavski's dry voice repeat those words when I was rehearsing the part of Kalenik. "You have just come out of a hospital, surely not a tavern. . . ." I never did get the better of that role, although Stanislavski himself demonstrated it until our sides split with laughter.

"No use stamping around to show a drunkard. A man who is drunk will keep trying to maintain his equilibrium and not to stagger. He will attempt to go along a straight line and fight the influence that is forcing him to zigzag. A general rule for playing drunks," said Stanislavski, "is to have him glue his feet to the ground. His legs are to be used only in most urgent cases, they are rooted to the spot, whereas his eyes, facial expression, neck and arms mainly convey his rhythm.

"Kalenik has glassy eyes and a constant urge to dance—a wild hopak—which for him constitutes a serious problem.

"You do not dance but keep puzzling over this complex problem, so that one is aware of your intense preoccupation. Some mysterious force suddenly drags you and carries you to one side, yet you do not see anything around you. You are in a dense fog and hear, vaguely, voices."

Before rehearsing any scene we always listened to the music.

"Let us study the music carefully, and see how many units there are in it," said Stanislavski. Then, after hearing it played over several times, he established the following:

"1. Kalenik tries to dance right where he is. With the words: 'Yes, but that's not the way to dance the hopak', he leans on his elbows, he meditates—'it didn't go right'. You will have to think up what to do next.

"2. He makes an effort, struggles to the centre of the stage. Finally he topples over.

"3. 'What is it that my pal keeps saying to me?' He lies there. Nothing is of any use!

"4. 'Oh but. . . .'' He is lying on his back, so he dances in that position, stamping his feet on the ground.

"5. He 'dances' on all fours."

Here the girls begin to sing about him: "Look here, girls. . . ."

Meanwhile the girls who were onstage when Kalenik began his dance coordinate everything they do with Kalenik's acting.

1. They listen to Kalenik as he comes near.

2. They whisper to each other, agree what to do.

3. They run away, hiding from Kalenik. One group goes to the left behind the fence and the cart, the other goes behind the house, the bridge, the well.

4. They peek at Kalenik.

5. They run away from Kalenik.

It is all a merry game.

To begin with the girls had a long rope which they threw diagonally across the stage from the well to the cart, and they kept Kalenik's feet tangled up in it. He cannot figure out what is preventing him from dancing, and when he falls he goes head over heels. He had been rehearsed to do this in exact time with the music and this always brought a roar of laughter from the audience.

Kalenik has an old coat which he drags around after him over the ground; his blouse is in tatters, only his trousers manage somehow not to fall off him. When he lets his coat drop for a moment one of the girls quickly ties it to the rope behind Kalenik's back. Then they begin another prank: He leans over to pick up his coat. Suddenly, like a live thing it slithers away over to the cart. When he manages finally to put his hand on it, it quickly crawls away to the well. Poor Kalenik is absolutely bewildered by all this deviltry.

Having fagged Kalenik out, the girls now begin to sing: "Poor old Kalenik!" and "Hop, hop, hop, tra-la!" and keep hiding from him, crouching behind the cart, beyond the bridge, behind the well. The game consists of Kalenik's hearing voices wherever he turns but being unable to see the girls as they keep crouching down again in their hiding places. He hears them on all sides but when he looks, he sees no one. Kalenik's whirling around and the popping up and down of the girls was so carefully rehearsed that his eye never caught any of them. It was all very funny but to Kalenik there was something strangely miraculous in it.

"It is not his legs which are drunk but his thought, his soul; that is the basis of this scene," said Stanislavski to the singer in the role of Kalenik.

After he had knocked at Hanna's door in error and said: "Open the door, woman, it's time for this Cossack to go to sleep," the girls lead him towards the cottage of the Headman, where he had intended to go, dragging his coat along behind him. The comedy line continues with the arrival of the Headman, who has stolen over to Hanna's cottage with the idea of trying to make love to her.

The emergence of the Headman from behind Hanna's house is quite unusual; he is crawling on all fours so that no one will see him and, almost prostrate on the ground, he knocks at her window.

"The old hog is rooting at her door and window," was how Stanislavski described the scene.

At the beginning of the scene there is a trio: The Headman who is knocking at the window, Hanna who is scolding the Headman for pestering her, and Levko who is watching him from a distance. Stanislavski arranged them in the following positions: the Headman, creeping around, calling Hanna and knocking first at one window and then another. Hanna replies, appearing always at a different window from the one where the Headman is knocking, and then she immediately disappears again. The Headman then quickly crawls to that window. Levko watches them both from his advantageous position on the roof of the cottage, onto which he has climbed from the other side.

A May Night, Act I (from the 1928 production): Outside Hanna's cottage, with the Headman in the foreground, Levko on the roof, and Hanna at the window.

The Headman tries to lure Hanna, telling her about his grand past when he was a guide to "Empress Catherine of sainted memory", and sat beside the imperial coachman.

"Sing that," said Stanislavski, "from the stoop, through a crack in the door."

When Hanna, who is a young and haughty Ukrainian girl, threatens to tell Levko all about this, the Headman is overcome with a fever of passion. He declares it in: "Love me, love me, darling girl, caress and pet me, my beauty," and this is done at a most rapid tempo, requiring the clear, almost frenetic enunciation of a patter song. All the strings in the orchestra accompany the Headman's absurdly passionate speech with throbbing, thumping strokes.

"Now go and crawl around those windows and grunt at each one with impeccable diction until the young people come and chase you away," said Stanislavski to the singer in the part of the Headman.

But although he staged this absurdity, he did not allow the actor to make himself absurd as an end in itself.

"The main object in these circumstances is not to play being funny but seriously to ask yourself what must be done if, in such circumstances and at the present moment, I wished to get to Hanna—that is, 'I' as I am today and not my image of the character. . . without borrowing any extraneous feelings, but using only my own. As soon as you leave yourself behind, everything becomes monotonous. But here and now if I try to get into her room, what must I do to enable myself to believe in my own actions?"

Hanna replies to the Headman from inside her cottage, Levko joins in from the roof, and the trio ends when a whistle calls in the youths who had put the Headman up to the precarious game he is playing. The Headman tears himself free from them with difficulty. This all happens at a rapid tempo (*presto*) and builds up to the finale of the act. A fight between Levko and the Headman explodes and the quiet of the May night is disturbed.

Levko calls to the other young men from the roof: "Hey there, you young fellows, I told you all to go to bed," and then lightly jumps to the ground. They are all grouped around the well to rehearse a ditty about the Headman. This song was sung in a friendly tone, loudly, with good diction, and it conveyed the impression of brash and gay foolery. But that was not enough for Stanislavski. His actors must create something. So he proposed the following scheme:

"The principal factor is the well-defined, brilliantly enunciated patter. The conductor must follow the actor. The voice that leads the couplet seems to be inventing, improvising: the whole scene is impromptu. They all follow the one who is doing the inventing. You must fix who comes first, and who next: but absolutely no gestures.

"Do not play gaiety but try to get inside the words. Levko is the leader. 'Thought that up—right?' And the others add on to it, think up new things."

While the young men are singing, learning their song as they stand in a group around the well, another group of young men comes onstage, played by apprentices of the Studio.

They begin to change into sheepskin coats turned inside out, and new, fantastic figures with brooms and pitchforks appear. At the end of the song a folk dance begins which demonstrates how such young men enjoy themselves at an outing.

"Now all hell breaks loose," was the description Stanislavski gave to this scene.

They dance on the roof, astride brooms, on top of the cart, on the well-stoop. In the very middle of the scene a skilled hopak dancer, borrowed for this production, vaults into the air above everyone's head. Unrestrained youthful gaiety is carried to such a high pitch of excitement that it splashes and cascades over the edge of the orchestra. Stanislavski was a past master in whipping up powerfully dramatic, boisterous scenes to the highest degree—he did not stop halfway. The finale suggests a rousing continuation of the "warfare" between these young men and the Headman and his gang, and it clearly indicates what the through-line of action for the whole opera will be.

Act Two

In the Sister-in-law's clean home a cordial conversation is taking place over a supper in honour of a newly-arrived guest—the Distiller.

The Distiller is smugly self-satisfied. In his makeup and figure he reminds one of a well-nourished hog. The Sister-in-law's cosy cottage is trimmed inside with flowers and in the entryway to the left one can glimpse smoked hams, bunches of peppers and onions. The blue light of a Ukrainian night shows through the windows.

The act begins with a brief prelude. There is a gay exchange in the orchestra among the flutes, oboes and violins, as they repeat a dance melody in which flowing movements alternate with abrupt, delicately leaping notes (staccato). The overall impression is that of the unending flow of a stream of music, rather like the unhurried, slightly eccentric conversation led by the Headman, the Distiller, and the Sister-in-law. They sit all in a row at the table, facing the audience, with the windows on one side. The Distiller is in the middle, between the Headman and the Sister-in-law, who are both making much of him.

"Since there will be 'warfare' here," said Stanislavski to his assistant directors, "the act should begin in an atmosphere of complete contentment and well-being."

After he scrutinized this scene, which had been rehearsed much earlier and even performed on occasion, Stanislavski began to do it all over from scratch, as if it had not gone through all those rehearsals already.

His indications were abrupt:

"Stress the native, local side! Of what does it consist? Naiveté, forthrightness. They are being introduced to a General (the Distiller) and they turn themselves inside out to make a good impression on him. They wait on him, fawn on him, in an obsequious manner."

Then he asked the actors gathered around him:

"Did you follow the through-line of action? Were you thoroughly amused by it? Did you divide the act up into episodes? Why did the Distiller come here? What sort of a guest is he? Are you interested in the objective chosen? Perhaps it can be compared to Stanislavski's going down to some small place in the sticks to start a new theatre?" He made no bones about equating himself with the Distiller in order to make the actors have a clearer idea of their objective. The Headman and the Sister-in-law are straining every nerve. What a guest! This is an event in that cottage.

Next Stanislavski insisted that his actors have their personal interpretations of the events on the stage, their own independent attitude towards the music, which went much, much further than a simple counting of measures.

It might have seemed that the supper conversation was flowing along very evenly and perhaps not too interestingly in the beginning of the act, but Stanislavski was able to uncover in this brief trio ever-newer colours and they, if one listened attentively, coincided exactly with what the orchestra was playing.

At first it was proposed that there would be a ceremonial greeting of the Distiller on his arrival. But Stanislavski, after having carefully listened to the music, decided to reject that variant. He said:

"No, they have been sitting at the table for some time. The first words of getting acquainted have been said. It is time to get down to business."

The business in question begins with the words: "Is it soon you plan to set up the distillery?" That phrase signals the beginning of the second act, and Stanislavski immediately posed the question:

"What is the Headman's main purpose? To court Hanna and obtain her affection, or to go into partnership with the Distiller and set up a tavern? Gogol hints at either solution. But don't confuse us. Proceed along the through-line of action, the thread of which you take into your own hands. Why do you need to do that? Because that is the only way to answer the question: What am I doing?

"Right now the Headman is expending all his energies on courting the Distiller; he's a toady. But in relation to younger people he's a tyrant and a stubborn fool."

Like all toadies and brazen people he is also a coward and Stanislavski holds his cowardice up to ridicule. But also, like others of his ilk, he speaks with succulence, using rounded phrases, pronouncing each word with vapid self-complacency. "Lard every word heavily," urged Stanislavski.

The future relationship between the Sister-in-law and the Distiller is very clearly hinted at in the first phrase: "And will you live here, friend, for all that time without a wife?"

"Will a romance blossom? Or will it not? Send up a trial balloon," said Stanislavski to the Sister-in-law. "A peasant woman like you enjoys a tasty dish."

The trio about a wife for the Distiller rolls along merrily. The cross-eyed Headman keeps looking the Distiller over, as though smelling him out, and the Sister-in-law looks at him the way a cat does at a piece of meat. Meanwhile the Distiller rocks with mirth. It's all so gay with the wine, the fat sausages in one's fingers, as the talk flows. A most expressive bit is the Distiller's story about the idiot Germans who thought they could make vodka "not with firewood, like honest Christians, but with some diabolical kind of steam." Here Stanislavski made the actors give a special flavour to each word so that it would reek with the "stupidity of those Germans". He described the Distiller in these words:

"He is a touring showman, he is dispensing 'enlightenment'. In his arrogant self-importance, he fancies himself a 'magician'! He is a super-salesman, a top-notch tavern keeper. And he is a supreme boor. For the Headman, his coming there is a tremendous event. He is bursting with pleasure—he is going to get his own tavern. He, the Distiller, will manufacture vodka for all of you; look at him with humility and enthusiasm."

About the relations between the Distiller and the Sister-in-law, Stanislavski suddenly had this to say:

"The scene is built around the fact that an agile, ingratiating cock-of-the-walk is flirting with a handsome, plump peasant woman. The Sister-in-law is a depraved creature, invites merchants to her house, is unfaithful. But you must not play depravity! Rather play Romeo and Juliet, for the Sister-in-law thinks she is irresistible. She does not run, she sways around in the house. You must have an attitude of deadly earnestness towards all her stupid words and actions—that is basic to your acting here," Stanislavski repeated several times with emphasis.

The last rolling phrase of the trio is interrupted by stumbling knocks on the bass viols, very reminiscent of both the shuffling, unsteady feet of a drunken man and also of some importunate thought. The knocking sounds are taken up by dragging, creeping, chromatic notes on the wind instruments which, like a fog, float up out of the orchestra. This bewildered, stupefied, dizzy drunkenness is described by the Rimski-Korsakov music with great humour.

Kalenik suddenly appears on the threshold of the door, thinking he has at last found his own cottage.

"You don't see anything in front of you," said Stanislavski in order to stress the man's drunken state, "not people, not the cottage, not the furniture. You are walking in a fog through a desert and you cannot distinguish a thing. The threshold seems to you to be a hillock, the doorjamb a tree. The lamp on the table is the moon."

Picking up the coat Kalenik has been dragging on the ground, Stanislavski began to creep around inside the cottage as if going through a thicket. His eyes were fixed on some mysterious point far in the distance at which he, rolling his tongue, his lower lip hanging down, his eyes watering, seemed to be peering.

While calling down every kind of curse on the Headman, who has been turned to stone by his astonishment, Kalenik moved on, looking for his cottage, straight towards the orchestra, but an invisible force grabbed him and turned him aside, towards the table, where he sat down oblivious of the presence of anyone else.

This point is reached when Kalenik says: "You woman up on the warm bricks over the stove—I'm not coming up to you. My legs ache. . . ."

Kalenik somehow thought he must be somewhere near his sleeping place, and Stanislavski gave him a tricky thing to do: He began to undress himself, pulling off his tattered shirt.

With the words: "Now that's what I like! He has come in and acts as if he were in his own home," the Headman took Kalenik by the scruff of his neck and prepared to throw him out of doors, like some old rag, but the Distiller spoke up in his defense: "Leave him alone, let go, brother, let him rest. He's a useful man. . . ." So the Headman pushed Kalenik onto a mat near the entrance.

"When drunken Kalenik came in," said Stanislavski, "the Distiller practically dissolved with emotion. Here was a real client! Worth his weight in gold! So make the Headman understand that Kalenik will be useful in their business. Then they will all be delighted!"

Kalenik lying near the threshold of the cottage is overcome with self-pity: "Something very like old age is coming!" Then he is seized with violent resentment against the Headman, and explodes: "I wish that a loaded cart would run over him, the one-eyed devil." But having reached that peak he composes himself for sleep. The Headman has jumped up preparatory to throwing him out when, to the accompaniment of two short chords like shattering glass, a large stone flies through the window into the cottage.

They all take refuge under the table. In the pause that follows, which is pregnant with malignant silence, the Headman crawls out on all fours from under the table and makes his way to the stone that is lying on the floor.

Kalenik is now forgotten and he can sleep quietly to the end of the act. But the peaceful and gay mood of the beginning of the act has been destroyed.

Fearful and ready to dodge again under the benches, the Distiller and the Sister-in-law crawl out like some kind of quadruped. The Headman says: "I'd like to crush him with this stone" and prepares to hurl it back out of the window, but the Distiller stops him. "God forbid, friend, that you bless anyone with such a blow."

They are frightened, but sit down again at the table to hear the Distiller's tale about the corpse with a dumpling in its mouth.

The story begins with the mysterious phrase: "Do you mean to say you do not know what happened to my late mother-in-law?"

He says the word "mother-in-law" with a quasi-tragic intonation. The Headman, thoroughly alarmed, asks hesitantly: "Your mo-o-other-in-law?"

"The old rhinocerous yawned with astonishment," suggested Stanislavski, in adding some colour to the Headman's words. "Your mo-o-other-in-law?" repeats the Sister-in-law in a voice faint from fright. They sit down and dare not move or breathe they are so frightened! The tale must be extraordinary, terrifying! "Are there perhaps some devils in it?" suggested Stanislavski.

The tale is about a guest "whose origin was unknown" who choked to death on a dumpling and died at once, just after the Distiller's mother-in-law had been thinking: If only you would choke to death on those dumplings. Every night after that the dead man sat astride the ridgepole of their cottage and gave his mother-in-law no peace.

"Tell us not only *what* you see but *how* you look at this whole picture. Perhaps you have some kind of a premonition?" said Stanislavski to the Distiller.

Now they are sitting at the table bunched up against each other with fright. They all repeat, their voices atremble, the last phrase: "And he had a dumpling in his teeth."

The tension in the atmosphere explodes in an abrupt blast. At the window, together with a noise of more shattered glass, appears a

terrifying head made out of a pumpkin, with glowing eyes. The boisterous song of the young men outside is now heard: "Our Headman is
grey-haired and cross-eyed. . . ." Inside, they listen transfixed to the
song; then, infuriated, the Headman rushes into the entryway, only to
find a lot of devils in sheepskins dancing; they grab the Sister-in-law,
wrap her in a sheepskin, and hand her over to the Headman, who,
thinking this is Levko, drags her into a closet and locks it. In the entry
there is a raucous free-for-all from which the Headman apparently
emerges as the victor.

The fight was carefully organized by Stanislavski. In such scenes he
never allowed any improvisations.

"Count the accented places in the music and plot all your actions
according to them. Clap out the rhythm in various ways and you will
find it will get control of you and synchronize your actions with the
music."

After the music had been repeated for us many times, that is to say
the young men's song, mostly with the orchestra, then Stanislavski
assigned an exact plot for each participant in the fight.

1. The Headman is lying down, the Sister-in-law is creeping about,
the Distiller is lying down.

2. Levko appears at the window. The Distiller says: "What a fine
song" and goes towards the entry.

3. The Headman rushes to first one window, then a second, and grabs
hold of one of the tenors in the chorus.

4. Levko is in the entry. The Distiller starts to back away from him.
The Headman hides. The Sister-in-law picks up a poker.

5. The bassos in the chorus appear first at one window, then another.

6. Levko is grabbed, and two members of the chorus seize the
Sister-in-law.

After the Headman's solemn announcement: "You'll not trick me!",
to a military march (with two French horns and a drum) the Clerk
approaches the Headman's cottage together with the village policemen
to find the real instigator of all the commotion.

"One blockhead has come to another blockhead," was the way
Stanislavski characterized this movement. Then he went on to explain
the importance of these comic roles:

"A character part is a mask behind which it is simple and easy for an
actor to point a figure at vice. At a masked ball one can say many things
one would have difficulty saying without the mask.

"In the mask of a character part you are called upon in this scene to
show up the very quintessence of stupidity (the Headman, the Clerk)
and also the true quality of a 'peasant woman' tinged with depravity
(the Sister-in-law), followed by that of the tavern-haunter, the brazen,
drunken boor. Make the necessary physical adaptations to the parts but

leave your own inner qualities intact. Let yourself be involved in 'small truths' on the stage and when you perform them with sincerity, you will be on the way to achieving the 'larger truths'.

"An actor who is not alive in a comic part while on the stage is likely to grasp at the externals of his character and its image. He proceeds in a routine, 'actory' way and that is bad.

"Yesterday, let us say, you were in a good mood during rehearsal. Today you wish to renew this and you try to get it back through external means. This is impossible. You have to make use of those same 'small truths' to win back your feelings. You must go through the same preliminaries as before which resulted in a fine, gay mood. In your every movement, gesture, it is not the end point that is interesting but all that leads up to the resultant effect.

"It is difficult to play comic parts so that you retain a physical fluency consonant with the music, that is to say creating images which are musical. Therefore you must avoid all coarse and forced exaggerations while still carrying out the essential qualities of your characters, especially Gogol characters, to the highest degree of expressiveness. To do this many rehearsals are necessary in order to find just the right movements and colours."

The two fools, the Headman and the Clerk, after first arguing about who has the rabble-rouser in custody, sing: "Light, light, light! Let's look at him" and they go single-file into the entry, with great care pull the bolt, and open the closet. Out flies the Sister-in-law like a cannon-ball, hurls herself against the Headman, and screams her *recitative*: "You, tell me, please, have you gone quite off your head?" The accompaniment is made up of buzzing sixteenth notes that make one think of an angry hornet. This made it possible for Stanislavski to fashion a striking scene out of the row between the Sister-in-law and the Headman. She chases him all around the cottage, pinches, punches him, makes vituperative remarks. It is altogether clear that he is completely dominated by her. "I hope the devils will push *you* around in the next world." With the concluding remark the orchestra goes into a powerful *sforzando* and she runs out of the cottage, banging the door after her.

"And she does it to her own hurt," added Stanislavski, "because she will immediately fall into the hands of the rebellious young men."

Shortly after she has left the scene she is heard screaming offstage. This may pass unnoticed, but if it does it will not be clear how she, instead of Levko, gets locked up again in the shed.

Stanislavski, however, by his staging and by the significant looks that are exchanged by everyone, stresses her scream and in this manner prepares the explanation of a new prank by the young men outside.

After the Sister-in-law goes offstage, the scene ends with a grouping of "the powers that be" for a crusade to punish and make an example of that devil in the sheepskin coat.

To the solemn accompaniment of the words: "Let everyone know what authority means!" the punitive expedition, in military formation, is launched under the command of the Headman, who goes out followed by those who had come with the Clerk as the curtain closes.

For the second scene in Act Two the set consists of a thatched barn in the foreground. Light from the moon and stars falls on the roof and on the dimly-seen, whitewashed wall of a cottage. The barn has a window which is boarded over.

The music for the beginning of this scene is mysterious and gives the impression of watchfulness and uncertainty. The bass viols and the cellos interrupt each other with the muted plucking of strings, as if they were creeping up to a cautious combination with the woodwinds. There is a long, sustained chord which suggests listening while remaining completely motionless. Everything is pregnant with fear, as if in the dark one might meet with demons.

The Headman with his "platoon", who were starting out so bravely and solemnly as they left the cottage in the preceding scene, are now obviously terror-stricken. They are all frightened by the dark, mysterious barn and they drop on all fours to go around it, to listen, to try the door and window. All is quiet, and that makes it all the more alarming!

The first cues: "Is he here?" "Yes!" "Halt!" are jerky and frightened in tone. Then they all in turn, beginning with the Headman, peek through the keyhole and then start back in horror. This is the beginning of the comic trio: "Satan! Satan! It's old Satan himself!" Now they are all sitting on the ground leaning against the barn wall, and they are holding a council of war. "They will have to burn Satan up right away," said Stanislavski, "otherwise they cannot hope for anything but their doom."

"Fire, fi-i-re!" wails the Headman in a heartrending cry. The sanest of them all is the Distiller—he is a man of action! He knows that you cannot destroy Satan with mere fire. "It is only with flames from a pipe that his power can be burned up."

The crowd onstage are galvanized into energetic action: the door of the barn must be covered with straw, lighted, not from the flame in a lantern but with sparks from the Distiller's pipe. This is all done to an agitated *allegro tempo*. The "platoon" still on all fours crawls around on the ground, giving the scene a weird animal-like character. At the height of all the commotion the muffled voice of the Sister-in-law is heard from inside the barn: "What are you doing, you people? I'm not a witch." This completely upsets the Headman, who crosses himself and then firmly states: "It's the Devil himself!"

Finally the cowardly Clerk, who is mortally afraid of sin, with chattering teeth makes the proposal: "If it . . . that is to say, whatever it is . . . in there . . . would agree to take an oath . . . under the sign of the cross . . . it would be proof positive that it's not a devil!" Meanwhile the "authorities," quaking in their boots, begin to draw magic circles around themselves and make crosses on the ground. The Clerk unfastens the hefty padlock on the barn door and a strange figure appears on the threshold—it really is like some kind of diabolical apparition. The Sister-in-law is dressed in a black sheepskin coat (with the wool outside) and trussed with ropes. Her head is tied up in a kerchief with the corners sticking out so that they look like horns, and her mouth is covered up with something—altogether her appearance is fantastic.

"Cross yourself!" the Clerk says in a loud whisper. During a considerable pause the Distiller unfastens the ropes and the shaggy creature crosses herself.

After the Sister-in-law is freed from the ropes and gets rid of the coat, she again favours the bewildered Headman with some sound cuffs and a torrent of crackling expletives.

The scene ends with the arrival of three policemen who yell: "We have caught him!" It turns out that their catch is none other than drunken Kalenik.

The disturbed night rolls on, but as the curtain is closing on this Act, one hears the Headman's orders: "Run! Fly! Do you hear, immediately run!" With this he orders all the frightened police to chase after the disturber of the peace.

Both scenes in this act represent the juxtaposition of the world of dull-witted and self-satisfied old men to the world of the young people. The counter through-line of action is that of the comedy characters—"Let everyone know, especially the young, what authority is"—whereas the straight through-line is that of Levko and his companions, who represent freedom.

Act Three

The scene designer for *A May Night*, Kurilko, was faced with difficulties that were of two kinds. They were connected with Stanislavski's high standards and with the extraordinarily meagre materials he had to work with on a small and poorly-equipped stage. On the stage Stanislavski had to create the atmosphere of a mystery-shrouded lake on a night when water sprites are abroad, and, in addition, an old manor house in a tumbledown, uninhabitable condition, which must be brought to life and lighted up.

By this marvelous, dream-created house the water sprites were to stage their dances, coming out of the water, but also swimming in the lake itself.

The plan for the stage design was, as usual, proposed by Stanislavski.

Down front and parallel with the curtain there was a flat dike that stretched clear across the stage. In the middle of it there was a small arched bridge across a stream which ran out of the lake, apparently right into the orchestra pit. The water and the bridge are masked at

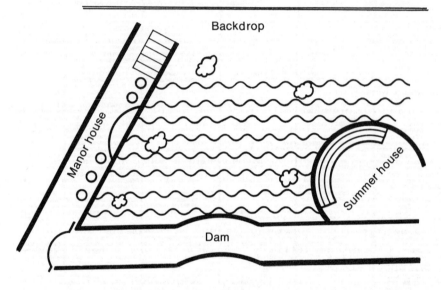

A May Night, plan for Act III.

either end by a plane tree with arrow-shaped leaves, such as grow in the Ukraine. On the right, as seen from the auditorium, the dike ends at a half-ruined circular summer house, drowned in the thick greenery of wild vines. On the left on the far side one sees the ruinous manor house with steps going down to the water's edge. Behind the dam there are a few half-drowned, thickset willow trees. They were built so that the water sprites could climb around in them and swing themselves on the branches. On the far shore one glimpses the village, the lights in the cottages. The moon casts its beams on the dark blue, glassy surface of the lake, on the tumbledown, overgrown summer house and the white walls of the manor house with black holes in them where the windows used to be. In the dim twilight it is all poetic and mysterious. Stage lighting, if handled by an artist, can perform miracles and Stanislavski paid very particular attention to it.

The curtain opens—it is dark, late at night. Stars twinkle, the lights from the cottages on the far side of the lake and the moonlight are reflected on the water. It is a place of solitude and quiet.

Rimski-Korsakov's music begins. The sounds are soft, reflective, long-sustained, growing in volume then fading away again in the distance; the notes on the French horns are like voices in a mysterious forest thicket; there are low sighs from the violins, like whiffs of cool air; then a pulsing *tremolo* from all the strings, like the rustle of awakening leaves or a tiny ripple on the surface of the lake lighted by the moon. Then there is a sound of lapping water in the reeds by the shore, from the oboes and flutes—it is all enchantment, the voices of the night bewitching our ears.

The picture painted in this way by the composer was called "A Ukrainian night and the songs of Levko".

"How quiet, how cool it is here!" marks Levko's entrance.

"No!" said Stanislavski interrupting the singer. "That was just any tenor singing and we have to have Levko, who, in the enchantment of this night, is tired from being pursued, who is resting here after all the fights and dances, and who, besides, is still dreaming about Hanna. All this must be conveyed in the very sound of your voice. Sing the *quiet* and the *cool* to us as you feel them. It is not sufficient for you merely to open your mouth and take in a deep breath."

After Levko had repeated the phrase many times, sought for fresh colours for it, for its singing quality, Stanislavski added:

"But do not attempt to substitute the sweet timbre of your voice for your beautiful feelings. *Make it a rule: When you are learning the text and music of a role, be extremely careful not ever to go over it by rote, but always combine it with the inner course of your part. Relate the enunciation, the text, the music, all to the through-line of action that goes through your whole role.* Your artistic creativeness lies in your showing us: This is how *I* interpret this thing. *A role is not made interesting by words alone but by what the actor puts into them.*"

This analysis of Levko's first phrase in the act took place beside the piano in the Studio, so that when the singer went onstage he was already in full possession of the understanding needed for every phrase he sang. His singing had to become visual, or else Stanislavski said: "I do not see what you are singing about, therefore I do not understand. You are not ready yet to go on the stage."

We must remember that at the end of the second act the chase for Levko was started again—by the Headman and the local police. Now we see something like a bear dashing to the summer house from behind a tree. This is Levko who has eluded his pursuers by turning his coat with the fur side out and who has sought refuge here; he turns and looks back to where the pursuit came from. Stanislavski adhered closely to the plot of the play, but embroidered on it with logically imagined events.

After the musical introduction, which paints a landscape in the terms of Gogol, Stanislavski said:

"How can we reproduce on the stage the sense of nature which we hear in the orchestra?" Then answering his own question he went on: "By the movements of Levko. He walks, he listens. . . . He is fascinated by the old manor house. He has come here at night. Perhaps it is all a dream?

"He is exhausted. Sleep overpowers him. He sings some phrases as if he were asleep."

When a line of conduct has been clearly established, when the music has been learned and a pattern of movement fixed, Stanislavski taught us not to rely on improvisation. As the singing score is all set, marked off in measures, musical periods, so all the *actions* of a singer should be carefully studied and combined with the music. When Levko entered, in this act, the following pattern was established:

He cautiously listens to what is behind him; he is saving himself from pursuit. He hides. He stops and listens. He takes three steps. Hides himself to keep safe from his pursuers. He hears something. There is a splash in the water—and Pannochka appears. Levko throws himself to the ground. Again he hears something. He flattens himself on the ground. He keeps his ears cocked, peeks out from under his sheepskin coat. Pannochka has come out and is on the steps; she climbs up them, lifting her veil. Levko lies still but has rolled himself in a heap like a hedgehog, listens, crawls forward for two steps. Again he listens, crawls four steps, then five. He listens, looks around. Raises his coat a bit. Pannochka passes (twelve chords), disappears in the distance. Levko looks around, uncovering half his face, raises himself slightly and lets the coat slip off his face, raises himself slightly and lets the coat slip off his head. Without moving he sings: "How quiet and how cool. . . ."

It is with such infinitesimal details that Stanislavski worked out a whole scene which is indicated in the libretto merely by the words: "Enter Levko."

"How quiet," he sings, lying on his coat. "Oh, dreams of my dear Hanna come. . . ." He gets up, throws his coat down by the summer house, sits on it, and sings his aria. He sings it almost like a lullaby and is himself lulled to sleep.

While he sleeps water sprites, half fish, half human, emerge from the lake.

Levko tries to throw off his drowsiness, he fights against sleep. "O moon . . ." is a song of great breadth. He sings it lying on his back, almost as if he were reclining on cushions in a carriage and riding alone. . . .

"Can you sing lying down?" asked Stanislavski.

"I can," replied Levko, and did.

"Splendid," said Stanislavski. "When our great opera producer Mamontov invited singers to perform for him he asked them if they could take a high note while turning a somersault. When he heard the indignant replies of the puffed-up singers he turned to Shalyapin and said: 'Fedya, you're a splendid singer, can you do a somersault right now here on the floor?' He could and he did."

Levko's pattern of action is now built around the fact that he longs to go to sleep, fights against his inclination, dozes, wakes up, and sings some phrases half drowsing. . . . Pannochka sings from the manor house. Levko is not sure whether what he hears is real or in a dream.

While he is dozing the house is transformed: delicate columns appear, there are lights in the windows, the water sprites are stirring around in the water. When he sings: "What is this? Am I dreaming?"—he jumps up, astonished, runs into the summer house where he hides himself and from there watches the fantastic goings on. The water sprites are awaking, coming to life, beginning to sing. They gradually emerge from the water, climb into the trees, warm themselves in the moonlight, dry their hair.

Stanislavski's water sprites were unusual creatures: they did not perform ballet steps, but rather they dove, played in the water, danced in a ring, swung on the branches of the trees.

"The water sprites emerge from the water," said Stanislavski to the women's chorus in making a picture for them of their performance, "but first we see only their fingers, then their hands, and then their heads. Forget that you are human beings. You have been drowned. Think of yourselves as animals—you are beautiful but half human, half fish. Remember the serpents that live in the water, crocodiles; recall their movements and why they make them. Think of fish, jellyfish and how they move about. Prepare exercises, sketches for water sprites—aquatic creatures.

"That is one part of your role, its characteristic part, but the other is this moment, this night. How is it going by, what is your line of action in it? You have been hibernating, you are numb, but now it is a warm night and you have risen to the surface. You are coming back to life. As you awaken you are blinded for a while, like salamanders; gradually you grow accustomed to the light, you take fright easily; look around as if you had entered some new realm. Half-wild, still-drowsy creatures, you slowly begin to be more like human beings. But you are still spiteful, you like to trick a handsome youth with the water. Each one of you had her own tragedy when she was on earth."

They have to swim up, raise themselves from the depths, so to say. This was accomplished by having light ropes rigged all the way across the stage in parallel lines about forty inches above the floor. These ropes were hung with lengths of tulle dyed the colour of water. Seen from the auditorium they gave the illusion of a surface of water. And on each of these riggings—there were seven or nine of them—the water sprites lay as if on the bottom of the lake. As they lay on mats they went through the motions of swimming, of leaping out of the water, then slowly emerging, climbing out onto rocks, shaking the water off themselves, getting up into trees, etc. The faces of the water sprites were covered with transparent gauze, which masked their features. In the blue night light this gave them the aspect of mystery-shrouded undersea beings. Their long hair was made of very fine cord, which looked heavy and rather like reeds. They wore tights and semitransparent drapery which gave their figures changeable outlines.

The overall effect, achieved especially by the fluent movements of the water sprites as they "swam", was startling and, above all, convincing in a truly fantastic way.

The first chorus of water sprites consists of three parts: the first is accompanied by waltz-like music: "We love to lure a fine young man with our singing, or frighten an old one away with our laughter"; the second is more emphatic and contains overtones of drama: "Let us forget how the young men fell in love with us, mocked us, and how we buried ourselves in the dark depths away from sorrow and the coils of grief. . . ." In this section there are outraged cries, there is suffering; in the third part the water sprites appear to have calmed down, they return to the theme of enticement. The staging of what the water sprites do and how Levko bears himself was worked out to correspond to these three parts of the chorus.

The first part was devoted to the awakening of the water sprites. They warm and dry themselves by the light of the moon.

The second part was taken up with their noticing Levko, who is watching them. So they begin to swim over to the summer house and crawl up near it, almost threatening him. After all, it was because of such young men that they all drowned themselves.

The third part of the chorus is of a softer, most alluring nature and this is reassuring to Levko. The water sprites caressingly try to lure him into the water and, out of curiosity, he is already on the brink of the lake, quite absorbed in looking at them as they walk on the dike; he looks at them as he would animals in a menagerie.

There was a definite pattern drawn for this "scene of the water sprites" and it was bound up with intergroup movements in accordance with each musical phrase.

Finally, they all vanish, not one is left. "What a marvellous, impossible dream", sings Levko, astonished by what he has seen. Immediately another marvel is revealed: a water sprite emerges from the water, swings on the branches of a willow tree, begins to call her comrades: "Oh come, maidens, come together, my pretty ones, let us dance in a ring." Again the sprites come out of the water, and they begin their dance with the words: "All on a midnight. . . ."

The music for the dance is still tentative, shy; it consists of three repeats, three couplets, and although it becomes progressively livelier it does not reach a point of gaiety or full energy. In it all there is still a plaintive sense of non-fulfillment.

The text of this song, as of all the other ritual songs in *A May Night*, is of folk origin and Stanislavski was particularly interested in this.

Stanislavski made no difference, when it came to the quality of performance, between a soloist and a member of the chorus. Once on the stage they ranked as equals from the point of view of being artists.

"There is nothing artistic in that! You have no line of inner vision! Why did you come here?" asked Stanislavski. "What do water sprites like? What do you imagine it to be? You must add a clear visual picture to what you do. You must know how to analyse the component parts of the music and then reflect them in your actions. It is very difficult for non-specialists to come to a deep comprehension of music. If you do not produce the words the audience will not hear anything but sounds, they will have no part in the musical action. If you do not love words, you will possess no diction. You are giving evidence of what one can call 'singers' psychology.' You are not pursuing the inner line of a water sprite's essential being, that is why the words mean nothing to you. A word here and there is audible, but not a single complete phrase. "I wish blah-blah-blah. . . ." (Here Stanislavski mumbled something with limp lips and everyone laughed). "Then I fall into a musical trance. I can fall asleep over such sounds. . . . But the aim of our Studio is to fight operatic routine and the idea that one only *hears* opera.

"Well now, back to the beginning!" This was the usual ending of the digression caused by the failures in a rehearsal. The work was then resumed and went on until we began to hear freshly-minted words and see faces enlivened by real feelings.

After the dance of the water sprites comes the meeting between Pannochka and Levko. All the other sprites vanish in the water, but Pannochka, who had secretly been watching the dance from the terrace of the old house and observing Levko, comes out to the edge of the terrace.

"This is poor Pannochka here before you," she says to Levko from above.

The whole manor house with its half transparent columns is bathed in a greenish light. Pannochka is silvery and pale blue, the features of her face are indistinct and her whole figure rather blends into her mysterious background so that she seems to be a ghostly apparition.

Levko in his wide trousers, with the lute-like instrument in his hands, watching the apparition with curiosity, is very reminiscent of one of Gogol's Cossacks, who are not "afeard of any devils".

"She is both a disembodied spirit and a human being," said Stanislavski, "who fixes one with her eyes—much like the ghost of Hamlet's father."

Stanislavski kept reminding us constantly that water sprites are not just ardent, joyous young girls who have nothing to do but dance. He advised each actress to recall something from her own past life which ended in tragedy and draw on it. Each of the water sprites must have gone through some such drama and is suffering from it. Pannochka's pain is even greater than that of the others.

"What is the line of your actions?" he asked Pannochka and then gave his own answer. "Study the facts. You came up out of the water to look at the house where you spent a happy childhood with your mother until tragedy overwhelmed you and you drowned yourself. You remember all this. Down in the water you go through terrible tortures, suffer endlessly reviving all the pain caused you by your stepmother. That is why you are vindictive. Your stepmother, your enemy, must be somewhere here. Now you see this young man, perhaps he will help you. But people are afraid of you. You have to find some way of communicating with a living human being. But you are—a shade! What means can you employ? You have the power of enchanting people, just as all water sprites do. Try this on Levko. You must draw him to you so that you can be saved."

Pannochka's charms begin to affect Levko; he jumps into the water and wades over to the house, clambering over stones. He even sings: "I am ready to do anything, Pannochka, anything you command me to do."

Pannochka asks him to play dance tunes on his instrument so the maidens can dance more freely.

Now Levko is in the midst of the sprites. He is standing on a rock some distance from the shore and he sings, to the accompaniment of his bandore, his dashing song: "Shines the golden moon." The sprites circle round him dancing. Then, as if to tease Levko, they sing: "He has forgotten his true love. . . ." and he repeats their words: "I have forgotten my true love."

It begins to look as if Levko will fall under the power of the water sprites. He is surrounded by them. He is in danger. After all, it is well-known that they are not friendly to human beings, that they take their revenge on them. In another moment they will seize and drag him down to the bottom of the lake. What saves him is the fact that Pannochka needs him to help find her wicked stepmother, a witch, and all the sprites obey Pannochka. At the instant of greatest danger to

Levko she asks the young man: "Oh, find for me my tormentor, I am stifled by her."

The plaintive words of Pannochka are accompanied by agitated arpeggios on the harps; she is suffering, languishing, and Levko is ready to do anything she asks. He is already half in love with Pannochka. Her charms are at work.

"Let us do the raven dance once more," the water sprites sing, and they begin a game which consists of one of them playing a raven and the others a mother hen with a brood of chicks. The raven tries to catch one of the chicks but no matter which way he turns, to the right, to the left, the chicks succeed in hiding behind their mother.

"Raven, raven, what are you doing?" "I am digging a pit." "Why, oh why, do you dig a pit?" "I'm digging for some treasure."

The witch, who is Pannochka's stepmother, offers to be the raven. Externally she looks like all the other water sprites but when she turns her back to the audience it becomes quite clear that she is the witch because the actress wears a terror-inspiring green mask with protruding teeth on the back of her head and on the back of her arms, above the elbow, she has claws attached (they are made of papier-mâché). She has only to turn her back to the audience and they see a terrible old witch. But she quickly turns around and the impression vanishes. Levko guesses that she is the witch, and at the end of the game, after Levko's exclamation: "There she is! There's the witch!" the water sprites fall on her and with wild laughter drag her down into the depths of the lake.

After the raven game and the unmasking of the witch the sprites disappear as the night ends. Dawn is at hand. For Pannochka the time has come for release and repose. She had watched the raven game with excitement from the house and now that the witch has been drowned she swims over to the dike where Levko is. Her face appears in the reeds near the edge of the water but the rest of her remains out of sight. Levko leans down to the water near her and it is then she says: "Oh, how light my heart and how comforted" and this is the beginning of a tender, brief duet at the end of which grateful Pannochka gives Levko a message for the Headman. Then, with the words: "Be happy with your Hanna, farewell," she swims off into the lake. The rays of the sun just rising above the water shine on her face, on Levko, and on the house, which during the raven game once more returned to its ruinous state; the columns and the windows have vanished. The May night is over. Morning has come.

Rimski-Korsakov wrote a musical description of the rising sun, during which Levko seems to rouse himself from a dream and looks around, trying to decide whether what he saw was real or not.

Yet in his hand he holds the message, and to the accompaniment of powerful chords from all the stringed instruments he sings, with wonder and joy: "No, no, it was not a dream. . . . I hold the message." The sounds from the orchestra swell into a tide of triumph and finally the theme is resolved in a majestic C-major chord.

But now at this moment of triumph comes the reckoning for the pranks of the past night. Together with an avalanche of sound the pursuing patrol swoops down on Levko to catch him at last.

"Just grab him! What are you so cowardly about? I wager he's no devil but a man." The last phrase is understood by the audience because Levko had earlier at a most critical moment turned his sheepskin coat with the fur out and that made him into a "devil". But the sun is filling the whole stage so brightly that no further mystification is possible. The trick has been shown up. The Headman is the conqueror now and the arrested Levko stands before him, held by four policemen.

The little bridge on the dike, so recently filled during the semi-darkness of night by all the water sprites, is now swarming with village people headed by the Headman and the Clerk. There is no wrack of fantasy left.

Now the Headman says menacingly to Levko: "So it is you who invent songs?" But at this point the Clerk intervenes to read Pannoch-ka's message, which he does with reverence and solemnity while sitting on the bridge, dangling his feet over the water. The others crowd around this one literate person in a scene that is reminiscent of the letter scene at the end of Gogol's *Inspector General*. Quite like the Mayor in that play the Headman proves quite hard-of-hearing when it says in the letter that he is an old fool. The gist of the letter, which purports to be from a high official, directs the Headman to repair the bridges on the highway, and also to have Levko marry Hanna.

Off in the distance are heard the voices of the village girls on their way to throw their wreaths into the lake. There are two women's choruses—one is approaching from the side of the summer house, and the other from the manor house. They are both singing the old ritual songs of the water sprites. Hanna enters with the girls. There is a joyful meeting with Levko—they will be married tomorrow! Now the stage is crowded with people, who all take part in the happiness of Hanna and Levko. The village girls are still carrying their wreaths, flowers, branches of birch. They all celebrate the young couple. This is the triumph, the victory of youth.

Against the background of all this rejoicing some comic episodes are still being produced by the Headman, Kalenik, and the Sister-in-law. The Headman goes around boasting about his being the guide of Her Imperial Majesty; Kalenik, who has been wandering around all night in search of his home, trumpets his especial theme: "I am my own Head-man"; and the Sister-in-law, still resentful of what was done to her, puts on a big scene of jealous rage for the Headman, that everyone is bound to see: "Where have you been rambling around all night, you cursed man? Go on, tell me!" And the Headman runs away from this spiteful woman while everyone laughs at him. He is completely disgraced.

Now the combined choruses sing a "gloria" to celebrate Levko and Hanna, who stand in the centre of the crowded stage. The girls throw their wreaths into the water and make wishes on them for future happiness. To add a gentle and humourous touch to the celebration Stanislavski had a little old man push his way through the crowd, settle down on the dike with his fishing rod to cast his baited hook down into the orchestra. The figure of a fisherman always carries an atmosphere of the quiet charm of the dawn of a new day. He cannot remain there long, for the swelling sounds of the finale of the opera will quickly overtake him. But in the orchestra a musician has a little silver fish ready, which he attaches to the old man's hook. As the finale brings down the curtain he hauls in his catch from the "water", it gleams merrily and makes an amusing and happy ending to A May Night.

When Stanislavski was working on his system of training creative actors, he approached the problems of production from different angles in order to work out in practice the basic ideas of his "system". He also applied this method in staging each production in his Opera Theatre in a different way. While Eugene Onegin and The Tsar's Bride were devoted in the main to the establishing of logical feeling translated into terms of action, in A May Night an entirely new approach is apparent.

The work on A May Night began with learning how to find the logic of action, the unbroken line of a role from beginning to end, and then developing it.

It would seem that the solution of the problem is more complex in an opera than in a drama. Nothing distracts a dramatic actor from the pattern for his role that he was worked out. His attention can be entirely concentrated on the characters with whom he is acting and on the actions they take.

But an actor in opera is not free to handle himself as he chooses on the stage. He is absolutely in the power of the rhythm of the music, the tempi set by the conductor. His relationship with his partners is also circumscribed by clearly defined intervals and pauses. Yet the art of an actor in opera consists in his achieving, despite these limitations, a sense of being free and maintaining the unbroken line of his life as the character he is playing.

Stanislavski conducted every rehearsal and did all of his directorial work along two parallel lines. He carried out the basic idea of a production to the point of its being a carefully put together and elegant creation. At the same time he taught his actors their technique, how to work on a part so that it would have the same full stature as a real, living entity. It was a distinguishing feature of Stanislavski's own work that he always combined teaching with directing in shaping a production.

The teacher role gave way to that of a director only when the performance had reached its culminating stage in final rehearsals. When a painter puts the finishing touches on his canvas they sometimes quite unexpectedly alter all that has been done previously and lend a new and keener impact.

Backstage these final rehearsals were called "infernal" as all that had been set previously was shaken up and rearranged. New demands were made on us until the performance really came to life and began to "sound".

So it was during the pre-opening night period when *A May Night* underwent a thorough revision and reevaluation of the work already done on it. Some actors who had prepared their roles for a whole year found themselves removed and their places taken by their understudies, who had been present at all rehearsals.

Staging was changed, and out of the strain and stress new scenes with new features were born and familiar patterns discarded.

If one missed one or two days of rehearsals one came back to the theatre to find much that was already quite unrecognizable.

"What do you mean, he cut *that* out?" one heard. "He did." "But *that other*, did he really cut it too?" "He did. And now the scene is entirely altered."

It seemed as though everything was being destroyed that had been so painstakingly built up for a whole year. It was very hard on the actors, who had conscientiously studied and worked and done everything the director had required of them. Now they were required to be even more flexible, to engage in bolder improvisation on the basis of the material already prepared. It now became quite clear which of the actors had really moved ahead in absorbing Stanislavski's technique and which had only taken refuge in "boning up" their parts. There was no quarter given to anyone now, regardless of rank.

It was a case of "martial law". If Stanislavski's day-to-day discipline was quite beyond the level of that in all other theatres, the discipline maintained in this time of preparation for a première was really military. Yet it was this heightened sense of self-discipline—the giving of one's all to that opening performance heedless of wounds to one's personal vanity, putting aside all false pride—that brought to a peak the joint creativeness of an ensemble for which Stanislavski always strove.

Stanislavski felt it was also a point of ethics for every actor and actress of the Studio not engaged in the performance to come to the theatre and help their comrades with their costumes or makeup. This too was a cardinal factor of the joint effort. He had no use for the actor or actress who could say: "I am not in this opera, there is nothing for me to do, I'll just come and see the performance." For Stanislavski that attitude was hostile to art and he was not to be reconciled to it.

All the participants in *A May Night* felt the effervescence that engulfed the whole theatre during these rehearsals. Sometimes it was very difficult for the actor-singers, the scene designer, and the entire production staff. Even Suk, the conductor, had to sit patiently at his desk and rest his baton until Stanislavski would ask the conductor's pardon for the delay and say: "Now let us go on."

In working on a production there seemed to be two Stanislavskis. The one was patient, a gentle teacher during the period of general preparation in the Studio rehearsal hall. He was almost paternal in his attentiveness, his uncomplaining explanations many times repeated, demonstrated, with a gentle smile and flashing eyes. One could make mistakes, learn and relearn how to avoid them. But when the production was transferred to the stage, when the run-through rehearsals began and the shaping of the whole was effected, then the Stanislavski who stood in the auditorium was no longer the teacher but the director. In return for all his patience in training his actors he now demanded instant adaptability to new conditions, fresh artistry, flexibility of temperament and technique.

"Since you have now come out onto the stage, please . . ." and there followed a series of dots which meant: "No more coddling, no more allowances made for anyone." He considered that enough time had been devoted to developing them.

The inner and outer lives of the actor-singers on the stage were subtly fused with the Rimski-Korsakov music. This made the performance of *A May Night* musical not only to the ear but to the eye, since Stanislavski took special care to have all the movements of the performers gently rhythmic as one of the indispensable conditions of acting in opera.

One of the reviews said: "It is necessary to note that, thanks to Stanislavski's system of acting, the precision of enunciation was carried to a point of perfect virtuosity. Undoubtedly this enables a wide audience to be drawn close to the whole action of the opera. What is also remarkable about this production is that there are no first and second rank divisions in performance. All the participants carry equal responsibility for it. . . ."

6

Boris Godunov

A MONTH AFTER *A May Night* had its première Stanislavski began to rehearse *Boris Godunov*, which by that time had been thoroughly studied and sketched out roughly by his assistants.

The organization and planning of work on each production was under the immediate supervision of Stanislavski, who kept an eagle eye on each so that there would not be any blank spaces left between one production and the next, which was already ripening. In his theatre work ran right along on a conveyor belt.

He felt that the right kind of organization was a primary condition for the creative growth of the theatre: "Everyone must always have a job in hand. No one should be wandering around aimlessly, waiting wearily for his next part." This was an oft-repeated remark of his.

All the preparatory work: the discussions about the aims and perspectives of each performance, the studying of the score, the acting and musical rehearsals—all this went on in the rehearsal room with the four columns where *Eugene Onegin* was first performed. Now the whole hall was included in the stage and Stanislavski's chair was placed against the long wall on one side, among those of the other directors of acting and musical training. This was arranged for a special purpose: "They will act less with their legs," said he. He objected strenuously to pointless wandering around the stage because he felt that the noise of steps interfered with an actor's concentration on his thoughts and inner impulses to action. The transfer of the rehearsals from this hall to the stage of the Opera Theatre was permitted only when each scene and the whole performance was solidly founded on inner logic and when the actor-singers were so well established in their parts that they would not be thrown off-balance by the influence of the public auditorium.

Before the *Boris Godunov* production there were grave doubts about it on the part of both the singers and the administration. From one angle there were elements of musical drama in Mussorgski's opera that seemed predestined to be staged by Stanislavski. The whole character of Mussorgski's way of writing, especially his *recitativos*, offered a tremendous expanse for the application of Stanislavski's principles of acting in opera.

On the other side one heard cautious, sceptical voices saying: "How can one produce *Boris Godunov* on such a small stage? And who can sing Boris after Shalyapin? Is this at all within the capabilities of such young singers?" and so forth. Still Stanislavski did undertake the production of *Boris Godunov*, with a young troupe, with youthful singers in the principal roles and he created a remarkable performance, free of all stale operatic conventions, and imbued with the real spirit of the 16th century.

Stanislavski's attitude towards Mussorgski's music was that of extreme veneration because he considered that the composer had contributed a new life to Pushkin's great work.

There was one more circumstance related to this opera which inclined Stanislavski to work on it. In 1927 it was announced that the well-known musicologist P.A.Lamm had prepared for publication the original score of *Boris Godunov*. As this first version was entirely unknown, inasmuch as the opera was always produced in the Rimski-Korsakov revision of the score, there was naturally a strong interest in Mussorgski's primary concept.

The first score was written by him in 1869 and it consisted of seven scenes: 1. Near the Novo-Devichiye Monastery; 2. The Coronation of Boris; 3. In a Monastery Cell; 4. In a Tavern; 5. In the Terem (Women's Quarters); 6. The Square in front of the Church of St. Basil the Blessèd; 7. A Session of the Duma and the Death of Boris. It was this version which was offered to the Imperial Opera and rejected.

Then the composer began to rewrite the opera, taking into consideration the suggestions and wishes of the Administration of the Imperial Theatres. The changes he made were substantial. He added the whole act in Poland (it was called "In a Forest Glade near Sokolniki on the Dnieper") and cut out the scene in the Square near St. Basil. He also quite revamped the scene "In the Women's Quarters" and this resulted in an alteration of the character of Tsar Boris himself.

This second version was finished in 1871 and the score was published by Bessel. Thus it was accepted as the basic text of the opera. Although one cannot but conclude that the second version had many valuable traits, still the first one threw into higher relief Mussorgski's innovations as a dramatist and it defined with greater clarity the relation between the hero of the opera, Tsar Boris, and the people. The second version reveals concessions made to the bureaucrats of the Imperial Theatres on whom the fate of the opera's production depended.

Rimski-Korsakov made his version in 1896, using Mussorgski's second score as his basis, but in his noble efforts to make the opera more popular, he retreated even further from the original idea it contained.

In his introduction to his version Rimski-Korsakov explained why he had undertaken the reworking of the score: "Practical difficulties, the fragmented quality of melodic phrases, the drawbacks in the vocal score, the rigidity of the harmonies and modulations, the mistakes in his knowledge of voice usage, the poor instrumentation."

Nevertheless many things that were held to be shortcomings in the opera by Mussorgski's contemporaries eventually were seen in quite a different light. The originality of Mussorgski as a composer and his innovations in musical forms broke up the old, rigid, generally accepted forms and opened new perspectives in the realm of musical drama. When he had finished his work on *Boris Godunov*, Rimski-Korsakov felt obliged to make the following reservation: "The present score does not destroy the original version, and therefore the work of Mussorgski is wholly preserved as the noble piece of work it is, worthy of respect and recognition."

After the Stanislavski Opera Theatre had made a careful comparison of the two versions, the preponderance of choice lay with the original score with the Polish scenes added.

In Mussorgski's own second version he began with the Pushkin text but then moved away from it in favour of a more melodramatic, less political implication in Boris's soliloquy, and showed him rather in the light of certain neurotic traits. In this second version he turned sharply away from the concept of "national musical drama" in the direction of the personal drama of a "criminal Tsar Boris", and here Stanislavski definitely preferred the first version of the opera.

"The general idea of our production," he said at the first rehearsal on February 21, 1928, "is to show the depth of Mussorgski's absorption in folk themes. *Boris Godunov* is a symphony. It is necessary to distinguish in it the various voices and to bring out all the shadings. The musical subtleties of the opera must be emphasized by means of the inner line of impulsion of each actor-singer."

In addition to the musical qualities of this work Stanislavski also was drawn to the Pushkin text. The problem of conveying Pushkin's words from the stage to the audience preoccupied and excited him throughout his whole life in the theatre. He often recalled his own failure to do this in *Mozart and Salieri* and the difficulties he had in staging *The Miser Knight*. He said that to project a Pushkin text from the stage was extraordinarily hard to do, and that he did not know, at the time, of any actors within whose capabilities the solution lay. The secret of handling Pushkin's poetry on the stage, in his opinion, lay in the revelation contributed by music.

After devoting his life to the study of the use of words in the theatre, and after all his attempts to achieve an effortless pronunciation of Pushkin's verse on the stage, Stanislavski now dreamed of really hearing it as it should be, set in Mussorgski's music. He expected to prove that here was the possibility for a fuller revelation of Pushkin.

In connection with this aspiration Stanislavski also dreamed of producing *The Stone Guest* with Dargomyshski's music.

"That is an opera which one hears and then leaves the theatre with the feeling that he has witnessed an extraordinary theatrical event; it has nothing to do with ordinary opera because the words are so completely merged with the music."

Because of their interrelationship, questions of musical speech in drama and dramatic expressiveness of words in opera were of equal interest to Stanislavski. Nevertheless he frequently pointed out that actor-singers were far better off then ordinary actors because they had such steady support from melody and accompaniment, albeit singers unfortunately do not always care enough about words on the stage.

"The whole of *Boris Godunov* needs to be based on dazzling diction. You need to know how to speak Pushkin's lines. There is very little staging involved. Everything is based on the words in the phrases! You are to pronounce the text in such a musical way that Pushkin's verse will be preserved. That is your main objective. And it is motivated by your psychology, your inner transitions. In contrast to all the former productions you have been in here, you will not be concerned with action but with conveying all the charm of Pushkin's poetry."

Stanislavski began with rehearsals of the most difficult scene, the conclusion. This scene was particularly exciting to all who worked on it and they were impatient to be rehearsed by Stanislavski himself.

"Splendid!" he exclaimed when the scene was sung for him, then he added: "It's a difficult scene." After that came the analysis of the work prepared by his assistants. "What lies at the heart of this scene? Mutiny and patriotism. At first there is rioting, looting. How are we to introduce the right shadings? All that you have done so far is in one tone, and it is all very loud. I cannot be sure which is the rioting, which the debauchery, which the scoffing and the hatred. If we follow only the line of sound-impressions it will be difficult to sort things out, so that is why we must follow the inner pattern, which gives the opera its revolutionary impact."

He half closed his eyes as if he had a vision, somewhere in the distance, of how the whole scene might look. Then he began to outline a picture:

"All the action takes place against the ruins of the house of Boyar Khrushchev, which has been almost burned to the ground. There is snow and trees scorched black by the fire. There is a stockade enclosure. Beyond it lies a road, a small elevation with burned birch and pine trees. In the distance there is a conflagration. It is night. The estate is being looted. Furniture, luxurious chairs, bags of loot are dragged onto the forestage. The house itself is almost all burned down. Chimneys stand out starkly. Perhaps only a doorway remains. A blackened tree, covered with snow. . . ."

Stanislavski could visualize things clearly, with every smallest detail, and see a whole setting in which action would take place, and paint the picture in such a way that it became an integral, familiar part of the production, as if it had always been there. His fantasy was always very logical and much more convincing than the directions in the libretto: "A woodland glade . . . a stump in the foreground."

"All such indications are crossed out," he used to say. "They were written by writers of no great brilliance" (this referred to librettists). "They did not know the stage."

Then Stanislavski had us go back to listening to the music. He never conceived of any action or emotion on the part of the characters apart from the music. His usual questions to both actors and musicians were : "What is the musical action here? How does the act unfold? Why are there these intervals, such as we find in *Parsifal?* What emotions do they express?"

The whole mood of the beginning of the act is defined by the word "riot". But Stanislavski immediately began to analyze the word so that there would be no such thing as rioting "in general".

He was a lifelong enemy of that expression "in general". So now he began to teach his singers how to discover the component elements of the concept "riot".

"How does one convey the idea of a riot? What is to be included in it?" Then he answered his own question: "Scoffing, hilarity, the humbling of one's enemy, torture, reproaches, joy, etc. The whole will add up to a riot."

Moreover, as was his custom, he drew parallels from the work of other artists and their creative processes. He was always trying to persuade his actor-singers to be artists themselves, to learn how to handle the subtlest shadings of colours, to be able to break up a colour into its constituent parts. "The drawing of a role", "the colours of a role" were expressions often on his lips.

"Actors usually proceed like children," he said. "They paint each thing in one colour: the sky is blue, the grass is green, earth is brown. But an artist combines colour tones. He has a most intricate range of colours on his palette. So don't paint your role just with primary colours."

In drawing a pattern and suggesting a series of objectives for each section of it, Stanislavski was really projecting the outline of a whole act.

"The sound of an alarm (we must get bells and match up their tones), a fire, a loud knocking. Something crashes. Havoc! Is this joyous or menacing?" Stanislavski asks the conductor. "It is more to our advantage to choose contrasting tones." Later on he proved that it was better to start the rioting off on a note of hilarity so that in the end it would be terrifying.

"A hilarious prank" is how he described the beginning of the scene. "There is a group of young men brawling, another is trying to stop them, others are fulminating, some have a large beam and are trying to break down a wall of the house. Still others are hacking away with axes. Some drag a trunk out of the house, smash it up. All this is done in the mood of rioting peasants thoroughly enjoying what they are doing, as only Russian peasants can."

The rehearsal of this bit (just one page of music before the chorus comes on) was repeated endlessly. The major part of Stanislavski's work was always devoted to the beginning of an act and until that was thoroughly established he refused to go any further.

"You're pretty quick with your looting," he said after watching the results of many such repetitions. "Criticize yourselves: As you played it, the trunk was falling apart to begin with and the contents were spilling out of their own accord. You kicked up a lot of dust but you quite overlooked the logic of the things done. Did you expend your temperament on showing off or on creating an image? Try not to act in such a hurry. That trunk is very heavy. How are you going to smash it up? With what?

"In life nothing happens all at once. You must learn to draw out each action on the stage. Try to find what it typifies. Don't push yourself, don't show yourself off until you have completely in mind how things happen in ordinary life. It is only the correct choice of your physical objective that will lead you to your super-consciousness, your creativeness, and your intuition. That is a law!

"The second moment [Stanislavski called the separate units of action 'moments'] is when they drag the Boyar out of his house. The tenors harass him cheerily, the bassos are glum. They pull him out as they would a dead cat. They set him up. They wipe their noses in a dark mood. They evidently intend to keep the game up for some time. After all, it will be a good performance—they are going to hang him. Here their joy takes on terrifying proportions. The women are all agog to see the spectacle. It's as though they had the Tsar himself in front of them. All the time there is an alternation of game-playing and sinister menacing. The bassos are for strangling him at once, the tenors, for prolonging the fun. Try to make a mock ceremony of it all. Jeer at him, lord it over him with great malice, amuse yourselves! Like a cat with a mouse—she clutches him then lets him go.

"The tortured Boyar waits for the final blow. His role is a tragic one in a brutal scene. It is important to maintain an atmosphere of anarchy throughout. There is no need here for set staging, all is dictated by inner emotional states. They are overjoyed that they have brought the beast to bay; he is trussed, helpless. The laughter is sneering.

"Bring out the meaning—your diction is halting," Stanislavski would stop them again and again. "Good diction is essential to the expression of clear meaning. Apparently you do not visualize what you are singing about."

The chorus sings: "So that the old man howl not too hard, so that his princely vocal chords be not torn, perhaps we'd better block up his throat. . . ." But Stanislavski stopped them at once: "I hear *owl* and it makes no sense." *H* is a treacherous consonant, so he proceeded at once to hold a session on polishing consonants. Then he went on: "Let me understand the inner meaning of what you are singing. The point is not in the volume of the sound but in its play of colour.

"Your faces are aflame with anger. But you are using irony and that is always difficult. Try singing *piano* (you want to skin the old cat, but do it gently). For now, use just one intonation, no words, just syllables like 'la-la-la', but convey the inner meaning of your intent."

Stanislavski tried all sorts of ways to induce the chorus to form phrases richer in coloration and not just formally correct.

"The first 'glorification' of the Boyar begins with a *pianissimo* and ends with a *forte-fortissimo*. How do you achieve this? The simplest manner is by volume of sound. But you can also do it with colours. Add a variety of moods so as not to restrict this multicoloured characterization to just one stress. This sort of training can be of the greatest benefit to a singer."

These and many other pointers were given by Stanislavski so that the words of the chorus would not be produced mechanically, so that they would be infused with vitality. It was only when his singers achieved this, he averred, that they would possess the brilliance of Shalyapin's diction, which distinguishes a true artist from an ordinary artisan.

"Now sing the 'Glory to the Boyar' ", he said on one occasion, "as if you were celebrating a great actor on the occasion of his silver jubilee."

In his search for true characterization and variety in these scenes, especially those with the chorus, the crowd scenes, he turned to the musical director of the opera with the question:

"Would it not be possible to assign various lines to individual singers in order to hold the 'density' of the chorus together for the

powerful finale; also to divide the chorus into groups for the purpose of
bringing out the conversational quality of the music?"

This method was used in the scene at the Novo-Devichiye monastery and that in the Duma. Wherever it was possible and in consonance
with the structure of the music in choral scenes, Stanislavski tried to put
life into the mass, to get away from uniformity and achieve an impression of the many facets of a crowd. Naturally this resulted in pitched
battles with the chorus masters, who defended to the last the procedure
of grouping the members of the chorus by the range of their voices and
demanded that the sopranos, altos, tenors, and bassos be kept in their
own niches, whereas Stanislavski was always trying to break up those
groupings, to mix them, to give actors the opportunity of being in
contact with one another, as in real life. This, naturally, called for a
great deal of extra work but it did not in any way jeopardize the overall
blending of the choral sounds.

In his asking to have the choral responses sung by individual voices
in the chorus, Stanislavski was restoring the original concept of the
composer which had been distorted in the early productions of the
opera. It was against such distortions (for which the all-powerful conductor at the Maryinski Opera in St. Petersburg was responsible, when
Boris Godunov was first produced there) that V.V. Stasov, as a passionate partisan of this new Russian music, voiced his protests: ". . . an
ignoramus conductor not only cut out all that did not find favour in his
very routine taste ... but he also distorted the deepest and most
characteristic intentions of the author; he had the whole chorus or a
whole group in the chorus sing what was supposed to be sung by
separate individuals. In doing this he quite perverted Mussorgski's
reforming innovation of having small, separate scenes inside the mass of
the chorus and turned the opera back into the routine ruts of ordinarily
accepted opera methods."

Having succeeded in getting his actor-singers to produce live, clear
words when they were going through their mock glorification of the
Boyar, Stanislavski then took up the injection of active, external
movements into their conduct.

"In this first part I see three separate actions:

"1. You squat around the Boyar and gaze at him as though you were
seeing him from a distance: Who is this? You consult with each other:
What is this, a tree, or a bush?

"2. During the soprano theme you crawl a little nearer. Aha! We see!
That's who it is! The Boyar himself! This is said with malicious irony.
Then you seem to tell each other who it is.

"3. You start a mock procession around him. You drape some matting
over him and so on."

But as soon as the actors began to move around on the stage a new problem arose, the solution of which Stanislavski felt was highly significant: how to relate the rhythm of external movement to the inner rhythm of feelings. They may coincide, or not, and this lends emphasis to the special character of each small unit. It is very simple to learn how to keep rhythm when singing or walking—that is marching. Stanislavski, however, was dead set against that primitive interpretation of rhythm onstage.

The analysis of the "glorification" scene shows the character of his directions.

The mock glorification of the Boyar was written by Mussorgski in a rather slow tempo (*andante cantabile*), whereas the inner emotional state of those singing cannot possibly be temperate. The whole act builds with mounting agitation, nervous tension. Yet Stanislavski was able to combine the slow, quiet external rhythm with an inner turmoil.

"This scene is in essence a revolt. You sing in quarter notes but inside you are throbbing in eighth notes or sixteenths. Don't interpret this rhythm externally, in terms of gestures. What you must find is the rhythm of your feelings. It is as if you had a metronome inside you. One move is ready to move on into several accelerated ones; whole notes threaten to break up into thirty-second notes. It is only by combining your rapid inner rhythm with your slow external rhythm that you can transform a quiet scene into a tempestuous one. It is a complex job, but if you can achieve this you will always be at ease onstage."

Stanislavski also reminded us that in seeking to express truthful feelings on the stage an actor can begin with his internal state and externalize his emotions or act in the reverse order, from external to internal emotions.

"If the music does not immediately suggest to you the right rhythm for your feelings then express them first externally while seeking a justifiable basis for them and that will create for you the inner emotion you need. If you accomplish your physical objective you will find that the reflex effect of this will be to stir your inner feelings.

"If you wind up a watch it will go of its own accord," he used to say. "Forget about any system of acting then, *for such a system's sole purpose is to give nature a free rein.*"

Stanislavski rehearsed the beginning of the above scene, which is the last in the opera, many, many times. He always came up with something that could be added to it, to illumine it, even if all that had gone before was well-performed. The actors who did not come on until the middle of the act very often were not able to rehearse their entrances, even though there was no time limit set by him to his rehearsals.

A rehearsal usually went on and on until one of his assistants, taking advantage of a pause, would cautiously suggest that the hour was late and that it was time to release the actors. Whereupon Stanislavski would pull out his watch with an alarmed expression—for some reason he kept it in a side pocket together with a large bunch of keys to his bookcases—and then he would hurriedly acquiesce: "Yes, yes, of course! Why didn't you speak to me sooner? Next time we will begin to rehearse where we leave off today; otherwise we will never move ahead." But the next time he still went back and rehearsed from the beginning.

When we did move on to the next scene, the arrival of Varlaam and Misail, Stanislavski remarked: "Remember, this opera is set in the Time of Troubles. There was a great deal of dissension among the people. Some were on the side of Boris Godunov, others were against him. You cannot tell who these men are who have arrived.

"You have dragged the Boyar out to hang him. Do not immediately abandon this enterprise. You have to have some basis for moving from one scene into the next. What is the line of your action here? To look, listen, warn! Try to look as if nothing were going on. You cock your ears. At first you do not grasp what is said, then finally it dawns on you. Slowly you move out of your mood of spite into one of hilarity. There are some who try to convince you the news is true and others who do not take it in. The entrance of Varlaam and Misail must be clearly seen. Do not put anything in the way that would block it. The points to be made are:

"1. The news of a new Tsar coming to power.

"2. The two drunken monks climb in over the fence, bringing the news about the new Tsar—this is a genre scene.

"3. Russia is falling apart! I'll smash it to bits!

"4. A drunken dance.

"Find different shades of colouring for all these bits so that the whole does not coalesce into a monotone. The idea of Varlaam's song is to rouse the people against Boris. This is done by both the monks with great skill. They are intent on stirring up a revolt and earning a hundred rubles. Those who are half drunk sit down, the rabble-rousers walk around. In order to see how a revolt swells you must show its gradations."

The scene here described, although it was fully finished, was never put on because of technical considerations. It would have necessitated an extended intermission just before the end of the opera which would have made Boris far too long. Stanislavski very reluctantly agreed to the cutting, but was somewhat compensated for the loss by the addition of the scene in the square near St. Basil the Blessèd.

In this period of work on Boris Godunov Stanislavski gave wide opportunities for his assistants and young directors to show their own initiative. The work on various scenes was divided among them. The mob scenes were handled with the main company by B.I. Vershilov, the deputy art director of the theatre; the "Tavern", "Cell", and the "Polish" scenes were rehearsed by Zinaïda Sokolova, Madame Meltser, and me. The second campany was trained by Madame V.V. Zalesskaya. Later Ivan Moskvin of the Moscow Art Theatre, an old friend and associate of Stanislavski, took a hand in some of the directorial work.

1. Near the Novo-Devichiye Monastery

The melody that begins the opera is plaintive, indeed heartrending. As mournful as the autumn song of a shepherd, a solo bassoon is heard. This melody as Mussorgski wrote it does not merge with a broad flow of music as it does in the Rimski-Korsakov orchestration. It is like a moan, broken into spasmodic pauses like heavy sighs.

This is the theme of a ruined Russia. It does not reoccur in the opera yet it has a kind of inner bond with the theme of the usurper which runs through the entire score in various forms and colours.

This somewhat distant similarity of the two themes is perhaps an allusion to the fact that the people's dream of freedom is bound up with their faith in the Tsarevich Dmitri, who has revolted against the despotism of Boris Godunov.

With the first sound of this plaintive melody the curtains part. There is no overture to the opera.

Onstage, squarely facing the auditorium, is the high wall of the monastery with a tower over the gateway. The wall runs almost parallel with the footlights. The main gates are shut and only a small low door in one fold is ajar. Near the gateway there is an old beggar woman squatting on the ground with a baby in her arms, waiting submissively and patiently for something.

With the next musical phrase a little beggar girl is seen limping along the wall. She drops to the ground and nestles close to the old woman. These two figures seem to be symbolic of a starving, suffering Russia.

From the cellos the melody passes to the clarinets, then on to the bass viols. As the theme spreads, grows in volume, we see a group of people being driven in by the bailiffs. In twos and threes the peasants, men and women, are thrust onto the stage, and gradually half of the space is filled with a crowd. The bailiffs use whips, kick the peasants in the back, force them to go down on their knees beside the monastery wall.

The theme swells, passes to the wind instruments and finally is taken up by the whole orchestra. A group of boyars, headed by Shuiski, appears. They go through the gate by means of the low door. In the absence of the bailiffs, who are driving another group of peasants off-stage, some inquisitive people try to peep through the crack of the door. But they are soon forced back.

Now the space in front of the wall is solidly filled with people. The head bailiff carries a heavy cudgel. He disappears behind the door under the tower and reappears to give orders to his underlings to go about and watch the people—there are many who may be thinking of some means of slipping away. Others are completely indifferent to whatever is demanded of them.

Suddenly the bailiff dashes out and yells: "What do you think you're doing? Standing around like a bunch of idols! Quick! Down on your knees! Spawn of Satan!" First reluctantly and then slowly under a rain of lashes from whips the "Spawn of Satan" sink down. The people look at each other. Then there is the first pregnant pause. At a signal from the bailiff the chorus begins to sing their insincere plaint: "To whom have you abandoned us, our father?" So far things go smoothly. After he has started the chorus with its quiet lamentations the bailiff with worried looks again disappears into the monastery.

As soon as he leaves the crowd disintegrates, it no longer has any resemblance to a group of the faithful praying for the Tsar; the chorus continues to sing smoothly but the intonations are impudent and insolent. The crowd of people who have been forcibly driven here begin to have a bit of fun. The peasant men and women who had been praying apparently so ardently now are like children tumbling over each other. The last chords of the chorus music are like pitiful moans but then comes bold, brazen music and one hears a voice yelling: "Hey! Mityukha, ho there, Mityukha! What are we all howling about?" The good-natured answer comes from a smiling young peasant: "How the hell should I know?" Then later comes the line: "I guess we are going to set a new Tsar on top of old Russia." Here Stanislavski had a dishevelled young fellow, carrying a flask of vodka, dash out of the crowd, bounce into the air in a wild kind of dance and sing that line. Then the small door in the big portal opens, the bailiff appears, and instantly they all fall into their former kneeling positions as suppliants. Under the glare of the bailiff's eyes they cough, sneeze, spit, clear their throats, and then take up their wailing chant once more.

In this way Stanislavski succeeded in lightening the leaven of the crowd with unexpected colours and thus showing the profound indifference of the people to the choice of a new Tsar, and the whole business of government, because in any case their lot would not be affected. During this whole scene the individual lines were sung by one or two voices in the chorus. This gave more liveliness to the crowd and that is what Mussorgski wished.

After this scene with the chorus, the bailiff and the prayers for the Tsar, the bent figure of an earnest old man, Shchelkalov, appeared on the tower over the gateway. The crowd stood up and the men doffed their headgear as they gaped and looked up to the fine-looking old boyar, who told the people that "the country was groaning under the evil of lawlessness" and that it was necessary to "accept the power of an overlord." His musical accompaniment is full of solemnity, prayerful in character, almost in the rhythm of a religious rite. He bows low to the people and they in return, despite the fact that they have no notion of what he has been saying, sigh and bow low to him while looking at each other covertly with questioning eyes.

The boyar leaves, the people stand around expectantly. Then a religious chant is heard from a group of "God's People" drawing nearer. The tatterdemalion with the flask of vodka hastily tells everyone that these "God's People" are a brotherhood of blind beggars. Then these "Fools of God" of old Russia, chanting the psalm "Glory be to Thee, all-powerful Creator. . . ." walk on one after another, handing out little holy images, small crosses, calling upon all to "array themselves in robes of light," to "exalt the image of the Lord". They are greeted with shy respect, and as "God's People" they are met with low bows, while the peasant women weep for no particular reason. Then the procession is admitted into the monastery where they will be placed, in their quality of "God's People", among the high and mighty near to the Tsar.

Once more the crowd is bewildered, and quite humbled now they hang their heads. The orchestra accompanies this sad mood with fragments of a mournful melody suggesting a desolated country.

Later on Mussorgski, who was a subtle composer of drama, produces in contrast a marvellous scene full of fun with Mityukha. The irrepressible power of Russian humour, which enabled the people to survive all the griefs of their history, resounds throughout this scene.

On one side of the stage a group of young fellows who have been bored by all the doings wink at each other then steal over to Mityukha, who has become interested in the holy images handed out by the blind beggars. They try to strike up a conversation with him: "Did you hear what the blind beggars were saying?" Mityukha answers firmly: "I did"—and thereupon he launches an explanation. But the more he "explains", the more evident it becomes that he did not understand anything. All he understood was that you must take your ikons and go, but where to go, or why, he could not explain. Stanislavski pushed this to the point of boisterous guffawing.

Then the bailiff appears on the tower and yells at the crowd below: "Hey you flock of sheep!" He brandishes his cudgel to reinforce his order that they present themselves in the Kremlin again the next day. "Do you hear me?" he asks and again flourishes his big stick. Everyone is disappointed: "We thought we'd be all through today and now we have to begin all over again."

The crowd slowly melts away, shouting remarks to one another, while the orchestra plays a melancholy melody of their prostrate country. When the stage is emptied, only the old beggar woman with the children remains near the gateway. She has sat down near the threshold of the little door in the big portal—she probably has nowhere to go. The rays of the setting sun, streaking down from the tower along the wall, light up her solitary figure. With this the melancholy melody in the orchestra fades out.

In this scene, as in the whole opera, there is revealed the deep chasm between the people and the Tsar and his boyars. The high monastery wall, in front of which the crowd was pushed around and forced onto their knees, symbolizes as it were their great differences and mutual misunderstanding.

Stanislavski used many tones to convey the helpless state of the Russian people.

2. The Coronation of Boris Godunov

The second scene of the opera was transferred by Stanislavski from the square outside the cathedral to the interior of the building. The footlights are where the altar screen would be so that the whole action takes place facing the audience.

The Patriarch's dais stands in the foreground. The setting retains the architectural lines and the inner decorative richness of the Kremlin churches. The walls and the supporting columns are all covered with frescoes and there are watch lights and lighted candles everywhere. In the front, to the right of the audience, is the tomb of one of the rulers of Russia, perhaps that of Tsar Fyodor, the predecessor of Boris Godunov. In the back of the stage there are open portals leading out to a porch where crowds have been gathered under the guard of bailiffs. When the curtain opens one sees preparations for the ceremony in course. Candles and watch lights are being lighted. People look around the stone pillars with curiosity. The centre of the church is empty but one has the feeling of impinging crowds, held in check by guards. The scene opens with the ringing of bells, which grows louder and louder and is finally incorporated in a tremendous orchestral chord. The orchestra is augmented by real bells brought from the Novo-Devichiye Monastery for the performances, bells which are famous for their mellow tones. During the pause which ensues, and while the atmosphere is still resounding from the bells, Shuiski hurriedly enters to a fanfare from the brasses: "All hail, Tsar Boris Fyodorovich! All glory to him!" Here

Boris Godunov, Scene 2: The Coronation of Boris. (Photograph reproduced from damaged plate.)

begins the triumphant glorification music of the Tsar. Against this background the Procession of the Cross enters the cathedral, which has been prepared for the Patriarch to preside over the coronation. A procession of noble boyars bearing heavy religious emblems slowly advances and is ranged in a semicircle around the cathedral walls. The remaining space is filled with the clergy of high rank and finally the Patriarch enters. Everything is now ready for the reception of the Tsar. As the chorus ends with "Glory! Glory! Glory!" and the bells ring resonantly Boris appears in the light of the entrance portal, preceded by four military attendants in white. Pale, with downcast eyes, holding the sceptre and orb in his hands he slowly mounts the steps of the

Patriarch's dais with the help of Shuiski and the Patriarch himself. The bells stop ringing. He is dressed in imperial robes and he faces the auditorium as if before the altar. The French horns play a long, even, impersonal note which is taken up by the violins and violas—it turns into the theme of Boris's gloomy introspection. "My soul is afflicted. . ." he says.

After the prayer: "O Righteous one, All-Powerful Father . . ." Mussorgski indicates a pause of a whole measure. Stanislavski used this pause to have Boris and everyone present go down on their knees. This is a moment of silent prayer after an unbroken, ever-increasing flow of music and the powerful climax of Boris's solemn invocation.

At the end of the prayer Boris lays the sceptre and orb on a salver presented to him by Shuiski ("It must be Shuiski, the Tsar-to-be; let him receive these emblems of imperial authority", said Stanislavski). Then Boris steps down from the platform of the Patriarch's throne to bow to the tomb. Beside him is Fyodor, now the legitimate heir to the throne. Only the audience has seen Boris's face, as all the others on the stage are behind him.

In keeping with Stanislavski's wishes, a makeup was devised for Boris that reflected his Tatar origins. He was also concerned with the stature of the Tsar. The singer who had this role (N.D. Panchekhin) was of medium height so special footgear was provided for him which made him appear taller without interfering with his natural way of walking. Stanislavski himself told the shoemaker what to do—first a sock with a special, high heel was prepared and then the outer shoe was designed to wear on top of that.

The novelty of this staging, the clear logic of the action, its complete fusion with the music really made it seem as if the scene had been written to be played inside the cathedral instead of out in the square as was usually done.

3. The Cell in Chudov Monastery

After the gorgeousness of the coronation scene the audience is shown the crypt-like monastic cell of Pimen. Stanislavski insisted that it be very small and be placed in a cellar-like spot. History indeed places it "underground".

To the production staff Stanislavski handed the problem of instantaneous changes of scenery and this was achieved by the use of a revolving stage on which the first three scenes were "loaded" before the opera began.

It took only about a minute to make a clean transition thanks to many rehearsals with the stagehands. The set for the cell had the sides

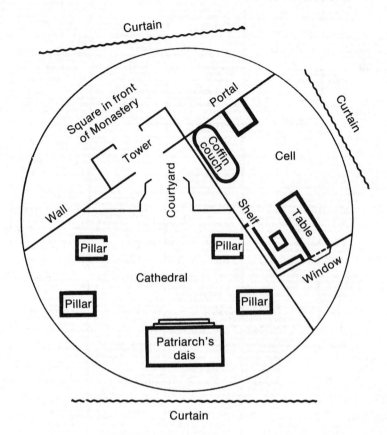

Boris Godunov, plan for the first three scenes.

brought forward so that the width of the stage did not exceed about nineteen feet.

Stanislavski spent a lot of time on the role of Pimen. His warmest, most concerned remarks were reserved for this part, and had he himself sung in *Boris Godunov* this would probably have been his chosen role. When he was portraying it during rehearsals he made an extraordinarily impressive figure out of Pimen.

"He is a hundred years old, his eyes look deep into the past. He sees things that those around him no longer can see. Present realities are practically nonexistent for him, except for his rolls of parchment and his quill. He does not notice anything in his surroundings, his movements are very slow. He is almost as if overgrown with moss. There is a small narrow table, or rather just a plank, attached on one end to the windowsill and held up at the other by a log of wood. On this plank and on shelves along the wall are rolls of manuscripts in sheaths of birch bark. Near the rear wall is Pimen's bed—a hollowed-out, coffin-like resting place covered with a piece of matting. A rushlight on the table illumines his face. All the rest of the cell is dark and will not have any light until the rays of dawn come through the window."

When the curtains open, the audience sees only Pimen's face and the shadowy outline of his figure. During his whole soliloquy all attention is centred on him. It is only when the muffled sound of singing somewhere at a distance in the monastery comes through to the cell from above that the audience is able to distinguish the vague figure of a man crouched under the table. There on some straw is a ragged, almost worm-like creature—who is destined to be the future Tsar.

After his startled awakening from a nightmare ("Always the self-same dream") the self-styled Pretender sticks out his head, covered with matted hair, to be blessed by Pimen. Only then does the squat, ungainly, almost misshapen figure crawl out from under a mat. Stanislavski stressed the contrast between the serene Pimen, so far removed from all earthly concerns, and the restless fugitive, with his darting eyes and his tormented mind full of magnificent and terrifying visions as Pretender to the throne.

"Listen to the verse you are singing," said Stanislavski to the Pretender. "What are the word-sounds that Pushkin uses when you describe Pimen: 'You fought under the battlements of Kazan, you repulsed the forces of Lithuania under Shuiski, you saw the court and luxury of Ivan'.

"Then what do you sing about yourself? 'From my young years I have wandered from cell to cell, a threadbare monk.' It is well-nigh impossible to render in reading all the beauty of Pushkin's verse—it only shines forth in all its glory when the words are blended with music."

From this ungainly, mystery-enshrouded figure crawling out from under a table in a small cell we will see emerge a proud and fascinating adventurer, who will know how to wear the robes and play the role of a tsar. It was this great range that Stanislavski sought to have his singer encompass.

For the time being, however, the Pretender is afraid to look straight at Pimen; he merely listens to the monk's tale about the murder of the Tsar's son. Leaning against a log of wood at the end of the table and trembling at his own question, he asks: "What was the age of the murdered Tsarevich?"

As Pimen answers: "He would be of your age and now on the throne," the flutes in the orchestra for the first time hint at the theme of the Pretender. In the libretto the rather precarious direction reads: "At Pimen's words, Grigori, the Pretender, majestically rises to his full height." To the actor attempting to execute these instructions Stanislavski immediately said:

"That's at once an operatic cliché. Why? You are already playing at being the Tsar—to all outward appearance. Is it as simple as that for a Pretender to climb onto a throne? Just by proudly standing erect? Your inner process must be much more complex than that. Express your own feelings and what you understand of your part."

When the solemn bells quietly begin to ring for early-morning mass and a vague beam of light slips across the damp wall of the cell, Pimen, tall and spare in his long black robe, stands up to go to church.

Grigori kisses his hand, gives him his staff, and respectfully accompanies the ancient monk to the door. When he has gone Grigori is transformed. He throws himself on Pimen's manuscripts and greedily devours their contents. His face lights up with predatory glee. He now grows to the dimensions of the terrible judge of Boris Godunov. The words: "Boris! Boris! May all around you tremble!" coming from his lips sound like a doomsday warning.

The sun now shines through the window and shows the ugly but powerful face of Grigori, whose eyes are fixed on a dark corner of the cell as if he saw there his fate.

4. The Tavern

In seeking, as always, a concise expression to sum up the essential meaning of a scene Stanislavski used for this one the word "trap". His plan was for a simple, peasant cottage interior with a large table at which all customers sat. Each person with his own preoccupations is clearly visible as he is placed right in front of the audience.

Behind the table are two windows and on one side there is a stove from which food is served. All action is centred around the table.

In the beginning an agile barmaid is fixing up herself and the place in expectation of the arrival of customers. Later on two vagrant monks, Varlaam and Misail, will sit at the table with their backs to the windows and still later the guardians of the law will be there.

The boisterousness of the vagrants and their song—Varlaam sings the famous "Whoever has been in the town, the old town of Kazan", as he keeps pouring out wine—is in contrast with Grigori's restrained and cautious bearing. He tries to keep as far away from the monks as he can while also keeping an eye on the window near which he is seated. He carries on a covert conversation with the barmaid against the background of Varlaam's drunken singing.

The director's problem here is not to let the drunken singing of the monks distract the attention of the audience from the development of the main theme of action which is carried forward by Grigori.

The police suddenly appear. This is the beginning of the dénouement of the main episode of this scene—the "drawing in of the net" which has to do with Grigori's fate.

"The police must appear without warning," said Stanislavski, "two at the windows, one in the doorway, and arrest everyone."

Two of the guards quickly climb in through the windows and settle themselves on the bench. Their leader comes through the door and five seconds later is sitting between the vagrant monks who are flanked by the guards and with all possibility of escape cut off. The staging was extremely simple, logical, rather amusing, and made it easy to guess what each actor was going to do: whether it was the zealous policeman, the slippery rascal Varlaam, bewildered Misail or assertive Grigori. This last, finding himself in a trap, draws a knife from his belt and, taking advantage of a moment of inattention on the part of the guards, jumps out one of the windows.

This scene always was very popular with audiences and was often played later on as a separate scene in recitals. Even without costumes or makeup the basic vividness of the effect remained.

5. The Terem—The Women's Quarters

For this scene, which is central to the whole opera, Stanislavski proposed the following plan to the scene designer, the conductor, and the cast: "The main motive force here is the torment in Boris's conscience. The key words are: 'If by chance even a single strain has appeared in thee. . . .' "

Then Stanislavski emphasized several points which unless they were brought out would leave the scene quite lifeless:

1. The death of his daughter's betrothed; 2. The cultural aspect. Boris teaches his son geography; 3. The opening up of Boris's conscience when he is alone—his first soliloquy. This whole aria embodies the clarity of his thought and inner conflicts; 4. It is obvious that he is preparing his son to succeed him; 5. The scene of the denunciation (this should be as vile as possible); 6. The Tsar receives a future ruler, the rivalry between two aspirants (arrival of Shuiski); 7. The change in Boris as soon as the Pretender is mentioned. This is the beginning of the Tsar's gradual downfall (his humiliating request, prayers, threats, the beast in him is aroused, his attack of illness). The scene in which there is laughter should be exploited. Shuiski is a good prosecutor. The attack—beginning of Boris's illness.

This short "outline of situations" summed up the basic points in the scene which would be developed in the course of rehearsals. A director first establishes a skeleton outline of the actions involved along which the main thread of the play will be woven.

Again as in *A May Night* Stanislavski, while frequetly using the phrase "the through-line of a role or a play", also stressed the gradualness of the transition from one emotional state to another. For example, in Boris's passing from the sanctimonious ruler to a groveling coward the singer has to feel his way through every step of the downward gradation. He pointed out at the same time that actors have a tendency to play "end results" and not the complex development of psychological, living feelings which lead to those results.

"You have to learn not to play a tsar in one spot and a coward in another, but all the 'twenty thousand shadings' [he loved the hyperbole of such numbers] which lie between the image of a tsar and a coward. This is of interest to me as a spectator because I wish to follow that path with you. . . ."

In choosing the scenery Stanislavski reasoned this way: Boris loves his children, he is preparing his son to be his heir; tortured as he is by his conscience he is prepared to suffer punishment, but he wishes to safeguard the throne for his son. In the last scene, just before he dies, he will say: "It is not for myself that I pray . . . but for my innocent, gentle, untainted children."

Where does he go when he seeks surcease from government problems and the lacerating claws of his soul, when he seeks peace and rest? To his children. In this scene we observe him as the affectionate father. The Tsarevich is studying geography. Where is this going on? Obviously his children have not come to him in his study, and indeed they were probably not allowed to go there, so he has come to them. So the set is something like a nursery. Here in his son's room, beside the boy's small bed, he suffers even more. He is tormented by the murder of another boy, like his own son. Therein lies a wealth of material for the inner creative state of a true actor.

The set for the room of the Tsarevich was painted by S.I. Ivanov, a splendid specialist in the old Russian style, who knew how to point up vivid spots of colour in the dark green-blue background of the chamber. He particularly enlivened the vaulted ceiling with flashes of dull gold and lent exquisitely colourful effects to the style of the stove.

On the wall near the canopied bed was a map and another lay unrolled on the floor. The Tsarevich, crawling over the latter, is colouring it. On the table are a globe and some books. And in the centre of the stage is a little chess table at which Boris teaches his son how to play. Between the decorated stove and the wall stands the Tsarevich's bed with its handsome canopy. On the left side of the stage one can see down a broad corridor which leads to other chambers in the Women's Quarters. Out there, sitting on a painted chest, is Boris's daughter, the Tsarevna Xenia, who is scarcely more than a little girl. She is weeping. Her nurse tries to comfort and distract her. At the other side of the stage the mood is different. The Tsarevich is studying. Tsar Boris enters from the corridor. He consoles his daughter, sets her on his knee as one would a child, kisses her. Then he gestures her away and sadly watches her go. After that he pulls himself together and with a buoyant manner goes over to his son. He tests his knowledge. It is like a lesson and the boy answers his father's questions. The father is pleased with his progress. They both stand in front of the map of the Russian Empire examining it like two rulers: the one the actual Tsar, the other the Tsar-to-be. Then picking up his colours and books the Tsarevich goes out leaving Boris alone. Here begins his soliloquy: "I have reached the pinnacle of power". Stanislavski purposely does not let Boris move here, or change his position, so that all attention is directed to the actor's face and the thoughts behind it. His frank confessions are interrupted by the arrival of a boyar bringing a denunciation of Shuiski.

"The boyar crouches beside Boris, whispers in his ear," said Stanislavski, "and as quickly, thinking himself unnoticed, vanishes as he had appeared. But Shuiski is already aware of him. We have seen Shuiski peering around the door as the boyar is whispering his denunciation.

"Now the two rivals, Boris and Shuiski, stand face to face—they are both calm, imperturbable. The one is haughty, the other respectful in manner.

"Do not forget that you are a future tsar and that you are a boyar of ancient lineage," said Stanislavski to Shuiski. "You're a descendant of Rurik. It would not be in keeping for you to be a downright scoundrel, a stealthy villain, the way Shuiski is usually portrayed. The calmer, wiser, more restrained you are the more excited Boris will become. The highest form of shrewdness is to know how to conceal your feelings. Maintain a most noble and imperturbable exterior. The Tsar will be insolent, offensive and you will calmly give him the kiss of allegiance, and bow. Later you will easily, caressingly, imperceptibly, push him off the throne.

"And you," said Stanislavski to Boris, "don't allow yourself to get alarmed at once by the very mention of the Pretender. Don't pump up a lot of fear immediately, the way most singers in the role do. You still do not fully understand the matter. When you finally do grasp it, you weigh it, and give your orders. Try to do it all step by step. . . ." At the end of the scene Boris almost throttles Shuiski, tries to force out of him whether the Tsarevich Dmitri was really murdered. Shuiski quietly smooths his clothing, kisses the Tsar's hand, and never even hints at having been offended. When the Tsar feels a seizure coming on he dismisses Shuiski, who however remains to watch Boris from behind the door.

In the hallucination scene at the end of the act Stanislavski called on Boris to show great boldness. When it was necessary he did not shrink from the most daring mise-en-scènes. Boris throws himself down on his son's bed, tries to hide from the imagined phantom in the curtains of the canopy. He tries to conceal himself in a corner of the chamber and when, apparently, he is chased from there by the ghost he overturns the chess table, scattering all the pieces on the ground. All this was played in an ever increasing tempo and made a powerful impression; when finally the exhausted Tsar is brought to his knees and begs for mercy, finally falling on his face, he becomes a pitiful figure.

This whole scene is full of such dramatic tension and covers such a wide range of emotions that it takes an actor with a great temperament to play it—also one who has complete control of words and voice, a singer and actor of high quality and mastery. The first of our singers to play this role of Tsar Boris was N.D. Panchekhin and he fully met all the requirements. He was an expressive and lifelike embodiment, the tragic image of this highly gifted although criminal ruler.

6. Marina's Bedchamber

In the next two so-called Polish scenes new characters are introduced: Marina Mnishek and a Jesuit priest called Rangoni.

The first scene is in Marina's bedchamber. There is a bed covered with a damask baldaquin, a gorgeous mirror with a gold frame and a painting, a prayer stool with a crucifix—these are the main accessories of the apartment,with a large, bright window in a gothic frame.

A women's chorus of Marina's attendants sings a light, half-dancing song: "Along the Vistula so azure blue, 'neath an elm so silvery . . ." as they dress their mistress. They bow low, they bend over as they adorn Marina with various ornaments. The capricious beauty in a dress of stiff gold damask puts on some of the ornaments and rejects others. Each attendant comes forward on her own musical phrase, in her own rhythm and character. Marina in her gorgeous attire and jewelry seems to be preparing for some ceremonial occasion. But Stanislavski stressed the fact that "Marina's capriciousness derives from nervousness, not boredom. She is very much on edge."

Having dismissed her fussing attendants she remains alone to rehearse her seduction of the Pretender, whereby she hopes to become the Tsaritsa of Moscow.

"This is a Tsaritsa-to-be," said Stanislavski, trying to get the actress-singer to feel that freedom a person has when, alone and talking to herself, she without any embarrassment shows her innermost desires. The grasping and shrewd Marina longs to be the Tsaritsa even though she knows that her future spouse is really only an adventurer.

At a rehearsal of this scene with Marina and Rangoni, Stanislavski said:

"I can make a suggestion to help you to look like a queen. Half gestures are unacceptable. From the very base of your arm, let your prana energy flow to the end of your outstretched hand, releasing all tension right down to the tips of your fingers. Remember: the fingers are all important. If the flow of your prana energy is permitted to go throughout your whole body, you will always be fluent in movement. Dancing and gymnastics cannot give you this plasticity as long as you do not possess an inner sense of movement. When you walk your energy must flow all the way from your spine down your legs. This is something you should be stubborn about acquiring. Only then will your body be flexible. Develop your hands, your fingers. The fingers are the eyes of the body. Try moving, sitting down, while feeling your prana coursing through you. When you are walking use your legs and feet right down to the end of your big toe. Let the rest of your body remain entirely free. And do not forget that the spine has a great part to play in plasticity. The flow of prana includes your backbone."

These precepts repeated, in essence, all the early exercises in developing body plasticity which Stanislavski had been doing with his young students for nearly fifteen years. His insistence on them was continual and was applied to all actor-singers whatever their parts.

Carried away by her role Marina dances around her room unaware of the covert observation of Rangoni, the Jesuit priest.

"First let him stick his nose out beyond the baldaquin enclosing her bed," said Stanislavski. "Instantly the playful Marina turns into an obedient Catholic, a daughter of the Church, and sees in the secret spy only an affectionate and sensitive pastor. Later, in the duet, we come to the tricky diplomatic game played by two cheats"—which is how Stanislavski put it.

The game is played with friendly faces, shrewd eyes, expressive terms. "It is a diplomatic duel," was Stanislavski's description. "They try to trick each other, and they both know this although they do not give the fact away."

So the duet moves along until Marina explodes, and begins to be insolent to the priest, and he in turn begins to threaten her. The struggle ends in a victory for the Jesuit. Rangoni, infuriated, holds a cross over the frightened Marina, as if to strike her head with it. When Stanislavski played this he was terrifying. Marina crawls on her knees to her prayer stool to invoke divine assistance; supercilious, capricious, false, vicious Marina is changed into a pitiful puppy fawning at the feet of the cynical Rangoni, who has grown into a terrifying, sinister figure. Of course, it was only thanks to Stanislavski's guiding instructions that it was possible to bring this scene to such a high level of significance, since the text as written by Mussorgski diverges greatly from the Pushkin original and the musical fabric of the scene is not at its best here.

"The scene is rather trite," said Stanislavski, "and everything happens without preparation. So we have to rely on characterization and expressive diction."

The through-line of action for Marina he summed up as her overweening desire to become the Tsaritsa.

"The whole role must be vividly coloured," he insisted. "She is a horrid girl who will insinuate herself into the devil knows what. She is chock-full of vice. The minor key in the music demonstrates her caprice. She is on edge, she has an important rendezvous tomorrow. What will happen if that falls through?"

The actress-singer in Stanislavski's view should make a beautiful wench of Marina, capable of torturing cats and sticking pins in her servants; what makes her interesting is the extent of her evil qualities. She does not love the Pretender but she thinks she will be a match for his evil intents.

7. The Scene by the Fountain

The set shows a fountain—a great silver figure of a woman with a jar in her hands. Nearby is a stone bench. In the background the greenery of a park, lights in the castle windows. Two flights of stairs lead down to either side of the fountain. It is night. The moon is up.

The scene is dramatically rather overburdened by the long conversation between the Pretender and Rangoni, as well as the arrival of guests and their dancing; it ends with more dancing and toasts in honour of Marina. In these delaying actions of guests moving around and dancing there is a distinct giving in, on the part of the composer, to old operatic traditions. Stanislavski retained only the waiting for the Pretender, the arrival of Marina, and their duet, which has in it the essence of the scene and moves the action of the opera forward.

The whole duet of Marina and the Pretender, accompanied by the moving Mussorgski music, depends on expressive words with scarcely any external movements. They both sat on the stone bench and did not walk around the stage.

"Use the words to draw the design of your thoughts, find the right shadings for your scorn of the Pretender," Stanislavski said to Marina.

The Pretender's declaration of love required a great amount of work.

"Why the saccharine smile on your face just because you are speaking of love?" Here Stanislavski had rough comments for all tenors and their rubber-stamp declarations of love. "After all you are saying: 'How tormented I have been, how long was my unfulfilled expectation' and so on. That's all about torment and suffering and your face is positively beaming."

At the end of the scene Rangoni again appears. His head emerges from behind a bush.

"He was sitting there all along, overhearing what you said," suggested Stanislavski.

The psychological pattern which Stanislavski gave to the scene had this basis:

"The psychology of the Pretender is rooted in fear. He thinks the beautiful Marina may send him packing. Like any high-school boy he prepares himself for their rendezvous. He hides, when he hears Marina's voice, and doesn't know how to behave."

These unexpected remarks were aimed at getting rid of the sugariness, the banality with which opera singers are so cursed when they sing love duets.

"You must act the inexperienced lover," concluded Stanislavski, "and in so doing you will destroy any banal romanticism. Marina will conduct herself majestically and thus embarrass the Pretender. Whatever he can say about love she knows already. She just sits and waits. And there should be very few gestures: 'Just tell me when you will be Tsar.' And all he does is swear that he truly loves her. All this is a very bourgeois porcedure to Marina. But when he sings: 'I am the son of a Tsar', he grows in stature and begins to punish her. At this point Marina produces no end of flattering bowings and scrapings, curtseys, as if she felt she must not let him slip through her fingers, he must quickly come to a decision."

It must be said that in neither of these two "Polish" scenes did one feel the conviction of dramatic reality which the Russian scenes so clearly brought out. The Polish spirit did not inform this part of the opera with the force evident in the others. The reason for this may lie not in the theatre, the scene designer, or the producer but in the composer, whose work in these Polish scenes is less profound than in the Russian ones.

8. Outside St. Basil the Blessèd

Perhaps the most expressive and starkly powerful scene of the opera, which reveals the tragic condition of the Russian people during the time of Boris Godunov, their voiceless conflict with the Tsar, is that outside the cathedral of St. Basil the Blessèd. S.I. Ivanov with outstanding ingenuity designed a set which, although it was less than thirteen feet in depth, gave the full illusion of the cathedral on a snowy winter morning in the half-light of daybreak. The outline of the cathedral is visible against a still-dark sky. There are glimmers of light through the barred windows, coming from candles and watch lights. Mass is in progress.

Boris Godunov, Scene 8: The crowd outside the Cathedral of St. Basil the Blessèd.

All around this handsomely decorated, snow-covered, dimly visible cathedral are hordes of beggars who have spent the night there. They are huddled against the walls, clinging close to each other, shivering in their hopeless despair, cold and starving. This filthy wave of humanity beats against the cathedral, from the windows of which blink cheerful and peaceful lights from burning candles. Inside the church it is probably warm and cozy. But the lights shining out only make the beggars feel chillier and more forlorn.

Several guards keep watch over the crowd. Some of them step across figures lying on the ground, lifting their caps apparently in a search for someone. The pervasive feeling is that the eye of the government is always open. Suddenly a young fellow is hauled out by the scruff of his neck but he snatches off his cap, tries to explain something, and then suddenly darts away in the shadowy spaces under the terrace around the cathedral. For a moment the crowd stirs, then again lapses back into immobility. All this goes on to the accompaniment of the tremulous, anxious music of the introduction to the opera. Now the figure of Mityukha, who was in the first scene, cautiously sidles, almost crawls, out of the cathedral. The crowd begins to talk about the anathema pronounced against Grigori. They are obviously all on the side of Grigori as Dmitri (the Pretender). Since Mityukha talks much too freely and too loudly, after the chorus has sung: " . . . Death to Boris and his whelps. . . ." the guards arrest him and take him away. The crowd subsides into huddled silence.

A pale ray of the rising sun falls on the half-witted Yurodivoy, who is standing holding an ikon on the path to the Kremlin. When some children steal a penny from him and he falls sobbing on the path, the boyars and attendants begin to stream out of the church. Mass is over. Finally the Tsar himself appears on the high porch before the cathedral. He has to pick his way through the dark mass of humanity sprawling on the ground, who suddenly come to life when they see him and begin to sing a chorus which is full of remarkable, tragic power: "Oh Father, our Provider, give us food for the love of Christ. . . ." The chorus begins in a whisper and then swells to a *fortissimo*. The growing resonance of the chorus is paced by a pattern of movements among the crowd. The people slowly rise, crawl to the feet of the Tsar, stretch out their pleading arms, and bar his path.

The Tsar is dressed in a sable hat trimmed with gleaming jewels and a gold brocade coat with sumptuous fur trimming. Overwhelmed by this dark and terrifying flood of filthy human beings, he tries to force his way through them but stumbles over the prostrate form of groaning Yurodivoy, the half-wit.

Bewildered, Boris begins to speak in kindly tones to him at first, but then he is at once taken aback by the half-wit's words: "The great ones will be killed just as you killed the little Tsarevich." As a French horn plays a solitary, mournful, long-drawn-out note the whole scene is swallowed up in a mist except for a narrow shaft of reddish light showing the head of the condemned Boris and the naive, shining face of the half-witted Yurodivoy.

The impact of this picture reached extraordinarily powerful dimensions. The dramatic solution and execution of this scene by the singers of the Stanislavski Theatre should be inscribed on the roster of their greatest artistic achievements.

9. The Duma and the Death of Boris

This scene of the Duma or Council to which the boyars have been hurriedly summoned is set in the uncertain light of early morning. The day is just beginning to break. In the Duma chamber the walls are lined with chest-like benches covered with red cloth. On the left is the Tsar's throne. At the entrance, a table where all the members of the council sign in. Overcoats and hats are piled up in corners or on the window-sills. On the walls are shelves with heavy volumes, books of laws and edicts.

The whole chamber, according to Stanislavski, is dingy; it is a workroom, there is nothing impressive about it. Only the throne is decorated with gold carvings. The state of mind of those present is that of worry and depression. This is an agitated morning—that was how Stanislavski described the atmosphere of the beginning of the scene.

"What does one hear in the preliminary music? Agitation, a kind of anxious, brooding mysticism—something sad, dark, is impending. One senses a coming tragedy. Things are not well with the Tsar. The fate of these boyars hangs on the life or death of Tsar Boris."

Now someone arrives, he says a prayer, bows, signs the book, and sits down. He whispers to his neighbour, then is concentrated again. They all sit around looking gloomy. The mood is funereal. They are all preoccupied with their thoughts. Someone asks a question, then forgets what he asked, twirls his beard. He does not even notice that he has tousled it in his nervousness. He looks around, then falls into meditation again.

"The thing to do is to alternate concentrated, deep thought with quick gestures. You sink into thought (a long note) then suddenly snap out of it with a quick movement. Begin with the measure before the gesture, take a dotted eighth note. Work out the technique for this," was Stanislavski's advice when the singer was finding the inner rhythm of agitation for the beginning of the scene.

The meeting opens with the arrival of Shchelkalov, who solemnly carries in the Tsar's edict with regard to the Pretender and reads it from the throne. Disputes are rife, they threaten to turn into violence—the agitation mounts.

"Do not forget the basic mood," Stanislavski reminds us. "Boris has poor support. Even here he stands alone." The boyars keep jumping up from their places (they all have brisk cues); they fly at each other in the council chamber like gamecocks. Shchelkalov has taken his place at his table, as secretary of the Duma; one after another they approach him with various proposals. The disputes end in a prayer to Heaven "to take pity on much-suffering Russia."

"The prayer of the boyars is a special rite," said Stanislavski. "This is a very important day."

They are all glad to see Shuiski arrive although they meet him with irritation.

"The brains of the boyars," said Stanislavski, "has come. Shuiski dominates the scene with his tale about Boris's illness—he does it sincerely but out of extraordinary shrewdness. His account arouses and upsets the boyars still further and they were already quite bewildered. The confusion in the council chamber is increased and into this atmosphere of great agitation Boris, now quite out of his mind and trying to escape from the importunate ghost of the murdered Dmitri, rushes in headlong.

"He is glimpsed first through an inside window in the chamber which opens onto a palace corridor, then he dashes into the council chamber and attempts to hide. He does not know where he is and since all the boyars have prostrated themselves on the ground he does not at first see anyone. The chamber appears to be empty."

Boris keeps making small signs of the cross over himself.

"Don't force your emotions," said Stanislavski to Boris, "but proceed along physical lines. Act as though the place were infested with rats, with demons. If you do this correctly the feelings will come along of their own accord."

Boris is in a dressing gown. When Shuiski gently speaks to him, and when the Tsar sees the heads of the boyars lifting from the ground he for a long time cannot think where he is and who these people are all around him. This is the moment of his awakening from a terrible dream—the moment when the sick man who has been in the grip of some terrible, frightful mania slowly returns to reality, pulls himself together, and is once more the Tsar. This was stunningly demonstrated by Stanislavski at one of the rehearsals.

After a long "Shalyapin style" pause Boris, now in his right mind, quickly adjusts his robe, then slowly walks to the throne, sits down, looks around the chamber at them all, and then, in a friendly tone, addresses the boyars: "I have summoned you. . . ."

It would seem that now the affairs of state would be taken up but the ever-"solicitous" Shuiski reports the arrival of an elderly monk, "a man of truth and counsel"—Pimen.

"Shuiski speaks to the Tsar as he would to a child," suggested Stanislavski. "It is necessary that the Duma and Boris himself receive Pimen as a counsellor and comforter. Pimen is presented almost as if coming from beyond the grave. He is a man of religion for whom there exists no earthly sovereign. He has come to reveal a secret and then depart. He gazes into space, sees no one. His unseeing eyes open and then close. This is the figure of fate. The role must be played with special quality."

Pimen's entrance was impressively prepared. All the boyars fall on their knees. The old man comes in supported by two youthful acolytes. He blesses the Tsar, places the stole on his head, as if preparing him for confession. From under it one sees the suffering face of Boris.

"I cannot breathe!"—Boris's last attack was treated by Stanislavski in an extraordinary and original way.

"Do not tear at the collar of your shirt to show you are suffocating. That is what all the other singers in this part do and that is just a stale cliché. Lean forward and fall as an ox does when he is butchered. The boyars catch you up in their arms."

Two benches from the foreground are quickly pushed forward by the boyars and covered with their fur coats, thus improvising a couch. Onto it they lay the Tsar—it is right in the centre of the stage—like a corpse with his feet toward the auditorium. They all leave and he is alone except for his two weeping children, who have come running into the chamber. Boris embraces them both, gives his last instructions to his son, and addresses a final prayer to heaven.

"The children are afaid of the dying man," said Stanislavski. "Xenia kisses him without looking at him and then hides behind Fyodor. Frightened, they slowly draw away from their father. Monks enter with a religious habit. A Kremlin bell tolls the death knell. Their father no longer belongs to them but is given over to the rites for the dead.

"Prepare a brilliant funeral," said Stanislavski. Monks enter with acolytes and candles. Some boyars carry the Tsar's robes, and emblems of authority, the sceptre and the orb, others carry religious vestments and the "Shima", the large black cloth which the monks lay on the dying man. For a second Boris regains consciousness, disturbs the rites by tearing off the black covering, protests violently, and struggles against death. But the spark of life does not last long and this outburst only hastens his inevitable end. The solemn ritual is resumed. The Patriarch now stands at the head of the couch, blessing the Tsar. Shuiski stands beside the bier holding the sceptre and orb on a tray. A ring of black-habited monks closes in nearer and nearer to the dead man. His bewildered, orphaned children stand apart. At the four corners and along the sides of the bier, as if it were a coffin, the monks place huge lighted candles as the last chords of music from the orchestra die away.

It was at the height of our work on *Boris Godunov*, when the production was ready to be transferred to the stage of the Studio Theatre, that Stanislavski, during the celebrations of the 30th Jubilee of the founding of the Moscow Art Theatre, played his last part. This was that of Vershinin in *The Three Sisters*, and at the end he was stricken with a severe heart attack. He never acted on the stage again and for a long time was unable to go on with his work as a teacher and director.

At this crucial moment, his old associate in the Art Theatre, Ivan Moskvin, came forward. The production of *Boris Godunov* was all rehearsed and ready, but the eye of an experienced director, when a transfer takes place to a larger stage, always sees things to be done.

Even the best models of stage settings require final and sometimes substantial adjustments both in construction and colours.

Moskvin had a deep knowledge of Russian history, his sense of what was true on the stage was absolutely sure, and moreover, he had a fine feeling for music—a characteristic of the Moscow Art Theatre of that time. His experienced eye could not be deceived by any falseness in emotions portrayed, so that Stanislavski had every reason to be confident that Moskvin would fulfill all of his hopes.

The natural trepidation felt by the whole company before the dress rehearsal of *Boris Godunov* was allayed by a letter sent by Stanislavski to the cast:

"My dear Students—*all* of you. I am writing this note on the sly without my doctor's knowledge, so do not give me away.

"I want you to know that it just seems to you that I am not right there—for invisibly, in my heart, I am present and in my thoughts I am going through everything with you. I can imagine just what is going on.

"You have been straightforward and conscientious in your attitude towards your work: You have not spared yourselves and now you have extricated yourselves from the difficult situation into which you were thrown by my illness.

"That is a great accomplishment. It proves that the Studio is full of life, energy, perseverance, and independence.

"You are splendid. This is a cause for great rejoicing to us all, particularly to me.

"What remains does not depend on us but on chance. But this much I do know: Work that is done wholeheartedly, with love, is never done in vain. Go out onto the stage boldly, knowing that the success of a production is not made by first performances but by many repetitions and by time. Today is only a dress rehearsal before an audience. And there may be ten or fifteen such previews ahead of you. It is only after that that your performance will be stabilized and will be established in the opinion of the public for years to come.

"When the curtain goes up or when each one of you makes his or her entrance, remember that this is not the all-decisive moment, it is merely your first appearance before a public which has already come to love you. . . ."

7

The Queen of Spades

THE REHEARSALS OF *The Queen of Spades* had already been started earlier in the same year of 1928, which had been one of boiling directorial activity for Stanislavski.

The preparation of this opera overlapped the intense work of finishing the *Boris Godunov* production. When a rehearsal for that would be finished and all the singer-actors who were performing that evening had left, Stanislavski would not return to his own study at once. He often settled himself in his big leather armchair, rattled the keys on his chain, and sat thinking about what should be done next. A conversation would spring up, perhaps about the current or future repertory for his Opera Theatre. Along with that he would reminisce about all sorts of incidents in his life in the theatre, in Russia and abroad. In the course of such talks he would share with us his ideas about *The Queen of Spades*.

"I see Herman not as a brilliant officer," said he, tapping on a nearby table. "He is a military engineer, perhaps, not good-looking, wears glasses, but has burning eyes, is gloomy, shy, irascible. He wanders through the park, avoids the company of such dashing gay blades as Tomski, Narumov. He sits on park benches among the nannies and their charges, who look with diffidence at this strange officer. This is a character part; he is no hero, or lover, as he is usually portrayed.

"As for the old Countess: late at night she sits up in her huge Louis Quatorze bed and looks like a wrinkled, little old woman, a little like a monkey. After they take off her wig she is quite bald. But when she dresses to go out in society she straightens herself up to become really tall and erect, and she walks cautiously for fear of falling to pieces. When I was in Nice I saw an old English lady on the Quai des Anglais. She was a hundred years old. She took a daily walk in a black suit regardless of the heat. She was as straight as a stick, and well-corseted to keep her erect. She never looked at anyone. At home, by herself, I rather imagine she took her uncorseted ease and relapsed into being a nonentity.

"I visualize too a simple girl, a dependent, brought up in the household. She lives in the entresol in very modest surroundings. She sleeps in a small bed behind a large screen. Her friends are shy schoolmates. Their games are the same as those of the girls who play in the courtyard. Lisa lives above the Countess's bedroom. When awakened by their noise the irascible old lady has to climb the winding stair up to Lisa's room. That is why she is always so cross when she appears."

The last scene in the gambling den, in contrast to the previous realistic details, became, in Stanislavski's vision, quite fantastic. Heaps of gold, conjured up by Herman's imagination, suddenly appear on all the gaming tables, and in the mirror there is a dim reflection of the Countess in a shroud. As he described these scenes to the cast Stanislavski roused their interest and created an atmosphere of fascinated anticipation, of impatience to begin to create. He tried (indeed it was natural to him) to excite everyone with each new piece of work, to make them all fall in love with it. He felt that this attitude of falling in love with a new production was a necessary element in creative work. "If you are not carried away by a new production in the theatre it will not amount to anything," he used to say.

That is why Stanislavski never decided about putting a new production into the repertory without taking into consideration the feelings of his actor-singers as to their attraction to it, sympathy for the idea, or even their warnings against it.

Whenever he assigned a role to a singer he first asked whether it had any attraction for him or her. He somehow imperceptibly succeeded in brushing away doubts, arousing convictions, imparting warmth, even fire. He would never tolerate indifference to a new role or to a whole new production: He felt that was the most harmful thing that could be.

We all had to be excited by the work in hand, and we all were supposed to care about a new production whether or not we were taking part in it.

So it was that gradually, unnoticed, the consciousness developed that we must stage *The Queen of Spades*, and by the time that *Boris Godunov* opened the preparatory work on this next opera was already in full swing. The painter A.Y. Golovin had agreed to design the sets. Conversations with a prospective designer, discussions about the general outline of the production, were usually begun before the actor-singers had begun to study their parts. Stanislavski felt that it was necessary that the participants, when they began to study the opera, should have a clear conception of the whole play, the character of the roles they were to play and the setting in which they would be called upon to perform.

His serious illness then removed him from all work in the theatre for two years.

It was necessary to stage *The Queen of Spades* without his help and guidance. This was, naturally, reflected in the fate of the opera. He had, to be sure, worked out in detail the plan for the first four scenes, he had conducted preliminary discussions and laid out in general terms the development of the whole production. It is, however, a long road and a complex one leading from plans and dreams for a new production to its concrete embodiment on the stage.

The extremely difficult production of *The Queen of Spades*, put on as it was without our supreme artistic adviser, turned out to be further hampered by the fashion of the moment, which decried the work of Chaikovski. In those days the opera that reigned on the boards of the Leningrad and Moscow opera theatres was *Johnny* and the proponents of its composer, Kshenek, lauded him to the skies and turned thumbs down on Chaikovski. Thus 1929 and 1930 turned out to be highly unfavourable years for the production of *The Queen of Spades*.

Another difficulty appeared when our scene designer, Golovin, was taken ill. His sickness chained him to his bed and we were deprived of the participation of a great artist in our work. The scenery was in the end executed by his assistant, M.P. Zadkin. The restricted size of the stage posed serious problems for both the scene designers and those now in charge of the production (Vladimir Alexeyev—Stanislavski's brother—B.I. Vershilov, and P.D. Rumyantsev).

Some scenes, like the "Barracks", the "Canal", the "Gambling Den" were successful but others—"The Park", "The Ball"—were not. The written instructions of Stanislavski often failed to solve certain practical problems and yet the theatre was unwilling to abandon his original plan of production; indeed it lacked the boldness to alter it.

To show the character of some of the complexities involved in this production here is a semicomic episode: In the third scene, "The Ball", all the ladies were in extremely voluminous crinolines, some five and one half to six feet in diameter. These impeded their movements, especially since there were stairs onstage leading from the palace into the park. One of the directors, in order to convince Stanislavski of the necessity of altering the staging plan for this act, wrote to him at Nice (where he was convalescing) and sent a map of the stage which was thickly covered with contiguous circles—all the crinolines with no space left between them. The author of the letter concluded that the stage must be rebuilt or else all the cast could not be crowded onto it.

To this Stanislavski replied: "Why do you write as if they could not all get onto the stage when your drawing shows that they did do so, and very well?"

Of course, had he been in the auditorium himself he would have noticed how inconvenient the preliminary plan was and would have made many changes, which is what he often did in other productions. But in these circumstances there were certain difficulties connected with the external aspect of the production which never were resolved. As for the inner line of the performance, the characterizations, the inter-relationships of the actor-singers—all this remained true to Stanislavski's basic concept and there was much that was both interesting and significant. This made it possible to keep *The Queen of Spades* in the repertory for ten years.

The first four scenes were worked out in detail by Stanislavski himself—all subtle lines of action and movement for the characters were there. Copies of his production plan were given to all his assistant directors who executed them. The last three scenes were prepared independently by his assistants but in the spirit of his vision of the whole opera.

If one takes a critical view of the results of the whole work done on the production, one is bound to note that the mass scenes in this opera—the chorus strolling in the summer garden, the chorus taking shelter from a thunderstorm, and finally the chorus of singers and guests at the Ball—were merely decorative in effect. They are needed only as a background against which events in the lives of Herman, Lisa, the Countess are developed. In these chorus scenes the "people" do not contribute to the development of events as they do, for example, in *Boris Godunov*, and it takes a very fine artist's hand to keep these crowd scenes from becoming static.

The small chorus scene of Lisa's friends, the dependents in the household of the Countess, came off with greater success than the central choral events, because it was easier to tie them in with the characters in the play.

As always Stanislavski's concept was signalized by originality and a deep penetration into the meaning of the events displayed. That intangible line between what is real and what is fantasy, between the logic of everyday life and the play of Herman's sick soul, which so clearly comes out in Pushkin's *Queen of Spades*, was reflected in Stanislavski's production plan. He did not resort to any directorial "stunts" in order to make the story mysterious and awesome, nor did he seek to create an atmosphere of madness around Herman. All life on the stage was directed so that the coherence and logic of events and actions were evident. At the same time, where clear reason could explain happenings with simple causes, Herman's diseased imagination, hypnotized by the mysterious past of the Countess and also by his dangerously inflamed ambition, saw all in a special light.

This circumstance very quickly led him away from his partly illusive love for Lisa, whose very name he confessed he did not know and did not wish to know, caused him to forget her completely, and pushed him to join his fate with that of the Countess. The character of the hero in this play is extremely complex; this is partly explained by his position as an insignificant young officer in aristocratic surroundings. But Herman is not simply an ambitious, impoverished young man set on breaking into high society. He is a hero of the early 19th century, in some respects reminiscent of Julien Sorel in Stendhal's *The Red and The Black*, set in the conditions of life in the days of Catherine the Great—this was a sop to the tsarist censor—and this somewhat beclouds the features of this character.

The author of the libretto, the composer's brother Modest Chaikovski, explains the alteration of the period in which the opera is set: "About the middle of December [1889] a consultation was held in the office of the Director of the Imperial Theatres ... where I read my scenario. It was here that the decision was made to change the opera from the times of Alexander I to the end of the reign of Catherine II as I had done for Klenovski. In keeping with this decision the third scene (the Ball) was radically altered and a scene along the Canal, which I did not have at all in my scenario, was injected. The rest remained as it was, with the exception of the above-mentioned two scenes. In addition, however, I.A. Vsevolozhski made many suggestions for detailed changes in the rest of the scenario."

This explains why there are certain deficiencies in the libretto. Although Peter Chaikovski overcame them by the power of his emotions and the sincerity of his feelings, these deficiencies nonetheless did show up when the libretto was subjected to painstaking study in the period of preparing the opera.

The traits of pertinacity, willful stubbornness in the character of Herman, attributed to him by Pushkin, were rather watered down in the libretto. Those traits retreat in the face of the agonized, lovelorn music in the first half of the opera, and this often impels singers in the role of Herman to convert themselves into the image of a sweetly-pitiful tenor-as-lover.

But Stanislavski pointed out the bond between the musical theme of Herman's first aria: "I do not know her name..." and the theme of "the three cards" and tried to convince his singers to seek out in the music qualities of pertinacity and energy and embody them in Herman to make a manly character of him.

Stanislavski did not pursue the idea of showing Herman as a madman, he only tried to create an atmosphere of tension around him thanks to which a man in the grip of a morbid idea would inevitably fall into the abyss of madness. The directorial plan for the first scene shows the Summer Garden and the disposition of the main characters in it.

Stanislavski worked out in detail the strolling of people in the Summer Garden, and thus created a natural, living background for the unrolling of the tragedy.

In his written plan there were directions for a variety of alternate stagings for this episode with the chorus. Here are the nurses with their children at play, the wetnurses with their charges in their arms.

"The nurses sing nonsense songs to the children," Stanislavski noted. "The children are hot, the nurses wipe off the perspiration and take the children's shirts off to replace them with dry vests so they won't catch cold. One of the children gets cooled off, snatches away the vest, and runs away to play. The children are given candy brought to the park in little paper cornucopias."

Then comes the chorus of the governesses: "Over in an open space they have organized a game for the children. Now they have come to take a rest. Perhaps some will stroll over to a baby carriage, or watch the children, or play with them. Their words make one feel that they are bored by the children. They gossip together, munch candy, read newspapers."

Next is the chorus of the wetnurses. "They walk around rocking their infants in their arms, or in their carriages, they change their diapers, give them pacifiers, nurse them, or give them a bottle."

In Stanislavski's staging of this scene not a vestige remains of the usual high-society promenade seen in ordinary productions of *The Queen of Spades*.

"Here come our soldiers!" and a group of boys in military uniforms marches out from the wings to face the children running (in a game) in the opposite direction.

The nurses, abandoning their charges, run to the balustrade to see the boy-soldiers march by. The governesses too stand up and watch, some of them putting up their lorgnons to get a better look.

The young soldiers drill in an opening behind a trellis. They march around to the blowing of trumpets. If there are many of them they can pass upstage along the middle path; but if there are only a few of them they can keep marching around the trellis with the same children circling it several times.

The nurses and governesses collect their belongings, wraps, baskets, toys, umbrellas, etc. and hurry after the departing children. They push the prams across the opening, some walking quickly, others more slowly.

Onstage there remain: on the right, one of the people out strolling, who is now reading a paper, and an old man, on the left, who moves over to a bench in the centre and goes to sleep.

All these suggestions were set down by Stanislavski in relation to the layout onstage.

"Herman at first mixes with the crowd of strollers, then he sits down on one of the benches.

"During the preceding scene, in keeping with the music, Herman, while waiting for Lisa and because he is so nervous (this is very obvious), jumps up again and walks to the archway leading out of the park, and looks off into the distance," wrote Stanislavski.

"At the beginning of the act, in the restaurant, almost all the tables are filled with members of the chorus (they can help out with the singing of the nurses as well as with that of the strollers in the park).

"Towards the end, when the boy-soldiers leave, Table A (on the plan) is freed and immediately a waiter prepares it to be occupied by Surin and Chekalinski.

"By this time Herman is seated on a round bench in the centre with his back to Chekalinski and Surin.

"Chekalinski and Surin play their scene together with perfect diction. They sit at the table and drink wine."

After this the production plan shows a drawing with Tomski's entrance.

"It would be ideal if the scenes between Herman and Tomski could be played in one place without moving around, except that Herman's fire and nervousness must not be diminished. To accomplish this everything must be transferred to the inner pattern of his part, expressing it through diction and coloration. When, because of the singing, it is necessary for him to stand up, it can be done. That is to say his nervousness and passion may bring him to his feet, then let him put his right knee on the bench and while in that pose continue his harangue of Tomski.

"If this cannot be done smoothly, then towards the end of his aria 'I do not know her name' Herman can move over to the right side of the stage (as seen from the auditorium), and Tomski would follow to go on with the conversation.

"You must find the right place in the music to introduce, without disturbing the scene, a few strollers into the vicinity so that the appearance of the chorus will not be too precipitate, will not appear as it were on order.

"Around the restaurant buffet, without disrupting the action, there can be some movement to and fro. Also beyond the balustrade people can be brought in. Besides at the back of the stage, where there is a cross path, people are constantly moving in either direction.

"Incidentally it would be simple, and have more basis, to bring forward from upstage small groups and arrange them on the right and left. There would be greetings exchanged, chatting, movements off in other directions. . . ."

Stanislavski again objected to the customary tendency in opera theatres to place the members of the chorus according to their voices, obliging the sopranos, altos, tenors, and bassos to stick with their own kind.

"Here husbands and wives will be seated at first," wrote Stanislavski. "They will sing while moving about intermittently. This will not be like a group of old women or old men singing together.

"The young gentlemen and young ladies will come over to them, also there will be children and grandchildren, and they must be mixed so that they will not wander around in herds.

"Some of the young people as they go by will stop and sit down with the older men and women. The older women will smooth the hair of the young girls, straighten their dresses, give them various instructions.

"It would help in setting up these little gatherings, and would put life in the pattern of the chorus, if some quite new words were written (if only for the chorus). . . .

"Against the background of the gay strolling crowds Herman is a dark spot.

"We must try, during the scene between Herman and Tomski, unobtrusively to move, in twos, threes, or more, the people away from this part of the stage, especially the left side (as seen from the auditorium) and clear the bench for the impending scene with Eletski. . . ."

After his duet Herman goes to greet Eletski and then Surin and Chekalinski.

Enter the Countess and Lisa. At a little distance behind them a footman carries their capes.

Herman jumps up in order to find out who is the fiancée of Eletski. There is an unexpected confrontation which frightens the Countess. She all but faints away. Lisa and the footman help her to sit down on the bench to the left.

The Countess lays her head on Lisa's shoulder. Eletski rushes off to get a glass of water. Then he stands near her, finally sitting down beside her still holding the glass.

Tomski, who has been watching the scene, has remained in the middle of the archway. Surin and Chekalinski also look on from where they are seated at their table.

This is how the quintet goes:

All the action is disclosed by diction, facial expression, eyes, and small gestures. The leader in verbal expression here, I think, is the Countess or Herman. Tomski moves over to greet the Countess. She puts some questions to him. (Meantime Eletski and Lisa have gone through the archway.)

Tomski gives his arm to the Countess and leads her back through the archway. Back there the old lady is given something more to drink. The footman has followed her.

"Herman never lets the Countess out of his sight and she keeps her eyes on him. Meantime Eletski accompanies Lisa. They walk by. Eletski's aria.

"Behind them walks the Countess supported by her footman. The moment when she passes Herman should be remembered later in the scene in the barracks. She looks closely at Herman.

"When the Countess passes Herman there should be a distant roll of thunder.

"Find the right place in the music when extras can hurry by trying to get away from the thunderstorm.

"Tomski's scene and his ballad upstage. [This ballad, "Once upon a time in Versailles", contains the dramatic kernel of the whole opera. It is the story of the Countess and her fabulously successful career as a gambler which is due to her possessing the secret of the "three infallible cards". Later, when Herman attempts to wrest this secret from her, the Countess dies. But she reappears as a ghost and divulges the secret to him: "The three, the seven, the ace!" In the last scene in the gambling room Herman wins prodigiously on the first two cards, but when he stakes everything on his last card, the ace, it mysteriously turns into the fateful Queen of Spades and all is lost.] Diction. Intonation. They drink and chat.

"Herman is now the focal point. At first he scarcely listens to Tomski, then his interest is deeply aroused. . . ."

In his notes directing *The Queen of Spades* Stanislavski touches mostly on questions of staging and does not go into the development of the inner pattern of each character. This production plan was laid out for assistant directors and actors who were already sufficiently versed in the essential meaning of the events. But the visual side of the production was thought out by him down to the smallest details.

After Tomski's song "Once upon a time in Versailles" Stanislavski made a note of the following lighting effects: sunset, impending thunderstorm, lights on the restaurant tables and also here and there in the park. In the background there were also dim lights from city buildings.

Then he continued with the staging:

"Herman as he listens moves closer. Standing behind a trellis he listens to the end of the song; then, as Tomski, Chekalinski, and Surin get up from their table he quickly crosses to the bench in centre stage.

"As Chekalinski and Surin go by they chat.

"Tomski puts on his overcoat near the buffet of the restaurant and walks off with the crowd. As he passes Herman he bids him good evening. But Herman is in a state of collapse, scarcely aware of what is going on around him. He is immersed in his thoughts and feels the shock of learning that Lisa is betrothed to Eletski, and also of meeting the old Countess.

"Now is a mob scene—and the thunderstorm. People stream from all sides towards the summerhouse. The ladies pin up their skirts, wipe their feet, wrap their bonnets in kerchieves, shake their umbrellas, hop over puddles. Or they prepare to move on and open their umbrellas to

The Queen of Spades, G. A. Yegorov as Herman.

cover themselves. The gentlemen wrap their high hats in handkerchieves and prepare to make a headlong exit, to the right, the left, or
upstage. Some nurses with prams are hurrying away belatedly.

"Against this milling crowd Herman remains a fixed point.

"Now at last he begins to look about and realize *where* he is and
what is going on around him. . . .

"I cannot define this any closer without the music.

"In the end he goes upstage, beyond the archway, seemingly calling
upon heaven and earth to hear his vow."

The scene designer, Zandin, used this outline as the basis for his set
for the Summer Garden. The park was not as extensively planted and
full of vegetation then as it is nowadays and as it is usually shown
onstage. It was laid out in a formal pattern in the style of the French
parks in the 18th century, carefully clipped, trimmed, and full of
geometric straight lines.

A semicircular summerhouse made of green latticework framed the
forestage; in the centre of it was a large decorative vase on a pedestal,
and around that ran a circular bench; this and the semicircular benches
on either side of the stage were planned for the use of the principal
characters.

The restaurant, a group of small tables out-of-doors where socially
prominent young people gathered and where Tomski was to sing his
"ballade", did not have quite the informal air that Stanislavski had
hoped for. Besides the singers were too far away from the centre of the
stage and that was not an advantageous position from which to sing.

The thunderstorm scene did not work out too successfully—this was
when the whole chorus was crowded into the summerhouse in the very
centre of the stage. The situation seemed rather forced inasmuch as the
summerhouse with its open latticework afforded poor protection from
the rain, and therefore there was no valid justification for keeping the
chorus there.

The first chorus, of people strolling in the park, was more successful.
In order to avoid static situations we introduced a number of panto-
mimed episodes among the young dandies courting the young women
and the central point in the chorus was the arrival of a high official—a
person on the order perhaps of Potemkin—who is greeted by the crowd,
who then follow after him when he leaves. This gave a touch of liveliness to the chorus who sing about the beautiful weather.

The famous quintet "I'm frightened", which is sung during the first
meeting of Herman and the Countess, was not well-based. Incidentally
the whole procedure here is so artificial in itself, is so far removed from
any reality, that it is on the whole extremely difficult to give it dramatic
validity.

The finale of the act—with flashes of lightning—coincides perfectly with the pattern of the music in the orchestra, with Herman left motionless in the centre of the stage. It was beautiful and impressive. Indeed the whole design of Herman's role in this act was artistically emphasized both by his inner expressiveness and his outward appearance (he stood out from the colourful crowd in his black uniform and great grey cape). He showed the character of an austerely reserved, determined, and passionate man and there was no place in it for exercising a tenor's charm or indulging in trite sentimentalities.

The main defect in this act was the unsuccessful execution of the scene design, which blindly followed Stanislavski's sketch, whereas it should have been reworked on the stage into something more appropriate to the time and place of action. This would not only have been more pleasing to the eye but also easier to act in for the singers.

Later in 1934, Stanislavski decided to restage *The Queen of Spades* and invited Pamfilov, a young painter, to design the sets. As a result of his work with the artist new models for the stage settings were approved.

The next scene, as Stanislavski conceived it, was to take place in the modest room in the entresol of a handsome city residence where Lisa, the ward of the despotic old Countess, lived.

He stripped Lisa and her companions of their luxurious white wigs, dressed them in simple gowns and in this way indicated that they did not belong to high society.

Lisa treats her maid Masha in a very simple, straightforward way, and talks with her frankly as she would with a close friend.

This is how Stanislavski outlined his ideas for the scene:

"Pauline and one other girl are onstage. They sing. The others are scattered around the room at random. Some are in the centre of the stage, others at a table where there are some sweets, someone is near the spinet, some are near the banisters of the staircase.

"Lisa looks pensive. She stands at the back of Pauline's chair—she had moved there after the first verse of Pauline's song—then takes her hands or sits on the edge of her chair. After the third verse Lisa goes off, looking both sad and pensive, to the alcove. . . . These moves are all to be made in the rhythm of the music. They will be noticed and will show up clearly Lisa's mood (in contrast to the vivacity of the other girls).

"Masha is near the stairs. During the scene she is almost constantly occupied (in rhythm with the music) in putting chairs back in their places or tidying up the table with the sweets on it, or straightening the rug.

"The girls gather round Pauline as she sings. When she stops they surround her, kiss her, and beg her to sing some more.

"But Lisa does not add her voice to theirs, she stands pensively in the archway of the alcove, leaning against one of the curtains.

"While Pauline is singing her ballad Lisa looks even more woebegone—almost with tears in her eyes she goes to her dressing table and unobtrusively wipes away a tear. Then she sits sadly down by the dressing table. When she stops singing Pauline runs over to her, covers her with kisses, and caresses her as they whisper together.

"One of their friends joins them. Meantime others have left their places. They form groups near the staircase railing. Two girls are at the spinet, another group of two or three are in the centre of the stage, and

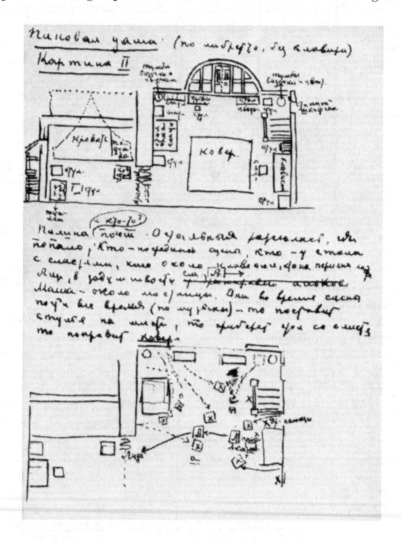

The Queen of Spades, plan for Scene 2 (Lisa's bedroom) as drawn by Stanislavski.

others are near the table with the sweets. They mill around, drink, crack nuts, eat sweetmeats. Two pairs walking up and down with their arms around each other exchange confidences. Someone goes out onto the balcony and walks up and down there.

"After the cue: 'What are you pulling such long faces about?' they begin to move all the chairs and clear the centre of the stage, setting the chairs along the walls. Masha busily helps them.

"Chorus with dance: They form a ring for a country dance. There are two girls inside the ring: one is the man and the other plays the peasant woman.

"To make this have a little piquancy the girls should all be very prim (but gay). This is an 18th-century country dance (it does not seem in the least peasant-like). The girl who plays the man twirls her imaginary moustache (which peasants would never do).

"It ends with general dancing and winds up in all kinds of foolishness; one of the girls lifts a corner of her skirt and tries to dance a trepak (sitting down and kicking out her legs). Another one behind is held up by two friends while she throws her legs around. One tries unsuccessfully to perform a trepak and sits down hard on the rug and roars with laughter. A third holds herself up between two chairs, as she tries to squat and kick her legs forward at the same time.

"In the midst of these outrageous doings in comes the governess.

"They all instantly scatter, some onto the balcony, others dash into the alcove, where several hide themselves in the folds of the curtains. Still others gather around Lisa and hurriedly straighten their dresses so that the governess will not notice how dishevelled they had become. Someone hides behind the spinet on a stool. (While the dancing was going on Lisa has been sitting still, in contrast to all the others, and whispering with a friend who has drawn up a chair to the dressing table to be near her.)

"The governess has come up from below on the inside staircase. Only her head is visible at first.

"She goes out onto the balcony and scolds the girls there. Then she goes over to the spinet. Meantime those who were on the balcony steal away playfully down the stairs (in accordance with the music and rhythm).

"The governess approaches the girl behind the spinet and gives her a scolding. She drops a beautiful curtsey and then when the governess turns elsewhere, also dashes merrily downstairs. The governess goes over to the alcove, pulls the curtains apart, and gives a piece of her mind to the girls hidden there. They drop elegant curtseys to her, say good-bye to Lisa, and primly march downstairs. But after a few steps they break into headlong flight.

"Having had her say, the governess now takes up her scrutiny of how Masha is removing the plates with the sweetments from the table; straightens a chair or two which are in disorder, and leaves. (Masha goes on straightening the room without interfering with the characters left onstage.)

"Lisa and Pauline are in the alcove. Lisa is sitting at her dressing table, removing a brooch and rings, preparing to undress.

"Lisa opens her window and speaks of the storm and the renewal of nature.

"After this (as Pauline speaks of her being bestowed on Eletski) they both move towards the staircase. They kiss each other. Lisa wants to accompany her downstairs but Pauline leaves her alone and goes away.

"Lisa returns to the alcove, unbuttons or unties her blouse; Masha follows and helps her take off her blouse and skirt (or at least unfasten them). If it can be fitted in, then let Masha carry away the blouse and skirt with her as she leaves.

"Lisa sits down at her dressing table and begins to brush her hair, weeping as she does it—and sings her aria. She frequently picks up her handkerchief and wipes her eyes. She walks to the window, still brushing her hair, and looks out.

"At the window Herman appears (the window is semicircular and reaches almost to the floor). Lisa snatches up a shawl from her bed. She does not have time to hide herself but pulls the curtains around her.

"At Herman's words: 'I beg of you—remain' Lisa wants to run out and get away, but Herman stops her.

"As Herman says: 'Oh, do not go away' Lisa (in rhythm with the music) tries to escape, wrapped in her shawl, and gets to the staircase. She goes down a few steps. You see only her head. Herman rushes after her, to bring her back.

"As Lisa says: 'Why, oh why are you here? Do go away' she waves Herman back as he tries to come near her.

"As he says: 'Cry out! Call everyone', Herman makes a definite advance towards her.

"Lisa runs away, pulling the curtain, and standing there holds the end of it so Herman, who is on the other side of the curtain, cannot penetrate farther into the alcove. He sings his aria 'Forgive me, O celestial being' on his knees in front of the curtain.

"Lisa looks out at him from time to time, from behind the curtain. She is irresolute, struggles with her own emotions. During his aria she moves over to her dressing table, weeping bitterly.

"Herman cautiously pushes the curtain aside, goes over to Lisa, and kneels before her.

"He may even kiss her hand.

"There is a knock, they are alarmed.

"Lisa dashes to the staircase.

"As Lisa says 'Flee', Herman wants to jump out of the window.

"Instead of: 'Too late', I would sing: 'What are you doing?' And as she sings Lisa dashes back to prevent the crazed man from jumping to certain death.

"As she sings: 'Come here' Lisa hides Herman in the folds of the curtain and goes over to open the door to the Countess.

"When she runs over to open the door, she stands so that the Countess is kept in the larger room. Various old women of her entourage are with the Countess. As she moves forward they precede her and light the way.

"In the end they are all in the positions indicated on the ground plan.

"Incidentally, it would be much better if the Countess were accompanied by only one attendant, an old crone like herself. The Countess examines all parts of the room. If there is time she may even look out onto the balcony. Then she enters the alcove. Lisa hastily places herself so that she protects Herman and the Countess will not touch the curtains or find a person hidden in the folds.

"The Countess leaves. Two of her attendants hurry on ahead, the rest follow after her. At the railing of the staircase, the Countess stops, makes the sign of the cross over Lisa, allows her to kiss her withered hand and herself kisses Lisa on the forehead. Meantime Herman sticks his head out from the folds of the curtain (on the alcove side) and sings his cue from there.

"I forgot to mention the Countess's first lines on entering: 'What, you are not asleep yet? Why are you still dressed?' They could be changed to: 'Why aren't you asleep; and why are you not undressed?'

"As Herman says: 'O, have pity on me' he moves quickly towards Lisa, who has locked the door but in coming back has prudently remained on the stairs (from which one can see only her head and shoulders).

"When Herman says: 'Then, you condemn me to death', Lisa moves toward him to restrain him. She is almost ill with anguish. Then Herman says: 'Pronounce my sentence and then I'll die' and rushes towards the window.

"As Lisa says: 'Heavens above!' she rushes after him, stopping in the archway almost ready to collapse.

"Herman: 'Farewe-ll!' and tries to get out of the window.

"Lisa replies: 'No, you shall live', and in a state of exhaustion sinks onto her bed.

"Herman moves over to her.

"When she says: 'I am thine' Herman sits down upon the bed beside her and they embrace."

In the setting forth of the director's plan there is not only the pattern of action but also a definition of the logic of behaviour for the main characters.

In the very first phrase of his notes is the expression: "Pauline and one other girl sing". This refers to the duet "It is already evening", and it shows that Stanislavski following the logic of events presumed that Lisa should not *sing* anything in the beginning of the scene. According to the libretto, Lisa is supposed to sing to Pauline, after her duet with the other girl, asking her to sing again alone, but Stanislavski gave Lisa's words to another member of the chorus.

In this way Stanislavski wished to point up Lisa's mood, her disturbed state after her meeting with Herman that morning and her becoming engaged to Eletski. Stanislavski was very particular about establishing the logic of behaviour for the main characters and when necessary, he even altered the text of the libretto, because he was fully aware of the fact that Chaikovski's brother Modest who wrote it was not an outstanding poet.

It was necessary for us to give a turn of 180 degrees to Stanislavski's plan for this scene. That is to say, we put the alcove on the right of the stage and the entrance from below with the staircase on the left. This was made necessary by the fact that it was impossible to make an opening through the floor at the point indicated by Stanislavski. One might suppose that such a circumstance would not be of significant importance and yet there was some kind of impalpable loss in the composition of this scene as a result of the switch.

In other details the whole scene was done exactly according to Stanislavski's plan—all his staging was convincing, lively, and gave evidence of the inner tensions in the action. It was easy to act in his mise-en-scène. The curtain which divided the stage into two parts made an excellent arrangement for the duet of Lisa and Herman. It was only at the very end of the scene that an alteration was made. "At the words 'I am thine' Herman sits down on the bed beside her and they embrace"; it was felt that this was not in accordance with the mounting storm of passion in the music which is expressed in the last lines of the singers. They slowly move towards each other, to this music, across the whole stage as if drawn against their wills by the force of the feelings that engulf them.

The next scene is a Court Ball and Stanislavski's concept of the set for it was that it should be designed with the magnificence and gorgeousness of the 18th century and be original in structure. The action was to develop on a grand staircase leading down from an upper terrace, and around a pool at its foot surrounded by green arbors. In the foreground is a lawn with chairs set about for guests where they could sit and watch the "pastorale" (masque) enacted on the grand staircase. The building in the rear was to be illuminated to show the shadows of people dancing; flags, a dark sky, fireworks—all this was to present a picture in the style of the "fêtes" held at Versailles in the 18th century.

That was how Stanislavski envisioned the set but his ideas were not entirely carried out. The stage itself was too small, there was no master scene designer of the calibre of Golovin on whom one could count to create such a complicated set—so the scenery was definitely scamped and, to be quite frank, the effect did not come off.

Stanislavski also made notes for directing this act:

"I do not believe that we have enough voices in the chorus. If we had I would place them on the upper terrace.

"While this chorus is singing various groups of people in costumes would be dancing (a quadrille). Several sets of dancers will have gone down into the park and sat down, after exchanging greetings with friends in masks and trying to puzzle out who they were. Here, at random, is a list of the various sets of quadrille dancers:

"1. A group of Chinese men and women with large parasols.

"2. A group of (Siberian) Samoyeds. Somewhere I have seen some amusingly naive costumes of Samoyeds of that period.

"3. Greeks, with spears and shields, among them Poseidon's son Chryssor. Greek women with flowers.

"4. Shepherds and shepherdesses (Pauline or others) with a flock of sheep—children in costumes.

"5. Herman enters alone in black (in domino and mask). In order to mark his entrance, which is important, let him arrive when there is no one else on the staircase. Have him come as early as possible because the conveying of the message must take place in the beginning, shortly after his entrance.

"6. A group of Cupids—Hymen and his suite (who will later be part of the finale in the pastorale masque).

"As they descend they mix with the others, meet others, play the parts indicated by their costumes, but at first one should see them all standing as groups, as if they were in a painting. . . .

"Meantime there must be time to put through a certain action which the public will notice: Herman appears, there is a figure (Lisa) sitting in the front row of chairs at the bottom of the staircase, next to another woman quite bedizened, extravagantly costumed, showing a scrawny neck in a very low-cut dress (the Countess). Lisa is uneasy, turns away to the right (of the audience) thinking that Herman will come down there. But he comes down to the left. Therefore Lisa turns abruptly left.

"Herman sits down on chair No. 11 and a masked person sits on No.12. No matter who that is. In any case Lisa moves through between the first and second rows of chairs and brushes Herman with her left shoulder in a way to be noticed by the audience.

"As she passes him she, for an instant, raises her mask but does it so that the person sitting in No. 12 does not see her face. . . Herman starts. Lisa sits down on No.13 and, unnoticed, holds out a note behind the back of the person in No.12 to Herman. Perhaps he does not at first notice her gesture. Let her make several tries. This must be done so that the audience will be sure to see it. This handing of the note must be very skillfully rehearsed.

"After receiving the note Herman gets up and retires into an arbor to have time to read it.

"Meantime the Master of Ceremonies appears at the top of the staircase and invites the crowds up the stairway. The only persons left in the foreground are Surin, Chekalinski, Tomski, and Lisa. Herman is in the arbor. The unknown person has gone up the staircase, also the Countess.

"Liveried footmen keep circulating with trays of sweetmeats, drinks, wine. Surin, Chekalinski, and Tomski stop a footman with a tray of wine. They retire into an arbor as a group, and the footman pours out wine for them.

"Surin, Chekalinski, and Tomski then mount the staircase while Eletski descends the other ramp and goes over to Lisa.

"As she says: 'No, Prince, later on, some other time, I beg of you. . . .' she jumps up and moves rapidly to the right side of the stage. But Eletski stops her, brings her back, she sits down, he sings his aria at first standing then sitting beside her. Herman is still reading the note in the arbor. His back is turned to the people watching the fireworks and his body conceals the letter from Lisa in his hand. In this way Herman is facing the auditorium and can sing directly to it.

"Meantime chairs No. 1, 2 and 3 have been occupied by people in frightening masks and costumes.

"Chekalinski and Surin cover their faces with masks and draw coverings over their hands (perhaps they can use what was worn by the witch in A May Night). They are at the opening of the arbor where Herman is sitting. He is alarmed. He moves back to Chair No.11 at the words: 'Are you not he, that third man, who filled with passion. . . .'

"The next cue, 'three cards, three cards, three cards' should be given to others, those who are sitting in chairs No. 1, 2, and 3. They all immediately turn and stare at Herman, assuming strange, exaggerated poses in their fearsome costumes, queer noses, beards as they sing the cue to him. As soon as they have done this, they turn away and disperse, walking in strange ways, and disappear in the crowds.

"This alarming effect can be heightened by the way it is lighted. Actually when the fireworks begin, coming from both the right and left wings and from beyond the auditorium (from above), the audience will constantly be bathed in multicoloured lights and flashes from reflectors or in some other way.

"At the moment when the horrible masks are making their effect let them be spotlighted and let Herman, in a state of alarm, dash into another arbor on the right.

"Meantime obviously artificial trees and bushes are being set out on the terrace at the top of the staircase, also down the sides of the steps. It produces the naive effect of a stage forest scene in the sentimental vein of the 18th century. They also set out some wooden figures of lambs.

"The Master of Ceremonies comes out onto the terrace, clears away all the crowd, and announces the beginning of the masque-pastorale.

"Keeping track of the music and its rhythm, the costumed guests hurry to occupy the seats at the foot of the stairs, crowding into the seats, filling the arbors wherever they can. The Countess sits down in No.17 and Herman occupies No.20. Surin is in No.5.

"In back people in dominoes and masks stand on stools and benches.

"During the finale of the masque-pastorale or during the new introductory music while the different costumed sets of quadrille dancers are going up the staircase, the Master of Ceremonies hurries out. The Empress has arrived. . . .

"The Master of Ceremonies then runs around to everyone asking that they remove their masks. But this is not so easy to do as they are tied on from the back. Only the Countess and Herman remove theirs promptly. Incidentally, Herman had already raised his mask up onto his forehead because he wished to read the letter over again. Herman sits all through the finale of the masque-pastorale with his back to the performers and facing the audience. He does this in order to conceal the letter he is reading from all those around him.

"The Countess, having removed her mask, is the first to stand up and leave. She brushes Herman as she passes him. They look at each other, take fright.

"Herman rushes to the left (seen from auditorium) to get away from her. He goes through the rows of chairs, facing us, the spectators. He looks with horror at the Countess, and she at him. Herman passes Surin, who half rises from his chair and whispers in Herman's left ear. After speaking his lines he quickly sits down again as if nothing had passed between them.

"Herman rushes off in a state of alarm. He hides in an arbor while all the other guests, at the invitation of the Master of Ceremonies, are hurrying up the staircase where lattice partitions are being set up for the arrival of the Empress.

"Without the musical score it is impossible to fix definitely how the crowd will be disposed on the terrace. . . .

"We have 1. the meeting between Herman and the Countess, and their avoidance of each other; 2. the scene between Herman and Surin and the ensuing lines of Herman.

"If we let the crowd get up earlier I am afraid the play between the soloists will be blurred.

"The forestage is emptied since everyone but Herman has mounted the staircase.

"Herman has hidden himself in one of the arbors.

"Lisa now comes out of the crowd and hurries to that same arbor. Herman wishes to come out to meet her but she pushes him back behind the greenery where he had concealed himself.

"Lisa herself sits down in the arbor and, leaning over, begins to whisper in a low voice without showing what she is doing. Meantime she passes a key to Herman (she is facing the auditorium).

"Herman now rushes like a madman up the staircase and tries to get through the lattice barriers. He is held back. He rushes down the stairs again seeking for a way out. Meantime the reception of the Empress is in progress at the top of the staircase."

This is how Stanislavski packed this scene with action, a scene which essentially contains no active dramatic events and is mostly diluted by picturesque episodes in the nature of "divertissements".

The scene in the bedroom of the Countess is one of the most perfect in Russian classic opera both as to the clarity of the dramatic pattern and the extraordinary and powerful enchantment of the music. Therefore it is a scene which singers can act in with ease.

In his exposition Stanislavski pointed up the "given circumstances" of the drama and led his actors along the line of the logic of events and physical actions, never making any mention of emotions, which, as he believed, would come to the fore of their own volition if the preliminary physical life of the role was properly organized.

Yet in his creation of this living logic on the stage he gave evidence of such virtuosity in his shadings that an actor who did no more that merely follow the given pattern conscientiously was bound to impress the audience. For example: Herman has to find a secret entrance "in the bedroom, near a portrait". Is it that simple to do when one enters a strange room with extraordinary furniture, with no illumination except from a watch light? Stanislavski set his actor the task of discovering that secret doorway—it was covered over—as a real life problem (like "a thief entering a strange apartment at night") and it had to be done in the rhythm and the mood given in the introductory music for this scene.

"Herman is in a mask and black domino," Stanislavski reminded the actor. "He has rushed here in a frenetic condition straight from the ball, trying to reach the house before the Countess arrives. He must cautiously and carefully examine, almost pass his fingers over, each painting, each protuberance, each bit of molding, and do it with the nervous, agitated feeling of secret fear and in the rhythm suggested by the music."

Short restatements of the tragic musical phrases alternate with bursts of muted violins which like a broad wave sweep along with Herman's tenseness. These are followed by slowly descending sequences, almost morbid throbs of a frightened heart, such as Chaikovski often used to express the agitated emotions of his principal character. In this atmosphere of tensely charged music the black figure in a mask— quietly stealing along the wall, carefully watching everything around him, keenly aware of all possible sounds, sometimes coming to a rigid state of immobility, and then finally vanishing through the secret door—grips the attention of the audience and holds them fixed on the seriousness of what is transpiring on the stage. The actor does not have to play anything; all he must do is faithfully execute his physical objectives in the rhythm of the music which accompanies them.

This is how Stanislavski, especially in the powerfully dramatic and psychological points in a play, knew how to protect his actor-singers from "acting mysteriously or mystically"—by keeping them on the plane of strictly concrete actions.

The way Stanislavski expounded this was as follows:

"There is the introductory music during which Herman (in black mask and domino) opens the concealed door, steals into the room and hides behind a screen.

"Only his head is visible. He can look around the room and sing his first five cues from behind the screen (with the main emphasis on diction and coloration).

"He has seen the portrait of the Countess. The whole of the ensuing aria is closely centred on the portrait. He will act as if he were drawn to it by some mysterious power. His whole meeting with the Countess has a sense of fatality about it. Herman, as if hypnotized, steals over to the armchair, kneels on the seat and rests his arms on the top of the back as he gazes intently at the portrait.

"Steps are heard. Perhaps he will try to get out (see the music) and rush first to the right then to the left. Finally he will slip to the back of the scene and hide somewhere out of sight of the audience (perhaps, let us say, behind a portière).

"The Countess's suite is made up almost exclusively of old women; of them all she is the most awful in appearance. She herself is still in her domino worn in the last act. No need here of a large chorus—six or seven, no more (that is if this fits the music). One would not want a strong chorus here. They are, after all, just a group of old women singing. They carry candles. This effect should be put to good use. Let Chinese-like shadows of the old women be reflected on the rather ghostly white canopy above the Countess's bed from the candles and the watch light in front of the ikons.

"The Countess uses high, built-up (cothurnus-like) shoes, so seems tall. This will make the entering procession more imposing. Let them walk around the bed, come out onto the forestage from the right (seen from the auditorium).

"They lead the Countess to her dressing table and disrobe her. The actual undressing is hidden by the bodies of her attendants. She is then seen in a long white gown. They remove her built-up shoes. The audience sees this. She now shrinks into the tiny, scrawny little figure described by Pushkin. They put a dressing gown on her—it does not make her look stouter but reduces her size still further.

"Meantime Lisa appears at the door to the right, still in her costume, on her way upstairs to undress. She has an exchange with one of the attendants. She is very nervous.

"Before Lisa leaves it would be desirable not only to have the Countess undressed but also to take off her wig, which leaves her practically bald with only a few wisps of hair. In this state she goes over to an armchair and sits down. During the end of the chorus of the old women and maids they will have put a night cap on her head and this will make her look quite ghostly. This must all be done in full view of the audience. The figures of the maids must not interfere.

"Or it might be better just to put her to bed as she is—a bald, tiny, shrivelled-up being (this last pleases me best).

"To go back to Lisa. She has partly opened the door to go up to her room; standing on the lowest steps, she chats with Masha. At the end of the dialogue she has all but disappeared.

"As the old Countess sings: '... enough of lies...' she sends away her attendants, who have turned back her bedcovers and are waiting to put her to bed.

"After the other maids are dismissed, only one, with a candle, remains and it is more or less to her that the Countess addresses her words.

"In the middle of the aria, look for a good place in the music, without stopping the singing, to lift her into her bed and cover her—a tiny, wizened, little old woman in her huge royal bed under a baldaquin.

"She sings the French love song lying down, almost half asleep. The two maids who had stationed themselves one at the head and one at the foot of the bed, shading the light from their candles with their hands, have tiptoed off. The others had left earlier.

"There is a good deal of introductory music during which Herman can begin to stir in the background. His shadow is thrown by the watch light onto the canopy over the bed. The shadow, at first large, grows smaller as he approaches and it also becomes most distinct.

"He shows only his face through an opening in the draperies around the bed.

"The Countess, terrified, hides under her coverlet. As he says the words: 'You can make the happiness of a whole life' etc., Herman opens the curtains wider and is visible down to his waist.

"The Countess looks out with one eye from under the covers (of course, this is on the side towards the audience). During his next lines Herman first stands, then kneels leaning against the bed.

"Meantime the Countess slowly pushes an emaciated foot out from under the blanket. One has the feeling that she may hope to slip out of her bed without being noticed.

"When Herman pronounces the words 'old witch' he puts one knee on the bed, leans towards her, pulls away the covers, and aims a pistol at her. The Countess grabs a small pillow, covers her face with it, and dies, with her left leg and left arm hanging down from the bed.

"Before Herman says: 'She is dead' he removes the pillow from her face and the ghastly corpse is revealed to the audience.

"You must find the right place in the music for Herman to try to flee. As he runs around he comes upon Lisa who has opened a door and is standing there with a candle.

"Herman is like a frightened child (if this fits the music); he points to the dead Countess, but is afraid to go near her.

"Before Lisa's words: 'Yes, she has died' he rushes across the stage. He hides behind a screen. Only his head is visible. He is like a child, or a drunkard, uncertainly pointing at the corpse but not leaving his refuge behind the screen.

"Lisa says to him: 'So that is why you are here', and kneels beside the dead Countess while Herman like a madman stays behind the screen and helplessly, quietly, stupidly, crazily repeats over and over: 'She is dead.' "

This was the end of all that Stanislavski left in the way of notes about *The Queen of Spades*. The other scenes were rehearsed in accordance with his oral directions.

The fifth scene, "In the Barracks", was designed with a sparse setting: there is a bed, a table, a coat rack with two overcoats, a large high wall in the middle of which is a door and opposite to it a large window. The cheerless aspect of the great window and the walls, and the whole place lighted by a single candle speak of Herman's solitary life, of his discomfort, of his disturbed state.

When Herman cries out: "I can bear it no longer" and dashes towards the door the shadow his figure casts on the high bare wall leads him to believe it is the ghost of the dead Countess. As he retreats from the door, in the direction of the forestage, the shadow increases and since he has thrown his cape about his shoulders he is reminded of the Countess in her dressing gown. This solution made it possible to avoid bringing the Countess onstage, which always makes a very coarse and unconvincing impression.

Before the Countess says: "I have come to you. . ." there is a great swelling of the theme of the tormenting fear and this musical pressure very successfully coincides with the enlargement of the shadow, which really becomes menacing in effect. Herman here acted with great expressiveness so that this scene together with that in the bedroom of the Countess could be considered the two most successful high points of the production.

The sixth and next to last scene is laid near a quay of the Neva and was beautifully handled with laconic restraint. In the foreground, at an angle to the footlights, there was a pavement with a stone quay; a stone bench, a street light, the statue of a lion with his paw on a cannonball completed the scenery downstage. In the background the dark waters of the Neva glistened and masts of ships with furled sails bobbed up and down. On the far shore was a faint glimmer of the steeple of the chapel in the fortress of Saints Peter and Paul. Dawn was beginning to break through the scudding clouds of a stormy sky. The impression was one of a deserted, comfortless place and reproduced graphically the exhaustion, loneliness, and hopelessness that enveloped Lisa as she waited for her meeting with Herman.

Lisa's nervously impetuous movements as she looks down the quay match very well the monotonous pulsing rhythm of the music that introduces her aria: "Midnight is almost here".

In the duet of Lisa with Herman, which is filled with dramatic feelings, the two singers were called upon to exercise a high degree of vocal and dramatic mastery. They had behind them considerable stage experience and they had been trained by Stanislavski, so they successfully measured up to the requirements of their parts. The production was put on in the absence of Stanislavski (who was convalescing abroad) and lacked an artistic overall finish but the actor-singers performed their roles with skill, thus taking a step ahead in establishing their young theatre.

The last scene is laid in a richly gilded and ornamented basement with a low, vaulted ceiling. It is full of tables at which, when the curtain opens, gambling is in full swing. Several tables have been pushed together to make one large one on which supper has been laid. This relates to the first chorus of the gamesters who sing: "We will drink and make merry" and also to Chekalinski's words: "Get down to work now, take your cards." After this the waiters quickly dismantle the supper table and gambling begins in earnest at the tables. Herman has come into this jolly atmosphere of "gamblers at work". Stanislavski's first idea was that mysterious things should occur here, or so Herman would imagine. Whenever he looked at the tables, especially towards the finale and during the toasting ("What is life?"), great piles of gold were supposed to appear and to gleam in a peculiarly brilliant way and Herman was to see the ghost of the dead Countess. This series of visions in the deranged mind of Herman was supposed, in Stanislavski's original plan, to take place in this scene and also in the "Barracks" scene. Here the whole funeral of the Countess and Herman's farewell to her were to have been seen by him (and by the audience) when thrown on a transparent scrim—as if to illustrate the words: "There is the church, the crowd, the candles. . . ." But in the process of working out the scene Stanislavski decided to take a strictly realistic approach and everything "mysterious" was thrown out. For this reason a cut was made in the finale of the opera—Herman's delirium, his farewell to Lisa, his sentimental remorse. (This section, which was not at all necessary, was written by Chaikovski for Nikolai Figner, who was a past master in singing such emotional melodramatic scenes.) Herman does not stab himself as is usual, he shoots himself, which is more in keeping with the conduct of a young officer of that time. After a lengthy pause the chorus begins the moving chant: "Lord, forgive him. . . ." All the tonalities were right, no violence was done to the score and the finale gained greatly in power.

After the chorus, as the last strains of music are played, all the gamblers slowly disperse, much shaken by Herman's death. The curtain closes with only Herman's body on the stage, lying among the strewn cards.

While the opera was being prepared Stanislavski was of course convalescing abroad. In his letters to those in charge and to the whole theatre company he tried in every way to keep up their spirits and energies.

One such letter was dated January 14, 1930, when work was at its height, and it expressed his basic creative ideas on producing operas:

"Dear friends and members of the Opera Studio:

"First of all I must admit that I miss you very much. The last time we were together was during the Art Theatre's (30 years) celebration and that was almost 14 months ago.

"Then I want to begin with sending you my thanks for your two collective letters.

"I am writing to show you my support even at a distance. I know that things are difficult and upsetting for you at this time, but that is not important, in fact it is a good thing. It is time for you to get used to being on your own, because I am getting on in years. My illness is a first warning, and while I am still able to be of help to you you must take on your own shape, train your own leaders, send them to me for direction, hammer out your disciplines, because your future lies in your unity and energy.

"Answer me this: Do you believe that the foundations of our theatre are right? Do you wish to work on some other basis? If the answer to this last is yes, then we must part as we shall not accomplish anything together. Do you believe that it is not the production itself, or the tricks of shrewd directors, or the reflection of contemporary and quickly-evanescent fashions in our art but the making of singer-actors who work on the organic rules of nature, of truth, of artistic beauty, who will provide our people and our art with the necessary kind of theatre? If you do believe in this then preserve, strengthen, love and defend the foundations of our art.

"Is our theatre needed, does it make any sense, without them? If not, then you yourselves will realize that its salvation lies in the principles on which it is founded.

"Therefore if you believe in the basis of our art and believe it to be true you will not wish to work in any other way. If you have learned to achieve your objectives by our methods then you can say to yourselves: We have done everything in our power and the rest is out of our hands. Why then should you feel any discouragement? Are you worried about success or the lack of it? Then you must know in advance that if you have invested great love in this new production, if you have been clearly conscientious about your work, the things that you know, the capacities given you by nature, then you will succeed sooner or later. So cast away all doubts and proceed straight to your goal without wavering or holding back.

"Perhaps you are concerned about the future of our theatre? In that case I want you to know—that in our times anyone who wishes to remain alive must to some degree be a hero. So be heroic in your own group, strong, resolute, closely-knit. Then you will sleep quietly because you will be capable of dealing with life, you will clear away all obstacles and come out whole. If a canoe founders under the first wave, does not succeed in riding it and moving forward, it has no value for navigation. You will have to understand that if your group is not solidly built and will go down under the first wave of assault that faces you, then its outlook for survival is poor and indeed it is foredoomed.

"So let your mutual bonds of artistry be strengthened. This is so important that it is well worth the sacrifice of self-love, caprice, favouritism, and all the other evils that can drive a wedge into your collective intelligence, your will, your feelings for each other—that can tear you apart, demoralize and destroy the lot of you. The principal thing is to organize yourselves well and in this I can help with advice.

"At present I am tired and cannot dictate further but from day to day I shall make notes on what I can be helpful with, even at a distance, in confirming your joint enterprise and developing your inner consciousness and sense of discipline.

"I embrace and love you.

C. Stanislavski."

This letter provided the answers to many questions affecting the immediate life of this young opera group, which was temporarily deprived of its guiding genius. But it also was of prime significance in laying down principles for the future of theatre in the Soviet Union.

8

The Golden Cockerel

The Golden Cockerel WAS Rimski-Korsakov's last opera, and a summing up, as it were, of that great composer's work in this realm.

Every line of the Pushkin tale used in the libretto is a whole scene and the carrying out of a poetic image. The principal character, the lever of all action—the Queen of Shemakha—is described in sparse outline and remains mysterious. Her main characteristic is embodied in the expression "she gleamed like the dawn as she quietly received the Tsar." The Tsar, standing before her, remained speechless "like a bird of night in the face of the sun." Dawn and the sun—that was her essence.

The kingdom of Dodon was already somewhat familiar from other tales of Pushkin. To reign "while lying on one's side", that was the dream of fairy-tale rulers. But the impact of the satire, with which the nitwit ruler is pictured in *The Golden Cockerel*, is more incisive here than in the other Pushkin stories. The kingdom of Dodon is that barbarous land where no ray of light has yet penetrated to waken it from its primitive state of stupidity, ignorance, and hypocrisy.

V.I. Belski, who was one of the best Russian librettists, a man well-versed in both dramatic composition and the art of poetic structure, developed and broadened the two contradictory elements of the fairy tale. The Queen of Shemakha acquired definite, visible features; she spoke and sang with the beauty and enchantment which corresponded to the qualities hinted at by Pushkin and conducted the scene with Dodon, in which her nature and character are fully revealed, in the way Belski and Rimski-Korsakov understood her or conjectured her to be. Her baffling, oriental beauty came to life in the words, the sounds, the music.

There is still another important and mystery-enshrouded figure in this fairy-tale world—the wizard-astrologer, who called into being all the characters in the tale and then at the end says: "But am not I, besides the Queen, the only living creature, and all the rest fancies, dreams?" He may have said this for the benefit of the imperial censor, who might easily have taken Dodon for a caricature of the Tsar.

"As a matter of fact," wrote Belski in his preface to the libretto of *The Golden Cockerel*, "were these two in a conspiracy against Dodon, or did their attack on the poor fellow coincide, quite independently and accidentally, unrelated to each other?—Pushkin does not in any way clarify this point. A detailed working-out for a stage production of the story could not stand on a shaky premise. It was necessary to decide on a complete preliminary solution of the riddle, as we chose. Although the very inexplicit quality of the tale did possess a kind of charm of its own, nevertheless, the compulsions of making a comprehensible play out of it outweighed this and obliged the author to put into so many words the meaning of what was transpiring on the stage."

In this delicate way the librettist clarified his right to carry out to completion the picture only lightly sketched by Pushkin.

The libretto was published by Jorgenson in 1908 and contains a "Note by the Composer".

Among the first points in the footnotes, mention is made of the composer's stipulation that cuts should not be made. Further, that speech, whispering, and exclamations used "to heighten the comic or dramatic or realistic colour of a given moment", should not be used to replace the *recitative* indicated; that the metronomic indications should be observed—in other words he lays down rules for the production of opera which have become the very ABC of our art. The fourth point deserves particular attention:

"As in previous prefaces to operas the writer emphasizes that in lyric or quasi-lyrical passages, the characters onstage but not singing should in no way distract the attention of the audience from the singing in progress by superfluous acting or any movements, inasmuch as an opera is above all a musical creation."

In our day one scarcely should need such instruction from a composer—or are there perhaps still some singers and directors who suppose that opera can be made better-dramatized by extraneous actions and ad-lib additions which bear no relationship to the music? That is the way directors from drama theatres are in the habit of proceeding if they are not versed in music and its laws.

The musical richness of this last opera score of Rimski-Korsakov is extraordinary. The variety and sharply characteristic definitions of the leading themes, the remarkable colourfulness of the harmonies and orchestration are all part and parcel of its inherent wealth. In this opera Rimski-Korsakov has even what one might call "leit-timbres", as in the characteristic orchestration of the music of the Astrologer (a combination of harps, bells, and string *pizzicati*). The sarcastic, grass-roots native character of the music for Dodon and his kingdom, the refined grace and tenderness of the Shemakhan Queen's melody, which glitters with chromatic, elemental beauty—all this is a wealth of material indeed for the use of the singers and their directors.

Stanislavski, who was so sensitively attuned to the most refined shadings of music, worked with particular satisfaction on *The Golden Cockerel* regardless of whether he was carried away by the colossal stupidity of Dodon or the fragrant charm of the exotic Queen of Shemakha. Everything in this fairy-tale opera inspired his fantasy, which flashed forth in this work with all its characteristic brilliance.

In the autumn of 1930, after an absence of two years because of his illness, Stanislavski returned to his work in his various theatres.

In this new phase he delegated more and more initiative to his assistants and to the young directors, although he continued to plan out and correct their work. More and more often he would say:

"Use me while I am still able to work; ask me more questions, absorb from me all that my fifty years of experience in the theatre has taught me."

During this period his visits to the Art Theatre and to his Opera Theatre as well became more and more infrequent, but rehearsal work hummed in his home, in his study, and in the big rehearsal hall where he came for work with larger groups. His activity now acquired a definitely pedagogic character, and it became more and more fruitful. He watched each rehearsal for opportunities to express himself in terms of principles of art, explaining how one should progress in this or that event. His own study was transformed into an academy of theatre art where important instructions were given not only to actors but also to musicians, scenic artists, and playwrights.

During this time the productions prepared in his rehearsal hall were then transferred to the stage of our theatre by his assistants. He listened to the opinions expressed by the many visitors to the operas whether they were or were not trained in theatre work. The models for the sets, the sketches for the costumes and makeup he examined in his own home. To this end the scene designers, costumers, and makeup people were summoned to his study where some overhead lights had been installed over his sofa to provide the necessary lighting.

The Golden Cockerel opened on May 4, 1932. It ranks with the more significant creations of Stanislavski in the last decade of his life. His bringing out of the inner meaning of the fairy tale was brilliant in execution and rich in subtleties; therefore, it was the more regrettable that this production was not kept for long in the repertoire of our theatre. This was due to the technical shortcoming of our stage, which resulted in unduly long intermissions.

This production is an example of the dangers that lurk in the gap between a creative concept and its fulfillment.

This fairy-tale opera as dreamed of by Stanislavski called not only for a metamorphosis of the stage but of the auditorium as well: The audience sitting out front was to feel that they had found themselves in a new world of fantasy. According to Stanislavski's plan when the first measures of the overture were being played the auditorium would be transformed into a mysterious island set in a sea: the walls of the auditorium were to be lighted in the blue tones that melt the horizon between the sky and the sea on a moonlit night—and the ceiling would become a star-studded firmament. An engineer from the Moscow Planetarium worked on this project.

The Astrologer then was to appear in his oriental robes and sheepskin hat, moving through the auditorium as the overture was being played—a dark figure against the pale blue background. He walked down the central aisle singing to right and to the left as he went his opening aria: "I am a wizard. By secret art I am endowed with gifts extraordinary. I can call forth a shade, breathe magic life into its breast. . . ." He announced himself as the complete master of the magic world which would now be revealed. His face was lighted by a skillfully concealed bulb in his tall sheepskin hat which operated on a pocket battery. At the end of the overture the lighting effects in the auditorium faded out and the action was transferred to the stage.

Unfortunately Stanislavski's imaginative concept was imperfectly carried out. Even though the ceiling of the auditorium could produce something of the illusion of a starry sky, the walls certainly did not convert into airy space. Probably many of the spectators never even suspected that they were supposedly on the island created especially for them.

The story of the design of the settings for *The Golden Cockerel* is an unusual and complicated one. From the beginning Stanislavski was preoccupied with the question of how to present the sharp contrasts between the realm of Dodon in the first and third acts, and the Queen of Shemakha's domain in the second. He was rather inclined to the idea that two different artists should design the sets: the one who would be well versed in the background and spirit of Russian fairy tales and the other who would know the Oriental world. He talked to various artists and tried out various versions. The sketches offered by Krymov and Lentulov were rejected, and further research did not produce any results until, after some time, M.S. Sarian sent a model from Erivan (Armenia) of the Queen of Shemakha's realm. The model was so unusual and beautiful that Stanislavski was quite carried away by it and decided to use it despite the fact that it did not fit into his plan for the production. This was one of the rare occasions when Stanislavski was so won over by the fantasy of an artist that he abandoned his own original plan and fitted the production to the invention of the artist.

Sarian's model represented a fantastically shaped mount which stood on a revolving platform. It was painted in various colours and as it turned it took on different shapes and tints. Mountain trails appeared, trees of strange outlines, shrubbery, caves. In one aperture in the rock the luxurious pavilion of the Queen of Shemakha was set up. She seemed to be living in this rock. Since it was built in such a contrived manner this model at first glance seemed to contradict the more realistic style of the whole production. Some of Stanislavski's assistants did not accept what they called "this painted cake". And indeed it did put one in mind of a fantastic confection. But Stanislavski never shrank from even the most fantastic artifice provided it led to the revealing of the spirit of a composition, so he announced that the work on the opera and the solution of how to handle the two "Russian" acts would go forward under the impetus of the Sarian invention.

It proved to be very difficult to combine the "Russian" acts with the one laid in Shemakha since the Sarian mount was built in a circle and the plan for the "Russian" scenes was not taken into consideration. After some hesitation Stanislavski decided to use the model prepared by S.I. Ivanov for the first and third acts, since he felt this was sufficiently fantastic in character.

Despite the directions in the libretto the action was removed from the "large palace chamber of the glorious Tsar Dodon where the Duma was in session" out into the garden in front of the palace. Stanislavski explained this change:

"If in the very beginning you show an interior with boyars sitting around on benches and a tsar on a throne then it becomes a routine stage-palace scene and there is nowhere for the action to flow. Therefore I shall show the Tsar sitting on the grass in the garden. After all, he has no interest in governing his kingdom properly. He wants to drink, eat, relax—in general 'eat sweetmeats and listen to fairy tales'. With us the action starts with him taking his ease."

The stage was set with a large, wide-branched apple tree full of apples in the centre. Under it was a couch on which Tsar Dodon was lying and enjoying the cool of the day. To the left was an entrance to the palace, a simple, wooden structure; to the right was a tower made of logs, perhaps a watchtower, or else some sort of superannuated observatory. There was an outside stairway leading to the top of the tower where the Astrologer lived. The garden was enclosed by a palisade fence. Beyond it was a space where the people and the army gathered. But only the nobles, the boyars, were allowed inside the royal garden enclosure.

The action began with a "session" of the Royal Duma which takes place in the shade of the apple tree. The boyars either sat or lay on the grass. It was there in the atmosphere of a hot day, indolence after a good meal, drowsiness, that they discussed the business of government. This comic "session" was accompanied by monumental foolishness: the Tsar's sons consulted with the boyars about how to get rid of the enemies. The brains of the "military council" were quickly exhausted and their thoughts were soon addled. Then a brawl broke out among the boyars, between the "partisans" of heavy kvas (a cider-like drink) and those of chick peas.

"This must all be played with utmost seriousness," Stanislavski kept reminding his singers. "The more stupid it is, the more earnest it will appear to be."

The brawl is interrupted suddenly by the completely enchanting music of the Astrologer. Over this dull-witted, narrow-minded, lazy group of people something like a precious veil is thrown, an unexpected weaving of sounds from the orchestra all of which is alien and incomprehensible to these stupid, fat creatures. At the same time a mysterious old man comes down from his high tower, a gentle but rather alarming apparition.

"The Astrologer is an awesome person out of the East," observed Stanislavski. "There is something akin to the Queen of Shemakha in him but there is also some sort of enmity towards her."

When he came down from his tower the Astrologer brought something covered by a bag. With gaping mouths the Tsar and his boyars looked at their mysterious guest. When he drew out of the bag a gleaming young cockerel who craned his neck around and preened himself, their mouths gaped even wider. It was with the aid of this cockerel that Dodon was enabled to govern his kingdom "while lying on his side" after thoughtlessly promising, in exchange for this gift, to carry out any wish of the Astrologer's as if it were his own.

To the accompaniment of the sound of bells the Astrologer returns to his tower, while down below the undisturbed, lazy life takes its usual course. The Cockerel crows somewhere up above out of sight. The Tsar listens to him, raises his head, then settles back on his couch under the apple tree and rolls over occasionally from side to side. Food is brought to him by his housekeeper Amelfa, who also carries his parrot. Amelfa in a pointed bonnet looks like a peasant woman made of clay. She treats the Tsar like an infant, leaning over the pillow on which he is lying. The Tsar begins to have visions, the magic of the Astrologer is beginning to take effect. After a quiet lullaby, during which everyone has dropped off to sleep, magic sounds are heard and strange colours pass over the stage. In his sleep the Tsar is restless, he fidgets around in his bed. A shadow is thrown on the white figure of Amelfa, standing at the head of the Tsar's bed—it is the outline of the Queen of Shemakha. In the twilight setting one seems to see a Persian-like female figure in a strange costume, and this is just the way the Queen of Shemakha will be dressed later on.

This is how the effect was produced: When Amelfa took up her place at the head of the Tsar's couch she unobtrusively threw a sheet over herself. It was on that surface that a colour slide was projected showing the Queen of Shemakha in exactly the same pose as that of Amelfa. There was a complete synthesis of the two figures. The vision appears imperceptibly and was projected from a lantern attached to the wall of the orchestra pit near the director's podium.

In his dream the Tsar attempts to embrace with his awkward arms the exquisite, flower-like figure but instantly the Cockerel begins to crow and raise an alarm. With the last chord of the Shemakhan music the vision vanishes and Amelfa once more emerges. It is evident that there is some bond between the Astrologer, this vision, and the Cockerel's crow calling the people to arms.

Beyond the palisade an excited crowd of people begins to gather. They call for the sons of Dodon, who in turn try to escape. They are caught and forcibly covered with armour. They take leave of their wives. Everyone sobs. The weeping warriors are set upon their steeds (these are outside the palisade and are just props) and the first army is dispatched. Once more quiet and sleep are restored; once more Amelfa tells a fairy tale and the Tsar is disturbed by dreams. Meanwhile the theme of the Queen of Shemakha is heard more loudly than ever, and again the figure of an Oriental maiden with her hair flowing down over her shoulders appears at the head of the Tsar's couch. Again he flails his arms around in fruitless atempts to embrace her. A second time his sleep is broken by the crow of the Cockerel with the warning to be on guard. Now Tsar Dodon himself will have to set out at the head of his army. Outside the palisade they lead on a richly-caparisoned steed. With the aid of about a dozen people he mounts the steed by climbing over the fence. A chorus sings a marching song: "Our Father Tsar! Hooray!" And Dodon leaves with his army, while behind him they sing: "Watch yourself, our Father dear, and stay in the rear, stay in the rear."

The set for the second act shows the fantastic mountain representing the realm of the Queen of Shemakha seen in a mysterious night lighting. The ground around the mount is strewn with Dodon's dead warriors, including both of his sons.

Great vultures are sitting in the semidarkness on the juts at the foot of the mount. They spread their wings and fly off. Stanislavski revelled in that sort of contrived effect. It is to this ill-fated battlefield, lighted by a moon far on the wane, that Dodon comes with his army.

All his soldiers crawl in on all fours. The chorus of the warriors sings: "Whispering terror in the voiceless night". They are full of fear and tense caution. This blends so well with their crawling movement it really seems as if it could not be otherwise.

Finally Dodon himself crawls in, feeling his way to the bodies of his dead sons. The "chieftain" Polkan arrives with a great cudgel and sets up a pitiful wailing lament. But in the music as well as on the stage the darkness begins to fade and the rising sun gilds the crown of the fabulous mount. Then all the colours of the rainbow begin to play over it, making it gleam like a precious jewel, slowly revealing the outline of the Queen's pavilion.

Now the army prepares for battle. They have dragged along a kind of cannon which looks like an antiquated stovepipe; they load it . . . but now on the very top of the mount, all glowing in the sunlight, appears the Queen of Shemakha herself. She is accompanied by a bevy of girls who look as if they had stepped out of a Persian miniature painting. Their gleaming beauty and graceful elegance contrast strikingly with the dark, crawling mass of Dodon's army lurking among the bushes, hiding away from the light, down at the bottom of the mount.

It is from the top of the patterned mount, surrounded by her friends and handmaidens who drape the slope with beautiful garlands, that the Queen sings her famous hymn to the Sun: "O answer me, All-seeing Star."

The scene of the meeting between the Queen and Dodon and his falling under her spell was worked out by Stanislavski with his virtuoso skill. The whole meaning of the fable, its inner motivation and moving force, lies in this duet and unless it is brought out there is no point to *The Golden Cockerel*. Since this scene has little external activity producers often make cuts here. But it did not seem long to Stanislavski, and he threw himself with great pleasure into working on it.

What preoccupied him particularly as rehearsals progressed was the maintaining of the very tenuous inner pattern of the roles of Dodon and the Queen of Shemakha within the framework of conditions on the stage. The actor-singers had to work this out for themselves, polish the faceted surface of their graceful movements, keeping them always related to the setting and the lighting. Stanislavski was extremely insistent on actors being aware of and feeling the impact of the setting. He never allowed any disjunction between actors and scenery.

There is a nostalgic lonely beauty contrasted with dull-witted triviality in the duet of Dodon and the Queen. Stanislavski had her constantly evince her revulsion and hatred for the stupid bestiality of Dodon. This makes the fable not only funny but also angry. It aroused in the audience the desire to destroy the stupid malevolence embodied in Dodon.

"For the Queen's role you have to find the two factors: one is a terrible yearning and the other is hatred, derision, of a beast," said Stanislavski in describing this part.

"And for your role," he added turning to Dodon, "you are playing one of those old men that try to look through a crack in a fence to see a young girl bathing and then suddenly find yourself thrown in the pool.

"You are acting out a fairy tale so you must do everything in an utterly serious manner and believe in everything you do.

"Now you, Queen of Shemakha, are telling Dodon about your yearnings, your loneliness (in your aria: 'Between the sea and the sky there hangs suspended a little isle') and all you get in response is his dull-witted stupidity. You must be quite taken aback by this. Remember that if you are not dismayed there is no point to the scene. It is your dismay that allows you to deride him and also to gain the audience's sympathy.

"Make a note of the highest and lowest points of longing and establish your actions and emotions in accordance with the degrees between then. There will be a long coherent line with differing states of feeling and different physical attitudes."

The Queen sings of her yearning for love and accompanies herself on a harp, in an attempt to arouse in Dodon some spark of aesthetic feeling. She asks him if he sang when he was in love. In reply Dodon says: "I sang a lot." She then enquires: "Well, how did you sing?" But Dodon only says: "I really can't recall." She caressingly says: "But tell me . . . more or less." Contrary to the libretto, which read: "Dodon picks up a psaltery," he takes up an oriental drum, with embarrassment squats down in front of it like a rabbit, and taps it with the sticks as he sings the words: "I shall always love you, if I don't forget you." This scene exposes Dodon for the half-witted fool he is and explains the "feline fury" of the Queen which Stanislavski directed her to show.

Stanislavski replaced the dance between Dodon and the Queen (Rimski-Korsakov asked in his introduction to the opera that it be arranged so as not to tire the singers) with a pantomime game: "I shall be a little fish and you the crab to catch me." Whereupon Dodon crawled around the Queen's tent on all fours trying with his claw-like arms to catch the little golden fish—the Queen. The Queen's entourage looks derisively at Dodon, so do his warriors. The Queen's maiden attendants, following their mistress's example, take possession of the warriors, drape them with oriental scarves, and begin to dance with them. Dodon as well as all his army are enchanted and dance boisterously as the mount begins to revolve. Next, the Queen begins to prepare for the journey to her nuptials with Dodon, followed by her outlandish suite: monkeys, dwarfs, giants. They set Dodon and the Queen on a throne placed on top of a litter and the procession starts for Dodon's kingdom as the curtain falls. It seems as though triviality has won the day and captured beauty.

In the beginning of the third act there is a sense of depressing languor, heavy foreboding. The Golden Cockerel, on which everything depended, is perched up on a high pole and makes no sound. Everyone looks up to it but it still remains silent.

Now to the music of the famous "March" a procession arrives outside the palisade. It is a motley lot of people, foreign-looking, bearing strange fruits from a strange land, outlandish costumes and at the end of it are Dodon and the Queen of Shemakha. They are seated side by side on their golden litter. Dodon has brought back a Queen for his realm. Even he is now all dressed in oriental fashion. His people look on him with alarm and sadness. Their Tsar is arrayed in a golden robe of oriental cut, he wears a white turban with a feather on his head. They are dumbfounded.

When the procession enters with Dodon and the Queen borne on high above everyone else, again that "terrifying Oriental personage", the Astrologer, appears. As in the first act he wears a tall sheepskin hat and a kind of red-coloured robe. He looks something like an ancient nomad. This beggarly old man now demands to be given the "Magical-flower", which is the Queen of Shemakha, because he wishes "to try out the married state." After a brief altercation with him the Tsar snatches the army chieftain's stout cudgel and strikes the Astrologer on

The Golden Cockerel, Act III (from the 1932 production): The death of the Astrologer.

the head with it. He falls to the ground between the Tsar and the Queen. The nuptials of the pair are ill-omened from the start. Dodon, bewildered in his awkward position, tries to kiss his bride.

Then comes the brutal dénouement. After the Queen's enraged outburst: "Curses on you, evil monster, and all your nation of fools", down from the sky (that is, from overhead on a well-greased wire) the Golden Cockerel drops straight onto the head of Dodon. There is a momentary blackout and then we see Dodon lying dead on the steps of his throne, dressed in his old Russian clothes (his oriental splendour is stripped off in the blackout)—and both the Astrologer and the Queen of Shemakha have vanished.

Before reaching the point of embodying a production in the movements of the actors onstage, a director must first conceive in his imagination the shape of the production. Stanislavski's genius lay in his capacity to make everyone engaged in a production active co-creators with him in his directorial concept. All dividing lines were wiped out between what he himself suggested or demonstrated and what the actors did on their own creative initiative or because of the logical necessities inherent in their parts. This is the overriding significance of Stanislavski's method of work in bringing forth an expression of collective art—which is the aim of theatre.